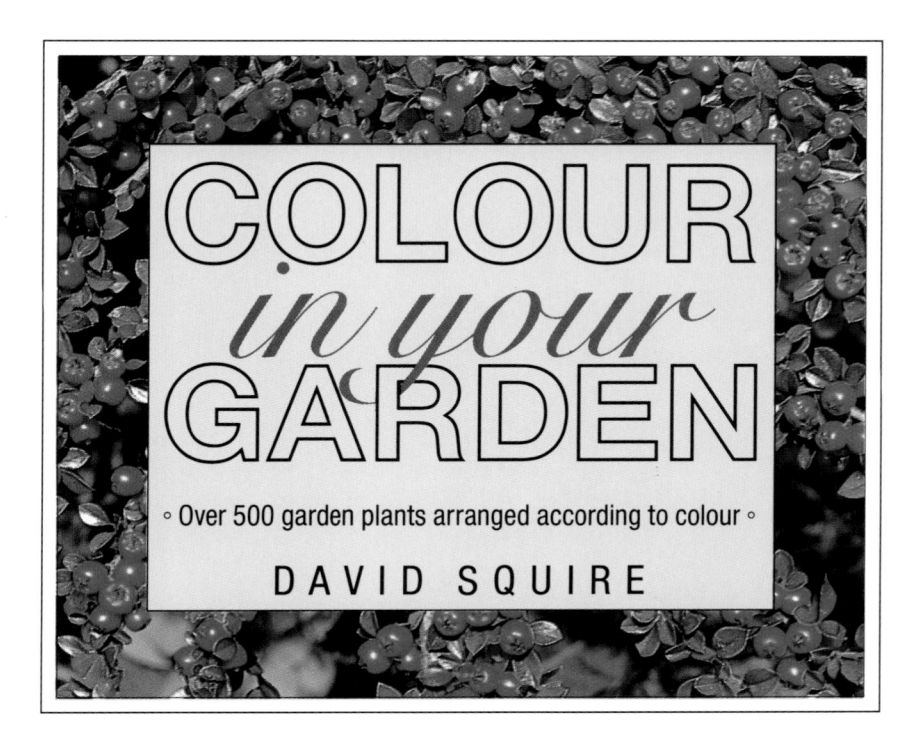

COLOUR
in your
GARDEN

◦ Over 500 garden plants arranged according to colour ◦

DAVID SQUIRE

a Salamander book

Published by Salamander Books Limited
LONDON • NEW YORK

Published by Salamander Books Limited
129-137 York Way,
London N7 9LG,
United Kingdom

© Salamander Books Ltd., 1991

ISBN 0 86101 564 9

Distributed by Hodder & Stoughton Services,
PO Box 6, Mill Road, Dunton Green, Sevenoaks, Kent TN13 2XX

CREDITS

Editors: Jonathan Elphick & Veronica Ross
Designers: Barry Savage & Rachael Stone
Typeset by: Barbican Print & Marketing Services Ltd.
Colour separation by: Melbourne Graphics Ltd & P & W Graphics, Pte. Ltd.
Printed in Belgium by: Proost International Book Production, Turnhout, Belgium

CONTENTS

Introduction

HOW TO USE THIS BOOK

Gardeners are like painters, but with a fresh canvas available to them only once a year. Borders are planned, plant and seed catalogues avidly searched and gleaned for more vibrant and long-lasting colours, and fellow gardeners consulted. But should you or your family have a predilection for certain colours, perhaps those that contrast with established plants in your garden or blend happily against certain colour-washed walls, then you need practical and visual help at your elbow. A reliable book which clearly portrays the range of garden plants within a particular part of the colour spectrum will be invaluable, and that is the purpose of this lavishly illustrated all-colour book. *Colour in Your Garden* comprises five chapters: *The Flower Border, Rock and Naturalized Gardens, Container Gardening, Walls and Trellises* and *Trees and Shrubs*. Within each of these chapters plants are grouped into several ranges of colour. These are *Reds and Pinks, Blues and Purples, Golds and Yellows, Greens and Variegated* and *Whites, Greys and Silvers*. Green and variegated plants are superb as features on their own or as backgrounds for other plants, perhaps creating exciting colour contrasts. This information enables single-colour theme gardens to be created, as well as providing the 'know-how' to mix-and-match plants.

The introductory pages explain the nature of light and colour, and how different colours are measured and defined, according to their hue, value and intensity. There is useful information on the use of colour in the garden, why some colours are dominant and the effects of bright sunlight and the shadows of evening. Planning colour with the aid of a *colour-circle* is explained, and the concept of complementary and harmonizing colours is discussed.

Colour in Your Garden reveals a wealth of plants for all parts of the garden: filling annual and herbaceous borders, adorning rock and naturalized gardens, bringing colour to window-boxes, hanging-baskets, troughs and other containers on patios and terraces, climbing walls and trellises or serving as a harmonious framework to knit together the various elements within a garden. Each plant is illustrated in full colour and clearly described, including its botanical and common names, height and spread (in metric and imperial units), cultivation and propagation. Within each colour range the plants are listed alphabetically according to their botanical names. At the base of each page there are valuable tips on using combinations of plants to create colour-contrasts, subtle harmonies, focal points and interesting shapes and patterns. Detailed all-colour border plans, showing how to arrange plants, enable everyone to create a colourful garden.

At the end of this book there are two comprehensive indexes. The first lists all common names, the second index is of botanical names, including synonyms (alternative names). The inclusion of the latter helps in the identification of plants botanists have recently re-classified and given new names, but which are frequently sold under their old, better-known names. This book is a valuable and informative addition to your gardening bookshelf, offering information which colourfully parades the 'know-how' that enables your garden to be transformed into a bright and colourful leisure area for the whole family.

Above: Cercis siliquastrum *This hardy deciduous tree is commonly known as the Judas Tree. During early summer, it bears lovely rich rose-pink flowers.*

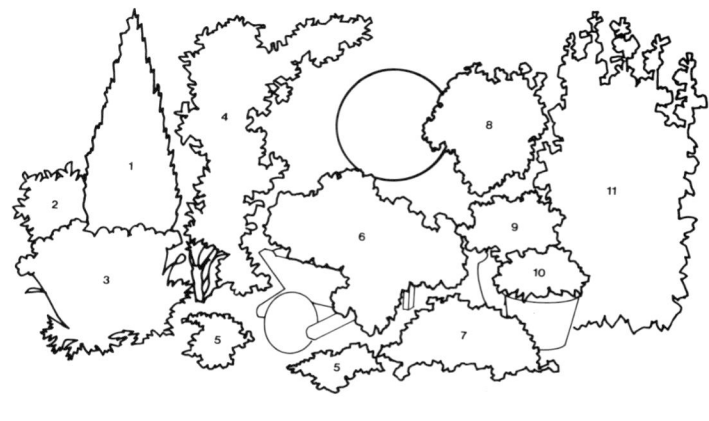

Above: Camassia quamash *This dramatic purple or blue flowered bulbous plant from North America brings colour to a border during mid-summer.*

Key:
1 *Juniperus chinensis* 'Pyramidalis'
2 *Fuchsia magellanica* 'Aurea'
3 *Papaver orientale* 'Mrs Perry'
4 *Clematis* 'Nelly Moser'
5 *Thymus drucei* 'Annie Hall'
6 Mixture of geraniums
7 *Helianthemum nummularium*
   'Raspberry Ripple'
8 Trailing lobelia, petunias, nasturtiums, geraniums and marigolds
9 *Geranium* Harlequin'
10 *Petunia* 'Honeybunch'
11 *Alcea rosea* (Hollyhock)

Introduction

SCIENCE OF COLOUR

What are light and colour?

The vast range of colours we see in our gardens and homes, with their near infinite subtleties of quality, shades of light as well as intensity, can be accurately measured. But what exactly are light and colour? To state coldly and scientifically that they are forms of electromagnetic radiation clearly disregards their beauty, but, technically speaking, that is their nature.

Electromagnetic radiation comes from the sun, and its range is wide, from gamma rays to low-frequency radio waves. But only a very small part of this extensive spectrum is in the form of visible light, from wavelengths at around 0.0004mm when the colour is deep violet, through blue, green, yellow, orange and red to deep red, with a wavelength of 0.0007mm.
See Diagram 1, below.

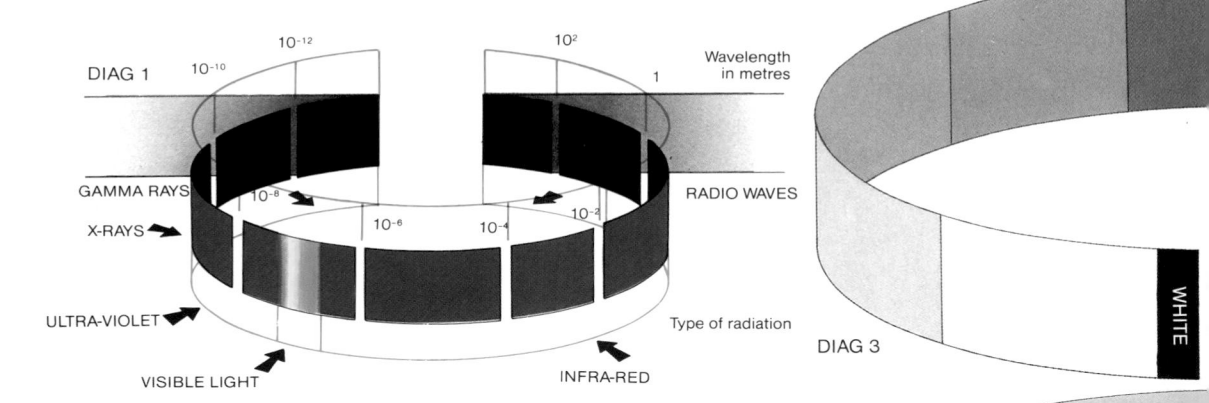

Defining colour

Colours can be conceived as having three dimensions - hue, value and intensity.

Hue

This first dimension is the quality by which colours are basically distinguished from each other, such as yellow from red, green, blue or purple. For convenience, the colours so defined are those that are easily recognized, such as red, yellow, green, blue and violet. However, the Munsell System in North America defines the principal hues as red, yellow, green, blue and purple, with intermediate ones as yellow-red, green-yellow, blue-green, purple-blue and red-purple. In reality these names do no more than define points in a continuous range of hues that form a transitional and continuous band of colour. They are best conceived as a circle of pure colour, containing no white, grey or black.

If a strip of paper with ten equal divisions is marked and coloured with the five principal and five intermediate hues of the Munsell System and held in a circle the continuous range of hues and their relationship to each other can be seen.
See Diagram 2, top right.

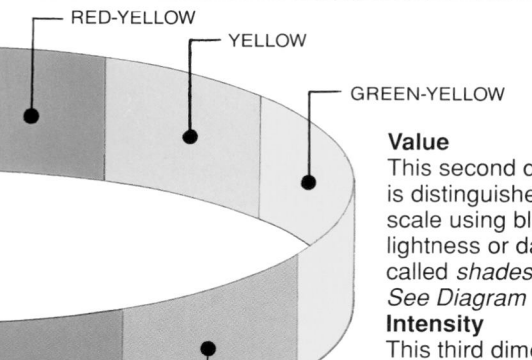

RED-YELLOW

YELLOW

GREEN-YELLOW

GREEN

BLUE-GREEN

BLACK

Value

This second dimension defines the quality by which a light colour is distinguished from a dark one. This is most easily depicted on a scale using black and white as the extremes. When defining the lightness or darkness within a colour, those with dark colours are called *shades,* while those that are light are *tints.*
See Diagram 3, centre left.

Intensity

This third dimension is also known as *saturation* or *purity,* and in North America as *chroma.* It defines the strength or weakness of a colour - its brightness or greyness. For instance, yellow can be highly saturated with colour, or the pigments slowly decreased to a point when it becomes light grey. Other colours will produce similar results, but dark hues such as red will become grey, and purple will become dark grey.
See Diagram 4, bottom left.

Colour absorption

When sunlight falls upon coloured surfaces a few of the colours present in the white light – which contains a mixture of all wavelengths of the visible spectrum – may be absorbed by the colour and not reflected. This process is known as *colour absorption* and tends to make primary hues such as red, blue and yellow more dominant.

When white light falls on a white surface, most of the rays are reflected and the subject appears white. This, however, does not apply to other surfaces. Yellow surfaces absorb the blues, indigos and violets in white light, reflecting mainly yellow as well as some green, orange and red.

Reds, the most colour saturated of all hues, absorb green and blue light but reflect red, while blue surfaces absorb red, orange and yellow rays, and scatter blue, together with green, indigo and violet.

This intensification of reds, blues and yellows tends to make them dominant. Fully saturated hues reflect no more than two of the primary colours, whereas pink, which is a desaturated red - a pastel shade - reflects all three of the primary colours but a greater amount of red.
See Diagram 5, below.

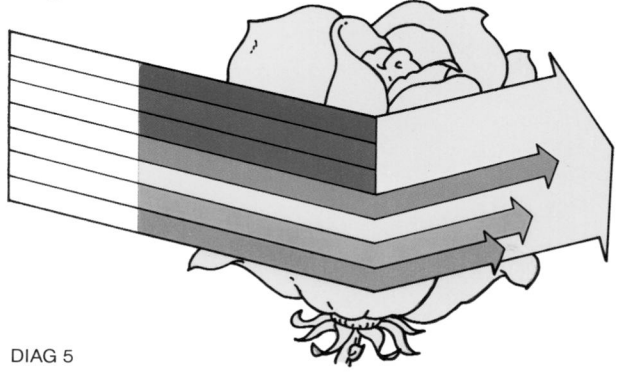

DIAG 5

Introduction

COLOUR IN THE GARDEN

Colour wheels

Colour wheels are frequently used to aid colour planning in the garden. When the great English scientist Sir Isaac Newton investigated light in the late 1600s, he made a wheel formed of seven colours (red, orange, yellow, green, blue, indigo and violet). During the late 1800s the American scientist A.H. Munsell researched colour assessment based on equal changes in the visual spectrum. He created a colour wheel formed of five principal colours (red, yellow, green, blue and purple, with intermediate ones between them). Other wheels have been created using four colours (red, yellow, green and blue). However, the easiest colour circle to use is formed of three basic hues (red, yellow and blue) with three secondary ones (orange, green and violet). The secondary colours are created by overlapping the basic hues.

These colour circles indicate complementary colours (those diametrically opposite) and those that harmonize with each other (those in adjacent segments). Complementary hues are those with no common pigments, while harmonizing ones share the same pigments. Therefore, it can be seen that yellow and violet, blue and orange, red and green are complementary colours, while yellow harmonizes with green and orange, blue with green and violet, and red with orange and violet.

This colour-circle is formed by mixing coloured paints, by the process known as *subtractive colour mixing*. The other method of creating colour is by projecting three separate coloured lights (red green and blue) onto a white surface. This process is known as *additive colour mixing* and creates colours with a different bias. *See Diagram 6, of a subtractive colour circle*, below.

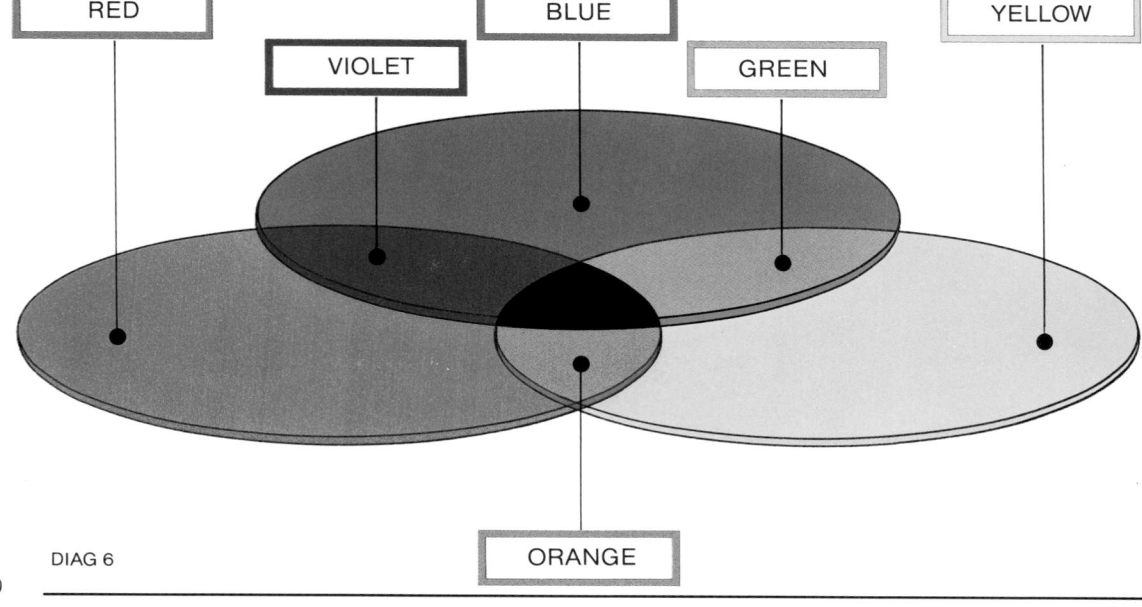

RED · VIOLET · BLUE · GREEN · YELLOW · ORANGE

DIAG 6

Below: Aubretia *The vibrant colour of this wall plant creates a dramatic effect above a planting of orange flowers.*

Shiny and matt surfaces

The surface texture of a leaf, flower or stem influences the reflected light and its effect on the eye. A smooth surface reflects light at the same angle at which the light hits it. This makes the light purer in colour than the same light reflected from a matt surface. There, the irregularities of the surface scatter the reflected light and create an impression of dullness. Another effect of different surface texture is that smooth surfaces appear darker and matt ones lighter. In Nature, however, few plant surfaces are as smooth as glass, and the scattering of reflected light occurs from most of them. *See Diagram 7, below*

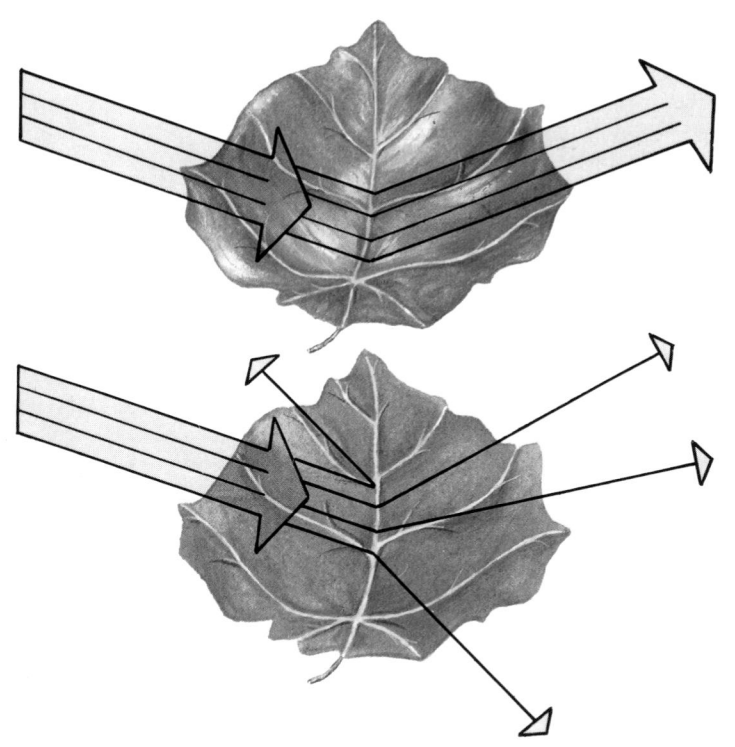

DIAG 7

The evening factor

The well-known delight of shepherds to have red sky at night, indicating a fine tomorrow, results from a clear sky as the sun's rays penetrate atmospheric particles and the air molecules themselves. Even though the sky appears blue, the rays become redder, because blue light is not created but scattered out of white light. This change to the violet end of the spectrum makes dark colours even darker. Blues and especially purples are made darker, while whites and yellows are not so dramatically affected. Conversely, bright sunshine glaring down at midday highlights light colours more than dark ones.

Above: Heliotropum x hybridum *This half-hardy perennial is usually grown as a half-hardy annual. Its flowers have a beautiful fragrance, said to resemble that of a cherry pie.*

Introduction

HARMONIES AND CONTRASTS

All colours have their own personalities: some are dominant, perhaps overpowering when *en masse*, others are demure and reserved, with a gentle and soft quality. Creating a balance of harmonies and contrasts throughout the garden, as well as in one particular area, is very important if it is to be a pleasing area for outdoor living.

White, grey and silver borders reveal a sense of space, coolness and serenity that no other colour can achieve. Consider the impression of unending space created by a snow-covered field, the coolness revealed in summer by silver and grey-leaved plants, and the serenity and tranquillity of a white-flowered climber trailing over an old white-washed brick wall. Areas of the garden totally devoted to white, grey and silver plants are fascinating and unusual, but do not plant all of your garden in this way. Use them in an area which is not immediately apparent, so that on turning a corner a display of relaxing colours comes as a surprise. Green foliaged plants harmonize with white and silver plants, offering a background that does not vie for attention or become dominant, yet one that reveals its own qualities of calm and a sense of continuation from season to season.

Reds are the most dominant of all colours in a garden and in a totally colour-saturated form are exceptionally strong and powerful, often overpowering to the eye. Strong reds need to be used with care, especially in large groupings. When seen against a mid-green background, densely-red flowers, such as poppies, have a three-dimensional effect and appear to stand out from the foliage and stems. Most red flowers however, are not totally colour saturated and appear as shades. Pinks, for example, are desaturated reds, which means that they contain only a small proportion of red pigments.

Golds and yellows are the brightest colours in a garden. Yellow flowers bring life and brightness, especially in spring and early summer. However, these colours have a vibrancy that can soon overpower and subdue demure and light colours, and therefore need to be used carefully. Soft yellows, however, happily blend with whites, silvers and greys, but ensure that the total area given to yellow is less than that allocated to the white.

Blues and purples have a range that extends from soft and gentle blues to strong and dominant purples. Indeed, such is the colour range that the spire-like heads of delphiniums when packed with deep purple flowers are even highlighted by blue sky. Shades at the pastel end of this range blend with the less dominant shades of yellow, but do not try to form a pot-pourri of dominant reds, purples and yellows - unless you have strong sunglasses!

Throughout this all-colour book we have both described individual plants as well as suggesting those which form pleasing colour and shape combinations with them.

Above: Rudbeckia 'Autumn Leaves' *This beautiful annual creates a distinctive splash of colour (centre) in a mixed border.*

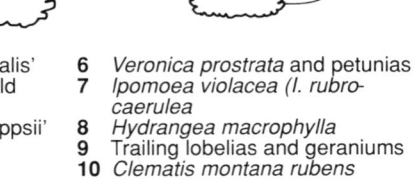

CHAPTER ONE

Above: Aster thompsonii nanus
*This lovely 20cm (8in) high rock
garden plant produces masses of
star-like lavender blue flowers.*

Key:

1 *Cupressus glabra* 'Pyramidalis'
2 *Euonymus fortunei.* 'Emerald and Gold'
3 *Chamaecyparis obtusa* 'Crippsii'
4 Agapanthus
5 *Thymus* 'E.B. Anderson'
6 *Veronica prostrata* and petunias
7 *Ipomoea violacea (I. rubro-caerulea*
8 *Hydrangea macrophylla*
9 Trailing lobelias and geraniums
10 *Clematis montana rubens*

THE FLOWER BORDER

Flower borders are invariably a medley of different types of plants. Early in the year many borders are packed with spring-flowering bedding plants such as wallflowers, double daisies, forget-me-nots, daffodils and tulips, while in summer they are awash with hardy annuals and summer-flowering bedding plants. Additionally, some borders are a mixture of shrubs and herbaceous plants, as well as quick-growing and colourful space fillers such as annuals and summer-flowering bedding plants. These 'mixed' borders are usually a pot pourri of different colours, with shrubs providing a framework of colour from year to year, while hardy and half-hardy annuals create attractive splashes of colour which can be changed each year.

As well as mixed-colour borders, single-colour theme ones are also possible. These are devoted to plants within a certain colour range, such as *whites, greys and silvers, pinks and reds, blues and mauves,* and *golds and yellows.* Additionally, *green foliaged plants* can be used to create borders with soft and gentle tones, as well as provide backcloths for more vividly-coloured plants. Some plants have *variegated foliage,* and as well as being visually dramatic on their own, they can be attractively harmonized with plainer-leaved types.

Within this chapter, plants are arranged according to their flower or leaf colours, enabling a paintbox of colours to be readily seen. Single colour-theme borders have immediate impact, thanks to their originality and eye-catching qualities, but they can often be further enhanced with small patches of harmonizing colours. For instance, blue borders are enhanced with patches of demure white or delicate pale lemon-yellow (but not blinding bright yellow, which commands too much attention in full sunlight and suppresses the beauty of pastel-blue tints). White and silvery borders, with their cool and spacious influence, can be given a slightly warm glow by introducing patches of pink or light blue flowers. Avoid strong colours, as these soon dominate and spoil a white-theme border.

Left: Summer-bedding schemes *need to create a mixture of colours, heights and textures, yet also be symmetrical and attractive.*

THE FLOWER BORDER

Acanthus mollis

Common Bear's Breeches (UK)
Artist's Acanthus (USA)

Acanthus plants are easily
recognizable by their long, upright
spires of tubular, rather foxglove-
like flowers and handsome leaves.
The most commonly grown species
is *Acanthus mollis*, with white and
purple flowers borne during mid to
late summer in 45cm (1½ft) long
spires. Others include *Acanthus
spinosus*, the Spiny Bear's
Breeches, and *Acanthus
longifolius*, the Long-leaved
Acanthus. Other common names
generally given to the whole group,
are Bear's Breech and Bear's Foot.
Height: 90cm (3ft)
Spread: 75cm (2½ft)
Cultivation: Deeply cultivated well-
drained soil and a sunny position
suit this plant. It can be left to form
large clumps; in autumn, cut these
down to soil-level.
Propagation: Although seeds can
be sown in spring in loam-based
compost in pots placed in a cold
frame, it is easier for the home
gardener to propagate by lifting
and dividing congested lumps in
spring.

Left: **Acanthus mollis** *This
dramatic herbaceous perennial
displays purple and white flowers
in long spires from mid to late
summer. In small gardens just one
plant is often enough, as the roots
can be invasive.*

Achillea millefolium

Yarrow (UK) Common Yarrow ·
Milfoil ·Sanguinary · Thousand
Seal · Nose Bleed (USA)

This is a well-known hardy
creeping herbaceous perennial; the
original wild species is often seen
as a weed in lawns, pastures,
meadows and grassy banks.
Several attractive forms are now
available and will enhance any
mixed or herbaceous border. The
deep green leaves provide a

Acanthus plants have had a marked influence on
architecture. The leaves of *Acanthus spinosus*, Spiny
Bear's Breeches, are said to have been the model for
decorations in the Corinthian style of architecture.

perfect foil for the 10cm (4in) wide flattened flower heads from mid to late summer. The form 'Cerise Queen' displays cherry-red flowers, and 'Kelway' clear red heads.

Height: 60-75cm (2-2½ft)
Spread: 45cm (1½ft)
Cultivation: Any well-drained garden soil and a position in full sun suits this tolerant plant. In autumn cut down the stems to soil level. Supporting the plants with twiggy sticks is necessary only in exposed areas. Remember to stake the plants early so that they grow up and through the supports.
Propagation: The easiest way to increase this plant is by lifting and dividing established plants in early spring.

Below: Achillea millefolium 'Cerise Queen' *This beautiful cherry-red form of the common Yarrow brings both colour and feathery deep green foliage to a mixed or herbaceous border.*

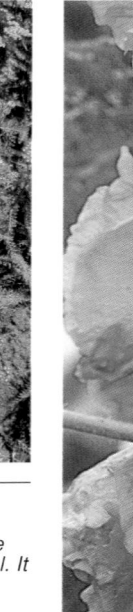

Right: Alcea rosea
This showy plant, often better known as Althaea rosea, can be grown as an annual or a biennial. It looks especially effective when planted against a wall, and is splendid for bringing late colour to a garden. It grows higher when cultivated as a biennial.

Alcea rosea

(Althaea rosea, Althaea chinensis)
Hollyhock (UK and USA)

This well-known hardy perennial is grown as an annual or biennial. Its funnel-shaped single or double pink flowers, to 10cm (4in) wide, are borne on short stalks from mid to late summer and even into early autumn. The light-green leaves have hairy surfaces.

Height: 2.1-2.7m (7-9ft) treated as a biennial; 1.3m (4½ft) treated as an annual.
Spread: 60cm (2ft)
Cultivation: Hollyhocks like fertile, relatively heavy, moisture-retentive soil and a sheltered position. They usually require staking when grown as biennials. They can be encouraged to flower for several years as perennials by cutting the stems down to within 15-20cm (6-8in) of soil-level after the flowers have faded. Hollyhocks treated in this way should be mulched with well-rotted manure or compost during the following spring and early summer. In exceptionally cold areas, cover the plants with cloches.

Propagation: To grow as an annual, sow seeds in late winter 6mm (¼in) deep in loam-based compost and keep at 10°C (50°F). When the seedlings are large enough to handle prick them off into pots and leave them in a cold frame to harden off. Plant out into the garden when all risk of frost has passed. To grow as a biennial, sow seeds 12mm (½in) deep in drills in the open garden in mid-summer. When the seedlings are large enough to handle – usually in late summer or early autumn – thin them out or transplant the young plants to 45-60cm (1½-2ft) apart. During spring of the following year set them in the garden. Remember that these plants will need staking. The supports should be unobtrusive.

Achillea millefolium is a delightful plant for the flower border with a medicinal past. Old English herbalists called it Nose-bleed because its leaves promoted bleeding when applied to the nose.

Alcea rosea, with its large flowers on long spires, blends with many autumn-flowered plants. When grown as an annual or biennial rather than as a perennial, it is less susceptible to rust disease.

THE FLOWER BORDER

Amaryllis belladonna

(*Hippeastrum equestre*)
Belladonna Lily (UK)
Belladonna Lily · Cape Belladonna ·
Naked-lady Lily (USA)

A bulbous, somewhat tender plant with mid-green strap-like leaves from late winter to mid-summer. In late summer, these die down and the fragrant trumpet-shaped satiny pale-pink 10-13cm (4-5in) wide flowers appear on bare stems, usually in clusters of three or four, sometimes up to twelve.
Height: 60-75cm (2-2¹/₂ft)
Spread: 30-38cm (12-15in)
Cultivation: Well-drained soil in a sunny and sheltered position is best. A site at the base of a south or west-facing wall is ideal. Late frosts will damage the early foliage. Set the bulbs in the soil in early summer, with 15-20cm (6-8in) of soil covering them. Remove dead flowers as they fade; also the leaves and stems when they die down.
Propagation: Clumps that become too large can be lifted in summer as soon as the leaves turn yellow. Divide and replant immediately.

Alstroemeria aurantiaca

Peruvian Lily (UK)
Peruvian Lily · Lily of the Incas
(USA)

A richly-coloured, fleshy, tuberous-rooted Chilean herbaceous perennial, the hardiest of all alstroemerias. The trumpet-shaped 4-5cm (1¹/₂-2in) wide flowers, borne from mid to late summer, boast a range of colours, from rich orange to orange-scarlet. The long, lance-shaped leaves are glaucous (blue-grey) beneath.
Height: 90cm (3ft)
Spread: 38-45cm (15-18in)
Cultivation: Alstroemerias prefer fertile, well-drained, light soil and a sunny or partially shaded position. Set new plants (preferably pot-grown) in position during spring, 10-15cm (4-6in) deep. To encourage the development of

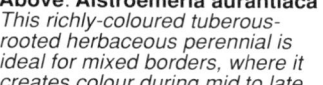

Above: **Alstroemeria aurantiaca**
This richly-coloured tuberous-rooted herbaceous perennial is ideal for mixed borders, where it creates colour during mid to late summer. The flowers are ideal for cutting for home decoration, when they last a long time in water.

further flowers, remove the blossoms as they fade, and in autumn cut the plants down to soil-level.
Propagation: New plants can be raised from seed sown in loam-based compost in spring and placed in a cold frame, but it is easier for the home gardener to lift and divide congested clumps in spring. Take care not to damage the roots. To produce a large number of plants lift and divide established clumps in mid-spring and pot up small individual pieces. Place in a cold frame.

Alstroemeria aurantiaca, with its vivid colours, needs a strong contrast from a large, spectacularly coloured shrub, such as the purple-leaved *Cotinus coggygria* 'Royal Purple'.

Amaryllis belladonna gained its common name Belladonna Lily in Italy from the fancied resemblance of its blend of red and white flowers to the complexion of a beautiful woman (*bella donna*).

Aster novi-belgii

Michaelmas Daisy (UK)
New England Aster (USA)

A beautiful and well-known herbaceous perennial. The original type came from North America and when introduced into Britain gained its common name because it flowers on Michaelmas (29 September), a significant feast day in the agricultural calendar. The plant has deep green, stem-clasping, slender-pointed leaves and 5cm (2in) wide flowers borne in dense clusters during late summer and early autumn. Many pink and red forms are available, including 'Carnival' (semi-double, cherry-red), 'Freda Ballard' (semi-double, red), 'Patricia Ballard' (semi-double, pink), 'Raspberry Ripple' (double, carmine-red), 'Winston S. Churchill' (double,

glowing ruby-red), 'Orlando' (semi-double, pink), 'Fellowship' (semi-double, pink) and 'The Cardinal' (single, deep rose-red). There is also a range of dwarf forms, 30-45cm (1-1½ft) high.

Height: 90cm-1.2m (3-4ft)
Spread: 45-60cm (1½-2ft)
Cultivation: Fertile, well-drained but moisture-retentive soil (especially in late summer) is essential, as is a position in full sun. Most of the tall varieties will need staking with twiggy sticks. Do this early so that the plants grow up through the sticks and eventually hide them. After flowering, cut the plants down to soil level. The clumps are best divided every three years to prevent the quality of the flowers from deteriorating. Replant only young parts from around the edges of the clumps as these are young and healthy;

discard the old central portions.
Propagation: This is easily done by lifting and dividing clumps in early spring, every three years. To produce large numbers of plants *Aster novi-belgii* is best increased by lifting and dividing healthy clumps in mid-spring every spring and separating the healthy outside parts into small pieces. These can be planted in a nursery bed if very small or planted into the border. Because they are small they will have to be planted close together.

Below: **Aster novi-belgii 'Orlando'** *This richly coloured semi-double pink variety of Michaelmas Daisy brings life and colour to borders in late summer and into autumn. Fertile, well-drained but moisture-retentive soil is essential, and a sunny position.*

Below: **Amaryllis belladonna** *This exotic-looking bulbous border plant is useful for providing late summer colour. It does well among shrubs that provide some protection or by a south or west-facing wall.*

Aster novi-belgii and **Aster novae-angliae** are superb for late colour. They are ideal for mixed and herbaceous borders, while the dwarf forms of *Aster novi-belgii* are ideal for small town gardens.

THE FLOWER BORDER

Canna x generalis

(*Canna x hybrida*)
Indian Shot (UK)
Common Garden Canna (USA)

An erect, large-leaved rhizomatous
hybrid, frequently used in summer-
bedding schemes. The leaves
reach 60cm (2ft) long and 30cm
(1ft) wide. There are two main
types of canna: those with purple
or brown leaves and those with
green ones. The 5-7.5cm (2-3in)
gladioli-like flowers are borne at the
tops of the stems during summer.
Outstanding forms include 'Assault'
(green leaves, red flowers),
'Bonfire' (green leaves, orange-
scarlet flowers) and 'President'
(green leaves, vivid scarlet
flowers).
Height: 90cm-1m (3-3¹/₂ft)
Spread: 38-45cm (15-18in)
Cultivation: During early spring,
plant the rhizomes in trays or large
pots of rich loam-based compost
and keep at 16°C (61°F). Before
planting them, give the rhizomes a
thorough soaking with water. They
will soon send up shoots; if more
than one shoot appears, split them
up and pot them. When they are
well established, pot them up into a
rich compost, and subsequently
into containers or beds where they
are to flower. Make sure you do not
do this until all risk of frost has
passed. In autumn, dig up the
plants or move them into a
greenhouse before the onset of
frosts.
Propagation: Divide the rhizomes
in early spring. Cannas can also be
increased from seed, although the
progeny will not resemble the
parents. Also, the seeds have
tough coats and require nicking
with a knife or soaking in water for
a day or so. Sow in late winter in a
high temperature.

Celosia argentea plumosa

(*Celosia argentea pyramidalis*)
Prince of Wales' Feathers ·
Feathered Cockscomb (UK)
Cockcomb · Feathered Amaranth
(USA)

A distinctive half-hardy annual
frequently grown as a houseplant but
also useful for summer-bedding
displays in mild areas outdoors.
Striking, feathery, 7.5-15cm (3-6in)
high flower plumes appear during late
summer in a range of colours. Good
forms include 'Apricot Brandy'
(orange-red), while others have mixed
colours – red, pink, yellow and orange
– as in 'Pampas Plume Mixed'.

Height: 38-60cm (15-24in)
Spread: 25-30cm (10-12in)
Cultivation: Fertile well-drained
soil and a sunny and sheltered
position are essential when
growing these plants outdoors. It is
not worth trying to grow them
outdoors in cold areas, as sudden
low-temperature spells soon check
their growth.
Propagation: During mid-spring,
sow seeds 3mm (¹/₈in) deep in
loam-based compost kept at 20°C
(68°F). When they are large
enough to handle, prick off the
seedlings into boxes or small pots
and slowly harden them off, without
sudden drops in temperature. Plant
them out into the garden when all
risk of frost has passed.

Cannas, with their dark foliage, can be used to create
an interesting summer-bedding scheme with an
edging of light blue lobelias and a carpet of scarlet-
flowered *Begonia semperflorens* 'Indian Maid'.

Crocosmia masonorum

Montbretia (UK and USA)

A hardy corm-producing border plant with strap-like leaves, patterned pleats and ribs. The flame-orange flowers are borne from mid to late summer at the tips of the arching stems. A similar though less hardy plant is *Crocosmia x crocosmiiflora (Montbretia crocosmiiflora)*. These are beautiful plants with 4cm (1½in) long trumpet-shaped flowers from mid to late summer. There are many exciting varieties, such as 'Bressingham Blaze' (orange-red), 'Emberglow' (orange-red) and 'Vulcan' (orange-red)

Height: 75cm (2½ft)

Spread: 20-25cm (8-10in)

Cultivation: Light, well-drained and fertile soil is best, but do not let the soil dry out during summer. Crocosmias appreciate a sunny position. Set the corms in position in early spring, 5-7.5cm (2-3in) deep and 15cm (6in) apart. In warm areas the plants can be left in the soil to form large clumps, but in exceptionally cold areas lift the plants in late autumn, dry off the corms and store them over winter. When storing the corms keep them neither too dry, or they will shrivel, nor too damp, or they will rot.

Propagation: Large clumps left in the soil can be lifted and divided just after flowering, or you can wait until spring.

Above: **Crocosmia masonorum**
This spectacular plant for summer colour is hardier than others of its genus. The flowers can be cut for house decoration. In mild areas it can be left in the ground to form large clumps.

Left: **Celosia argentea plumosa 'Apricot Brandy'** *This distinctive half-hardy annual needs a warm and sheltered position. The plume-like flowers last for many weeks in summer and contrast well with the light green foliage.*

Celosia argentea plumosa is often used in formal bedding schemes, but it can also look effective planted as a filler in mixed borders or with hardy annuals. Take care not to overwater plants.

Crocosmia x crocosmiiflora forms a stately display in mixed borders. Several varieties are available, including 'Bressingham Blaze' (orange-red flowers) 'Emberglow' (orange-red) and 'Vulcan' (orange-red).

THE FLOWER BORDER

Cuphea miniata

A spectacular Mexican half-hardy perennial grown as a half-hardy annual. Cupheas bear slender-pointed mid-green leaves covered with white bristles. During mid-summer and into autumn, they produce a fine display of bright-red 4cm (1½in) long tubular flowers. Often grown as a pot plant for a cool greenhouse or conservatory, they can also be used in summer-bedding schemes. The form 'Firefly' has brilliant scarlet flowers.
Height: 45-60cm (1½-2ft)
Spread: 38-45cm (15-18in)

Cultivation: Any ordinary garden soil suits cupheas, and they can be grown in full sun or light shade.
Propagation: During spring, sow seeds 6mm (¼in) deep in loam-based compost at 15°C (59°F). When they are large enough to handle, prick the seedlings off into loam-based compost and harden them off in a cold frame. After all risk of frost is over, set the plants out in the garden. Alternatively, the seedlings can be pricked off into small pots of loam-based compost, and potted up into larger pots as the plants grow. When they have become sizeable plants they can be taken indoors.

Left: Cuphea miniata 'Firefly'
This busy, highly branched hardy annual bears masses of bright scarlet flowers during summer. It is best planted in the centre of the annual border as it does not require staking.

Dahlia

These reliable and well-known garden flowers can be divided into two main groups: those that can be grown as half-hardy annuals for use in bedding schemes; and those that are best grown as perennials in mixed borders, mingling with herbaceous plants and flowering shrubs.
BEDDING DAHLIAS
These half-hardy perennials from Mexico are grown as half-hardy annuals, displaying 5-7.5cm (2-3in) wide single, double or semi-double flowers from mid-summer to autumn. There are many varieties in a wide colour range, in mixed and self-colours.
Height: 30-50cm (12-20in)
Spread: 38-45cm (15-24in)
Cultivation: Well-cultivated, fertile, compost or manure-enriched soil and a sunny position suits bedding dahlias. If the soil is too rich, however, the plants produce excessive foliage at the expense of flowers. There is no need to stake them – unlike the large border types. Removal of dead flowers encourages the plants to produce further blooms. Water the plants during dry spells.
Propagation: During late winter and early spring, sow seeds 6mm (¼in) deep in a loam-based seed compost at 16°C (61°F). When they are large enough to handle, prick off the seedlings into boxes or small pots of loam-based compost and slowly harden them off in a cold frame. Set them out in the garden as soon as all risk of frost has passed.
BORDER DAHLIAS
These are half-hardy tuberous plants, easily damaged by frost, that quickly bring colour to the garden. There are several classifications and many varieties.

Cuphea also does well as a pot plant for the home or greenhouse. Sow seeds in spring and prick out the seedlings into small pots of loam-based compost. Pot up into larger pots when the roots become pot-bound.

Anemone-flowered
(60cm-1m/2-3¹/₂ft): These have double flowers with flat outer petals and short, tubular inner ones. Flowering is from mid-summer to the frosts of autumn.

Ball-type (90cm-1.2m/3-4ft): As the name implies, these have ball-shaped flowers, with tubular, blunt-ended petals. There are *Small Ball* types with blooms 10-15cm (4-6in) wide, and *Miniature Ball* forms with flowers up to 10cm (4in) wide.

Cactus and Semi-cactus
(90cm-1.5m/3-5ft): These are sub-divided into five groups, *Miniature* (blooms up to 10cm/4in wide); *Small* (blooms 10-15cm/4-6in wide); *Medium* (blooms 15-20cm/6-8in); *Large* (blooms 20-25cm/8-10in wide); and *Giant* (blooms 25cm/10in or more wide). Cactus types have petals rolled back or quilled for more than half their length. Semi-cactus types have similar petals, but quilled or rolled back for less than half their length.

Collarettes (75cm-1.2m/2¹/₂-4ft): These have blooms with a single outer ring of flat ray florets, with a ring of small florets in the centre, forming a disc.

Decoratives: These have double flowers without central discs. They are formed of broad, flat ray florets. This group is further divided into: *Miniature* (90cm-1.2m/3-4ft): These have flowers up to 10cm (4in) wide. *Small* (1-1.2m/3¹/₂-4ft): Flowers 10-15cm (4-6in) wide. *Medium* (1-1.2m/3¹/₂-4ft): Flowers 15-20cm (6-8in) wide. *Large* (1-1.5m/3¹/₂-5ft): Flowers 20-25cm (8-10in) wide. *Giant* (1.2-1.5m/4-5ft): Flowers 25cm (10in) or more wide.

Paeony-flowered (up to 90cm/3ft): The flowers are formed of two or more rings of flat ray flowers, with a central disc.

Pompon (90cm-1.2m/3-4ft): The flowers closely resemble those of *Ball* types, but are more globular and are no more than 5cm (2in) wide. The florets curl inwards for their entire length.

Single-flowered
(45-75cm/1¹/₂-2¹/₂ft): These display

flowers up to 10cm (4in) wide, with a single row of petals arranged around a central disc.

Cultivation: Well-drained soil, with plenty of moisture-retentive compost or well-decomposed manure added, is required. Include a sprinkling of bonemeal before setting the tubers in the ground during mid to late spring at 10cm (4in) deep. If sprouted tubers are used, take care that they are not planted too early, or frost will damage them. The young plants will need staking for support. Nip out the growing tips of all shoots to encourage sideshoots to develop, and if you want large flowers, remove sideshoots and buds from around the developing flowers. The removal of dead flowers helps the development of further flowers.

Above: Dahlia 'Bishop of Llandaff' *This is a paeony-flowered type with rings of flat crimson petals surrounding a central core of stamens. Its foliage is dark and although it is a dahlia used in bedding schemes, at 75cm (2¹/₂ft) high it grows taller than most varieties used for bedding.*

In autumn, carefully dig up the tubers about a week after the foliage has been blackened by frost. Remove soil from the tubers and store them upside down for a few weeks to encourage them to dry out. Then place them in boxes of peat in a dry, frost-proof position until the following year.

Propagation: The easiest way for the home gardener to do this is to divide the tubers in spring.

Formal planting schemes for bedding dahlias are easy to create. One example is as a carpet of salmon-pink and cherry-red dot plants, with an edging of pale blue lobelia.

Ball types to look for include 'Alltami Cherry' (small ball, vivid scarlet), 'Biddenham Serene' (small ball, dark crimson), 'Direct Hit' (miniature ball, scarlet) and 'Valerie Buller' (miniature, plum red).

THE FLOWER BORDER

Above: **Dahlia 'Alva's Doris'**
*A beautiful bright crimson small
cactus dahlia,10-15cm (4-6in)
wide. It rises to 1-1.2m (3 ½-4ft)
high with a spread of 75cm (2 ½ft)
wide. It is dominantly coloured.*

Left: **Dahlia 'Geerling's Elite'**
*A brilliantly-coloured free-flowering
collarette variety, this has orient-
red petals tipped buff, and a buff
collar. It rises to 1m (3 ½ft) and is
ideal for setting towards the front of
a mixed border.*

Decorative types to look for include 'Hamari Girl'
(giant dec., pink), 'Jo's Choice' (miniature dec., red),
'Festive Season' (small dec., yellow and red) and
'Liberator' (giant dec., rich crimson scarlet).

Top right: Dahlia 'Scarlet Comet'
An anemone-flowered variety with brilliantly-coloured flowers formed of an inner ring of petals that surround the centre like a halo. It is ideal for bringing an intense splash of colour to a border.

Right: Dahlia 'Salmon Keene'
This cactus-type displays the rolled or 'quilled' petals distinctive of this group. It produces attractively spiked flowers that will enhance a border.

Cactus types to look for include 'Athalie' (semi-cactus, pink blends), 'Elmbrook Rebel' (giant semi-cactus, deep red),'Doc Van Horn' (large semi-cactus, pink) and 'Alva's Doris' (small cactus, blood red).

THE FLOWER BORDER

Euphorbia griffithii 'Fireglow'

Spurge (UK)

An attractive perennial with lance-shaped, mid-green leaves and orange-red bracts at the top of the stems during early summer.
Height: 60-75cm (2-2½ft)
Spread: 60-75cm (2-2½ft)
Cultivation: Fertile, well-drained soil and a position in full sun suit euphorbias. Set the plants in position in spring or early autumn.
Propagation: The plants are easily increased by lifting and dividing large clumps in spring or autumn.

Dicentra spectabilis

Bleeding Heart (UK and USA)

This widely grown Chinese and Japanese herbaceous perennial has long been known as Bleeding Heart, but at the turn of the century it was the North American *Dicentra canadensis* that laid claim to this common name. *D. spectabilis* is often called Dutchman's Breeches, but this name is more accurately applied to *D. cucullaria*, another North American plant. At one time *D. spectabilis* was aptly called Chinaman's Breeches, which accurately related to the region from which the plant came. But whatever its common name, this plant is a most attractive addition to any garden. Its grey-green, finely-divided and rather fern-like leaves are a perfect foil for the 2.5cm (1in) long, pendulous, rose red, heart-shaped flowers, borne on arching stems during early to mid-summer.
Height: 45-75cm (1½-2½ft)
Spread: 45cm (1½ft)
Cultivation: Rich, well-cultivated fertile soil and a sheltered, sunny or partially shaded position suit this plant. The roots are somewhat brittle, so the plants are best left undisturbed once established.
Propagation: It is easily increased by carefully lifting and dividing established clumps in spring or autumn.

Above: **Dicentra spectabilis**
This well-known and distinctive hardy herbaceous perennial with dainty flowers needs well-cultivated fertile soil in full sun or partial shade. The flowers appear from early to mid-summer.

Below: **Euphorbia griffithii 'Fireglow'** *This unusual perennial has red-tipped shoots that arise from the soil. In early summer the appearance of the foliage is enhanced by strikingly attractive, bright orange-red bracts.*

Dicentra cucullaria, or Dutchman's Breeches, is native to North America and was once commonly found wild in New York State. Its Dutch connection is that New York was once called New Amsterdam.

Freesia x kewensis

This well-known South African tender, corm-bearing plant produces the sweetly-scented 2.5-5cm (1-2in) long fragrant blooms so often sold as cut flowers for home decoration. These hybrids, often known as *Freesia x hybrida*, have narrow mid-green leaves and, when planted outside in spring, produce flowers during late summer. They are not hardy enough to be left outside all year. Many forms are available, in a wide colour range. Red and pink varieties include 'Red Star' (red), 'Rose Marie' (rose-pink), 'Madame Curie' (red) and 'Nieuw Amsterdam' (magenta).

Height: 45-60cm (1½-2ft)
Spread: 13-20cm (5-8in)
Cultivation: Fertile, light, sandy soil and a sheltered sunny position suit freesias. During spring, plant the corms about 5cm (2in) deep. Use small twiggy sticks to support the foliage, and in autumn, when the foliage has turned yellow, lift the plants and corms. Dry off the corms and remove the offsets. In mild areas and in well-drained light and sandy soils it is possible to leave the corms outside all winter. Corms planted in late summer to early autumn will flower in late spring. Although freesias can be induced to flower in a greenhouse, a temperature of 5°C (45°F) is needed. Plant the corms in boxes or pots of loam-based compost in late summer and early autumn to bring about flowering from mid-winter to spring. Ensure you maintain the right temperature.
Propagation: Although seeds can be sown in late winter and spring, it is easier for home gardeners to remove the corms and offsets and to replant these in spring.

Euphorbia griffithii provides a screen of leaves from soil level to the orange-red bracts at the tops of shoots. Its clear outline allows it to be positioned just 30cm (1ft) in from the edge of a border.

THE FLOWER BORDER

Above: Galega officinalis
These plants have a sprawling habit, but create a superb colour patch, with their small pea-shaped flowers borne on branching stems with attractive, narrow leaves.

Galega officinalis

Goat's Rue (UK and USA)

A bushy and sprawling hardy herbaceous perennial with light green, short-stalked, compound leaves formed of many leaflets and best seen at the back of a border. During mid-summer it produces dense clusters of pale lilac or white flowers in short spires. The form 'Her Majesty' is well-known for its soft lilac-blue flowers.
Height: 1-1.5m (3½-5ft)
Spread: 75cm (2½ft)
Cultivation: Any well-drained garden soil and a position in full sun or light shade are suitable. Ideally, position it for a dominant display, with a grouping of three or five plants at the back of the border. After flowering, cut the stems down to soil level.
Propagation: Although it can be increased by sowing seeds in spring in a nursery bed, it is much easier to increase by lifting and dividing large clumps in spring or autumn.

Galega officinalis best displays its charms at the back of a border. The lilac-blue forms look best set against a high old brick wall whereas the white form is superb with a backcloth of clear sky.

Large-flowered gladioli are ideal for setting in mixed borders, where they create bright colour while shrubs and border plants are becoming established. Set them in groups of one colour rather than a mixture.

Gladiolus: Large flowered Hybrids

Sword Lily (UK)
Corn Flag · Sword Lily (USA)

These are the well-known, large-flowered, corm-bearing plants that create such spectacular displays from mid to late summer. The erect spikes of flowers are often 50cm (20in) long, formed of florets 10-18cm (4-7in) wide in a wide colour range, with many lovely reds and pinks. These include 'Aristocrat' (velvety garnet-red), 'Dr Fleming' (light salmon-pink with cream throats), 'Jo Wagenaar' (blood-scarlet, with a velvety sheen), 'Life Flame' (vivid red), 'Ardent' (cherry-red), 'Flos Florium' (salmon-pink), 'Memorial Day' (reddish-magenta) and 'President de Gaulle' (orange-red).
Height: 75cm-1m (2½-3½ft)
Spread: 20-25cm (8-10in)
Cultivation: Ordinary well-drained garden soil and a position in full sun assure success for this reliable favourite. Plant the corms in mid-spring, 10cm (4in) deep in heavy soil but 15cm (6in) in light soils. Anchored at these depths, the plants will not require staking in sheltered areas. In exposed positions, support the stems with small canes. After flowering, when the foliage turns yellow, carefully dig up the plants and allow them to dry for a week or so. Cut off the stems 12mm (½in) above the corms if they have not already broken off, and remove all soil. Then store them in shallow boxes in a cool and vermin-proof position. It should also be dry.
Propagation: In autumn, when the corms are lifted and dried for storage, remove the cormlets from around them. During spring, plant these in drills 5cm (2in) deep in a nursery bed.

Left: Gladiolus 'Aristocrat'
This is a beautiful large-flowered gladiolus that gives a reliable garden display. The colour range is wide and includes many red and pink shades.

Above: **Godetia grandiflora 'Dwarf Vivid'** *This beautiful hardy annual grows well in most soils. Avoid excessively rich ones that encourage leaf growth at the expense of flowers.*

Godetia grandiflora

(Godetia whitneyi)

This beautiful, compact, hardy annual from western North America has light green, lance-shaped leaves that present a superb foil for the 5cm (2in) wide rose-purple, funnel-shaped flowers during mid-summer and into late summer. Many single and double varieties are now available, in a wide colour range. These include 'Dwarf Vivid' (dark pink), 'Crimson Glow' (crimson) and 'Sybil Sherwood' (salmon-pink).
Height: 30-38cm (12-15in)
Spread: 20-25cm (8-10in)
Cultivation: Light and moist soil and a position in full sun suit it best. Avoid excessively rich soils that encourage lush foliage at the expense of flowers.
Propagation: In late spring, sow seeds 6mm (¼in) deep where they are to flower. When they are large enough to handle, thin out the seedlings to 15cm (6in) apart.

Above: **Godetia grandiflora 'Sybil Sherwood'** *This is a beautiful hardy annual that produces a mass of single salmon-pink and white flowers from mid to late summer. It creates delicately-coloured mounds.*

Godetia grandiflora can also be grown as a houseplant. Sow seeds thinly in pots or boxes of loam-based compost in late summer. Pot up the seedlings and grow them on in a cool greenhouse.

THE FLOWER BORDER

Hemerocallis 'Pink Damask'

Day Lily (UK and USA)

A superb hardy herbaceous perennial with stiff, arching, bright green sword-like leaves and lily-like flowers, 13-21cm (5-7in) wide. This form develops warm pink flowers with yellow throats during mid to late summer. Other pink and red forms include 'Holiday Mood' (bright red), 'Hornby Castle' (deep brick red with a yellow throat), 'Morocco Red' (dusky red with a yellow cup), 'Stafford' (deep red with an orange throat) and 'Pink Prelude' (pink).

Height: 75-90cm (2½-3ft)
Spread: 45-60cm (1½-2ft)
Cultivation: Good garden soil that does not dry out during summer and a position in full sun or light shade are best for Day Lilies. Once planted, they can be left in the same position for many years. In autumn cut the plants down to soil-level.
Propagation: Day Lilies are easily increased by lifting and dividing overcrowded clumps in spring or autumn. Replant the divided roots immediately.

Heuchera sanguinea

Coral Flower · Coral Bells (UK)
Coral Bells (USA)

This bright and cheerful hardy perennial from Mexico and Arizona has attractive, evergreen, round or heart-shaped, dark green leaves. The small, bell-shaped, bright red flowers are borne in lax heads on long and wiry stems from mid-summer to autumn. Several superb forms are available, including 'Firebird' (intense deep red), 'Red Spangles' (crimson-scarlet), 'Scintillation' (pink, tipped red),

Left: Heuchera sanguinea 'Red Spangles' *This is a beautiful Coral Flower with crimson-scarlet flowers borne on slender stems from mid-summer to autumn. Light soil is needed: do not plant in a clay soil.*

Hemerocallis are admirable for setting in a mixed or herbaceous border, to which they contribute both height and colour. Also, their stiff, upright form means they look good alongside paths.

Heuchera sanguinea is a delight at the edge of a border and can be blended with yellow roses, such as Rosa 'Buff Beauty'. It also looks good mixed with the magenta-flowered *Geranium psilostemon*.

Kniphofia

Red Hot Poker · Torch Lily · Flame Flower (UK)
Torch Lily · Poker Plant · Red Hot Poker · Tritoma (USA)

These well-known hardy herbaceous perennials produce distinctive poker-like heads from mid-summer to autumn. There are many hybrids, as well as true species, in a height range from 45cm-1.5m (1½-5ft). In colour they range from yellow and orange to red, and include 'Samuel's Scarlet' (height 1.5m/5ft, flowers bright scarlet-red), *Kniphofia uvaria* (90cm/3ft, red orange and yellow), *Kniphofia macowanii* (75cm/2½ft, deep orange-red), *Kniphofia nelsonii* 'Major' (75cm/2½ft, flame red), *Kniphofia rufa* (60cm/2ft, yellow tipped red), *Kniphofia praecox* (1.5-1.8m/5-6ft, brilliant scarlet).

Cultivation: Kniphofias like well-drained, fertile soil in full sun. It is essential that the soil does not remain wet during winter. Give the plants a mulch of well-rotted manure or compost in spring.

Propagation: The easiest way to increase the plants is by lifting and dividing large clumps in late spring. True species breed true from seeds, which can be sown 12mm (½in) deep in seedbeds in spring.

'Splendour' (salmon-scarlet) and 'Sunset' (bright red).
Height: 30-45cm (1-1½ft)
Spread: 38-45cm (15-18in)
Cultivation: Well-drained relatively light soil in full sun or light shade suits heucheras best. Set new plants in the soil in spring or autumn. After flowering, cut down the stems.
Propagation: Heucheras are easily increased by lifting and dividing old plants in spring. This usually needs to be done every three or four years, particularly when the crowns appear to rise out of the ground. Heucheras can also be raised by sowing seeds in early spring boxes of loam-based compost placed in a cold frame. When large enough to handle, plant out seedlings into a nursery bed. Plants will be ready for the garden in autumn.

Above: Hemerocallis 'Pink Damask' *An eye-catching Day Lily, this variety boasts warm pink flowers with yellow throats. It is ideal for planting and leaving in one position for a long time. The flowers last for only a day, but are quickly replenished by further flowers that create colour over a period of several months in summer.*

Right: Kniphofia praecox
This beautiful tall herbaceous perennial has stiff stems bearing torch-like brilliant scarlet flowers in late summer and into early autumn. They look best when planted in a dominant display with the bright torch-like heads silhouetted against blue sky, and are ideal for use in island beds where the plants are grown without supports.

Kniphofias are superb in a bed of their own using, just one species or variety. They are at their best when filling a bed that slopes down to water, but also look good in large gaps left between paving slabs.

THE FLOWER BORDER

Lilium 'Enchantment'

This distinctive and widely-grown hardy Asiatic stem-rooting lily, bears heads of up to sixteen cup-shaped, nasturtium-red flowers up to 15cm (6in) wide in mid-summer. Another superb lily from the same group is 'Cover Girl', with stunningly attractive, demure-pink flowers.

Height: 90cm-1.2m (3-4ft)
Spread: 20-30cm (8-12in)
Cultivation: Fertile, well-drained soil in full sun or light shade assures success. Set the bulbs in position, 10-15cm (4-6in) deep, from late autumn to early spring. Although it must be well-drained, the soil should also retain moisture, so during spring and summer keep the surface well mulched with peat or compost. Ensure the soil is moist before adding this moisture-retentive material. In sheltered gardens the lilies do not need staking, but on windswept sites - which really should be avoided - support from thin bamboo canes may be necessary.
Propagation: Every three or four years, lift and divide the congested clumps during late autumn or early spring.

Lavatera trimestris

(*Lavatera rosea*)
Mallow (UK)

This is one of the most beautiful of all hardy annuals, with a bushy habit and pale green, smooth, roughly heart-shaped, lobed leaves. The 10cm (4in) wide, glowing pink flowers are borne profusely from mid to late summer from the leaf-joints of the top leaves. Several forms are available, including 'Silver Cup' (silver-pink) and 'Sutton's Loveliness' (rose-pink).
Height: 60-90cm (2-3ft)
Spread: 45-50cm (18-20in)
Cultivation: Moderately rich garden soil and a sheltered but sunny site are best for mallows.
Propagation: During mid and late spring, sow seeds where the plants are to flower, setting them 12mm (½in) deep. When the seedlings are large enough to handle, thin them to 50-60cm (20-24in) apart.

Above: **Lavatera trimestris** '**Silver Cup**' *This beautiful hardy annual is a gem in any garden, and is also ideal as a cut flower for home decoration. Avoid sowing the seeds in very rich soil, which encourages lush leaf growth at the expense of flowers.*

Below: **Lavatera trimestris** *A superb setting for this hardy annual is to contrast it with the woolly grey-leaved hardy shrub* Ballota pseudodictamnus.

Lavatera trimestris, like many delicate pink flowers, needs careful positioning if it is not to be dominated by other colours. Mix it with grey foliage plants, such as the low shrub *Ballota pseudodictamnus*.

Lilium 'Enchantment' is ideal among rhododendrons and azaleas beneath a light canopy of tall pines. Lilies are useful for extending colour in a group of azaleas, which often look bleak in mid-season.

Linum grandiflorum 'Rubrum'

Scarlet Flax (UK)
Flowering Flax (USA)

This hardy annual with 4cm (1½in) wide, single, saucer-shaped scarlet flowers comes from Algeria. The flowers are borne from mid to late summer on wispy stems above a mat of narrow, pale green, pointed leaves. So wispy are the stems, even the slightest breeze sets them moving.

Height: 38-45cm (15-18in)
Spread: 20-25cm (8-10in)
Cultivation: Any good well-drained soil in full sun suits flaxes.
Propagation: During spring or early summer, sow seeds 6mm (¼in) deep where the plants are to flower. When they are large enough to handle, thin the seedlings to 13cm (5in) apart.

Below: Linum grandiflorum 'Rubrum' *This spectacular hardy annual has bright scarlet flowers from mid to late summer. A sunny position is essential for the rich colouring of the flowers.*

Below: Lilium 'Enchantment'
This really spectacular Asiatic lily, has clustered heads of cup-shaped flowers up to 15cm (6in) wide. It delights in a sunny position.

Above: Lilium 'Cover Girl'
An appealing Asiatic lily, this variety has large, wide open flowers that provide colour in a border in sun or light shade.

Lilies need moist soil and by setting them amid low, large-leaved plants, such as hostas, the ground will stay cool and damp. Variegated forms will supply colour when the lilies are not in flower.

Linum grandiflorum can also be grown as a pot plant for spring colour. Sow seeds thinly in late summer; thin to six seedlings per pot when large enough to handle and grow in a cold greenhouse.

Lobelia cardinalis

Cardinal Flower (UK)
Cardinal Flower · Indian Pink (USA)

A stunningly impressive though short-lived North American hardy herbaceous perennial with erect stems bearing oblong, lance-shaped, mid-green leaves and brilliant scarlet, 2.5cm (1in) wide, five-lobed flowers during mid to late summer.

Height: 75-90cm (2½-3ft)
Spread: 30-39cm (12-15in)
Cultivation: Rich, fertile, moist soil and a partially shaded position suit this plant. Fork in generous amounts of peat or well-rotted manure when preparing the soil. Set the plants in position in spring.
Propagation: In near-frost-free gardens the plants can be left in the soil throughout winter, but in all other areas dig up the roots in autumn and store them throughout winter in a cold frame or greenhouse. In spring, separate the rosettes and box them up in peaty soil until well established. They can then be planted in the garden.

Left: **Lobelia 'Cherry Ripe'**
This is one of the best known and spectacular of the many hybrids of Lobelia cardinalis *and* Lobelia fulgens, *producing brilliant scarlet flowers in late summer on stems up to 1.2m (4ft) high.*

Lychnis coronaria

(*Agrostemma coronaria*)
Crowned Campion (UK)
Rose Campion · Mullein Pink ·
Dusty Miller (USA)

This beautiful, short-lived perennial has silvery, woolly-textured, lance-shaped, leathery leaves and 12mm (½in) wide, rich crimson, rather bell-shaped flowers, borne in loose round heads from mid to late summer. The form 'Abbotswood Rose' boasts sprays of intense rose pink, while 'Atrosanguinea' has strong red flowers.
Height: 45-60cm (1½-2ft)
Spread: 30-38cm (12-15in)

Lobelias are named in honour of the Belgian botanist Matthias de Lobel (1538-1616). He went to England in 1584, and became physician to James I of England (James II of Scotland).

Lychnis coronaria is perfect for filling gaps in borders, where it blends well with many plants, including Rosemary *(Rosmarinus officinalis),* achilleas, Red Hot Pokers and African Lilies.

Cultivation: Any well-drained garden soil in full sun or light shade suits lychnis. In exposed areas it requires support from twiggy sticks, and removing dead flower-heads prevents the formation of seeds.

Propagation: Because it is only short-lived as a perennial, it is best grown as an annual. Sow seeds in late winter in loam-based compost at 13°C (55°F). When they are large enough to handle, prick out the seedlings into boxes of loam-based compost and slowly harden them off, eventually in a cold frame. Plant them out into the garden during late spring at 23-30cm (9-12in) apart. Alternatively, sow the seeds in mid-summer where the plants are to flower the following year. Thin the seedlings when they appear to 23-30cm (9-12in) apart.

Lythrum salicaria

Purple Loosestrife (UK)
Purple Loosestrife · Spiked Loosestrife (USA)

A beautiful resilient and reliable hardy herbaceous perennial with lance-shaped, mid-green leaves and handsome, reddish-purple flowers, borne in spires 23-30cm (9-12in) long during mid-summer and into early autumn. Several superb forms are available, including 'Firecandle' (intense rosy-red), 'Lady Sackville' (bright rose-pink), 'Robert' (clear pink) and 'The Beacon' (deep rose-crimson).

Height: 75cm-1.2m (2½-4ft)
Spread: 45cm (1½ft)
Cultivation: Moisture-retentive soil in a sunny position suits it best, although it does quite well in ordinary garden soil. After flowering, cut back the stems to soil-level.
Propagation: The roots can be divided in spring or autumn, but often old clumps become very woody and difficult to divide. Instead, take cuttings 7.5cm (3in) long from the base of the plant during spring and insert them in pots placed in a cold frame.

Above: Lychnis coronaria 'Abbotswood Rose' *This short-lived perennial displays loose heads of intense rose-pink flowers from mid to late summer. The silvery foliage is an attractive bonus with this border brightener.*

Below: Lythrum salicaria 'Firecandle' *This popular herbaceous perennial displays intense rosy-red flowers from mid-summer to early autumn. It does not grow well in deep shade, preferring a sunny position.*

Lythrum salicaria does best when grown in moist soil, where it enjoys the company of polygonums, *Euphorbia palustris* with its sulphur-yellow flower heads, and a range of moisture-loving grasses.

THE FLOWER BORDER

Nerine bowdenii

This pretty South African bulbous plant from Cape Province is not totally hardy in extremely cold areas. It has narrow, strap-like, mid-green leaves which develop after the flowers appear from late summer to early winter. The distinctive rose or deep pink flowers are each formed of six strap-like petals usually twisted at their ends. They are borne in heads of up to eight flowers, at the end of stiff stems up to 60cm (2ft) long. The most popular form is 'Fenwick's Variety', with deep pink flowers.

Height: 50-60cm (20-24in)
Spread: 15-20cm (6-8in)
Cultivation: Any good well-drained soil and a sunny position against a south or west-facing wall are suitable. Once established, the plants can be left in position to produce a spectacular display. However, when they are too cramped and congested, the number of flower stems decreases.
Propagation: Every four or five years, lift and divide overcrowded clumps. The plant can also be increased by sowing the soft, fleshy seeds in loam-based compost during late spring.

Macleaya microcarpa

(*Bocconia microcarpa*)
Plume Poppy (UK)

A large, graceful, hardy herbaceous perennial from Northern China, somewhat resembling *Macleaya cordata*. However, *M. microcarpa* has feathery pink plumes with a bronze appearance that makes it quite distinctive and the flowers are produced a couple of weeks earlier, from mid to late summer. They are best positioned at the back of a border, where they can be given plenty of room. The plume-like heads flower above other plants and create a very attractive background. These plants spread by invasive underground suckers.

Height: 1.5-2.4m (5-8ft)
Spread: 90cm-1m (3-3½ft)
Cultivation: Rich, fertile relatively light soil suits the Plume Poppy. Give it a site sheltered enough to prevent its tall stems being blown and battered by strong wind. Twiggy sticks are needed to support the plants. In autumn, cut them down to soil-level.
Propagation: The invasive roots can be lifted and divided in spring or autumn, and for the home gardener this is the easiest method. Alternatively, 5-7.5cm (2-3in) long cuttings from basal shoots can be taken in early summer and inserted in pots containing equal parts of peat and sharp sand, placed in a cold frame. Pot up the plants when they are well rooted.

Above: Macleaya microcarpa
A beautiful herbaceous perennial with feathery plumes. It is an invasive plant and because of this it is not very well suited to small gardens.

Top right: Nerine bowdenii
An eye-catching bulbous plant for autumn flowers. It needs a warm sunny and sheltered position, and the leaves appear after the flowers.

Right: Paeonia officinalis 'Rubra Plena' *A beautiful large-flowered herbaceous perennial sometimes called the Old Double Crimson Paeony, with crimson-red flowers in early to mid-summer. Once established it is best to leave it alone, undisturbed.*

Macleaya microcarpa is ideal for filling a large corner position against a wall. Its tall flower plumes are ideal for breaking up the often imposing nature of a large brick wall.

Nerine bowdenii is best given a relatively narrow border against a warm wall all to itself. Its late flowering makes it a tricky plant to combine effectively with others.

Paeonia officinalis

Common Garden Paeony (UK)

A distinctive and well-known herbaceous perennial, more popular in the past than today, but still deserving a position in a mixed border, where it often appears more at home than in a traditional herbaceous border. The large, deeply incised mid-green leaves are a perfect foil for the 13cm (5in) wide, single crimson flowers that appear on stiff stems in early to mid-summer. This form, however, is rarely seen and it is the forms such as 'Rubra Plena' (crimson-red), 'Rosea Plena' (deep pink) and 'Alba Plena' (pink at first, fading to white) that are mainly grown. *Paeonia lactiflora,* also known as *P. albiflora,* is another herbaceous perennial and rises to about 60cm (2ft) high. The true type bears 7.5-10cm (3-4in) wide single, white and scented flowers in early summer. However, there are many forms in pink and red, which can be up to 18cm (7in) wide. These include the double and scented 'Albert Crousse' with bright pink flowers; 'Bower of Roses' with rose-crimson double blooms, 'Bowl of Beauty' displaying soft pink semi-double flowers with golden stamens; 'Globe of Light' with pale rose-pink blooms; 'Karl Rosenfeld' displaying wine-red double flowers; 'Lady Alexandra Duff' with soft pink double and scented flowers; the single blue-pink 'Pink Delight'; 'President Roosevelt' with deep red double flowers; and the well-known 'Sarah Bernhardt' with scented, double, pink flowers. These are dominantly-flowered plants and soon create interest in the garden.

Height: 75-90cm (2½-3ft)
Spread: 90cm (3ft)
Cultivation: Paeonies thrive in a rich, well-drained but moisture retentive soil in full sun or light shade. When preparing the soil, dig in plenty of well-rotted manure or compost.
Propagation: During early spring or autumn, lift and divide large clumps.

Paeonia officinalis is originally a native of Southern Europe, from France to Albania. The true species is difficult to obtain, though there are several excellent hybrid varieties.

THE FLOWER BORDER

Papaver orientale

Oriental Poppy (UK and USA)

This hardy and stunningly attractive herbaceous perennial with rough, bristly, hairy stems and leaves is a wonderful scene-setter. The mid to deep green leaves are deeply incised, with the 9-10cm (3½-4in) wide scarlet flowers with black centres appearing during early to mid-summer. There are now many forms to choose from, including 'Enchantress' (carmine-pink), 'Allegro' (bright orange-scarlet), 'Goliath' (crimson-scarlet), 'Ladybird' (vermilion-red), 'Marcus Perry' (orange-scarlet), 'Turkish Delight' (flesh pink) and 'Cedric's Pink' (pink and curled petals with a purple-black blotch at the base).
Height: 60-90cm (2-3ft)
Spread: 60-75cm (2-2½ft)
Cultivation: Any good well-drained garden soil and a position in good light suit Oriental Poppies. Remove all dead flowers.
Propagation: The easiest way to increase Oriental Poppies is by lifting and dividing congested plants during spring. Alternatively, sow seeds thinly during summer, 6mm (¼ in) deep, in a well-prepared seedbed outdoors. When the seedlings are large enough to handle, thin them to 15cm (6in) apart. In autumn or spring, transfer them to their flowering positions.

Phlox paniculata

(Phlox decussata)
Phlox (UK)
Perennial Phlox · Summer
Perennial Phlox · Fall Phlox (USA)

A well-known and reliable herbaceous perennial for borders, which produces abundant displays of dense 10-15cm (4-6in) heads of 2.5cm (1in) wide flowers from mid to late summer above mid-green, lance-shaped leaves. The range of colours is wide, from white to purple, and red and pink forms include 'Vintage Wine' (claret red), 'Starfire' (deep red), 'Fairy's Petticoat' (shell-pink), 'Windsor' (clear carmine), 'Mother of Pearl' (pink), 'Pinafore Pink' (bright pink), 'Prospero' (pale lilac), and 'Red Indian' (deep crimson).
Height: Range of varieties from 60cm to 1.2m (2-4ft)
Spread: Range of varieties from 45 to 60cm (1½-2ft)
Cultivation: A fertile, well-drained but moisture-retentive soil in full sun or light shade assures success. Give the plants a mulch of well-decomposed compost or manure in spring to help reduce the loss of moisture from the soil. During dry summers, water the soil. In exposed areas, support the plants with twiggy sticks, and in autumn cut down the plants to soil level to tidy them up.

Propagation: Phlox are often infested with microscopic worm-like creatures called eelworms. Although these plants can be increased easily by lifting and dividing congested clumps in spring or autumn and replanting the young outside parts, if the parent plants are infested the new plants will also have the same problem. In such circumstances, it is better to propagate by taking root cuttings in winter or early spring. Cut the thicker roots into 12mm (½in) pieces and place in loam-based compost at 13°C (55°F). Cover the compost lightly. When shoots from these roots are 6.5cm (2½in) high, move the boxes to a cold frame to harden off. Plant out into nursery rows in late spring and leave for a couple of years before transplanting to the permanent site. Herbaceous phloxes can be grown from seeds, but named forms will not breed true. However, if you like to experiment when raising plants, phloxes can be easily grown by sowing seeds in loam-based compost during late spring. Place the sown boxes in a cold frame. Prick off the seedlings into further boxes when large enough to handle, and when growing strongly plant out into a well-prepared nursery bed. Set out in the garden during the autumn of the following year.

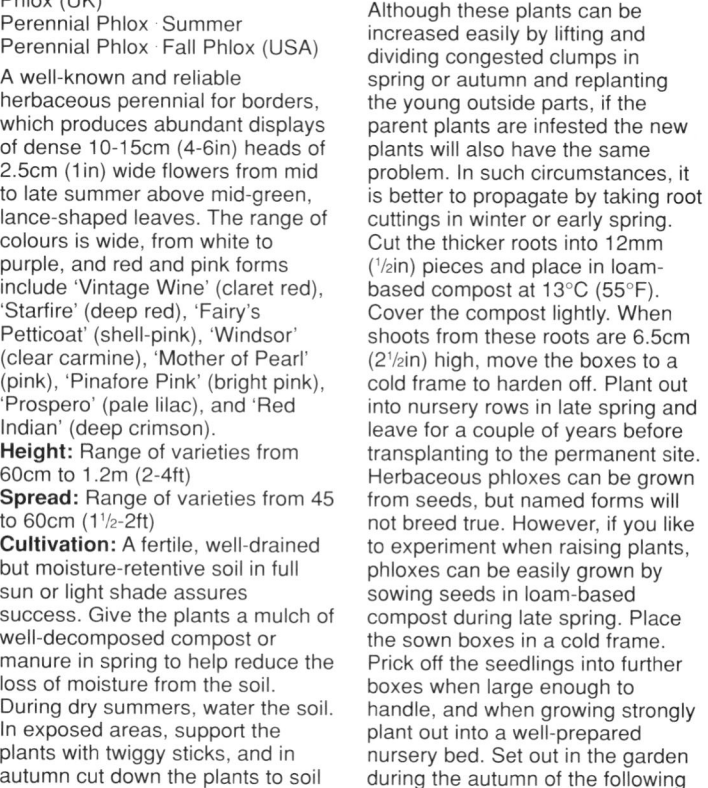

Left: Papaver orientale
Few herbaceous perennials capture as many early to mid-summer glances as this Oriental Poppy. There are several varieties available, in a wide colour range.

Right: Phlox paniculata 'Vintage Wine' *This claret-red variety is one of the best known forms of this beautiful herbaceous perennial for herbaceous or mixed borders.*

Far right: Polygonum amplexicaule 'Atrosanguinea' *This herbaceous perennial gives a ground-covering of deep green leaves with spires of red flowers.*

Papaver orientale needs a rustic, cottage garden setting to show off its charms – it never looks as good in a formal setting. When allowed to splay outwards over an old brick path, it is a delight.

Polygonum amplexicaule 'Atrosanguinea'

Mountain Fleece (USA)

A beautiful Himalayan herbaceous perennial with deep green, heart-shaped, long and tapering, pointed leaves. This form displays 15cm (6in) long spikes of red flowers during mid-summer and early autumn. The form 'Firetail' creates attractive bright crimson-scarlet spikes, while 'Inverleith' which grows to 30cm (1ft) bears red poker-like flowers on leafy mounds. The form *P. amplexicaule* 'Pendula', also sold as *Polygonum* 'Arum Gem', displays branching stems bearing dangling tassels of bright pink flowers from mid-summer to autumn. The plant is ideal for a small garden.

Height: 90cm-1.2m (3-4ft)
Spread: 60-75cm (2-2$\frac{1}{2}$ft)
Cultivation: Fertile, moist soil in full sun or partial shade is needed. After flowering, cut down the stems to soil-level.
Propagation: This plant is best increased by lifting and dividing the more congested clumps in autumn or spring.

Polygonum bistorta, the Snakeweed or Bistort, is another widely-grown species, mainly in the variety 'Superbum'. It is a mat-forming plant with light green leaves and spikes of pink flowers.

THE FLOWER BORDER

Potentilla atrosanguinea

Himalayan Cinquefoil (UK and USA)

A delightful Himalayan herbaceous perennial; the original form is little grown itself but it has given rise to a wide range of hybrids. They have grey-green, somewhat strawberry-like leaves, with the flowers borne in loose sprays of single or double flowers in heads up to 45cm (1½ft) wide, from mid to late summer. Varieties to look for include 'Flamenco' (large, single, intense red flowers), 'Gibson's Scarlet' (single, brilliant-red) and 'Glory of Nancy' (semi-double, crimson maroon).

Height: 45-60cm (1½-2ft)
Spread: 38-45cm (15-18in)
Cultivation: Potentillas will do well in a fertile, well-drained soil in full sun. Each spring, mulch them with well-rotted manure or compost, and in dry weather water the plants thoroughly.
Propagation: The easiest way for a home gardener to increase them is by lifting and dividing large clumps in spring or autumn.

Above: Potentilla atrosanguinea 'Gibson's Scarlet' *The single brilliant-red flowers of this distinctive herbaceous perennial are a joy from mid to late summer. The strawberry-like leaves supply an ideal foil for the flowers.*

Left: Sedum spectabile 'Autumn Joy' *This is one of the easiest to grow and amenable of all garden plants, never failing to create interest through its autumn heads of salmon-pink flowers.*

Sedum spectabile

Ice Plant (UK)

This is one of the most reliable and attractive of all border perennials. It probably gains its common name Ice Plant from its glistening, blue-grey foliage. During late summer and autumn, it bears dense 7.5-15cm (3-6in) wide heads of pink

Potentilla nepalensis has also produced some superb herbaceous perennials, like 'Roxana' (pink, brown-red and orange flowers) and 'Miss Willmott' (cherry pink). Both are 60cm (2ft) high.

Sedum spectabile mixes well with several blue plants, such as rose-purple colchicums and the stiff, upright spires of violet bead-like flowers borne by *Lirope muscari,* the Lily Turf.

flowers flushed with a mauve tinge. Several superb forms are available; perhaps the best known is 'Autumn Joy' with flowers that change from pale rose to a beautiful salmon-pink. 'Carmine' has bright carmine flower heads, 'Meteor' deep carmine-red heads and 'Brilliant' deep rose ones. As a bonus, they are attractive to bees.

Height: 30-45cm (1-1½ft)

Spread: 45cm (1½ft)

Cultivation: Any ordinary well drained soil and a position in full sun are suitable. Set new plants in position during spring or autumn. In spring, remove the dead flower heads.

Propagation: The easiest way for a home gardener to increase sedums is by lifting and dividing established clumps in spring or autumn. Alternatively, take stem cuttings 2.5-7.5cm (1-3in) long in late spring and insert them in pots of sandy compost in a cold frame.

Schizostylis coccinea

Kaffir Lily (UK)

Crimson Flag · Kaffir Lily (USA)

A well-known South African rhizomatous-rooted herbaceous perennial with mid-green, sword-like leaves and long stems bearing star-shaped 4cm (1½in) wide rich crimson flowers in late autumn and early winter. The flowers are arranged in spikes about 15cm (6in) long. The form 'Major' displays extra-large red flowers on strong stems, 'November Cheer' has pink flowers, 'Viscountess Byng' bears pale pink blooms, and 'Mrs. Hegarty' pale pink flowers.

Height: 60-90cm (2-3ft)

Spread: 30-38cm (12-15in)

Cultivation: Moist, fertile soil and a position in full sun are essential. It is vital that the soil is kept moist, so each spring give it a mulch of compost or peat. In autumn, cut the plants down to soil-level.

Propagation: During spring, lift the plants and divide them into pieces, each containing five or six shoots. Replant these pieces before their roots become dry.

Above: **Schizostylis coccinea 'Major'** *This vivid-red South African plant needs moist, fertile soil. As well as providing late season flowers for the garden it is ideal for use as a cut-flower.*

Schizostylis coccinea is in flower at the same time as the Michaelmas Daisy *Aster novi-belgii*. Soft blue asters blend well with schizostylis, and with silver-leaved *Santolina chamaecyparissus*.

THE FLOWER BORDER

Sidalcea malviflora

Checkerbloom (USA)

An erect, slender, rather twiggy-stemmed hardy herbaceous perennial from Western North America. The mid-green lower leaves are roundish, with five to nine shallow lobes. The funnel-shaped, 5cm (2in) wide, mallow-like pink flowers appear in clustered spires towards the tops of the stems from mid to late summer. Several forms are available including 'Croftway Red' (deep rich red), 'Loveliness' (shell-pink), 'Nimmerdor' (tapering spires of deep pink flowers), 'Oberon' (clear pink), 'Rose Queen' (rose-pink) and 'William Smith' (warm salmon-pink).

Height: 75cm-1.2m (2½-4ft)

Spread: 45-60cm (1½-2ft)

Cultivation: Ordinary garden soil suits this plant, but it must not be in full sun or strong shade. A position with light speckled shade in soil that does not dry out during summer is ideal. Twiggy sticks are needed to support the plants.

Propagation: It is easily increased by lifting and dividing congested clumps in mid-spring, replanting only the pieces from around the outside. It can be increased from seeds sown in spring in a cold frame, but named forms do not come true in this way.

Above: Tigridia pavonia 'Rubra'
The beautiful plant is only half-hardy and requires a warm position. It produces a succession of vividly coloured flowers, each lasting only a day but followed by others to give colour over a long period. The strange markings and spots on the flowers amply justify the plant's common name Tiger Flower.

Left: Sidalcea malviflora
The mallow-like pink flowers of this herbaceous perennial are borne on tall stems. After the delicately coloured flowers have faded, cut down the stems to 23cm (9in) of soil-level to encourage the development of lateral shoots.

Tigridia pavonia

Tiger Flower · Peacock Tiger Flower · Flower of the Aztecs (UK) Tiger Flower · Shell Flower · One-day Lily (USA)

This is one of the brightest and most eye-catching of all summer flowering bulbous plants. Originating from Mexico and Peru, it is only half-hardy. The long sword-like mid-green pleated leaves grow up to 60cm (2ft) high. From mid-summer to autumn, it produces 10cm (4in) wide yellow flowers spotted with crimson-brown. These are formed of three large petals and three small ones. Each of these flowers lasts for one day, but fortunately each stem

Sidalcea malviflora, with its delicate pink flowers, needs careful positioning in a border if it is not to be dominated by strong colours. An old brick wall provides an attractive background.

Tigridia pavonia does not grow too well with other plants: its colour and shape are dominant and can all too easily overwhelm other plants. It is best grown against a warm wall and given a spot to itself.

Above: Tulip 'Trance' *This Division 3 tulip has startling coloured flowers in mid-spring. It prefers a sunny position where there is some lime in the soil. 'Van der Eerden' is another superb red tulip in this division.*

Tulips

The range of these much-loved spring bulbs is extensive. They can be used in bedding schemes during spring, or in mixed borders, rock gardens, tubs and troughs, as well as indoors during winter and early spring. There is a wide range of species, and in addition botanists have classified those that have been created by bulb experts. There are many different divisions encompassing the wide range of flower sizes, shapes and heights. These are:

Division 1: Single Early (15-38cm/6-15in): The single flowers appear in spring when grown outdoors, or during winter indoors. Each flower is 7.5-13cm (3-5in) wide and sometimes opens flat when in direct and full sun. Many varieties are available, including some fine red and pink ones, as well as white, yellow, orange and purple.

Division 2: Double Early (30-38cm/12-15in): The double flowers appear in spring when grown out-of-doors in bedding schemes, or earlier when forced indoors. Each flower is 10cm (4in) wide and rather like a double paeony. The colour range is wide, including pink and red.

bears up to eight flowers. Several forms are available in red or scarlet, such as 'Liliacea' (reddish-purple with white variegations), 'Rubra' (orange-red with red and yellow spotted centres) and 'Speciosa' (scarlet with yellow and red centres). *Tigridia pavonia* is only one of a genus formed of about twelve species, all coming chiefly from Mexico but some also from Guatemala. Except for the Tiger Flower, which is descriptively known as the Jockey Cap in New Zealand, they are rarely grown in Britain and really need the benefit of a frost-proof greenhouse, although they can be planted outdoors in spring and lifted for storage in a frost-proof place during autumn.

Height: 45-60cm (1½-2ft)
Spread: 20-25cm (8-10in)
Cultivation: Rich, well-drained soil and a warm, sunny position are best. Plant the bulbs 7.5cm (3in) deep during spring, and after flowering lift and store them in a frost-free and vermin-proof place during winter. Only in exceptionally warm areas and when grown against a west or south-facing wall can the bulbs be left in position during winter.
Propagation: When the plants are lifted and divided in autumn, detach the young offsets from around the sides of the mother plants and re-plant them separately during the warmer spring weather.

Blue, scarlet and gold mixtures can be created by a carpet planting of a pale blue Forget-me-not *(Myosotis)* and a planting of the scarlet and gold single early tulip 'Keizerskroon'.

THE FLOWER BORDER

Above: **Tulip 'Aladdin'**
*A lily-flowered tulip from Division 7
with a typical waisted appearance
and pointed petals. 'Dyanito' is
another lily-flowered tulip in this
division, and 'Queen of Sheba' is
red, with orange edges.*

Division 3: Mendel
(38-50cm/15-20in): These flower
later than the previous types, with
rounded, 10-13cm (4-5in) wide
flowers on quite slender stems.
Colours include white and red, as
well as yellow. They look like a
cross between single early types
and Darwins.

Division 4: Triumph (up to 50cm/
20in): These bear angular-shaped,
10-13cm (4-5in) wide flowers on
strong stems in mid-spring. Colours
include yellow, gold and lilac, as
well as pink and red.

Division 5: Darwin Hybrids
(60-75cm/2-2½ft): These are
among the most large flowered and
brilliant of all tulips, with flowers up
to 18cm (7in) wide during mid-
spring. There are multi-coloured
forms, as well as orange purple,
yellow and red varieties.

Division 6: Darwin
(60-75cm/2-2½ft): These are
widely used in bedding schemes,
producing rounded flowers up to

13cm (5in) wide in late spring.
Varieties are available in white,
yellow and purple, as well as multi-
colours and pink and red.

Division 7: Lily-flowered
(45-60cm/1½-2ft): These are
characterized by the narrow waists
of the flowers, also the pointed
petals that curl outwards, reaching
20cm (8in) wide during mid-spring.
They look distinctive when massed
in a bedding scheme. Colours
include white, orange, yellow and
multi-coloured forms, as well as
shades of red.

Division 8: Cottage (up to 90cm/
3ft): This old grouping has oval or

rounded flowers 10-13cm (4-5in)
wide in mid-spring. The petals
sometimes have a hint of fringing
at their tips, and are looser than in
other forms. Flower colours include
white, pink, yellow, lilac and green,
as well as red.

Division 9: Rembrandt
(75cm/2½ft): These are tulips with
'broken' colours. The rounded,
13cm (5in) wide flowers have vivid
splashes of colour on the petals
during mid-spring. Base colours
include white, orange, yellow, pink,
violet and brown, as well as red,
with eye-catching broken colours
superimposed.

For a **yellow, orange-red and blue mixture** try a
deep blue Forget-me-not *(Myosotis)*, orange-red
'President Hoover' and the yellow 'Mrs. John T.
Scheepers'. Both of these are in Division 8.

Above: **Tulip 'Orajezon'** *A superb* Division 6 *tulip used in bedding schemes where it flowers in late spring. Tulips in this division are probably the most widely grown and popular for setting in spring bedding displays.*

flat, giving the appearance of a water-lily. They open in spring on sturdy stems, and are ideal for fronts of borders, rock gardens and containers. Most have two-coloured flowers.

Division 13: Fosteriana varieties (45cm/1½ft): These are derived from *Tulipa fosteriana* and produce large blunt-ended flowers in red and yellow in mid-spring.

Division 14: Greigii varieties (25cm/10in): These are mainly derived from *Tulipa greigii,* bearing brilliant, long-lasting red, yellow and near-white flowers in mid-spring. The petals reach 7.5cm long when the flowers are fully open.

Cultivation: When grown in the garden, select well-drained soil, preferably facing south and in a sheltered position. Set the bulbs 15cm (6in) deep during early winter. Space them 10-15cm (4-6in) apart. Remove dead flowers and dig up the bulbs when the leaves turn yellow. However, if the bed is needed earlier, dig up the bulbs as soon as flowering is over and heel them into a trench until the foliage has yellowed and died down.

Division 10: Parrot (45-60cm/1½-2ft): These have flowers up to 20cm (8in) wide, easily recognizable by their feather-like and heavily-fringed petals, appearing in mid-spring. The colour range includes brilliant white, orange, yellow and purple, as well as red and pink.

Division 11: Double Late (45-60cm/1½-2ft): These have very large and showy double flowers, somewhat resembling paeonies and up to 20cm (8in) wide. They remain in flower for a long period during mid-spring. Colours include white, orange, yellow and violet, as

Above: **Tulip 'Ida'** *A Division 4 tulip with a yellow base dramatically streaked red. This Triumph tulip flowers in mid-spring and thrives in full sun. Other Triumph tulips include 'Rose Korneforos' (rose-red) and 'Edith Eddy' (red with white edges).*

well as pink and red. Also, some are multi-coloured, with stripes and edgings.

Division 12: Kaufmanniana varieties (10-15cm/4-10in): These have been developed from *Tulipa kaufmanniana,* and have fine-pointed flowers that open nearly

For a **blue and red spring-bedding mixture,** perhaps at the top of a dry stone wall, try blue *Aubrieta deltoidea* and the Division 13 tulip 'Red Emperor', a tulip derived from *Tulipa fosteriana*.

THE FLOWER BORDER

Propagation: The easiest way is to remove off-set bulbs clustered at the bases of the bulbs. These can be planted in a nursery bed to develop into flowering-sized bulbs.

Right: **Tulip 'Allegretto'**
This double late tulip from Division 11 *is flamboyant, with long-lasting flowers during spring. 'Brilliant Fire' displays red flowers, and has the benefit of being scented.*

Below right: **Tulip 'Flaming Parrot'** *An exciting* Division 10 *tulip with a yellow and white background vividly striped red. Many Parrot tulips are bicoloured, and when fully open may measure up to 20cm (8in) wide.*

Below: **Tulipa greigii** *A superb species tulip with grey-green lance-shaped and distinctively veined leaves. The blunt-pointed orange-scarlet flowers appear in mid-spring. It is the parent of many hybrids in* Division 14, *and itself is well worthy of a prominent position in a rock garden.*

For a **salmon, orange-red and yellow mixture** try a carpet of the salmon *Cheiranthus cheiri* 'Easter Queen' and a mixture of the orange-red 'President Hoover' and the yellow 'Mrs. John T. Scheepers'.

Above: Tulip 'Greenland'
A demure tulip from Division 8 *that reveals green stripes on a pink background. Other outstandingly attractive pink Cottage tulips include 'Palestrina' (salmon-pink) and 'Mirella' (deep salmon-pink).*

Further plants to consider

Anemone x hybrida
(*Anemone japonica · Anemone x elegans*)
Height: 60-90cm (2-3ft) Spread 30-45cm (1-1½ft)
A hardy herbaceous perennial with several pink forms, including 'September Charm' (clear pink), 'Queen Charlotte' (semi-double and pink) and 'Max Vogel' (pink).

Bergenia cordifolia
Height: 30cm (1ft) Spread: 30-38cm (12-15in)
A well known hardy herbaceous perennial with large, mid-green, leathery leaves and lilac-rose flowers in dome-shaped heads during spring. The hybrid 'Ballawley' bears large red flowers.

Centranthus ruber
(*Kenthanthrus ruber*)
A hardy herbaceous perennial with long, strong stems displaying star-shaped, deep pink or red flowers from mid to late summer. Unfortunately, the leaves have an unpleasant smell when crushed, so set it to the back or middle of the border.

Geum x borisii
Height: 30cm (1ft) Spread: 30-38cm (12-15in)
A beautiful hardy herbaceous perennial bearing 2.5cm (1in) wide orange-scarlet flowers during early summer and often intermittently into late summer.

Monarda didyma
Oswego Tea · Bee Balm · Sweet Bergamot (UK and USA)
Height: 60-90cm (2-3ft) Spread: 45cm (1½ft)
A hardy herbaceous perennial with beautiful whorled heads of flowers from mid-summer to early autumn. Pink and red forms include 'Cambridge Scarlet' (bright scarlet), 'Croftway Pink' (rose pink), 'Melissa' (pale pink) and 'Pillar Box' (bright red).

Pyrethrum roseum
Height: 60-75cm (2-2½ft) Spread: 45cm (1½ft)
A spectacular hardy herbaceous perennial displaying bright green feathery leaves. During mid-summer it bears 5-6.5cm (2-2½in) wide, daisy-like, single or double flowers. Pink and red forms include 'Brenda' (single, cerise-pink), 'Bressingham Red' (single, crimson-scarlet), 'Eileen May Robinson' (single, clear pink), 'Kelway's Glorious' (single, crimson-red), 'J.N. Twerdy' (double, deep red) 'Madeleine' (double, clear pink) and 'Venus' (double, shell-pink).

Verbascum x hybridum 'Pink Domino'
Mullein (UK and USA)
Height: 90cm-1.2m (3-4ft) Spread: 38-45cm (15-18in)
A superb hardy hybrid herbaceous perennial with beautiful deep rose-pink flowers during mid to late summer.

If you like a **yellow and scarlet and gold mixture** try the stunning combination of a planting of a yellow viola and the scarlet and gold 'Keizerskroon'. The latter is a single early tulip from Division 1.

Above: Agapanthus praecox
This half-hardy evergreen creates dense 5-7.5cm (2-3in) wide heads of pale blue flowers during mid to late summer.

Agapanthus x 'Headbourne Hybrids'

African Lily (UK)

This popular hybrid is hardier than most other species. Like its relatives, it has long, strap-like mid-green leaves, with stunningly attractive deep violet-blue to pale blue flowers held in large heads like upturned umbrellas during mid to late summer.
Height: 60-75cm (2-2¹/₂ft)
Spread: 45-60cm (1¹/₂-2ft)
Cultivation: Fertile, well-drained soil and a sheltered position are needed. The foliage dies down in autumn, with fresh leaves appearing in spring. Ensure that the soil is not waterlogged during winter.
Propagation: The easiest way to increase it is by lifting and dividing established clumps in late spring, just as the new growth makes an appearance.

Right: Agapanthus x 'Headbourne Hybrids' *A beautiful hardy herbaceous plant but it does not like water-saturated soil during winter. The flowers, borne in inverted umbrella-like arrangements, appear on stout stems during mid to late summer.*

Aconitum wilsonii

Monkshood · Wolf's Bane · Helmet Flower (UK)
Aconite · Monkshood (USA)

This erect hardy herbaceous plant has deeply divided dark green leaves and 5cm (2in) high amethyst-blue hooded flowers during late summer and into early autumn. Several varieties are available including 'Kelmscott Variety' (lavender-blue) and 'Barker's Variety' (deep blue).
Height: 1.2-1.8m (4-6ft)
Spread: 45-60cm (1¹/₂-2ft)
Cultivation: Deep, fertile, moisture-retentive soil in slight shade suits it best. Do not allow the

Above: Aconitum wilsonii
A stately and erect herbaceous perennial, displaying amethyst-blue hooded flowers during late summer and into autumn. It gets one of its common names, Wolf's Bane, from its poisonous roots.

soil to dry out, and cut the plants down to soil-level during autumn.
Propagation: It is easily increased by lifting and dividing established clumps in spring or autumn. Seeds can be sown in boxes of loam-based compost in spring and placed in a cold frame, but this method takes a couple of years to produce flowering-sized plants that will create a worthwhile display.

Aconitum napellus is another Monkshood, with deep-blue flowers during mid-summer. It blends well with a backcloth of the Venetian Sumach or Smoke Tree, *Cotinus coggygria* 'Foliis Purpureis'.

Agapanthus blends well with yellow-flowered and silver-foliaged plants. For silver foliage choose *Stachys lanata*, while *Achillea filipendula* 'Coronation Gold' with its flat flower heads provides an ample splash of yellow.

Ageratum houstonianum

(*Ageratum mexicanum*)

A half-hardy annual with mid-green, hairy, heart-shaped leaves and 7.5-10cm (3-4in) wide clusters of powdery bluish-mauve flowers from early to late summer. Several superb forms are grown, including 'Blue Cap' and 'Blue Danube'.

Height: 13-30cm (5-12in)
Spread: 20-30cm (8-12in)
Cultivation: Moisture-retentive soil is best, and a position in full sun or partial shade. Do not set the plants in heavy shade. Removing the dead flower heads helps to extend the flowering season, and this is especially important where the plants are being grown in containers on a patio.
Propagation: During late winter and early spring, sow seeds thinly 3mm (⅛in) deep in pots of loam-based seed compost kept at 10°C (50°F). When the seedlings are large enough to handle, prick them off into boxes and harden them off in a cold frame. Plant them out when all risk of frost has passed.

Below: **Ageratum houstonianum 'Adriatic Blue'** *A well-known half-hardy annual for summer-bedding schemes. It is especially eye-catching as a border edging and looks good alongside gravel paths.*

Ageratum houstonianum can be used in many bedding combinations. Try an edging of ageratum with a carpeting of orange or salmon antirrhinums and dot plants of *Abutilon striatum* (*A. thompsonii*).

THE FLOWER BORDER

Anchusa azurea

Alkanet · Italian Bugloss (UK and USA)

A brightly coloured hardy herbaceous perennial with lance-shaped mid-green leaves, rough and hairy stems, and large bright blue flowers similar to Forget-me-nots displayed in large heads during mid-summer. There are several superb varieties, including 'Morning Glory' (bright blue), 'Opal' (soft blue), 'Royal Blue' (rich royal blue) and 'Loddon Royalist' (gentian-blue).
Height: 90cm-1.5m (3-5ft)
Spread: 45-60cm (1½-2ft)
Cultivation: Deep, fertile, well-drained soil in a sunny position is best. Anchusas need support from twiggy sticks; in autumn cut down the stems to soil-level.
Propagation: It is easily increased from root-cuttings. These are best taken in winter, cutting the roots into 5cm (2in) long pieces. At the stem end of each cutting make a flat cut at right-angles to the stem, while at the root end form a slanting cut. This helps to sort out the cuttings if they become mixed up. Insert them flat end upwards in pots or boxes of loam-based compost, and put them in a cold frame.

Aster amellus

Italian Starwort (UK)
Italian Aster (USA)

This well-known herbaceous perennial from Italy displays rough-surfaced grey-green leaves and 5-6.5cm (2-2½in) wide daisy-like flowers with golden-yellow centres during late summer and into autumn. Several superb forms are available including 'King George' (soft blue-violet), 'Nocturne' (lavender-pink), 'Sonia' (large and pink) and 'Violet Queen' (compact and dwarf).
Height: 45-60cm (1½-2ft)
Spread: 38-45cm (15-18in)
Cultivation: Well-drained but moisture-retentive soil and a sunny position suit it best. It dislikes excessive water during autumn and winter. In late autumn, cut down the stems to soil-level.
Propagation: Dividing established clumps in spring is the easiest method of increasing this plant.

Below: Aster amellus 'King George' *A large-flowered aster this variety has remained popular since it was first bred in 1914. It displays soft blue-violet flowers with dramatically contrasting golden-yellow centres.*

Above: Anchusa azurea *The beautiful blue flowers appear during mid-summer, creating a strong colour impact. The plants need support from twiggy sticks inserted at an early stage so that they can grow up through them.*

Anchusa azurea looks spectacular when grown against a backcloth of yellow foliage, such as that of the Golden Privet *(Ligustrum ovalifolium* 'Aureum'). Lady's Mantle *(Alchemilla mollis)* is small enough to be set around the front of the anchusa.

Asters are among the brightest flowering plants in our gardens, and suit bold plantings in a herbaceous or mixed border. A few asters are small enough to be planted in a rock garden setting, such as *Aster alpinus* which is only 1.5cm (6in) tall.

Above: Aster amellus 'Nocturne'
This is an especially good form that has a compact and bushy habit with semi-double lavender-pink flowers. Free-draining soil is essential for this late summer and autumn-flowering plant to produce a good display. Unfortunately, in areas of high rainfall the flowers tend to become sodden with water and to be weighed down. This can be prevented by covering the flowerheads with plastic sheeting.

Aster x frikartii

This brightly-coloured hybrid aster between *A. amellus* and *A. thomsonii* reveals 5cm (2in) wide blue daisy-like flowers with orange centres during late summer and well into autumn. The variety 'Mönch' produces masses of clear lavender-blue flowers with yellow rayed centres.
Height: 75cm (2½ft)
Spread: 38-45cm (15-18in)

Above: Aster x frikartii 'Mönch'
A superb hybrid aster bearing lavender-blue flowers during late summer and into autumn.

Cultivation: Fertile, well-drained soil and a sunny position suit this flower. Dry soil in late summer spells doom, but at the same time excessive wetness from ill-drained soils is also detrimental. Despite its height it does not need staking. In autumn, cut the flowered stems down to soil-level. *Aster x frikartii* blends well with late-flowering plants; some combinations are given at the base of the page. For a really stunning arrangement, use a mixture of *Anemone x hybrida* 'September Charm' with clear pink flowers, *Aster x frikartii* 'Mönch' and the pink *Nerine bowdenii* 'Fenwick's Variety'. Set these in front of the Chinese shrub *Hydrangea villosa*, which bears loose heads of pale purple flowers in late summer and early autumn. Even a single combination of *Aster x frikartii* 'Mönch' and the white *Anemone x hybrida* 'Honorine Jobert' looks lovely.
Propagation: Dividing established clumps in spring is the easiest method of increasing this plant. Alternatively, take basal cuttings in spring and put them in a frame.

Aster x frikartii is useful in herbaceous or mixed borders, and can be grown with many other plants such as *Anemone x hybrida*, *Nerine bowdenii* 'Fenwick's Variety', *Acanthus mollis* and *Sedum maximum* 'Atropurpureum'.

THE FLOWER BORDER

Borago officinalis

Borage (UK)
Talewort · Cool-tankard (USA)

This is a hardy annual, well-known as a culinary herb, with leaves used when young and fresh to flavour salads and fruit cups. They have a flavour reminiscent of cucumber and are large, oval, green and covered with hairs. The five-petalled, blue, 18-25mm (³/₄-1in) wide flowers appear in pendulous clusters from mid-summer onwards. White and purple forms are also available.
Height: 45-90cm (1¹/₂-3ft)
Spread: 30-38cm (12-15in)
Cultivation: Although this plant will grow in most soils, it does better in well-drained ground in a sunny position. It is well suited to a sunny bank or for a warm mixed border.
Propagation: During spring, sow seeds in shallow drills where the plants are to flower. When they are large enough to handle, thin the seedlings to 25-30cm (10-12in) apart for strong, healthy growth.

Campanula lactiflora

Milky Bellflower (UK)

This beautiful hardy herbaceous perennial has stems smothered in small light green leaves. The miniature bell-like light lavender-blue flowers appear during mid-summer. There is a wide range of varieties including 'Prichard's Variety' at 90cm (3ft) with lavender-blue flowers, 'Loddon Anna' at 1-1.2m (3¹/₂-4ft) with flesh-pink flowers, and 'Pouffe' at 25cm (10in) with light lavender-blue flowers.
Cultivation: Fertile deeply-cultivated and well-drained soil in full sun or slight shade suits it. But ensure that the soil does not dry out during summer. The tall-growing varieties

Borago officinalis, like many other seed-raised culinary and medicinal herbs, can be used in mixed borders or in odd corners, especially when a separate herb garden cannot be given entirely to them.

Above: Campanula lactiflora 'Pouffe'
A beautiful dwarf and hummock-forming campanula with light lavender-blue flowers during mid-summer. Other forms of this campanula rise to 90cm-1·5m [3-5ft].

Campanula medium

Canterbury Bell (UK and USA)

Most gardeners know this lovely old hardy biennial, with an upright stance and 2.5-4cm (1-1½in) long bell-shaped blue, pink, white or purple flowers from late spring to mid-summer. The best known form is the so-called Cup-and-Saucer variety, 'Calycanthema'. 'Bells of Holland', 38cm (15in) high and with a conical growth habit, has a mixture of single flowers in shades of blue, mauve, rose and white. Another form, 38-50cm (15-20in) high, is 'Dwarf Musical Bells' with multi-coloured bell-like flowers smothering the plants in blue, white and pink.
Height: 45-90cm (1½-3ft)

Above: Campanula medium
This reliable old favourite hardy biennial should find a place in any garden. It is ideal for filling bare areas in mixed borders, or as a high edging to paths.

Spread: 38-45cm (15-18in)
Cultivation: Moderately rich, well-drained soil in a sunny position suits this lovely plant.
Propagation: From spring to early summer, sow seeds 6mm (¼in) deep in a prepared seedbed. After germination and when large enough to handle, thin the seedlings to 23cm (9in) apart. During autumn, plant them into their flowering positions when the soil is in a workable condition.

need support in exposed areas.
Propagation: The easiest way to increase it is by division of large clumps during spring or autumn. Alternatively, take 4-5cm (1½-2in) long cuttings in spring, inserting them in pots of equal parts peat and sharp sand and placing these in a cold frame. When the plants are well grown, set them into their permanent positions in the garden. Alternatively, grow on the plants in a nursery bed before final planting.

White or yellow-flowered plants look superb with this blue herbaceous perennial. The tall-growing forms blend well with *Lilium regale* and the Madonna Lily, *Lilium candidum*. They can also join shape-contrasting but similarly-coloured plants to create blue textures.

Campanula medium is ideal grown as bold clumps in a mixed border, where it will bring colour while permanent plants are developing, perhaps blending with other ephemeral plants such as Love-in-a-mist *Nigella damascena* and Candytuft *Iberis umbrellata*.

THE FLOWER BORDER

Above: Centaurea moschata 'Dobies Giant' *An easily-grown hardy annual bringing large fragrant flowers in pastel tints to the garden from early summer to autumn.*

Centaurea moschata

(Centaurea imperialis)
Sweet Sultan (UK and USA)

This beautiful plant, native to the Eastern Mediterranean, is grown as a hardy annual. From early summer to autumn it displays sweetly-scented cornflower-like flowers in shades of purple, pink, white or yellow. The flowers, up to 7.5cm (3in) wide, are borne above the narrow grey-green leaves that display toothed edges. Another, more commonly grown relative is the Cornflower or Bluebottle, a native of Europe, with bright blue flowers.
Height: 45-60cm (1½-2ft)
Spread: 25-30cm (10-12in)
Cultivation: Fertile well-drained garden soil and full sun suit it. Removing dead flower heads helps to prolong the lives of the plants. In exposed areas they will need support from twiggy sticks.
Propagation: During spring, sow seeds where they are to flower. Set them in shallow drills, thinning the seedlings to 23cm (9in) apart when they are large enough to handle.

Ceratostigma plumbaginoides

This hardy sub-shrubby perennial from Western China has wide lance-shaped mid-green leaves that become tinged with red during autumn. The terminal clusters of blue flowers appear from late summer onwards, and it is a useful plant for bringing late colour to rock gardens and mixed borders.
Height: 25-30cm (10-12in)
Spread: 30-38cm (12-15in)
Cultivation: Light soil and an open but slightly sheltered position suit this attractive plant.
Propagation: It is easily increased by lifting and dividing clumps in spring, just before shoots appear.

Above: Centaurea cyanus 'Tall Double Mixed' *This hardy annual is very reliable and seldom fails to create a dominant display with its striking flowers in shades of blue, maroon, red, rose and white from early summer to autumn. It rises to about 90cm (3ft) high if the soil is kept moist, slightly less than this in dry conditions. In England it is known as the Cornflower, and in North America as the Bluebottle.*

Below: Ceratostigma plumbaginoides *A pretty hardy sub-shrub, ideal for late blue colour in a rock garden. Its foliage is a delight in autumn, when tinged with red, and it looks superb positioned at the base of a wall.*

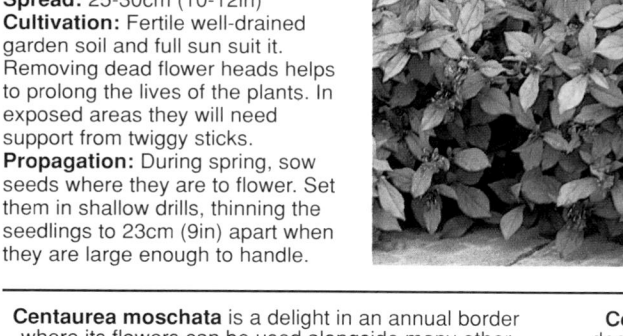

Centaurea moschata is a delight in an annual border where its flowers can be used alongside many other hardy annuals without any fear of its colour dominating its neighbours. It is good for cut flowers, so plant it within arm's length of scissors.

Ceratostigma willmottianum is a half-hardy deciduous shrub with diamond-shaped stalkless leaves. It bears terminal clusters of small rich blue flowers during mid-summer, and is ideal in a mixed border or even in a herbaceous mixture.

Chelone obliqua

Turtle-head (UK) · Turtlehead ·
Snakehead (USA)

This interesting, rather curious
looking hardy herbaceous perennial
has 2.5cm (1in) long deep rose
snapdragon-like flowers during late
summer. These are borne on stiff,
erect stems, from joints also bearing
dark green lance-shaped leaves with
serrated edges. *Chelone lyonii*,
another North American native, is a
hardy herbaceous perennial with
terminal clusters of 2.5cm (1in) long
pink flowers from mid-summer to early
autumn. The plant eventually rises to
about 75-90cm (2½-3ft) high.
Height: 60-75cm (2-2½ft)
Spread: 30-38cm (12-15in)
Cultivation: Fertile, light, well-drained
soil is needed, together with a position
in full sun or light shade. In wind-
protected gardens it may not require
support from twiggy sticks, but in cold
and exposed areas this becomes
essential. In autumn cut down the
stems to soil level.
Propagation: It is easily increased by
division of the roots during spring or
autumn, replanting only the young
parts from around the outside of the
clump. Alternatively, seeds can be
sown under glass in 15°C (59°F) in
early spring. Using this method takes
two years to produce flowering-sized
plants.

Chelone obliqua is best planted in a mixed or
herbaceous border, alongside colour-contrasting and
vigorous herbaceous plants such as the Shasta Daisy,
Chrysanthemum maximum.

THE FLOWER BORDER

Above: **Dahlia 'Gypsy Dance'**
A bedding variety ideal for the front of a border or in bedding schemes during summer. The small highly-coloured flowers are available in single and double forms.

Dahlias

These fast-growing garden favourites can be divided into two main groups: those grown as half-hardy annuals for use in bedding schemes and those that are best in mixed borders, mingled with herbaceous plants.

BEDDING DAHLIAS
These half-hardy perennials from Mexico are grown as half-hardy annuals, displaying 5-7.5cm (2-3in) wide single, double or semi-double flowers from mid-summer to autumn. There are many varieties in a wide colour range, in mixed or self-colours.
Height: 30-50cm (12-20in)
Spread: 38-45cm (15-24in)
Cultivation: Well-cultivated, fertile, compost or manure-enriched soil and a sunny position suit bedding dahlias. Soil too rich, however, will create excessive foliage at the expense of flowers. There is no need to stake them, unlike the larger border types. The removal of dead flowers assists in

the development of further blooms. Water the plants during dry periods.
Propagation: During the late winter and early summer sow seeds 6mm (¼in) deep in a loam-based seed compost at 16°C (61°F). When they are large enough to handle, prick off the seedlings into boxes or small pots of loam-based compost and slowly harden them off in a cold frame. Set the plants out in the garden as soon as all risk of frost has passed.

Above: **Dahlia 'Kay Helen'**
A ball type with very neat and compact blooms that look equally good in the garden or cut and displayed in a vase indoors. Dahlias thrive in rich soil and need a sunny position. The globular flowers are produced on stiff stems that with this variety carry the flowers above the foliage. To encourage rapid growth the soil must be carefully enriched before planting with the addition of bulky, well-rotted compost or manure worked in well with a fork.

Ball-type dahlias are available in a variety of colours.
They grow quickly from seed, and are useful in
providing colour throughout the summer, and make
attractive cut flowers.

Left: **Dahlia 'Earl Marc'** *A distinctive semi-cactus, not as quilled or tubular as the cactus types. The flowers have flatter petals.*

BORDER DAHLIAS

These half-hardy tuberous plants, though easily damaged by frost, are unsurpassed for bringing colour to a garden quickly. There are several classifications and many varieties. Indeed, each year hundreds of new varieties are introduced by dahlia specialists, while others are no longer marketed. When the dahlia was first grown as an exhibition flower in the early 1800s it consisted solely of ball types. To indicate their value, some new varieties were sold for as much as a guinea. At first no classification was recognized for the ball types, or for various other types of dahlia that were produced. However, catalogues were soon issued by traders in dahlias and these contained a rough classification. In 1904 the British National Dahlia Society in conjunction with the Joint Dahlia Committee published a classified list called the Classification and Description of Dahlias.

Anemone-flowered (60cm-1m/ 2-3½ft): These have double flowers with flat outer petals and short, tubular inner ones. Flowering is from mid summer to the frosts of autumn.

Ball-type (90cm/3ft): As implied, these have ball-shaped flowers, with tubular petals displaying blunt ends. There are *Small Ball* types with blooms 10-15cm (4-6in) wide, and *Miniature Ball* forms with flowers up to 10cm (4in) wide.

Cactus and Semi-cactus (90cm-1.5m/3-5ft): These are divided into five groupings – *Miniature* (blooms up to 10cm/4in wide); *Small* (blooms 10-15cm/4-6in wide); *Medium* (blooms 15-20cm/6-8in wide); *Large* (blooms 20-25cm/ 8-10in wide); and *Giant* (blooms 25cm/10in or more wide). Cactus types have petals rolled back or quilled for more than half their length. Semi-cactus types have similar petals, but quilled or rolled back for less than half their length.

Dwarf dahlias are thought to have been developed from low-growing forms found in 1750 on the lower slopes of the Sierra del Ajusca mountains in Mexico. The plants were said to be about 38-45cm (15-18in) high.

THE FLOWER BORDER

Collarette (75cm-1m/2½-4ft): These have blooms with a single outer ring of flat ray florets and a ring of small florets in the centre, forming a disc.
Decorative: These have double flowers without central discs. They are formed of broad, flat ray florets. This grouping is subdivided into:
Miniature (90cm-1.2m/3-4ft): these have flowers up to 10cm (4in) wide.
Small (1-1.2m/3½-4ft): flowers 10-15cm (4-6in) wide.
Medium (1-1.2m/3-4ft): flowers 15-20cm (6-8in) wide.
Large (1-1.5m/3½-5ft): flowers 20-25cm (8-10in) wide.
Giant (1.2-1.5m/4-5ft): flowers 25cm (10in) or more wide.
Paeony-flowered (up to 90cm/3ft): flowers formed of two or more rings of flat ray florets, with a central disc.
Pompon (90cm-1.2m/3-4ft): flowers closely resemble those of *Ball* types, but are more globular and do not exceed 5cm (2in) wide. The florets curl inwards for their entire length.
Single-flowered (45-75cm/1½-2½ft): flowers up to 10cm (4in) wide, with a single row of petals arranged round a central disc.
Cultivation: Well-drained soil, with plenty of moisture-retentive compost

or well-decomposed manure added, is required. Add a sprinkling of bonemeal before setting the tubers 10cm (4in) deep in the soil during mid to late spring. If you are planting sprouted tubers, take care that you do not plant them too early, as frost will damage them. The plants will need staking. Nip out the growing tips of all shoots to encourage sideshoots to develop. If you want large flowers, remove sideshoots and buds from around the developing flowers. Removing dead flowers helps in the development of further blooms. In autumn gently dig up the tubers about a week after the foliage has been blackened by frost. Remove soil from the tubers and store them upside down for a few

Left: Dahlia 'Scaur Princess'
A beautifully-coloured type which brings distinction to any garden.

Dahlias are superb for filling large blank areas in mixed borders, where they create spectacular colourful displays during late summer and into early autumn until frosts damage them. They are soon blackened by frost.

Left: Dahlia 'Vicky Jackson'
A decorative cactus, producing masses of flowers from mid-summer onwards until the frosts of late autumn.

Right: Dahlia 'Willo's Violet'
A beautiful pompon type, with deep violet flowers and a height of about 1m (3½ft). It is excellent as an exhibition dahlia.

weeks to dry them out. Then place them in boxes of peat in a dry, frost-proof position until the following year.

Propagation: The easiest way for the home gardener to do this is to divide the tubers in spring.

Dahlias in floral art: As well as creating colour in the garden the flowers of dahlias are ideal for decorating the home. The art of presenting dahlias for room decoration is not difficult, and part of the skill in using them relies on the choice of colours. Blue flowers, whatever their tone, need to be carefully used as the colour tends to fade in artificial light. Purples and mauves, however, can be used subtly, especially where they echo the same tones in the room. However, when used with white-flowered dahlias, which both lighten and dramatize the arrangement, the effect can be quite different. In contrast, other colours such as yellow and orange are much warmer and radiate a strong feeling of cheerfulness. Those flowers rich in scarlet, however, can create the effect of warmth in rooms facing east and north and not subjected to strong summer sunshine. Rooms facing north or east generally benefit from warm colours, such as orange, scarlet, yellow and amber, whereas cool colours such as pale mauve, lilac-pink, purple shades and lavender are better in south and west-facing rooms. If strong coloured blooms are used they can be given even greater impact by mixing them with pastel coloured flowers.

Collarette type dahlias originated in the municipal gardens of the Parc de la Tete d'Or at Lyons, France, during the last years of the last century. Specimens of these plants arrived in Britain in 1901.

THE FLOWER BORDER

Left: **Echinacea purpurea** *This stately herbaceous perennial is justifiably famous for its richly coloured flowers, from mid-summer to autumn. The cone-like orange centres to the flowers are a particularly attractive feature.*

Echinacea purpurea

Purple Cone Flower (UK and USA)

A well-known hardy herbaceous perennial, formerly called *Rudbeckia purpurea*. Its upright stems bear purple-crimson daisy-like flowers 10cm (4in) wide, at their tops from mid to late summer. The lance-shaped, dark green leaves are slightly toothed and rough to the touch. Several superb varieties are

Echinacea purpurea is a dominant flower, with the erect stems often holding the flowers high above neighbouring plants, like islands of colour. Surrounding plants should have subdued colours.

available, including 'Robert Bloom', (carmine-purple), 'The King' (crimson-purple) and 'White Lustre' (white petalled with deep orange centres).

Height: 90cm-1.2m (3-4ft)
Spread: 60-75cm (2-2½ft)
Cultivation: Well-drained fertile soil and a sunny position are essential for success. Set the plants in position in spring, and in autumn cut their stems down to soil-level.
Propagation: Although it can be increased from seeds sown in spring at 13°C (55°F), division of established clumps during spring or autumn is a much easier method. Use only the young parts from around the outside of the clump for replanting in the border.

Above: **Echinops ritro**
This hardy herbaceous perennial is highly cherished by flower arrangers. The globular flower heads appear during mid-summer and last a long time after cutting.

Left: **Echium plantagineum 'Monarch Dwarf Hybrids'**
A hardy dwarf mixture, up to 30cm (1ft) high these hybrids produce flowers in many pastel tints. When grown in a sunny position, they seldom fail to attract bees.

Echinops ritro

Globe Thistle (UK)
Small Globe Thistle (USA)

This hardy herbaceous perennial has deep green, thistle-like leaves and round, 4-5cm (1½-2in) wide, steel-blue flowers held on stiff stems during mid-summer. Bees find the flowers especially attractive.
Height: 90cm-1.2m (3-4ft)
Spread: 60-75cm (2-2½ft)
Cultivation: Most soils are suitable, but they should be well-drained and in full sun. This is a plant that is self-supporting and therefore ideal for island beds. During autumn, cut the plant down to soil-level.
Propagation: It can be increased from root-cuttings taken in late autumn, inserted in sandy compost and placed in a cold frame before

planting out in the garden. But the division of established clumps in spring or autumn is a much easier and quicker method.

Echium plantagineum

(*Echium lycopsis*)
Viper's Bugloss (UK and USA)

This distinctive hardy annual from Europe has mid-green leaves and upturned blue or pale purple bell-shaped flowers from mid-summer onwards. Although it normally grows up to 90cm (3ft), several lower-growing forms at 30cm (1ft) are available, including 'Blue Bedder' and 'Monarch Dwarf Hybrids' with blue, pink, lavender and white flowers. Several other species of echium can be grown in the garden, including the bushy, hardy biennial *Echium rubrum*. From early to mid summer it displays 12mm (½in) long, bright red tubular flowers with eye catching yellow stamens. Another species, *Echium vulgare,* the Common Viper's Bugloss is a hardy biennial, but is invariably grown as an annual. It is relatively short (60cm/2ft high) bushy and compact and bears tubular, 12mm (½in) long, purple-budded, violet flowers from mid to late summer. *Echium vulgare* and *Echium plantagineum* are both natives of the British Isles. *E. vulgare* is found in grassy places on light soils near the coast, while *E. plantagineum* grows in sandy areas near the sea, in the South-west.
Height: 75-90cm (2½-3ft)
Spread: 45cm (1½ ft)
Cultivation: Light, dry soil and a sunny position are needed, although partial shade also suits it.
Propagation: During spring, sow seeds 6mm (¼in) deep in their flowering positions, thinning the seedlings to 15cm (6in) apart. Seeds can also be sown in autumn, but wait until spring before thinning them. For earlier flowers, sow seeds in loam-based seed compost in late winter or early spring at 13°C (55°F). Prick out the seedings into boxes when they are large enough to handle, and harden them off before planting them out.

Echinops ritro is best planted in large clumps, where its dominant flower heads blend with a background grouping of *Campanula lactiflora* with small bell-shaped light lavender-blue flowers.

Echium plantagineum in one of its dwarf forms is of greater use in a garden than taller types. It is ideally suited for annual borders, and also for bringing height and shape contrast to small ornamental grasses.

THE FLOWER BORDER

Eryngium bourgatii

Sea Holly (UK)
Eryngo (USA)

This hardy herbaceous perennial
has stiff, upright and branching
bluish stems bearing spiny, holly-
like leaves and silver-blue, thistle-
shaped flower heads during mid to
late summer.
Height: 38-45cm (15-18in)
Spread: 30-38cm (12-15in)
Cultivation: It grows best in fertile
well-drained soil in a sunny
location. Only in exposed areas will
it need support from twiggy sticks.
In autumn, cut down the plant to
soil-level.
Propagation: It can be increased
by taking root cuttings in autumn
and inserting them in pots of equal
parts peat and sharp sand. Place
them in a cold frame during winter
and set the plants out into their
permanent sites in the garden
when they are well-grown.

Right: Eryngium bourgatii
*This hardy herbaceous perennial
displays strikingly attractive foliage
and flower heads, much cherished
by flower arrangers for home
decoration.*

**Below right: Eupatorium
purpureum 'Atropurpureum'**
*This exciting hardy and reliable
herbaceous perennial with purplish
foliage and rosy-lilac flowers is
admirable for mixed or herbaceous
borders, as well as wild gardens.*

Eupatorium purpureum

Joe Pye Weed (UK)
Joe-pye Weed · Sweet Joe-pye
Weed · Green-stemmed Joe-pye
Weed [USA]

This handsome upright hardy
herbaceous perennial from North
America has purplish stems
bearing slender and pointed mid-
green leaves. Fluffy, branching, 10-
13cm (4-5in) wide heads of rose-
purple flowers are borne from mid
to late summer. The form
'Atropurpureum' bears rosy-lilac
flowers and purplish leaves.

There are several other superb **Sea Hollies,** including
Eryngium alpinum, with frilled collars around the bases
of its steel-blue flower heads, and *E. x oliverianum*
which is graced with deep blue heads.

Eupatorium purpureum is a dominant plant, often
standing above its neighbours. In a mixed border, its
height and colour create a pleasing combination with
the blue *Hydrangea macrophylla*.

Height: 1.2-1.8m (4-6ft)
Spread: 75-90cm (2½-3ft)
Cultivation: Any good relatively moisture-retentive and fertile soil suits it, in full sun or light shade. During autumn cut down the stems to soil-level. It benefits from a mulch with well-rotted manure or garden compost every spring. Before applying it, however, hoe the surface to remove all weeds.
Propagation: It is easily increased by lifting and dividing established clumps in autumn or spring.

Left: **Festuca glauca**
This densely-tufted perennial grass is ideal for the front of a border. To create an impressive clump, use three or five plants, each 20cm (8in) apart.

Festuca glauca

Sheep's Fescue · Blue Fescue (UK and USA)

This hardy perennial grass forms a striking clump of bristle-like blue-grey leaves. It is ideal for planting at the edge of a border, where it can be used to soften harsh edges, and blend well with gravel paths. During summer it is adorned with oval, purple spikelets of flowers.
Height: 20-25cm (8-10in)
Spread: 15-20cm (6-8in)
Cultivation: Well-drained light soil and a sunny position are best.
Propagation: Seeds can be sown in a sheltered border, planting the seedlings out into a nursery bed when they are large enough to handle. It is generally easier, however, to lift and divide large clumps in spring or autumn.

Filipendula purpurea

(*Spiraea palmata*)

A handsome, though dominating, hardy herbaceous perennial with large lobed leaves held on crimson stems and surmounted by large flat heads of small carmine-rose flowers during mid-summer.
Height: 75cm-1.2m (2½-4ft)
Spread: 75-90cm (2½-3ft) and more
Cultivation: An ideal plant for rich, fertile, moisture-retentive soil in partial shade, perhaps in a wild garden or at the side of an informal garden pond.
Propagation: It is easily increased by lifting and dividing large clumps in autumn or spring.

Left: **Filipendula purpurea**
An impressive herbaceous perennial for a fertile moist, cool position in slight shade. Its carmine-rose flower heads form a dominant display during mid-summer.

Festuca glauca is superb for a colour contrast with yellow-flowered plants, such as Golden Garlic *Allium moly*, which is also known as Yellow Onion. Position the grass in front of the allium.

Filipendula rubra is another attractive filipendula, with large pinkish flower heads up to 28cm (11in) across. It is widely grown in the form 'Venusta' with deep pink flowers. It loves moist soil and slight shade.

THE FLOWER BORDER

Gladiolus byzantinus

Sword Lily (UK)

This hardy and reliable gladiolus has 25-38cm (10-15in) long flower spikes loosely packed with up to twenty plum-coloured 5-7.5cm (2-3in) wide blooms during mid-summer. The narrow, sword-like and upright ribbed leaves rise to 60cm (2ft).
Height: 60cm (2ft)
Spread: 13-18cm (5-7in)
Cultivation: Rich, fertile, well-drained but moisture-retentive soil and full sun suit it best. The corms can be left in the soil from year to year, and in light soils it is best to plant them 15cm (6in) deep – 10cm (4in) in heavy soil – so that they are self-supporting and do not become blown over. In heavy soil, place a handful of sharp sand under each corm when planting it. Remove dead flower stems after flowering and cut down the yellowed foliage to soil-level in autumn – but not too early or it will not have transferred its food content to the corms, which act as storage organs to help the plants survive winter.
Propagation: Every four or five years lift the plants in autumn and remove the little cormlets attached to the corm. Dry them and replant them in spring in sand-lined drills in a nursery bed.

Above: **Gladiolus byzantinus** *This small-flowered gladiolus flowers much earlier than its large-flowered relatives. Well-drained soil and a position in full sun assure success.*

Hosta rectifolia 'Tall Boy'

Plantain Lily (UK)
Plantain Lily · Day Lily (USA)

These hardy perennials with beautiful leaves, variegated in some varieties, were once known as *Funkias*. This species displays broad lance-shaped mid to dark green leaves and tall, upright flower stems bearing 5cm (2in) long violet-mauve flowers in slender spikes during mid-summer. Several other hostas, including *H. crispula*, have ·purple flowers. During mid to late summer this plant reveals lilac-purple flowers above its dark green, white-edged leaves, the feature for which it is mainly grown.
Height: 1-1.3m (3¹/₂-4¹/₂ft)
Spread: 75-90cm (2¹/₂-3ft)
Cultivation: Well-drained but moisture-retentive soil enriched with leafmould and in a lightly shaded position suits it.
Propagation: In spring, lift and divide large clumps. This variety can be raised from seed, but variegated hostas do not come true from seed.

Hostas are among the most attractive of border flowers for naturalized or woodland settings, or even large rock gardens. The variegated types, such as *Hosta fortunei* 'Albopicta' are especially attractive.

Left: **Hosta rectifolia 'Tall Boy'**
*This beautiful violet-mauve
flowered plant is ideal for a wild
garden, where the soil does not
become dry during summer.
Even when not in flower the foliage
forms a dominant display,
especially in early summer.*

Right: **Hosta 'Halcyon'**
*This attractively-flowered hosta
creates a dominant display in a
slightly-raised border where the
leaves can spread safely without
being trodden upon or splashed
with soil during heavy rainfall. Here
it is planted against the grass
Hakonechloa macra 'Albo-aurea'
with narrow bronze-tinted,
variegated green and buff leaves.
This grass looks good positioned at
a corner.*

Iberis umbellata

Candytuft (UK)
Globe Candytuft (USA)

This well-known highly-fragrant
hardy annual from Southern Europe
has mid-green, pointed, narrow
leaves. The 5cm (2in) wide
clustered heads of purple, white and
rose-red flowers appear from early
summer to autumn from successive
sowings. It is an annual that is well
known to children and often the first
plant they sow. It soon germinates
and forms an edging for the side of
a path. Alternatively, set it in bold
drifts towards the front of a border.
Height: 15-38cm (6-15in)
Spread: 23cm (9in)
Cultivation: Well-drained, even
poor soil in full sun suits it. Remove
dead flower heads to extend the
flowering season.
Propagation: From late spring to
early summer, sow seeds in shallow
drills where the plants are to flower.
The seeds take ten to fourteen days
to germinate. When the seedlings
are large enough to handle, thin
them to 20-23cm (8-9in) apart.

Right: **Iberis umbellata** *This
easily-grown and highly fragrant
hardy annual flowers over a long
period from successive sowings. It
is superb for planting in poor soils.*

Iberis umbellata is a very amenable plant and
associates with many others, such as Canterbury
Bells (*Campanula medium*), Clarkia (*Clarkia elegans*)
and Virginian Stock (*Malcolmia maritima*).

THE FLOWER BORDER

Incarvillea mairei

(*Incarvillea grandiflora brevipes I. brevipes*)
Trumpet Flower (UK)

This herbaceous perennial has attractive, deep green, pinnate leaves and bears rich pinkish-purple flowers with long tubular yellow throats during early to mid-summer.

Height: 30cm (1ft)
Spread: 20-25cm (8-10in)
Cultivation: Fertile, well-drained light soil in full sun assures success. During spring, plant the fleshy roots 7.5cm (3in) deep, and in cold areas protect the young and newly emerging shoots and leaves with a cloche or layer of straw. In particularly cold places they may require protection throughout winter. Often the new shoots are slow to emerge from the soil in spring, so take care not to damage them with early spring cultivations.
Propagation: Although the crowns can be lifted and divided in spring, they are sometimes tough and difficult to split. Instead, sow seeds in a prepared seedbed in spring, transplanting them the following spring to their permanent positions.

Right: **Incarvillea mairei** *This is a beautiful herbaceous perennial for the front of a border, or even for a rock garden where extra height is desired. The yellow-throated pinkish-purple flowers appear during early to mid-summer.*

Right: **Iris douglasiana**
This beautiful Californian iris needs limy (alkaline) soil and forms a large clump of colour in early summer. The plants are often short lived, but can be easily raised from seeds. The flowers are superb for home decoration.

Iris douglasiana

This beardless hardy iris from California has slender, coarse, deep green leaves that are normally evergreen and spread out to a width of 60cm (2ft). The 7.5cm (3in) wide flowers are borne in fours or fives on branched stems. They are in shades

Incarvillea delavayi is another well-known species, rising to 60cm (2ft) and displaying 5-7.5cm (2-3in) long rose-pink flowers during early summer. This species is taller than *Incarvillea mairei*.

Iris douglasiana is ideal for setting around rhododendrons, where it helps to produce ground cover and to create colour when some of the rhododendrons have finished flowering.

of blue-purple and lavender, with distinctive veining on the 'falls' (the three outer petals), and appear from early to mid-summer.

Height: 30-45cm (1-1½ft)
Spread: 60-75cm (2-2½ft)
Cultivation: This iris tolerates a little lime in the soil, and needs full sun or partial shade. However, it also grows well in neutral or slightly acid soil.
Propagation: It tends to be short-lived, but fortunately it is easily increased from seed sown during autumn in boxes of loam-based compost kept at 10°C (50°F). Alternatively, lift and divide the rhizomes in autumn, but take care that they do not dry out before becoming established.

Iris sibirica

Siberian Iris (UK and USA)

This versatile iris is suitable for a herbaceous border as well as the margins of an informal pond. The slender, sword-like, mid-green leaves die down in winter. The flowers are about 6.5cm (2½in) wide and are borne during mid-summer. In the original species, they are in various shades of blue, with white veining on the 'falls' (the three outer petals). Because the original species hybridizes freely, usually only hybrids are available. Good ones are 'Heavenly Blue' (rich azure blue), 'Cambridge' (pale blue), 'Ottawa' (clear light blue), 'Tropic Night' (velvety violet) and 'Perry's Blue' (deep blue).

Height: 75cm-1m (2½-3½ft)
Spread: 45-60cm (1½-2ft)
Cultivation: It grows best in moist soil, but will also perform well in a herbaceous border, where it does not usually grow so high. Plant the rhizomes 2.5cm (1in) deep in the soil during autumn or spring.
Propagation: It is easily increased by lifting and dividing congested clumps in late autumn or spring. Replant the divided rhizomes 2.5cm (1in) deep. Large clumps tend to become hollow and bare at their centres, and are therefore best lifted and divided at least every four or five years to keep them healthy.

Above: **Iris sibirica 'Heavenly Blue'** *This is a hardy iris for a border or the moist margin of a pond. Its rich blue flowers are borne two or three to a stem above the grassy sword-like leaves.*

Iris sibirica, planted in a moist area, mixes well with yellow-flowered plants such as the fragrant Himalayan Cowslip *Primula sikkimensis*, and *P. helodoxa*. It also looks good in a border against an old wall.

THE FLOWER BORDER

Liatris spicata

Blazing Star · Gayfeather · Spike
Gayfeather (UK)
Blazing Star · Button Snakeroot
Gay-feather (USA)

This hardy, tuberous-rooted, herbaceous perennial has small, strap-like, narrow, mid-green leaves. It bears dense, 15-30cm (6-12in) long, paintbrush-like spikes of pinkish-purple flowers during late summer and early autumn on stiff, leafy stems. A similar plant, *Liatris callilepis*, has bright carmine flower heads. The form 'Kobold' is even more attractive, with frothy bright carmine flower spikes, often up to 30cm (1ft) long. It grows well even on poor soil. When planted in a small grouping, it creates a superb splash of mid-summer colour. This attractive variety has the advantage of growing to only 60cm (2ft) high, whereas the original species, *Liatris callilepis*, rises to 90cm (3ft) and requires much more room, being better positioned in a flower border than in a rock garden. Another species, *Liatris graminifolia*, is not so widely grown. During late summer and into early autumn it produces purple flower spikes, surrounded by rather sparse leaves attractively covered with white spots. This species has the advantage of growing well in poor and dry soils.

Height: 60-90cm (2-3ft)
Spread: 38-45cm (15-18in)
Cultivation: Ordinary garden soil – not too heavy – and a position in full sun suit the Blazing Star.
Propagation: During spring lift and divide established clumps. To ensure the clumps are readily identified, mark them in autumn. Alternatively, wait until late spring before dividing them, when the young shoots will be apparent.

Left: Liatris callilepis 'Kobold'
The frothy flowers of this tuberous-rooted herbaceous perennial are a delight during mid-summer to early autumn. The flowers are useful for home decoration.

Liatris spicata is ideal for the front of a mixed or herbaceous border. Suitable companions include Red Hot Pokers (*Kniphofia*), *Bergenia* 'Silberlicht' and the Oregon Grape *Mahonia aquifolium*.

Linum narbonense

Flax (UK and USA)

This well-known hardy perennial has narrow, lance-shaped, grey-green leaves and graceful, arching stems that usually die back in winter in colder climates but may persist throughout winter in milder regions. The 2.5-3cm (1-1¼in) wide rich blue flowers, borne at the tops of the stems, appear throughout the summer months. *Linum perenne* is another hardy and perennial flax, rising to 30-45cm (1-1½ft). It has narrow lance-shaped greyish-green leaves and 2.5cm (1in) wide sky-blue flowers during mid to late summer. Like *Linum narbonense* it is also short-lived, but can be easily raised from seed. *Linum usitatissimum*, the Common Flax or Linseed, is a pale-blue-flowered hardy annual. It rises to about 60cm (2ft), with slender stems bearing 12mm (½in) wide, saucer-shaped flowers during

Above: **Linum narbonense**
Although tall, this Flax is suitable for a rock-garden. The flowers, borne at the ends of long stems, appear throughout summer.

mid-summer. *Linum austriacum* is another soft-blue flowered plant, but is a hardy perennial and has 2.5cm (1in) wide heads in mid-summer.
Height: 30-60cm (1-2ft)
Spread: 30-38cm (12-15in)
Cultivation: Ordinary well-drained garden soil and a sunny position suit Flax best. It will tolerate both slightly acid and limy soil.
Propagation: During early summer, sow seeds 6mm (¼in) deep in a prepared seed bed. When the seedlings are large enough to handle, thin them to 20-23cm (8-9in) apart. In autumn, transfer them to their flowering positions. The plants are quite short-lived, so it is best to buy fresh plants every three or four years and replace old ones.

Liriope muscari

Turf Lily (UK and USA)

This hardy, compact and clump-forming evergreen perennial has dark green grass-like leaves and upright stems, which bear 7.5-13cm (3-5in) long spikes of bell-shaped, lilac-mauve flowers from late summer through to autumn. The species *Liriope spicata* is quite similar, but with more erect and narrower leaves. From late summer and into autumn it displays 5-7.5cm (2-3in) long spikes of bright mauve, bell-shaped flowers. It is slightly shorter than *Liriope muscari*, rising to a height of 38cm (15in).
Height: 30-38cm (12-15in)
Spread: 38-45cm (15-18in)
Cultivation: Well-drained light and fertile soil in full sun or slight shade suits it well. Remove the flower heads when they fade.
Propagation: During spring, lift and divide congested clumps.

Linum narbonense, with its cottage-garden appeal, is at home by the side of an old-looking flight of steps against a weathered wall or as a perfect foil for grey-leaved plants.

Liriope muscari is ideal for the edge of a border or alongside a path. It harmonizes well with the Autumn Crocus (*Colchicum autumnale*), *Nerine bowdenii* or *Sedum* x 'Autumn Joy'.

Lupinus polyphyllus 'Russell Hybrids'

Lupin · Lupine (UK)
Lupine (USA)

These hardy herbaceous perennials are familiar to most gardeners. Their slender, upright spires of blue or red mid-summer flowers are borne above mid-green leaves formed of a circle of 10 to 17 leaflets. Many superb blue forms are available, such as 'Blue Jacket, 'Freedom', 'Jane Eyre' and 'Josephine'.

Height: 90cm-1.5m (3-5ft)
Spread: 60-90cm (2-3ft)
Cultivation: Well-drained moderately fertile soils are best, in full sun or light shade. Set the plants in position in autumn or spring, and cut them down to soil-level in autumn.

Propagation: Increase named forms from 7.5-10cm (3-4in) long basal cuttings in spring, inserted in pots of sandy soil and placed in a cold frame. When the cuttings are rooted, pot them up into small pots of loam-based compost. Plant them into permanent positions in autumn or spring when the soil is workable.

Right: Lupinus polyphyllus 'Russell Hybrids' *These hardy herbaceous perennials are popular and reliable plants for any garden, providing a mass of colour. They grow equally well in slightly acid or neutral soils, and in full sun or light shade.*

Left: Nemophila menziesii
This hardy annual has a rather spreading growth habit and bears sky-blue buttercup-like flowers from early summer onwards. It is ideal for edging an annual border or even a mixed border.

Nemophila menziesii

(Nemophila insignis)
Baby Blue Eyes (UK and USA)

This bright-eyed hardy annual from California has light green deeply-cut feathery foliage and 3cm (1¼in) wide, sky-blue flowers with white centres from early to late summer.

Lupinus polyphyllus 'Russell Hybrids' mixes with a wide range of herbaceous plants. Highlight the flowers by planting it against a dark green hedge, or use its own foliage as a backcloth for lower-growing plants.

Nemophila menziesii has flowers that are not colour dominant, so it can be mixed with plants such as the Poached Egg Plant (*Limnanthes douglasii,*) with its yellow-centred white flowers.

Nicandra physaloides

Shoo-fly Plant · Apple of Peru (UK and USA)

This hardy annual from Peru is vigorous and strong growing, its spreading shoots bearing oval, mid-green leaves with finely-toothed, wavy edges. The pale-blue, bell-shaped, 4cm (1½in) wide flowers have white throats, and appear from mid to late summer. These are followed by non-edible apple-shaped green fruits that can be dried for home decoration. It is said to gain the name *physaloides* from the resemblance of the fruits to those of *Physalis alkekengi*, commonly called Chinese Lantern or Bladder Cherry.
Height: 75-90cm (2½-3ft)
Spread: 38-45cm (15-18in)
Cultivation: Rich, moist soil and a sunny position are the keys to success. When preparing the flowering position, fork in plenty of well-rotted compost.
Propagation: During late winter or early spring, sow seeds 3mm (⅛in) deep in trays of loam-based seed compost kept at 10°C (50°F). When the seedlings are large enough to handle, prick them off into seed-boxes and put them in a cold frame to harden them off. Set the plants in the garden during late spring. Alternatively, sow seeds in late spring where the plants are to flower, 6mm (¼in) deep. Subsequently, thin the seedlings to 25-30cm (10-12in) apart.

Height: 18-23cm (7-9in)
Spread: 15-20cm (6-8in)
Cultivation: Although this annual grows in ordinary garden soil, it does even better in fertile, moisture-retentive soil in full sun or slight shade. Sandy soils enriched with plenty of compost are also suitable.
Propagation: During spring and early summer, sow seeds 6mm (¼in) deep in their flowering positions. When the seedlings are large enough to handle, thin them to 15cm (6in) apart. As well as being suitable for sowing in the garden, this annual can also be

greenhouse. To grow such plants sow seeds thinly in 13cm (5in) wide pots of loam-based compost in a cold frame during late spring or early summer. When they are large enough to handle, thin the seedlings to three in each pot. Make sure the greenhouse is not kept too hot.

Right: **Nicandra physaloides**
This tall, vigorous, branching hardy annual needs space in which to develop properly. The pale-blue, bell-shaped flowers are borne over many weeks, from mid to late summer.

Nicandra physaloides gains one of its common names, Shoo-fly Plant, from its ability to repel flies. It makes a lovely choice for the back of a border, with its attractive bell-shaped flowers.

Polemonium foliosissimum

Jacob's Ladder (UK)
Jacob's Ladder · Greek Valerian (USA)

A hardy herbaceous perennial from North America, Jacob's Ladder has stiff, upright stems bearing leaves formed of narrow dark green leaflets. From early to late summer, it bears 12mm (½in) wide mauve-blue flowers in clustered heads. The handsome flowers are highlighted by orange-yellow stamens. An early form is 'Sapphire', with light blue saucer-shaped flowers.
Height: 75-90cm (2½-3ft)
Spread: 45-60cm (1½-2ft)
Cultivation: Rich, deep, loamy soil in full sun assures success. These plants soon exhaust the soil, which will need annual mulching or feeding with fertilizer.
Propagation: The easiest way to increase this plant is by lifting and dividing established clumps in autumn or spring.

Below: Polemonium foliosissimum
This herbaceous perennial is ideal for any border and flowers over a long period of time. It needs rich soil, because the roots quickly exhaust the supply of nutrients.

Physostegia virginiana

(*Dracocephalum virginianum*)
Obedient Plant (UK)
Obedience · False Dragonhead
Lion's-head (USA)

This distinctive hardy herbaceous perennial bears long spires of mid-summer tubular pink-mauve flowers above large, glossy, dark green, coarsely-toothed leaves. The plant gets its common name from its flowers, which have hinged stalks and can be moved from side to side, remaining as positioned. Several forms are available, including 'Rose Bouquet' (pink-mauve), 'Summer Spire' (deep lilac-purple) and 'Vivid' (deep pink).
Height: 45cm-1m (1½-3½ft)
Spread: 45-60cm (1½-2ft)
Cultivation: This plant needs

Above: Physostegia virginiana 'Rose Bouquet' *A native of North America, this popular hardy herbaceous perennial bears spires of mauve-pink, tubular flowers which resemble small snapdragons.*

ordinary fertile garden soil that does not dry out during summer. During autumn, cut it down to soil-level.
Propagation: It is easily increased by lifting and dividing plants in autumn or spring. Alternatively, during spring, take 5-7.5cm (2-3in) long cuttings, insert them in pots of sandy compost and place these in a cold frame. When the cuttings are rooted, pot them up and plant them out into their flowering positions in autumn. In cold areas with wet soil, plant them during spring.

Physostegia virginiana is a reliable plant for a mixed or herbaceous border. The deep lilac-purple variety 'Summer Spire' needs non-conflicting colours set around it at a lower level.

Polemoniums come mostly from North America, but *Polemonium caeruleum* originated in Europe and Asia as well. It gained its first name from King Polemon of Pontus, an ancient country in North-east Asia Minor

Above: **Salvia x superba** *This hardy eye-catching herbaceous perennial forms a dominant splash of colour in any border.*

Above: **Salvia viridis** *is a beautiful hardy annual with pale pink or purple flowers which feature especially striking coloured bracts at the tops of the stems. It is raised as a half-hardy or a hardy annual, and it delights in a sunny and well-drained position in the garden.*

Salvia x superba

(*Salvia virgata nemorsa*)
Long-branched Sage (UK)

A dominant planting of this superb hardy herbaceous perennial will immediately attract attention. Its erect stems bear abundant, rich violet-purple flower spires at their tops all summer through, so set it at the edge of a border. Dwarf forms rise to less than half the height of the type plant, and include 'Lubeca' (violet-blue, 75cm/2½ft high) and 'East Friesland' (violet-purple, 45cm/1½ft high).
Height: 45-90cm (1½-3ft)
Spread: 45-60cm (1½-2ft)
Cultivation: Rich, well-drained but moisture-retentive soil in full sun assures success. Dry soils are not suitable. Staking with twiggy pea-

sticks is necessary for tall-growing forms in exposed areas. Cut down old stems to soil-level in late autumn.
Propagation: It is easily increased by lifting and dividing congested plants during autumn or spring.

Salvia viridis

(*Salvia horminum*)

This hardy annual from Southern Europe bears 12mm (½in) long pale pink or purple flowers from mid to late summer. It is better known, however, for its 4cm (1½in) long brightly coloured terminal bracts (modified leaves), which can be dried with the stems for home decoration. There are several fine forms, with a range of coloured bracts, such as 'Blue Bouquet' (rich purple-blue bracts) and 'Rose

Bouquet' (rose-carmine bracts).
Height: 38-45cm (15-18in)
Spread: 23-30cm (9-12in)
Cultivation: Ordinary well-drained soil in full sun suits it. To encourage well-branched plants, pinch out the growing tips when the plants are only a few inches high.

Propagation: During late spring or early summer, sow seeds 6mm (¼in) deep where the plants are to flower. When the seedlings are large enough to handle, thin them out to 23cm (9in) apart. You can raise earlier-flowering plants by sowing seeds thinly in trays of loam-based compost at 18°C (64°F) during late winter or early spring. When the seedlings are large enough to handle, prick them off into pots of loam-based compost and place them in a cold frame to harden off.

Salvia x **superba** demands space to be at its best. Plant it at the front of the border, with tall light blue delphiniums at the back and a sandwich of yellow achillea between them.

Salvia viridis, better known as *Salvia horminum*, is best used to create dominant colour at the tops of its stems. It is more often grown for its coloured bracts than for its flowers.

THE FLOWER BORDER

Above: **Trachymene caerulea** *The delicate heads of small lavender-blue flowers appear from mid-summer to autumn. This is a useful plant for bringing delicate blue shades to flower arrangements.*

Above: **Tradescantia virginiana 'Isis'** *This well-known Spiderwort has striking purple-blue flowers during most of summer. Well-drained but moisture-retentive soil ensures success with this reliable plant.*

Right: **Tulip 'Lilac Time'** *This beautiful tulip from Division 7 is distinctive, with its mauve, lily-like flowers. Flowers in this division are usually 15-20cm (6-8in) wide and appear in mid-spring.*

Trachymene caerulea

(*Didiscus caeruleus*)
Blue Lace Flower · Queen Anne's Lace (UK)
Blue Lace Flower (USA)

This is one of the most delicate and pretty of all half-hardy annuals. It forms a bushy plant with light green, deeply-divided foliage. The small dainty, lavender-blue flowers are displayed in heads 2.5-5cm (1-2in) wide and appear from mid-summer to autumn. They are suitable for cutting for home decoration, but the leaves and stems are sticky to touch.
Height: 45cm (1½ft)
Spread: 25-30cm (10-12in)
Cultivation: Ordinary well-cultivated garden soil and a sunny, sheltered position suit it.
Propagation: During late winter and early spring, sow seeds 3mm (⅛in) deep in trays of loam-based seed compost at 16°C (61°F). When the seedlings are large enough to handle, prick them out into small pots or boxes of seed compost. Plant the young plants out into the garden as soon as all risk of frost has passed.

Tradescantia virginiana

Spiderwort · Trinity Flower (UK)
Common Spiderwort · Widow's Tears (USA)

This hardy herbaceous perennial with smooth, glossy, strap-like, dull-green leaves and long lasting, 2.5-4cm (1-1½in) wide, three petalled flowers, is a delight throughout summer and into autumn. It is the hybrids from *T. virginiana* or *T. x andersoniana* that are mainly grown. Some botanical authorities suggest these hybrids are derived from the former species, while other botanists name the latter as a parent. Whatever their origin, the resulting plants are superb and include 'Carmine Glow' (carmine), 'Isis' (purple-blue), 'Iris Pritchard' (white, stained azure blue) and 'Purewell Giant' (carmine-purple).
Height: 45-60cm (1½-2ft)
Spread: 45cm (1½)
Cultivation: Ordinary garden soil, well-drained but also moisture-retentive, is best. In late autumn, cut the plants down to soil-level.
Propagation: Lift and divide congested clumps in spring.

Tulips

The range of form and colour of these well-known hardy bulbs is as wide as their possible uses in the garden. They can be used in bedding schemes during spring, in mixed borders or rock gardens, and in tubs or troughs for brightening up a patio in spring. There is a wide range of species, and in addition botanists have classified those that have been created by bulb experts into fifteen divisions, encompassing the wide range of flower sizes, shapes and heights. These are:
Division 1 – Single Early (15-38cm/6-15in): The single flowers appear in spring when grown out-of-doors, or during winter indoors. Each flower is 7.5-13cm (3-5in) wide and sometimes opens flat when in direct and full sun. Many purple varieties are available, as well as ones with white, pink, red, orange and yellow flowers.
Division 2 – Double Early (30-38cm/12-15in): The double flowers appear in spring when grown out-of-doors in bedding schemes, or earlier when forced indoors.

Trachymene caerulea from Australia soon attracts attention when grown in a dominant drift among hardy annuals or in a mixed border. It can also be grown in pots in an unheated greenhouse for summer colour.

Tradescantia virginiana and **T. x andersoniana** are ideal for a mixed or herbaceous border. Many plants combine well with them, including border geraniums and *Campanula lactiflora* 'Pritchard's Blue'.

Division 10 – Parrot (45-60cm/ 1¹/₂-2ft): These bear flowers up to 20cm (8in) wide in mid-spring, easily recognizable by their feather-like, heavily-fringed petals. The colour range includes brilliant white, pink, orange and yellow, as well as some lovely purples.

Division 11 – Double Late (45-60cm/ 1¹/₂-2ft): These have very large and showy double flowers, similar to paeonies and up to 20cm (8in) wide. They remain in flower for a long period during mid-spring. There are some stunning violet varieties, as well as white, orange, pink, red and yellow ones. There are also multi-coloured forms, with stripes and edgings.

Division 12 – Kaufmanniana varieties (10-25cm/4-10in): These have been developed from *Tulipa kaufmanniana*, and have fine-pointed flowers that open nearly flat, giving the appearance of water-lilies. They appear in spring on sturdy stems and are ideal for fronts of borders, rock gardens and containers. Most have two-coloured flowers.

Division 13 – Fosteriana varieties (45cm/1¹/₂ft): These are derived from *Tulipa fosteriana* and display large blunt-ended flowers in reds and yellows in mid-spring.

Division 14 – Greigii varieties (25cm/10in): These are mainly derived from *Tulipa greigii*, and produce brilliant red, yellow and near-white long-lasting flowers during mid-spring.

Cultivation: When growing tulips in the garden, select well-drained soil, preferably facing south and in a sheltered position. Plant the bulbs 15cm (6in) deep during early winter, spacing them 10-15cm (4-6in) apart. Remove dead flowers and dig up the bulbs when the leaves turn yellow. However, if the bed is needed earlier, dig up the bulbs as soon as flowering is over and heel them into a trench until the foliage has yellowed and died down.

Propagation: The easiest way is to remove the bulb offsets clustered at the bases of the bulbs. Plant these in a nursery bed and leave them to develop into flowering-sized bulbs.

Each flower is 10cm (4in) wide and rather like a double paeony. The colour range is wide, including good purple varieties, as well as red, violet, pink and yellow ones.

Division 3 – Mendel (38-50cm/15-20in): These flower later than the previous types, with rounded 10-13cm (4-5in) wide blooms on somewhat slender stems. Colours include white and red, as well as yellow. They look like a cross between single early types and Darwins.

Division 4 – Triumph (up to 50cm/ 20in): In mid-spring these bear angular-looking 10-13cm (4-5in) wide flowers on strong stems. There are lovely lilac-flowered varieties, as well as red and pink ones.

Division 5 – Darwin Hybrids (60-75cm/2-2¹/₂ft): These have some of the largest and most brilliant flowers, up to 18cm (7in) wide; they appear during mid-spring. There are multi-coloured forms, as well as purple, red, orange and yellow varieties.

Division 6 – Darwin (60-75cm/2-2¹/₂ft): These are extensively used in bedding schemes, producing

rounded flowers up to 13cm (5in) wide in late spring. There are some excellent purple varieties, also yellow, white, pink and red ones.

Division 7 – Lily-flowered (45-60cm/1¹/₂-2ft): These are characterized by the narrow waists of their flowers, also by the pointed petals that curl outwards as much as 20cm (8in) during mid-spring. They look especially attractive when massed in bedding schemes. Colours include white, orange, red, yellow and multi-colours.

Division 8 – Cottage (up to 90cm/ 3ft): This old grouping has oval or rounded flowers 10-13cm (4-5in) wide in mid-spring. The petals sometimes have a hint of fringing, and are looser than those of other varieties. As well as lilac, flower colours include green, white, pink, red and yellow.

Division 9 – Rembrandt (75cm/ 2¹/₂ft): These tulips all have 'broken' colours. The rounded 13cm (5in) wide flowers display vivid splashes of colour on the petals during mid-spring. Base colours include violet, as well as brown, white, orange, red, yellow and pink.

For a **blue and gold display** try the dark blue Darwin tulip (Division 6) 'La Tulipe Noire' with the orange Siberian Wallflower *Cheiranthus x allionii* 'Golden Bedder'. For extra shades of blue, add a few Forget-me-nots *(Myosotis)*.

For a **mixture of creamy-white and blue,** try planting a bed with the mauve-blue Parrot tulip (Division 10) 'Blue Parrot', dark purple Darwin tulip, (Division 6) 'Queen of Night' and the Wallflower 'Ivory White'.

THE FLOWER BORDER

Right: Veronica prostrata **Right: Veronica prostrata** *This beautiful ground-covering veronica produces masses of small deep blue flowers from early to mid-summer There are several superb forms, including a very low-growing type.*

Veronica prostrata

(*Veronica rupestris · V teucrium prostrata*)

A hardy mat-forming alpine veronica, this is a distant form of the Hungarian, or Saw-leaved, Speedwell from Southern Europe and Northern Asia. It is useful as a ground cover plant, displaying toothed mid-green leaves and 5-7.5cm (2-3in) long spikes of deep blue flowers from early to mid-summer. Several reliable forms are available, including 'Spode Blue' (clear pale blue), 'Rosea' (deep pink), 'Alba' (white) and a dwarf form 'Pygmaea' (5cm/2in high, with deep blue flowers).
Height: 10-20cm (4-8in)
Spread: 38-45cm (15-18in)
Cultivation: Any well-drained garden soil and a sunny position suit it.
Propagation: During mid-summer, take 5cm (2in) long cuttings and insert them in pots of equal parts peat and sharp sand. Place the pots in a cold frame and when the cuttings are rooted, pot them up singly into loam-based compost. During the following spring, plant them out into the garden.

Veronica spicata

Spiked Speedwell (UK)

An upright slim-flowered hardy herbaceous perennial, this veronica is well-suited to the front of a border. It displays long, toothed, lance-shaped, mid-green leaves. The narrow, 7.5-15cm (3-6in) long spires of small blue flowers are borne throughout mid-summer. Several superb forms are worth growing, including 'Blue Fox' (ultramarine blue) and 'Barcarolle' (rose-pink).
Veronica longifolia is another purple-blue-flowered border plant. It rises up to 1.2m (4ft) and bears 15cm(6in)

long terminal spires of flowers from early to late summer. To create a dominant clump, set the individual plants about 45cm (1½ft) apart.
Veronica virginica is another good border species, with pale blue spires of flowers.
Height: 30-45cm (1-1½ft)
Spread: 30-38cm (12-15in)
Cultivation: Well-drained but moisture-retentive friable soil in full sun or slight shade assures success. In late autumn, cut the stems down to soil-level.
Propagation: During spring, lift and divide congested clumps – you can usually do this every three or four years. This ensures healthy plants.

Top right: Veronica spicata
This is a reliable hardy herbaceous perennial for the front of a border, where it can display its spires of small blue flowers to advantage during mid-summer. There are several excellent varieties from which to choose.

Right: Catananche caerulea
This beautiful short-lived perennial brings a wealth of colour to a border. It is also excellent as a cut-flower, and can be dried for winter decoration in the home. The flowers appear during summer. For details see under **Further plants to consider** *on the opposite page.*

Veronica prostrata blends well in a rock garden with yellow-flowered plants such as *Linum flavum*, with 2.5cm (1in) wide mid-summer flowers, and the ever-reliable *Hypericum olympicum*, with golden-yellow flowers.

Further plants to consider

Ajuga reptans
Bugle (UK) · Carpet Bugleweed (USA)
Height: 10-25cm (4-10in)   Spread: 30-50cm (12-20in)
A well-known, soil-smothering, hardy herbaceous perennial, with
whorls of blue flowers borne on upright stems during mid-summer.
The form 'Atropurpurea' is distinctive, with purple leaves.

Campanula persicifolia 'Telham Beauty'
Peach-leaved Campanula (UK) · Peach-bells · Willow Bellflower
(USA)
Height: 60-90cm (2-3ft)   Spread: 30-38cm (12-15in)
A delightful perennial, with an evergreen basal rosette. The rich
blue, 2.5cm (1in) wide, saucer-shaped flowers appear during mid-
summer. 'Pride of Exmouth' displays rich lavender-blue flowers.

Catananche caerulea
Cupid's Dart (UK and USA)
Height: 45-75cm (1½-2½ft)   Spread: 45-60cm (1½-2ft)
A short-lived herbaceous perennial with narrow, lance-shaped
leaves and lavender-blue flowers during summer. The form 'Major'
bears richer blue flowers.

Delphinium elatum
Height: 90cm-1.5m (3-5ft)   Spread: 45-60cm (1½-2ft)
The actual species is seldom grown, but it is the well-known
Belladonna and *Elatum* (also known as 'large-flowered') types that
are widely grown. The range of blue-flowered forms is wide, including
'Blue Tit' (indigo-blue), 'Blue Jade' (sky-blue), 'Page Boy' (brilliant
mid-blue), 'Blue Bees' (bright pale blue), 'Bonita' (gentian-blue),
'Wendy' (gentian-blue, flecked purple), 'Cressida' (pale blue with a
white eye) and 'Mullion' (cobalt-blue with a dark eye).

Geranium x magnificum
(*Geranium ibericum* · *Geranium platypetalum*)
Height: 45-60cm (1½-2ft)   Spread: 45-50cm (18-20in)
An eye-catching hybrid geranium, with violet-blue 2.5cm (1in) wide
flowers during mid to late summer.

Geranium pratense 'Johnson's Blue'
Height: 38cm (15in)   Spread: 38-45cm (15-18in)
A well-known light-blue mid-summer flowering hardy herbaceous
perennial. The flowers are borne amongst mid-green five or seven-
lobed leaves.

Limonium latifolium
Sea Lavender · Statice (UK)
Height: 60cm (2ft)   Spread: 45-60cm (1½-2ft)
A distinctive hardy perennial, formerly classified as *Statice*. From
mid to late summer, it displays lavender-blue flowers in large, loose
heads. Two good forms are 'Violetta' (violet) and 'Blue Cloud'
(lavender-blue).

Veronica spicata is a British native plant that gains
its second name from the spike-like arrangement of
its flowers. The related *V. beccabunga* acquired its
unusual name from the old word *beck*, 'a rill or ditch'
and *bung*, 'a purse'.

THE FLOWER BORDER

apart when they are large enough to handle. In autumn, plant out the established plants in their flowering positions. In cold areas, wait until spring to do this.

Left: Achillea filipendulina 'Coronation Gold' *The eye-catching deep yellow saucer-like flower heads of this hardy herbaceous perennial are superb when the sun sets their bright colour alight. The flowers are excellent for floral arrangements, especially those that are dried for winter decoration.*

Top right: Alchemilla mollis *This beautiful herbaceous plant is ideal for setting alongside a crazy-paved garden path where it helps to soften the appearance of the surface and to fuse the border with the path.*

Alchemilla mollis

Lady's Mantle (UK and USA)

This hardy herbaceous perennial has beautiful light green and hairy leaves, shallowly lobed, and tiny sulphur-yellow star-shaped flowers 3mm (1/8in) wide, borne in frothy sprays from early to mid-summer.
Height: 30-45cm (1-1½ft)
Spread: 30-45cm (1-1½ft)
Cultivation: Well-drained but moisture-retentive soil in full sun or slight shade are needed. In exposed areas, this plant may require support from twiggy sticks, and in autumn cut down the whole plant to an inch or so above the level of the soil.
Propagation: Seeds can be sown in boxes of loam-based compost in early spring and placed in a cold frame. When they are large enough to handle, prick out the seedlings into boxes of compost, later setting the plants in nursery rows. In autumn, or spring in cold areas, set the plants in the garden. Large clumps can be lifted, divided and replanted in autumn or spring. However, do not lift and divide them during wet or cold weather.

Achillea filipendulina

(*Achillea eupatorium*)
Fern-leaf Yarrow (UK and USA)

This hardy herbaceous perennial displays 10-15cm (4-6in) wide, plate-like, lemon-yellow heads at the tops of upright, stiff stems from mid to late summer. The mid-green, deeply indented, feathery leaves are clustered up the stems. Several superb forms are available, including 'Coronation Gold', with deep yellow flowers, and 'Gold Plate', also with deep yellow flowers.
Height: 90cm-1.2m (3-4ft)

Spread: 75-90cm (2½-3ft)
Cultivation: Well-drained or even dry soil suits it, and a position in full sun. During early winter, cut back dead stems to soil level.
Propagation: Most gardeners will find it simplest to propagate yarrow by lifting and dividing the congested clumps in spring. Replant only the young parts from around the outside. Select pieces with four or five shoots.

Alternatively, seeds can be sown 6mm (¼in) deep in a prepared seedbed during late spring and early summer, thinning the seedlings to 25-30cm (10-12in)

Achillea filipendulina contrasts well with plain backgrounds and differently-shaped plants. For instance, the achillea's flowers are highlighted by a beech or yew hedge. They are also attractive when set with tall variegated grasses.

Alchemilla mollis is a useful plant which blends with many other plants, such as *Centranthus ruber* 'Albus' and roses, Red-hot Pokers (*Kniphofia*), and *Salvia haematoides*.

Right: Argemone mexicana
This annual is excellent for hot and dry places. Its beautiful, prickly, silvery-green leaves are able to roll up slightly to conserve moisture. The large lemon-yellow flowers appear during summer.

Argemone mexicana

Devil's Fig · Prickly Poppy (UK)
Mexican Poppy (USA)

Few plants are as distinctive as this hardy annual. Its prickly silvery-green glaucous leaves are borne on sprawling stems, with the saucer-shaped flowers appearing from early summer onwards. They are lemon-yellow, scented and poppy-like, 9cm (3½in) wide.
Height: 60cm (2ft)
Spread: 30-39cm (1-1¼ft)
Cultivation: Well-drained, light, relatively dry soil and full sun assure success. Remove dead flower heads to encourage others to develop.
Propagation: During spring, sow seeds in the border where the plants are to flower. Thin the seedlings to 30cm (1ft) apart when they are large enough to handle. Alternatively, sow seeds in boxes of a loam-based seed compost during early spring, keeping them at 18°C (64°F). When large enough to handle, prick out the seedlings into boxes of loam-based compost and harden them off in a cold frame. Plant them in spring.

Above: *The delicate sulphur-yellow flowers of* Alchemilla mollis *stand above the light green hairy leaves and form a pleasing combination with the rich royal-purple flowers of* Tradescantia 'Isis'. *The dull green strap-like leaves of the tradescantia complete the picture.*

Argemone mexicana is best grown with other plants in an annual border. Do not let other plants crowd and hide the attractive leaves. It survives hot, dry, inhospitable places.

Calendula officinalis

Pot Marigold · English Marigold (UK)
Pot Marigold (USA)

This is one of the best known and most reliable hardy annuals, with light green, pungent, lance-shaped leaves. The daisy-like, pastel-coloured flowers in yellow or orange, up to 10cm (4in) wide, appear from early summer to autumn. There are many varieties, including 'Lemon Gem' with yellow flowers, 'Fiesta Gitana' displaying pastel colours in cream, yellow, gold and orange, 'Orange King' in deep orange, and 'Geisha Girl' with reddish-orange blooms. The dwarf types do well in containers such as tubs and window-boxes. The taller ones are best in a border.
Height: 30-60cm (1-2ft)
Spread: 30-45cm (1-1½ft)
Cultivation: Like many other annuals, Pot Marigolds grow well in poor, free-draining soils. But in a medium-rich, well-drained soil in full sun they do even better. They can even become a problem, creating masses of self-sown seedlings, but this can be dealt with by removing dead flowers. Pinching out the growing tips of young plants encourages the development of side-shoots.
Propagation: During spring, sow seeds 12mm (½in) deep where the plants are to flower. When the seedlings are large enough to handle, thin them out to 30cm (1ft) apart. To raise plants for containers, pot up seedlings in small pots before setting them in containers. If you would like to raise plants for very early spring flowering, you should sow seed in the border during late summer and early autumn.

Centaura macrocephala

Yellow Hardhead · Yellow Hardweed (UK)

A handsome, hardy herbaceous perennial with 7.5-10cm (3-4in) wide, yellow, thistle-like flower heads at the top of upright, stiff stems during mid-summer. The rough-surfaced, stiff, elongated lance-shaped leaves clasp the stems right up to the flower heads. When cut, the flowers last well in water, and bees find the flowers very attractive.
Height: 90cm-1.5m (3-5ft)
Spread: 45-75cm (1½-2½ft)
Cultivation: Light, fertile, well-drained soil and a sunny position are essential. On exposed sites, you will need to support the plants with twiggy sticks. Centaureas benefit from being lifted and divided in early spring every four years or so.
Propagation: Seeds can be sown in spring in boxes of loam-based compost and placed in a cold frame. When they are large enough to handle, prick off the seedlings into boxes of compost. When they are well grown, plant them out into a nursery bed to remain for the rest of the summer. Set the plants out in the garden in autumn. Alternatively, lift and divide established clumps in spring.

Calendula officinalis has long been grown amid old-style borders packed with annuals and border plants. It gains its common name, Pot Marigold, from being grown in earlier times in pots for use in the kitchen.

Centaurea macrocephala does well when filling bare areas between roses. The stiff stems of the centaureas allow the handsome flowers to appear between the rose blooms.

Above: **Cladanthus arabicus**
This delightful hardy annual has orange buds opening to golden-yellow, fragrant flowers in succession throughout summer. A light soil and plenty of sunshine are essential. Remove dead flower-heads to encourage the development of further blooms.

Left: **Centaurea macrocephala**
Favoured by nectar-seeking bees the thistle-like yellow flower heads are often 7.5-10cm (3-4in) wide. They are borne on stiff stems, and are ideal as cut flowers, lasting a long time in water. The leaves form an attractive foil for the brightly-coloured flowers.

Cladanthus arabicus

(*Anthemis arabica*)

A bright hardy annual from Spain, with daisy-like, 5cm (2in) wide, fragrant, single flowers from early to late summer, and light green feather-like foliage.
Height: 75cm (2½ft)
Spread: 30-38cm (1-1¼ft)
Cultivation: Light, well-cultivated slightly acid soil in full sun is best. Rich soils tend to encourage a mass of foliage at the expense of flowers.
Propagation: During spring, sow seeds where the plants are to flower. Sow the seeds in drills, thinning to 30cm (1ft) apart.

Cladanthus arabicus is an ideal plant to choose for the centre or rear of an annual border, because it displays an overall mound shape. It tends to sprawl at its sides, quickly merging with neighbouring plants.

THE FLOWER BORDER

Above: **Coreopsis verticillata**
The finely-divided deep green leaves are very distinctive and from early summer to early autumn, starry yellow flowers are borne on stiff stems. It is ideal for use in floral arrangements.

Coreopsis verticillata

An attractive, busy, long-lived, hardy herbaceous perennial from the eastern United States of America, with distinctive, deep green, finely-divided leaves. The bright yellow, star-like flowers 4cm (1½in) wide, appear over a long period, from early summer to early autumn.
Height: 45-60cm (1½-2ft)
Spread: 38-45cm (1¼-1½ft)
Cultivation: Well-drained fertile soil in a sunny position suits coreopsis. Fortunately, it does not require staking in any but the most exposed sites. Cutting flowered stems back to soil-level encourages the development of further shoots. In early winter cut all stems down to soil-level.
Propagation: It is easily increased by lifting and dividing established and congested clumps in spring. Ensure each new piece has several strong healthy shoots. Do not let the roots dry out.

Above: **Dahlia 'Claire de Lune'**
This beautiful anemone-flowered dahlia grows up to 1m (3½ft), with pale sulphur-yellow flowers, shaded cream. It has strong stems, and is ideal as a cut flower.

Below: **Dahlia 'Yma Sumac'**
This is a bright decorative with double flowers. Decorative dahlias have a range of flower sizes, from l0cm (4in) in Miniatures, to 25cm (10in) or more in Giants.

Coreopsis verticillata is ideal in a mixed border producing a long-lasting display of colour. It tends to form an abrupt, regular block of upright colour, presenting a clear outline.

New dahlia varieties are introduced every year, and many of the less good ones are abandoned. To ensure you buy up-to-date, reliable varieties send for a catalogue from one of the major dahlia growers.

Dahlias

These bright flowers can be divided into two main groups: those which can be grown as half-hardy annuals for use in bedding schemes, and those which are best in mixed borders, mingled with herbaceous plants and flowering shrubs.

BEDDING DAHLIAS

These half-hardy perennials from Mexico are grown as half-hardy annuals, displaying 5-7.5cm (2-3in) wide single, double or semi-double flowers from mid-summer to autumn. There are many varieties in a wide colour range, in mixed or self-colours.

Height: 30-53cm (1-1¾ft)
Spread: 38-45cm (1¼-2ft)
Cultivation: Bedding dahlias need well-cultivated, fertile, compost or manure-enriched soil in a sunny position. Soil too rich, however, will create excessive foliage at the expense of flowers. There is no need to stake them—unlike the large border types. Removing dead flowers helps the development of further blooms. Water the plants during dry periods.
Propagation: During late winter and early spring, sow seeds 6mm (¼in) deep in a loam-based seed compost at 16°C (61°F). When they are large enough to handle, prick off the seedlings into boxes or small pots of a loam-based compost and slowly harden them off in a cold frame. Set the plants out in the garden as soon as all risk of frost has passed.

BORDER DAHLIAS

These are half-hardy tuberous plants, easily damaged by frost, which quickly bring colour to the garden. There are several classifications and many varieties.
Anemone-flowered
(60cm-1m/2-3½ft): These have double flowers with flat outer petals and short, tubular inner ones. Flowering is from mid-summer to the frosts of autumn.
Ball-type (90cm-1.2m/3-4ft): As their name implies, these have ball-

shaped flowers, with tubular, blunt-ended petals. There are *Small Ball* types with blooms 10-15cm (4-6in) wide, and Miniature Ball forms with flowers up to 10cm (4in) wide.
Cactus and Semi-cactus (90cm-1.5m/3-5ft): These are divided into five groupings, *Miniature* (blooms up to 10cm/4in wide); *Small* (blooms 10-15cm/4-6in wide); *Medium* (blooms 15-20cm/6-8in wide); *Large* (blooms 20-25cm/8-10in wide); *Giant* (blooms 25cm/10in or more wide).
Collarettes (75cm-1.2m/2½-4ft): These have blooms with a single outer ring of flat ray florets, with a ring of small florets in the centre, forming a disc.
Decoratives: These have double flowers without central discs. They are formed of broad, flat ray florets. This grouping is further divided into:
Miniature (90cm-1.2m/3-4ft): These have flowers up to 10cm (4in) wide.
Small (1-1.2m/3½-4ft): Flowers 10-15cm (4-6in) wide.
Medium (1-1.2m/3½-4ft): Flowers 15-20cm (6-8in) wide.
Large (1-1.5m/3½-5ft): Flowers 20-25cm (8-10in) wide.
Giant (1.2-1.5m/4-5ft): Flowers 25cm (10in) or more wide.
Paeony-flowered (up to 90cm/3ft): The flowers are formed of two or more rings of flat ray florets, with a central disc.
Pompon (90cm-1.2m/3-4ft): The flowers very much resemble those of *Ball* types, but are more globular and are no more than 5cm (2in)

Above: **Dahlia 'Primrose Bryn'**
This semi-cactus type has beautiful flowers. All dahlias are useful for the colour they bring to the garden, right up to the frosts of autumn.

wide. The florets curl inwards for their entire length.
Single-flowered (45-75cm/1½-2½ft): These display flowers up to 10cm (4in) wide, with a single row of petals arranged around a central disc.
Cultivation: Well-drained soil, with plenty of moisture-retentive compost or well-decomposed manure added, is required. Include a sprinkling of bonemeal before setting the tubers 10cm (4in) deep in the ground during mid to late spring. If sprouted tubers are used, take care that they are not planted too early, or frost will damage them. The young plants will need staking. Nip out the growing tips of all shoots to encourage sideshoots to develop, and if you want large flowers, remove sideshoots and buds from around the developing flowers. The removal of dead flowers helps the development of further flowers. In autumn, dig up the tubers carefully about a week after the foliage has been blackened by frost. Remove soil from the tubers and store them upside down for a few weeks to encourage them to dry out. Then place them in a frost-proof place.
Propagation: The easiest way for the home gardener to do this is to divide the tubers in spring.

Dahlias are natives of Mexico, where they grow in sandy meadows at about 1525m (5000ft) above sea-level. They were first brought to England by way of Spain, by the Marchioness of Bute in 1789.

THE FLOWER BORDER

Doronicum plantagineum

Green Leopard's Bane · Leopard's Bane (UK)
Leopard's Bane (USA)

This is one of the earliest-flowering hardy herbaceous perennials, revealing heart-shaped, bright green, shallowly-toothed leaves surmounted by single, golden-yellow, daisy-like flowers, 6.5cm (2¹/₂in) wide, during late spring and into early summer. Several superb forms are available, including 'Miss Mason' (bright yellow flowers), 'Spring Beauty' (deep yellow and double) and 'Harpur Crewe' (7.5cm/3in wide gold flowers).
Height: 45-60cm (1¹/₂-2ft)
Spread: 38-45cm (1¹/₄-1¹/₂ft)
Cultivation: Leopard's Bane appreciates fertile, moisture-retentive, deeply-cultivated soil in full sun or light shade. In autumn cut the plants down to soil level. They may need tidying up earlier in the year if other plants are to be set close to them.
Propagation: The easiest way to increase them is by lifting and dividing congested plants during autumn or early spring. Replant young pieces from around the edges of the old clump.

Above: Doronicums
The cheerful yellow flowers carry on after early daffodils are over.

Above: Doronicum plantagineum 'Miss Mason' *The yellow, daisy-like flowers of this early-flowering herbaceous perennial are a welcome sight in spring. They are excellent as cut-flowers.*

Doronicum plantagineum 'Miss Mason' is ideal for harmonizing with spring-flowering bulbs such as tulips. These will hold their heads above the doronicums, giving added height and interest.

Eschscholzia californica

Californian Poppy (UK and USA)

This delicate, highly attractive perennial from western North America is commonly grown as a hardy annual. It has attractive, finely-cut, fern-like, blue-green leaves, and from early summer to autumn it shows saucer-shaped, bright orange-yellow flowers with silky petals, 7.5cm (3in) wide. An added attraction is the crop of blue-green seedpods, each 7.5-10cm (3-4in) long. Several varieties are available, including some lovely clear yellow and orange flowered forms.

Height: 30-38cm (1-1¼ft)
Spread: 23-30cm (9-12in)
Cultivation: Light, sandy, poor soil and a sunny site are needed.
Propagation: From early spring to early summer, sow seeds 6mm (¼in) deep where the plants are to flower. When they are large enough to handle, thin the seedlings to 15-23cm (6-9in) apart.

Below: Eschscholzia californica
The original Californian Poppy has been developed into a range of colours. Dry, light, poor soil and plenty of sunshine assure success. It often produces self-sown seedlings in subsequent years.

Above: Helianthus annuus 'Sungold' *This low-growing sunflower, with double golden-yellow flowers up to 15cm (6in) wide, grows only 60cm (2ft) high. Many other varieties grow up to 3m (10ft). Sunflowers seldom fail to capture the attention of children, and are an ideal introduction to gardening. Tall-growing varieties are excellent for creating a short-lived screen in the garden. Set the plants in groups rather than in rows for the best effect. Make sure you give them firm support in the shape of stout canes with secure ties.*

Helianthus annuus

Sunflower (UK)
Common Sunflower · Mirasol (USA)

Popular in children's drawings and gardens the world over, this hardy annual from America bears gigantic, daisy-like flowers, 30cm (1ft) or more wide, singly at the tops of stems up to 3m (10ft) high. Flowering is from mid to late summer. There are many varieties, such as 'Autumn Beauty' (1.8m/ 6ft), with sulphur-yellow flowers stained copper-bronze, 'Sungold' (60cm/2ft), with double golden-yellow flowers up to 15cm (6in) wide, and 'Russian Giant' (2.4-3m/ 8-10ft), yellow-flowered.
Height: 90cm-3m (3-10ft)
Spread: 45-60cm (1½-2ft)
Cultivation: Well-drained soil in full sun suits the sunflower best. Remove dead flower heads and support the plants with stout canes or stakes.
Propagation: During early spring and into early summer, sow seeds 12mm (½in) deep. Thin the seedlings to 30-45cm (1-1½ft) apart when they are large enough to handle. Perennial sunflowers are best increased by lifting and dividing the plants during autumn or early spring, but they can also be propagated in the same manner as for the annual types.

Eschscholzia caespitosa is another species, with finely-cut blue-green leaves and yellow flowers, 2.5cm (1in) wide. A dwarf, only 13cm (5in) high, it is ideal for bare patches in a rock garden, or as a border edging.

Helianthus annuus, the sunflower, is often grown on its own in a sunny corner of a garden. But some varieties are superb at the back or centre of an annual border, mixing well with colour contrasting annuals such as *Celosia argentea plumosa.*

THE FLOWER BORDER

Left: **Limonium sinuatum 'Gold Crest'**
A yellow-flowered form of the Sea Lavender, with flower heads which are often dried for floral decorations during winter. Its unusually shaped foliage and bright flowers make it a superb choice for a border.

Right: **Narcissus 'Rembrandt'**
*This is a large daffodil from **Division 1,** with rich yellow flowers and frilled trumpets. It is superb for setting in mixed borders, or naturalizing in grass. One flower is produced on each stem. It looks best when planted in dominant clusters, rather than singly over a large area.*

Limonium sinuatum 'Gold Coast'

Sea Lavender (UK)

This hardy perennial, usually grown as a half-hardy annual, has bright yellow flowers in 10cm (4in) long clusters on erect stems from mid to late summer. It is one of the everlasting flowers, dried and used for home decoration in winter. For this purpose, cut the flower stems just before the flowers are fully open and, holding them upside down, tie them in bundles. Hang these up in a dry, airy shed until all moisture has gone. There are many other varieties, with flower colours including pink, lavender, white and dark blue, as well as various shades of yellow.
Height: 38-45cm (15-18in)
Spread: 30-38cm (12-15in)
Cultivation: Sea Lavender likes light, well-drained soil in full sun.
Propagation: Sow seeds 6mm (½in) deep during late winter and early spring, in a loam-based seed compost at 16°C (61°F). When they are large enough to handle, prick off the seedlings into boxes of loam-based compost and harden them off in a cold frame. Plant them out in the garden in late spring. Alternatively, sow seeds in spring *in situ*, but flowering is later.

Limonium sinuatum is only one of the everlasting flowers. Others include *Helichrysum bracteatum, Helipterum roseum* and *Xeranthemum annuum*, with purple flowers.

Narcissus

Daffodils (UK and USA)

Much-loved heralds of spring, these are all bright-faced flowers with central trumpets, in various sizes. There are many different species, from 7.5-45cm (3-18in) high. In addition, there are the many garden types, again in a range of shapes and sizes, which

---

Below: **Narcissus 'Fortune'** *A large-cupped daffodil from* **Division 2.** *This well-known daffodil with yellow petals and trumpets in shades from orange to red is ideal for mixed borders and naturalizing in grass. One flower is produced on each stem.*

---

have various classifications. Flower size ranges from 2.5-10cm (1-4in) wide, with one or several flowers on each stem, blooming from late winter to late spring.

DIVISION 1 – TRUMPET DAFFODILS (38-45cm / 15-18in): These are of garden origin and produce just one flower on each stem. The trumpet is as long or longer than the petals. They have been further divided into subsections: those with all-yellow trumpets, bicolours, white-trumpeted, and reversed bicolour trumpets.

DIVISION 2 – LARGE-CUPPED DAFFODILS (38-55cm /15-22in): These are large-cupped, with one flower on each stem and with the trumpet more than one-third the length of the petals. These are further divided into yellow large-cupped, coloured cups, bicoloured large-cupped, bicoloured red-cupped, and white large-cupped.

DIVISION 3 – SHORT-CUPPED DAFFODILS (36-45cm /14-18in): These have just one flower on each stem, with the cup part less than one-third of the length of the petals. Again, they are sub-divided, into coloured small-cupped bicoloured small-cupped and white small-cupped.

DIVISION 4 – DOUBLE DAFFODILS (30-45cm /12-18in): These have double flowers, with one or more blooms on each stem.

DIVISION 5 – TRIANDRUS DAFFODILS (up to 30cm / 12in):These are derived from *Narcissus triandrus*, distinguished by swept-back petals, and with two or three flowers on each stem.

DIVISION 6 – CYCLAMINEUS NARCISSI (20-38cm /8-15in): These are known for their long trumpets and swept-back petals, and are subdivided into those flowers where the trumpets are more than two-thirds the petal length, and those which are less.

DIVISION 7 – JONQUILLA NARCISSI (28-43cm /11-17in): These are of garden origin and developed from *Narcissus jonquilla*. They have two to four

Daffodils are universally admired. Spring has truly arrived when banks and beds glow with these beautiful flowers, many in shades of yellow. Forsythia blends well with daffodils.

Daffodils harmonize with many small-flowered and low-growing bulbs, such as the blue-flowered *Chionodoxa luciliae*. To create further interest, set these two bulbs near a blue-flowered, spring-blooming, deciduous shrub.

THE FLOWER BORDER

flowers on each stem. The flowers are highly scented and up to 5cm (2in) wide.

DIVISION 8 – TAZETTA NARCISSI (38-43cm / 15-17in): These are descended from *Narcissus tazetta*, with its characteristic bunched appearance. They are highly scented, and divided into two main types: those resembling *N. tazetta* and those developed from crossing *N. tazetta* and *N. poeticus*. These latter ones are known as poetaz narcissi.

DIVISION 9 – POETICUS NARCISSI (35-43cm /14-17in): These are of garden origin and are characterized by white petals and frilled bright red cups. They are delightfully scented.

DIVISION 10 – WILD FORMS AND HYBRIDS (7.5-45cm / 3-18in): Within this section are the species narcissi, encompassing all the wild forms, wild hybrids, and all the miniature types. Many are superb in a rock garden or naturalized in an alpine meadow.

Cultivation: They can be grown in many ways—for instance, in rock gardens, in alpine meadows, filling gaps in borders, or naturalized in woodland. The bulbs grow best in rich, well-drained soils in slight

Below: **Narcissus 'Irene Copeland'** *A double narcissus from **Division 4**, with camellia-like yellow and white flowers. Its form is attractive and contrasts well with the trumpet types. Another good variety is 'Mary Copeland' which has orange and white flowers.*

Above: **Narcissus 'Grand Soleil d'Or'** *A bunch-flowered narcissus from **Division 8**. It develops several flowers at the top of each flower stem, and makes a dominant display. It is slightly tender and therefore best grown in pots in the house or conservatory.*

shade. Sprinkle a general fertilizer over the soil before planting them during late summer and early autumn. Set the bulbs in holes three times their depth. (For example, it is best to set a 5cm (2in) deep bulb in a hole 15cm (6in) deep, covered with 10cm (4in) of soil.) You should set large-flowered types 10-20cm (4-8in) apart, and the smaller species types 5-7.5cm (2-3in) apart. Most daffodils should be left where they are planted for several years. If you are growing the bulbs in shrub borders, rather than in grass, plant them slightly deeper to ensure they are not damaged by hoeing during summer. After flowering, leave the foliage to die down naturally. The best-sized flowers are produced from bulbs in their second year

Narcissus poeticus 'Actaea', the Poet's Narcissus, is highly fragrant, and superb when set in large drifts in a wild garden. Bulbs are ideal for bringing splashes of colour to informal areas during spring.

after planting. However, to prevent the bulbs forming large and congested clumps in borders, lift and divide them every four years. Lift them as the foliage turns yellow. If they are left in the soil to be lifted later, mark the position, because otherwise they will be difficult to find.

Propagation: Lift and divide congested clumps after flowering, when the foliage has turned yellow.

Below: **Daffodils** *and* **forsythia** *are the epitome of spring to many gardeners. They are easy to establish and grow in a garden and seldom fail to create spring colour. Plant the daffodils in front of the forsythia in clumps rather than rows to achieve a natural effect.*

Above: **Narcissus 'Bartley'** *This highly distinctive small narcissus from* **Division 6** *has* Narcissus cyclamineus *as a parent. The petals sweep back from the trumpet. Set near the front of the border.*

Narcissus cyclamineus, with petals that curl back sharply on themselves, brings life to rock gardens and protected corners during spring. In warm and mild areas, it may appear as early as the end of winter. *N. cyclamineus* 'February Gold' mixes well with small crocuses.

THE FLOWER BORDER

Phlomis russeliana
(Phlomis viscosa)

This distinctive hardy herbaceous perennial has large, wrinkled mid-green leaves and hooded tubular flowers, each 2.5-4cm (1-1¹/₂in) long, borne in circular tiers up the stems during mid-summer. They resemble the flowers of Jerusalem Sage (*Phlomis fruticosa*).
Height: 75cm-1.2m (2¹/₂-4ft)
Spread: 75cm (2¹/₂ft)
Cultivation: Any good garden soil and an open, sunny position suit this plant.
Propagation: Seeds can be sown in a loam-based seed compost during spring and placed in a cold frame. But the easiest method of propagation is to lift and divide congested clumps in spring.

Right: Phlomis russeliana *The distinctive whorls of hooded yellow flowers appear in tiers up the stout stems. The attractive seedheads are useful for flower arrangements and can be used green or dried.*

Left: Oenothera missouriensis *This eye-catching, spreading herbaceous perennial from the Americas has bright canary-yellow flowers, 6.5-7.5cm (2¹/₂-3in) wide. These are produced during early and mid-summer.*

Above: Phlomis fruticosa *is the Jerusalem Sage, with whorls of yellow flowers in mid-summer.*

Oenothera missouriensis

Evening Primrose (UK)
Evening Primrose · Sundrop (USA)

A superb, mat-forming, low-growing herbaceous perennial with lance-shaped mid-green leaves and bright canary-yellow flowers, 6.5-7.5cm (2¹/₂-3in) wide. It has reddish stems and blooms during early and mid-summer. The flower buds often have red spots on their undersides. Unlike many Evening Primroses, it opens its flowers during the day as well as in the evening.
Height: 13-18cm (5-7in)
Spread: 45-60cm (1¹/₂-2ft)

Cultivation: Well-drained soil is essential, because the roots tend to rot during winter in a damp, waterlogged situation. Raised beds, therefore, are often the best places, or a rock garden. During late summer or early winter, cut the plant to soil-level.
Propagation: Seeds can be sown in spring, and the containers put in a cold frame. When they are large enough to handle, set the seedlings in a nursery bed until autumn. They can then be planted into the garden. Alternatively, divide established clumps in spring. This is the best method for named varieties of many oenotheras, as they do not breed true from seed.

Oenothera missouriensis is best seen in a raised bed. This ensures good drainage and brings the beautiful flowers nearer eye-level. Its spreading nature allows it to be blended with other plants including *Lysimachia nummularia*, Creeping Jenny.

Phlomis fruticosa, the Jerusalem Sage, is an evergreen shrubby plant, with whorls of yellow flowers, 2.5-3cm (1-1¹/₄in) long. It blends well with the silver and greyish-leaved *Lavandula angustifolia* and *Cistus purpureus*.

Above: **Rudbeckia fulgida 'Goldsturm'** *This superb bright-coloured form has flowers up to 13cm (5in) across. 'Deamii' is another good form, with flowers 7.5-10cm (3-4in) wide, borne in abundance.*

Rudbeckia fulgida

(*Rudbeckia speciosa·Rudbeckia newmanii*)
Coneflower (UK)

This well-known herbaceous perennial has mid-green, lance-shaped leaves and yellow to orange flowers, 6.5cm (2½in) wide, from mid to late summer. The flowers have distinctive purple-brown cones at their centres – hence the common name.
Height: 60-90cm (2-3ft)
Spread: 45-60cm (1½-2ft)
Cultivation: Coneflowers need well-drained but moisture-retentive, fertile soil in an open and sunny position. Support the plants with twiggy sticks and remove dead flower heads to encourage others. Cut the stems down to soil level during early winter.
Propagation: Seeds can be sown in spring or late summer, but for home gardeners the easiest way to increase this plant is by lifting and dividing established clumps in autumn or spring. Replant only the young parts from around the edges of the clump.

Rudbeckia fulgida blends well with the 45-60cm (1½-2ft) high herbaceous perennial *Aster amellus* 'King George', which has violet-blue flowers. *Aster x frikartii*, with wide orange-centred blue flowers, 5cm (2in) wide, is another good companion.

THE FLOWER BORDER

**Right: Rudbeckia hirta
'Marmalade'** *This is a beautiful
border plant creating a bold splash
of golden-yellow, peppered with
black cones. The flowers give the
impression of peering upwards.
They are excellent cut flowers.*

Rudbeckia hirta

Black-eyed Susan · Coneflower
(UK and USA)

This short-lived North American
perennial is grown as a hardy
annual. It has mid-green, lance-
shaped leaves on bristly stems.
During mid-summer and into early
autumn it bears golden-yellow
flowers, 7.5cm (3in) wide, with
brown-purple cones at their
centres. Many forms are available.
'Marmalade' has brilliant yellow
flowers with black centres, and
'Rustic Dwarfs' boasts shades of
chestnut, bronze and yellow.
Height: 30-90cm (1-3ft)
Spread: 30-45cm (1-1½ft)
Cultivation: These plants need a
well drained, preferably deeply-
cultivated, soil in an open and
sunny position. Remove dead
flowers during the summer to
encourage further flowers, and cut
dead stems down to soil level in
early winter. In exposed and windy
regions tall forms will need
supporting with twiggy sticks. Put
these in early so that the plants can
grow up and through them. If you
put them in too late, the sticks will
not become covered with leaves
and flowers and detract from the
appearance of the display.
Propagation: During late winter
and early spring, sow seeds 3mm
(⅛in) deep in loam-based compost
kept at 16°C (61°F). When the
seedlings are large enough to
handle, prick them out into boxes
of compost and harden them off in
a cold frame. Plant them out into
the garden when all risk of frost
has passed. Alternatively, sow
seeds 6mm (¼in) deep during
spring where the plants are to
flower, thinning them to 30-45cm
(1-1½ft) apart.

Sanvitalia procumbens

Creeping Zinnia (UK)

This is a beautiful, low-growing
hardy annual, with miniature,
single, rudbeckia-like yellow
flowers with black centres (2.5cm/
1in wide) during mid-summer. The
form 'Flore Pleno' has double
flowers. The flowers appear slightly
above the pointed, oval, mid-green
leaves, borne on trailing stems.
Their dwarf habit makes the plants

Left: Sanvitalia procumbens
*This hardy Mexican annual has
miniature rudbeckia-like flowers
during mid-summer. Like many
other Mexican plants, it needs
a position in full sunshine.*

ideal for the edges of borders, in
beds of annuals, rock gardens, and
even in containers where they can
trail over the side.
Height: 13-15cm (5-6in)
Spread: 15-20cm (6-8in)
Cultivation: Light but moisture-
retentive soil in full sun suits
sanvitalias best.
Propagation: During spring, sow
seeds thinly and shallowly where the
plants are to flower. When the
seedlings are large enough to
handle, thin them to 7.5-10cm (3-
4in) apart. Seeds can also be sown
in late summer in the open soil, but
the seedlings need cloche protection
during winter. Thin them out in spring
rather than autumn. Sanvitalias can
be grown to flower in hanging
baskets. In such circumstances
plants will be needed for setting in
the container early in the year. Sow
seeds at 13°C (55°F) during early
spring and prick off the seedlings
into pots. Harden off the plants and
set them out in the container as
soon as all risk of frost has passed.

Rudbeckia hirta is ideal for providing late colour in
the garden, at a time when many border plants are
past their best and the garden generally looks bare
and colourless.

Sanvitalia procumbens is superb in the garden, but
equally eye-catching as a pot plant indoors or in a
greenhouse. Sow seeds in late winter or early spring in
13°C (55°F), pricking out the seedlings three to a 15cm
(6in) pot.

Left: Solidago x 'Goldenmosa'
*This superb Golden Rod, with
frothy flowers in 15-23cm (6-9in)
long heads during mid to late
summer, gains its varietal name
from mimosa, which it resembles. It
is ideal in flower arrangements.*

Solidago x 'Goldenmosa'

Golden Rod (UK and USA)

This well-known hardy herbaceous
perennial displays tiny yellow
flowers in clustered feathery
plumes during mid and late
summer. The narrow, lance-
shaped, yellow-green leaves rise
from soil level to the dazzling
display of flowers. Its strong stem
makes it an excellent cut plant.
Height: 75-90cm (2½-3ft)
Spread: 60-75cm (2-2½ft)
Cultivation: Any good, fertile, well-
drained garden soil in full sun or
slight shade is suitable. Support
from twiggy sticks is necessary
only in windy and exposed areas.
During late autumn or early winter
cut the stems down to soil level.
Propagation: During autumn or
spring, lift old and congested
clumps and divide them. Replant
only the young parts.

Above: **Solidago 'Crown of Rays'**
*is a welcome sight in summer with
its cheerful golden-yellow flowers.*

Solidago x 'Goldenmosa' blends with pink and white
flowers. For example, you could try the pink-eyed
white *Phlox maculata* 'Omega' and the white flowers
of the Obedient Plant, *Physostegia virginiana*
'Summer Snow'.

THE FLOWER BORDER

Tagetes erecta

African Marigold (UK)
African Marigold · Big Marigold
Aztec Marigold (USA)

A well-known, half-hardy, much-branched annual from Mexico. Its lemon-yellow, daisy-like flowers are about 5cm (2in) wide, and last from mid-summer to autumn. The glossy, dark green leaves, deeply and finely-divided, are strongly scented. There are many types, including single and double-flowered forms, with flower colours from yellow to orange. They also range in height from semi-dwarf (30-38cm / 1-1¼ ft) to normal types (60-90cm / 2-3ft).
Cultivation: Most moderately-rich soils are suitable, and an open position in full sun.
Propagation: During late winter and early spring, sow seeds 6mm (¼ in) deep in loam-based seed compost kept at 18°C (64°F). When the seedlings are large enough to handle, prick them out and harden them off slowly in a cold frame. Plant them out as soon as all risk of frost has passed.

Thalictrum speciosissimum

Dusty Meadow Rue (UK)

For distinction and elegance, few plants surpass this hardy herbaceous perennial, with its heads of frothy yellow flowers 15-23cm (6-9in) long, during mid to late summer. The blue-grey leaves are long-lasting and deeply-divided and are borne dramatically on upright, stiff stems.
Height: 1-1.5m (3½-5ft)
Spread: 60-90cm (2-3ft)
Cultivation: Thalictrum prefers a good, well-cultivated fertile, moist soil and a position in full sun or light shade. In exposed areas it will require support from canes or stout twiggy sticks. In spring give a top-dressing of peat or well-decomposed compost, and in early winter cut the stems down to soil level. When staking the plants, do not leave it until late in the season as they grow quickly and may be blown over easily.
Propagation: Seeds can be sown in spring, and the container placed in a cold frame, but the easiest way to propagate is to lift and divide congested clumps in spring and replant them firmly.

Tagetes erecta can often be a difficult neighbour for other bedding plants because of its dominant size and colour, but it is useful for bringing bold colour splashes to mixed borders. You could also have a border full of these plants.

Thalictrum speciosissimum, like most yellow-flowered plants, associates well with blue flowers. Michaelmas Daisies and Delphiniums with strong blue-coloured flowers are excellent companions for it.

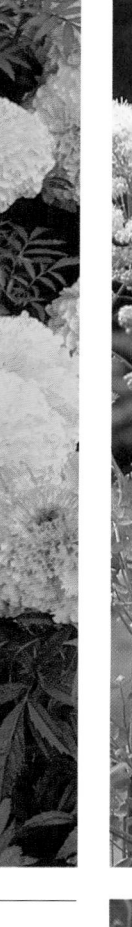

Trollius x cultorum

Globe Flower (UK and USA)

This is a delightful hardy herbaceous perennial, with large, globe-shaped pale yellow to orange flowers during late spring and early summer. The deeply-cleft and toothed mid-green leaves are a perfect foil for the buttercup-like flowers. Several superb varieties are available, including 'Fire Globe' (deep orange), 'Goldquelle' (golden-yellow), 'Salamander' (fiery orange), 'Canary Bird' (pale yellow) and 'Orange Princess' (orange-yellow).

Height: 60-75cm (2-2¹/₂ft)
Spread: 45-60cm (1¹/₂-2ft)
Cultivation: Rich, fertile, moisture-retentive soil and full sun or slight shade provide the best conditions. If stems are cut off at their bases after flowering, further flowers will develop.
Propagation: The easiest way for home gardeners to increase this plant is by lifting and dividing established clumps. Replant the young pieces from around the outside of the clump.

Below: Trollius x cultorum 'Fire Globe' *A beautiful hardy herbaceous plant for fertile, moist areas in the garden. It does well in damp areas around a garden pond. This variety flowers in spring at a height of 75cm (1¹/₂ft).*

Above right: Thalictrum speciosissimum *This eye-catching plant is much prized by flower arrangers. Its delicate, long-lasting foliage, closely resembling that of the Maidenhair Fern, is very attractive.*

Far left: Tagetes patula 'Queen Bee' *This yellow and red double crested French Marigold rises to about 25cm (10in) and flowers throughout summer. Its compact but well-branched growth makes it a superb choice for any flower border, where it can be used as dominant edging.*

Trollius flowers look good mixed with blue-flowered plants, but it is essential that the blue is strong enough not to be dominated by the yellow. *Iris latifolia* (*Iris xiphioides*) is the right blue and, like *Trollius*, likes damp soil.

THE FLOWER BORDER

Tulips

The range of these much-loved spring bulbs is extensive. They can be used to flower in spring in bedding schemes, mixed borders, rock gardens, tubs and troughs, or indoors for winter and early spring flowers. There is a wide range of species, and botanists have also classified those created by bulb experts. There are fifteen different divisions, encompassing the wide range of flower sizes, shapes and heights. These are:

DIVISION 1 – SINGLE EARLY (15-38cm/6-15in): The single flowers appear in spring when grown out-of-doors, or during winter indoors. Each flower is 7.5-13cm (3-5in) wide and sometimes opens flat when in direct and full sun. Many yellow varieties are available, as well as white, pink, red, orange and purple.

DIVISION 2 – DOUBLE EARLY (30-38cm /12-15in): The double flowers appear in spring when grown out-of-doors in bedding schemes, or earlier when forced indoors. Each flower is 10cm (4in) wide and rather like a double paeony. The colour range is wide, including some fine yellows.

DIVISION 3 – MENDEL (38-50cm /15-20in): These flower later than the previous types, with rounded 10-13cm (4-5in) wide flowers on quite slender stems. Colours include white and red, as well as yellow. They look like a cross between single early types and Darwins.

DIVISION 4 – TRIUMPH (up to 50cm / 20in): These bear angular-looking 10-13cm (4-5in) wide flowers on strong stems in mid-spring. Colours include pink, red and lilac, as well as yellow.

DIVISION 5 – DARWIN HYBRIDS (60-65cm / 2-2¼ft): These are among the largest-flowered and most brilliant of all tulips, with flowers up to 18cm (7in) across during mid-spring. There are multi-coloured forms, as well as yellow, orange, red and purple varieties.

Above: Tulip 'Golden Apeldoorn'
These Darwin Hybrids from **Division 5** *are superb in formal bedding displays, with flowers up to 18cm (7in) wide during mid-spring. These are borne on tall stems.*

DIVISION 6 – DARWIN (60-75cm / 2-2 ½ft): Widely used in bedding schemes, these produce rounded flowers up to 13cm (5in) wide in late spring. Varieties are available in white, pink, red, purple and multi-colours, as well as the yellow ones.

DIVISION 7 – LILY-FLOWERED (45-60cm /1½-2ft): These are characterized by the narrow waists of the flowers, also by the pointed petals which curl outwards, reaching 20cm (8in) during mid-spring. They look distinctive when massed in a bedding scheme. Colours include white, orange, red and multi-coloured forms, as well as yellow.

DIVISION 8 – COTTAGE (up to 90cm / 3ft): This old group has oval or rounded flowers, 10-13cm (4-5in) wide, in mid-spring. The petals sometimes have a hint of fringing, and are looser than in other forms. Flower colours include white, pink, red, lilac and green, as well as yellow.

DIVISION 9 – REMBRANDT (75cm / 2½ft): These are tulips with 'broken' colours. The rounded flowers, 13cm (5in) wide, have vivid splashes of colour on the petals during mid-spring. As well as yellow, base colours include white,

orange, red, pink, violet and brown.

DIVISION 10 – PARROT (45-60cm /1½-2ft): These have flowers appearing in mid-spring, up to 20cm (8in) wide, easily recognizable by their feather-like and heavily-fringed petals. The colour range includes brilliant white, pink, orange, red and purple, as well as yellow.

DIVISION 11—DOUBLE LATE (45-60cm/1½-2ft): These have very large and showy double flowers, somewhat resembling paeonies and up to 20cm (8in) wide. They remain in flower for a long period during mid-spring. Colours include white, orange, pink, red and violet, as well as yellow. Some are multi-coloured, with stripes and edgings.

DIVISION 12— KAUFMANNIANA VARIETIES (10-25cm / 4-10in): These have been developed from *Tulipa kaufmanniana*, and have fine-pointed flowers which open nearly flat, giving the appearance of a ▶

Vividly coloured **Darwin Tulips,** such as the dark red 'Scarlett O'Hara', combine well with white Pansies. The tulip flowers stand above the Pansies, allowing their heads to be seen through the tulip stems.

Tulips blend with a carpet planting of Daisies (*Bellis perennis*). Blue Parrot types make an eye-catching arrangement. Even two blues together – Forget-me-nots and Blue Parrot Tulips—are attractive.

Right: Tulipa marjoletti
This is a species, and there are more than thirty different types widely available. It grows to 60cm (2ft) and bears 5cm (2in) long blooms with pointed petals during late spring.

Below: Tulip 'Gold Medal' *Large and showy double flowers from* **Division 11***, these resemble paeonies and are up to 20cm (8in) wide. They remain in flower for a long period. However, in areas of high rainfall they can be weighed down by water.*

Tulips are the traditional companions of Forget-me-nots and Wallflowers. Cottage-type Tulips, with their large egg-shaped heads on stout stems, stand proudly above these underplantings.

Tulipa greigii hybrids can be mixed with Grape Hyacinths and *Alyssum saxatile* in beds with dry stone walls on one side, or in large containers. The alyssum helps to soften the container's edges.

THE FLOWER BORDER

water-lily. They open in spring on sturdy stems, and are ideal for fronts of borders, rock gardens and containers. Most have two-coloured flowers.

DIVISION 13—FOSTERIANA VARIETIES (45cm /1½ft): These are derived from *Tulipa fosteriana* and have large blunt-ended flowers in yellows and reds in mid-spring.

DIVISION 14—GREIGII VARIETIES (25cm /10in): These are mainly derived from *Tulipa greigii*, and have brilliant long-lasting yellow, red and near-white flowers. The petals reach 7.5cm (3in) long in mid-spring, when the flowers are fully open.

Cultivation: Select well-drained soil, preferably facing south and in a sheltered position. Set the bulbs 15cm (6in) deep during early winter. Space them 10-15cm (4-6in) apart. Remove dead flowers and dig up the bulbs when the leaves turn yellow. However, if the bed is needed earlier, dig up the bulbs as soon as flowering is over and heel them into a trench until the foliage has yellowed and died down.

Propagation: The easiest way is to remove the offsets clustered at the bases of the bulbs. These can be planted in a nursery bed to develop into flowering-sized bulbs.

Above: **Tulip 'Yellow Empress'**
This beautiful and distinctive **Division 13** *tulip has long-lasting flowers of medium size in mid-spring. The flowers grow best in full sun.*

Below: **Tulip 'Giuseppe Verdi'**
These small **Division 12** *flowers open like water-lilies in full sun. They are ideal for the front of borders as well as rock gardens and containers.*

Verbascum bombyciferum

(Verbascum 'Broussa')
Mullein (UK and USA)

This is a distinctive biennial Mullein (some are perennial) with attractive oval and pointed silvery leaves. The silvery, woolly stems are erect, and during summer their tops are clothed with sulphur-yellow, saucer-shaped flowers, 5cm (2in) wide, with pronounced stamens.
Height: 1.2-1.8m (4-6ft)
Spread: 60-75cm (2-2½ft)
Cultivation: Mulleins prefer a well-drained soil in full sun. Stake the plants in exposed areas and where the soil is rich and moist.
Propagation: Sow seeds thinly in late spring in boxes of loam-based compost, placing them in a cold frame. As soon as the seedlings are growing strongly, plant them out into a nursery bed. In autumn, set out the plants into their flowering positions.

Right: **Verbascum bombyciferum**
This is a bold architectural biennial raising spires of sulphur-yellow, saucer-shaped flowers with prominent stamens during early to mid-summer. The silvery leaves, covered with hairs, are a further delight.

Red Tulips set in a sea of yellow Polyanthus look superb, or try an underplanting of gold *Cheiranthus x allionii* (Siberian Wallflower) and blue Forget-me-nots, with Cottage Tulips 'President Hoover' (orange-red) and 'Mrs. John T Scheepers' (yellow).

Yellow backgrounds are very striking: you could try an underplanting of a yellow Viola, with the Single Early Tulip 'Keizerskroom' (with yellow and red flowers) above it.

Further plants to consider

Asphodeline lutea
(Asphodelus luteus)
Asphodel · King's Spear · Jacob's Rod (UK) Asphodel · King's Spear (USA)
Height: 90cm-1m (3-3½ft) Spread: 75-90cm (2½-3ft)
An upright, stately herbaceous perennial with dark green grassy leaves and fragrant, star-like, bright yellow flowers arranged up stiff stems during mid-summer.

Buphthalmum salicifolium
Willow-leaf Ox-eye (UK) Thoroughwax (USA)
Height: 45-60cm (1½-2ft) Spread: 60-75cm (2-2½ft)
A hardy herbaceous perennial which spreads by underground runners. It is ideal for moist soils. During early to mid-summer it bears bright, golden-yellow, daisy-like flowers, which measure 4cm (1½in) across.

Digitalis grandiflora
(Digitalis ambigua)
Yellow Foxglove (UK and USA)
Height: 60-90cm (2-3ft) Spread: 38-45cm (1¼-1½ft)
A perennial with pale creamy-yellow, foxglove-like flowers, 5cm (2in) long, during mid to late summer. The flowers are borne on spikes up to 60cm (2ft).

Helenium autumnale 'Golden Youth'
Height: 75cm (2½ft) Spread: 38-45cm (1¼-1½ft)
A beautiful free-flowering, hardy herbaceous perennial with large yellow, daisy-like flowers during late summer and into autumn. There are several other good yellow-flowering forms, such as 'Butterpat' and 'Wyndley' (yellow and copper).

Heliopsis scabra
Orange Sunflower (UK) Oxeye (USA)
A beautiful hardy herbaceous perennial, ideal for brightening up a border during mid to late summer, with large, daisy-like yellow flowers. Varieties to consider include 'Gold Plume' (rich yellow), 'Goldgreenheart' (lemon-yellow) and 'Incomparabilis' (orange-yellow).

Hunnemannia fumariifolia
Mexican Tulip Poppy (UK) Mexican Tulip Poppy · Golden Cup (USA)
Height: 45-60cm (1½-2ft) Spread: 38-45cm (1¼-1½ft)
A beautiful poppy-like hardy annual with finely-cut, blue-green foliage and cup-shaped yellow flowers on long stems during late summer.

Verbascum thapsus, the Great Mullein from Europe, has yellow flowers and thick woolly leaves and was called Bullock's Lungwort. It was also associated with witches and earned the name Hag-taper.

THE FLOWER BORDER

Abutilon striatum 'Thompsonii'

Also known as *Abutilon thompsonii*, this foliage plant is often grown in a greenhouse or conservatory as well as a 'dot' plant in a summer bedding display. This plant is grown with a single upright stem from which arise maple-like, mid-green leaves heavily mottled and splashed with creamy-yellow. When grown with summer bedding plants, it is planted amid a sea of colour-contrasting half-hardy annuals.
Height: 0.9-1.2m (3-4ft)
Spread: 38-60cm (15-24in)
Cultivation: Plant in fertile, moisture-retentive soil, as soon as all risk of frost has passed. Invariably, the planting is carried out in combination with summer-bedding displays.
Propagation: During mid-summer take 7.5-10cm (3-4in) long cuttings from stock plants (taking cuttings from those plants in summer-bedding schemes would ruin their

Above: Abutilon striatum 'Thompsonii' *brings height and distinction to summer-bedding displays. Its variegated leaves create colour and interest throughout summer.*

appearance). Insert them in equal parts moist peat and sharp sand, and place in 16°C (61°F). When rooted, pot up into a loam-based compost and over-winter in a frost-proof glasshouse or conservatory.

Amaranthus caudatus 'Green Form'

This attractive form of the crimson-flowered Love-lies-Bleeding is distinctive, with a restful appearance that creates a superb background for other hardy annuals. Often sold as 'Viridis', it has light green leaves and long tassel-like, pale green flowers from mid to late summer.
Height: 0.9-1.2m (3-4ft)
Spread: 38-45cm (15-18in)

Abutilon striatum 'Thompsonii' is excellent as a 'dot' plant in a sea of summer-bedding plants. Its height and colour bring an attractive contrast to the red-flowered *Salvia splendens*.

Amaranthus caudatus 'Green Form' with its beautiful green leaves and tassel-like flowers, creates a superb backcloth for other annuals, such as nasturtiums, marigolds and clarkia.

Cultivation: Grow in fertile, deeply-cultivated, moisture-retentive soil. However, it also succeeds moderately well in poor ground.

Propagation: Sow seeds *in situ* in drills 3mm (⅛in) deep and 30cm (12in) apart in spring. When the seedlings are large enough to handle, thin them first to 10cm (4in) then 30-38cm (12-15in) apart. Alternatively, sow seeds 3mm (⅛in) deep in seed compost in early spring and place in 15°C (59°F). When large enough to handle, prick out seedlings into seedboxes. Slowly harden off the young plants and plant into the garden as soon as all risk of frost has passed.

Left: Amaranthus caudatus 'Green Form' *This beautiful green-flowered form of Love-lies-Bleeding is eye-catching in a sea of low-growing hardy annuals, especially those with yellow or white flowers.*

Above: Euphorbia wulfenii *When planted at the top of a flight of steps, so that it is readily seen and dominates the eye, this bushy, shrubby perennial has few equals.*

Euphorbia wulfenii

This 'architectural' shrubby perennial creates a bushy shape formed of bluish-green leaves massed on stiffish stems. During mid-summer, the stems are headed by 20-23cm (8-9in) of bright, eye-catching, yellowish-green bracts.

Height: 0.9-1.2m (3-4ft)
Spread: 0.9-1.2m (3-4ft)
Cultivation: Plant in well-drained soil in a sunny position. It dislikes disturbance, so once established leave it alone. Small plants establish themselves easier and more rapidly than large ones.
Propagation: During late spring, take 7.5-10cm (3-4in) long basal cuttings and insert in equal parts moist peat and sharp sand. Place in a cold frame.

Euphorbia wulfenii creates a dominant splash of colour, contrasting well with silver-leaved plants, such as *Santolina neapolitana* and *Santolina chamaecyparissus* both with feathery and finely-dissected leaves.

THE FLOWER BORDER

Left: Hakonechloa macra 'Aureola' *This brightly-coloured grass-like perennial is very attractive when planted in a slightly raised bed. The leaves cascade to soften the edges of the border.*

Miscanthus sinensis 'Silver Feather'

A superb grass-like perennial, ideal for creating a screen of narrow, bluish-green leaves, or as a specimen in a border. In addition to the attractive leaves, during autumn it bears plume-like, silvery flower heads.

Hakonechloa macra 'Aureola'

This beautiful, variegated perennial grass creates a dominant feature, with narrow, long, green leaves almost entirely striped in bright yellow. Its nature is to cascade and sprawl, and is ideal for softening the edges of borders. It is also ideal in raised borders.

Height: 25-30cm (10-12in)
Spread: 0.9-1.2m (3-4ft)
Cultivation: Plant in any good, moisture-retentive soil, preferably in full sun.
Propagation: Lift and divide congested plants in spring.

Hakonechloa macra 'Aureola' harmonizes with *Hosta ventricosa* 'Aureo-marginata'. The narrow leaves of this grass-like plant create eye-catching contrasts with many hostas.

Miscanthus sinensis 'Silver Feather' is the parent of several superb forms, including 'Silver Feather' with large plume-like flower heads, and 'Zebrinus' which reveals foliage with longitudinal white stripes.

Height: 1.5-1.8m (5-6ft)
Spread: 1.5-1.8m (5-6ft)
Cultivation: Plant in moisture-retentive, fertile soil, preferably in full sun. In late winter, cut down all shoots to soil-level.
Propagation: Lift and divide congested clumps in early spring.

Below: Miscanthus sinensis 'Silver Feather' *This large member of the grass family creates a dominant feature in a mixed border. During autumn it develops large, silvery flower heads.*

Phormium tenax 'Variegatum'

New Zealand Flax (UK and USA)

This superbly architectural half-hardy evergreen perennial from New Zealand develops tall, sword-like, stiff and leathery leaves striped with green and yellow. From mid to late summer plants develop dull-red flowers on tall branching stems. However, these plants are mainly grown for their attractive foliage. Other attractive varieties of this species include 'Maori Sunrise', with a pinkish glisten to its leaves and an apricot band, edged in light bronze; 'Sundowner' with wide leaves which reveal a greyish-purple midriff and creamy-pink outer band; and 'Yellow Wave' with golden-yellow leaves with green outer edges. *Phormium cookianum* is another attractive species. 'Cream Delight' has leaves with

Above: Phormium tenax 'Variegatum' *creates colour throughout summer, displaying long sword-like leaves, striped yellow and green.*

green edges and a broad creamy band in the centre, while 'Tricolor' has bright green leaves edged in red and striped with white.
Height: 1.8m (6ft)
Spread: 1.2-1.5m (4-5ft)
Cultivation: Plant in fertile moisture-retentive soil in full sun. These plants are not fully hardy, and benefit from a mulch of straw or bracken over their crowns in winter. As soon as the flowers fade, cut off the main stem close to its base.
Propagation: Lift and divide congested plants in spring, replanting the young parts from around the outside. Ensure that each new part has three or four leaves.

Phormium tenax 'Variegatum' creates such a distinctive splash of colour that it is spoilt if other plants are positioned too close to it. Also, it is best seen in a bold, dominant display.

Yucca filamentosa 'Variegata'

A variegated form of Adam's Needle, also known as Needle Palm, that creates an eye-catching feature in a border. This upright hardy evergreen shrub develops stiffly erect, sword-like green leaves with broad cream and yellow edges. An additional attraction is the creamy-white, bell-shaped flowers which are borne on long upright stems during mid-summer. Young plants do not develop flowers.

Above: Salvia officinalis 'Icterina' *The brightly-variegated leaves of this sage are highlighted by planting the normal grey-green, wrinkled-leaved type around it. Avoid planting other variegated plants close to it, as they visually compete with each other.*

Salvia officinalis 'Icterina'

This variegated form of the common sage creates a wealth of leaves variegated green and gold. Sages are hardy, dwarf and dome-shaped, semi-evergreen plants. They are ideal for creating colour alongside paths, and especially at their junctions. Other colourful forms include 'Tricolor', with grey-green leaves splashed creamy-white and suffused pink. For young leaves suffused soft purple grow 'Purpurascens', widely known as the 'Purple-leaved Sage'.

Height: 45-60cm (1½-2ft)
Spread: 45-60cm (1½-2ft)
Cultivation: Plant in well-drained (but not parched) soil in full sun. If groups of three or five plants are planted together, spaced about 38-45cm (15-18in) apart, a large mound of foliage is created. Pinch off flowers, which appear during summer.
Propagation: During late summer take 7.5cm (3in) long heel-cuttings and insert in equal parts moist peat and sharp sand. Place in a cold frame. When rooted, pot up into small pots, planting into the garden in spring.

Salvia officinalius 'Icterina' develops into a low-growing mound that soon encroaches on the edges of paths. It is therefore best planted where paving slabs are used as an edging to a border.

Height: 0.9-1m (3-3½ft)
Spread: 0.75-1m (2½-3½ft)
Cultivation: Plant in well-drained soil in full sun. Do not attempt to prune or trim this plant.
Propagation: In spring, remove sucker-like shoots from around the plant's base and plant in a nursery bed for about three years.

Below: Yucca filamentosa 'Variegata' *This variegated evergreen plant has such eye-appeal that it readily captures attention. The sword-like green leaves have cream and yellow edges.*

Further plants to consider

Aruncus dioicus
(*Aruncus sylvester*)
Goat's Beard (UK) · Goatsbeard (USA)
Height: 1.2-1.5m (4-5ft)   Spread: 60-90cm (2-3ft)
An outstandingly attractive vigorous, hardy herbaceous plant with light green leaves up to 30cm (12in) long with individual leaves to 5cm (2in) long. During mid-summer creamy-white flowers in narrow plumes are borne in lax heads up to 25cm (10in) long.

Astrantia major 'Variegata'
Height: 60-75cm (2-2½ft)   Spread: 38-45cm (15-18in)
This variegated form of the herbaceous perennial Masterwort is especially attractive in spring and early summer when the foliage is relatively young. The mid-green, lobed leaves are striped and splashed with yellow. It is also often known and sold as 'Sunningdale Variegated'.

Brunnera macrophylla 'Variegata'
Height: 30-45cm (12-18in)   Spread: 45-50cm (18-20in)
This large-leaved herbaceous perennial has matt-green, heart-shaped leaves variegated cream. The best leaf colours are produced when the plant is growing in light shade. It has the bonus of bearing sky-blue, forget-me-not-like flowers during early and mid-summer.

Macleaya cordata
Plume Poppy (UK and USA) Tree Celandine (USA)
Height: 1.5-2.4m (5-8ft)   Spread: 0.9-1.5m (3-5ft)
This hardy herbaceous perennial has very large, deeply-lobed lower leaves, bronze above and grey beneath. During mid and late summer, small ivory flowers are borne in plume-like heads.

Miscanthus sacchariflorus
Height: 2.1-3m (7-10ft)   Spread: 60-90cm (2-3ft)
This tall, hardy, herbaceous perennial grass is ideal for creating a high screen of narrow, arching, mid-green leaves with pale mid-ribs. When grown as a screen, space the plants 60cm (2ft) apart in a single row. Alternatively, a thicker hedge can be created more rapidly by setting the plants in two rows, 45-60cm (1½-2ft) apart.

Scrophularia aquatica 'Variegata'
Height: 60-90cm (2-3ft)   Spread: 45-50cm (18-20in)
An outstandingly attractive variegated herbaceous perennial, with dark green leaves splashed with cream. It grows in most soils, but avoid those that are dry.

Sedum spectabile 'Variegatum'
Height: 38-50cm (15-20in)   Spread: 38-45cm (15-18in)
A beautiful variegated form of a well-known herbaceous perennial widely-grown in borders. The glaucous-green leaves are variegated buff-yellow. During late summer and autumn it bears heads of pink-tinged flowers.

Yucca filamentosa 'Variegata' creates such a dominant colour display that it captures attention from surrounding plants. Plant it in a sea of visually non-competing, low-growing, all-green plants.

THE FLOWER BORDER

Left: Anaphalis triplinervis
During mid-summer, bunched heads of white flowers appear above silvery-grey leaves. It harmonizes with the goblet-like rosy-purple flowers of Colchicum speciosum. *Plant these in clusters in front of the anaphalis.*

Anaphalis yedoensis

Pearl Everlasting (UK)
Everlasting · Life Everlasting (USA)

Hardy herbaceous perennial with 'everlasting' flowers formed of inconspicuous flowers surrounded by papery, modified leaves called bracts. These are long-lived and do not fade quickly. The white flowers can be dried, surviving almost indefinitely. These appear from mid-summer to early autumn in 7.5-10cm (3-4in) wide heads above narrow, lance-shaped, stem-clasping, grey-green leaves.
Height: 60cm (2ft)
Spread: 38-45cm (15-18in)
Cultivation: Well-drained soil and a sunny position are needed, although it tolerates slight shade. Do not plant it under trees. During late autumn cut back plants to soil-level. Fresh plants can be planted in autumn or spring.
Propagation: The easiest way to increase it is by lifting and dividing old and congested plants in autumn or spring. Replant only young parts from around the outside of the clump. Alternatively, sow seeds in loam-based compost in seedboxes in spring and place in a cold frame. When established, transplant the young plants to a nursery bed until they are large enough to be planted into the garden, in autumn or spring.

Anaphalis triplinervis

Pearly Everlasting (UK)
Everlasting · Life Everlasting (USA)

An attractive hardy herbaceous perennial wlth narrow, silvery-grey, lance-shaped and stem-clasping leaves. The undersides are covered with white, woolly hairs. During mid-summer bunched heads of white flowers are borne in 7.5-10cm (3-4in) wide heads.
Height: 30cm (12in)
Spread: 38cm (15in)

Cultivation: Well-drained soil and a position in full sun suits it, although slight shade is acceptable as long as it is not under trees. Water dripping on the leaves soon spoils them. Set new plants in position in autumn or spring.
Propagation: During autumn or spring, lift and divide established plants. Replant only the younger parts from around the outside of the clump. Alternatively, in spring sow seeds in loam-based seed compost. Place in a cold frame.

Left: Anaphalis yedoensis *This grey-leaved herbaceous perennial is widely-grown for its attractive foliage, as well as the heads of white flowers which appear from mid-summer to early autumn. Give it a sunny position.*

Anaphalis margaritacea, previously known as *Gnaphalium margaritaceum* and *Antennaria margaritacea*, is a popular species, with grey-green leaves and pearly-white flowers in mid-summer.

Anaphalis yedoensis like other species in this genus, have 'everlasting' flowers which are popular for winter flower arrangements. The flowers are inconspicuous, and it is the bracts that create the display.

Artemisia absinthium 'Lambrook Silver'

A hardy shrubby deciduous border plant with beautiful silvery-grey, finely-divided leaves. During mid and late summer it develops small, round, yellow flowers.
Height: 75-90cm (2½-3ft)
Spread: 90cm (3ft)
Cultivation: Ordinary well-drained soil and a position in full sun suits it. Although having a shrubby habit, it is best cut back to near ground-level in autumn.
Propagation: In late summer take 7.5-10cm (3-4in) long semi-hardwood cuttings and insert in equal parts moist peat and sharp sand. Place in a cold frame and pot up the cuttings individually when rooted.

Right: Artemisia absinthium 'Lambrook Silver' *This shrubby artemisia creates a stunningly attractive beacon of silver-coloured foliage throughout summer. It is further enhanced during summer with yellow flowers.*

Artemisia ludoviciana

White Sage (UK and USA)
Western Mugwort · Cudweed (USA)

A bold clump of this hardy herbaceous perennial seldom fails to capture attention. The deeply divided leaves are woolly and white, with silvery-white flowers during late summer and early autumn.
Height: 1.2-1.5m (4-5ft)
Spread: 38-45cm (15-18in)
Cultivation: Light, well-drained soil in full sun suits it, avoid cold and wet positions. In autumn, cut down stems to soil-level.
Propagation: In autumn or spring, lift and divide congested clumps.

Left: Artemisia ludoviciana *An herbaceous artemisia which closely resembles* Artemisia gnaphalodes, *but reveals deeply-divided lower leaves.*

Artemisia absinthium 'Lambrook Silver' creates a superb background for dark-leaved plants such as *Sedum telephium maximum* 'Atropurpureum' with broad, purple leaves and dark purple stems.

Artemisia ludoviciana is enhanced by a background of yellow flowers, such as those of achilleas and rudbeckias. A foreground of sedums create additional colour in autumn.

THE FLOWER BORDER

Above: Aruncus dioicus *A hardy and reliable herbaceous perennial which yearly creates a wealth of creamy-white, tassel-like flower heads above masses of light and somewhat fern-like light green leaves.*

Aruncus dioicus

(*Aruncus sylvester/Aruncus vulgaris/Spiraea aruncus*)
Goat's Beard (UK)
Goatsbeard (USA)

This hardy herbaceous perennial is native to a wide area of the northern hemisphere. During summer it develops lax flower heads formed of creamy-white, tail-like plumes. These appear above the light green, somewhat fern-like leaves which are borne on stiff, wiry stems. Male and female flowers develop on different plants, with the male flowers being more feathery than the female ones.
Height: 1.2-1.5m (4-5ft)
Spread: 60-90cm (2-3ft)
Cultivation: Moisture-retentive, rich, light soil in slight shade suits it best. During autumn, cut down all stems to soil-level. New plants are best set in position in autumn or early spring.

Propagation: It is easily increased by lifting and dividing congested plants in spring. Replant only the young parts from around the outside of the clump. The centre parts are old and woody.

Chrysanthemum maximum

Shasta Daisy (UK)
Max Daisy · Daisy Chrysanthemum (USA)

This well-known and widely-grown hardy herbaceous perennial creates an eye-catching display of single white flowers, 6.5-7.5cm (2½-3in) wide, from mid to late summer. Each flower has a golden eye. The range of varieties is wide, including single, semi-double and double types. Ones to look for include 'Snowcap' (intensely white flowers on dwarf plants about 50cm/20in high) and 'Wirral Supreme' (double, white flowers on plants 90cm/3ft high).
Height: 75-90cm (2½-3ft)
Spread: 45-50cm (18-20in)
Cultivation: Well-drained, fertile, slightly chalky soil is best, preferably in full sun. In late autumn, after plants have started to die back, cut down the stems to soil-level.
Propagation: Lift and divide plants every three years, replanting young parts from around the outside. Do not leave plants so that they form large, woody clumps that become full of old stems at their centres.

Right: Chrysanthemum maximum *This Shasta Daisy has white flowers which are especially attractive when seen against a blue sky. Divide clumps every few years, before they become full of old woody stems.*

Cimicifuga racemosa

Black Snake Root · Bugbane (UK and USA)
Black Cohosh (USA)

This North American hardy herbaceous perennial creates a mass of tall, branching stems which bear feathery spires of creamy-white flowers during late summer. Fluffy flowers are borne above somewhat fern-like, mid-green leaves. Other species include *Cimicifuga americana* (also known as *C. cordifolia*) which grows 0.6-1.2m (2-4ft) high and with creamy-white flowers, and *Cimicifuga japonica* at 0.9-1.2m (3-4ft) high and with snow-white flowers. All of these cimicifugas are attractive with delicate looking but hardy foliage.
Height: 1.2-1.8m (4-6ft)
Spread: 60-75cm (2-2½ft)
Cultivation: Plant in light, rich, deeply-cultivated and moisture-retentive soil. Once established, plants do not like to be disturbed. Cut down the stems to soil-level in late autumn or early winter.
Propagation: Lift and divide established clumps in autumn or spring.

Aruncus dioicus is ideal for planting in boggy areas around ponds, especially where naturalized areas merge with pools. Its height creates a natural looking backcloth for other plants around the pond.

Chrysanthemum maximum is further enhanced when yellow flowered plants such as the herbaceous perennial *Coreopsis verticillata* is set in front of it. A border edging of *Lamium maculatum* 'Album' completes the scene.

**Left: Cortaderia selloana
'Sunningdale Silver'** *The feather
plumes of this member of the grass
family are especially attractive
when highlighted by the sun. Don't
crowd other plants in front of it.*

Cortaderia selloana

(*Cortaderia argentea*)
Pampas Grass (UK and USA)

An eye-catching and distinctive
hardy perennial from the pampas
of Argentina that seldom fails to
create interest in a garden. It is
ideal for planting by the side of an
informal garden pond or as a
specimen plant in a well-manicured
lawn. Silky, plume-like, silvery
flower heads, sometimes 45cm
(18in) long, are borne from late
summer to late autumn at the tops
of long, stiff, upright but arching
stems. The flower heads usually
remain throughout winter and are
especially decorative when
covered by frost or snow. There are
several varieties, including 'Pumila'
at 1.2-1.8m (4-6ft) high and
'Sunningdale Silver' at 2.4-3m (8-
10ft) high and with large, white
plumes.
Height: 1.8-2.4m (6-8ft)
Spread: 1.5-2.1m (5-7ft)
Cultivation: Plant in light, fertile,
well-drained soil, during mid-spring.
Prune established plants in early
spring. Wear stout gloves to
remove old stems that will have
started to die down. Do not cut
down the stems - just pull them.
Propagation: In spring, lift and
divide established clumps that
have become too large. However,
take care not to spoil the shape of
the clump. Usually, clumps are not
disturbed until they are too large,
when the whole clump is lifted - not
an easy task - and young parts
from around the outside replanted.

Right: Cimicifuga racemosa *This
cimicifuga creates a bold display of
mid-summer, snow-white flowers at
the tops of long stems. Plant it in a
large group, near to the front of a
border, where it creates an eye-
catching feature.*

Cimicifuga racemosa has a blackish, stout, rhizome
with a bitter, slightly disagreeable flavour. The roots
have been used in the treatment of snake bites, as well
as acting as a sedative and improving the appetite.

Cortaderia selloana is native to the vast plains of
South America. It was introduced into Europe in 1843,
when the Scottish botanist James Tweedie (1775-
1862) sent seed to the Glasnevin Botanic Garden, near
Dublin, Eire.

THE FLOWER BORDER

Propagation: During late spring and early summer take 7.5cm (3in) long cuttings from basal shoots and insert them in equal parts moist, peat and sharp sand. Place in a cold frame. Pot up when rooted and during summer plant into a nursery bed until large enough to be set in the garden, preferably in spring when the soil is starting to become warm.

Left: Gypsophila paniculata *The misty, delicately presented, white flowers of this border plant are aptly described by its common name - Baby's Breath. Another name, Chalk Plant, indicates its liking for chalk.*

Onopordum acanthium

Ornamental Thistle (UK)
Scotch Thistle · Cotton Thistle (UK and USA)
Silver Thistle · Oat Thistle · Gentine Thistle (USA)

A distinctive hardy biennial that seldom fails to attract attention. Its densely branched and erect grey stems bear broad, jaggedly-lobed and spined, silvery-grey leaves. From mid to late summer it bears purplish-mauve to pale lilac, thistle-like flowers up to 5cm (2in) wide, at the tops of stems.
Height: 1.5-2.1m (5-7ft)
Spread: 75-90cm (2½-3ft)
Cultivation: Fertile, moisture-retentive soil in full sun or light shade suits it. Poor soil does not encourage the development of strong stems and large plants. To prevent plants seeding themselves, cut off flower-heads immediately flowering finishes.
Propagation: During early summer sow seeds 6mm (¼in) deep in a well-prepared seedbed outdoors. The seeds take up to five weeks to germinate and, when the seedlings are large enough to handle, thin them to 30cm (12in) apart. In autumn, transplant them to their permanent positions, 75cm (2½ft) apart.

Gypsophila paniculata

Baby's Breath (UK and USA)
Chalk Plant · Gauze Flower (UK)

A well-known and widely-grown border plant with grass-like, stiffish, grey-green leaves and white flowers in summer.

Height: 60-75cm (2-2½ft)
Spread: 75-90cm (2½-3ft)
Cultivation: Well-drained, slightly chalky soil suits it, but avoid those which are heavy. Plants respond to deeply-cultivated soil to which has been added compost or manure. When plants are young, insert twiggy sticks around them so that the shoots grow through them.

Gypsophila paniculata is ideal for creating a bold, large splash of white at the front of a border. It blends well with yellow-flowered herbaceous plants like *Helenium autumnale* with its late-summer flowers.

Onopordum acanthium is generally considered by Scottish antiquarians to be the thistle depicted in the badge of the House of Stuarts. Later it came to be regarded as the national emblem of Scotland.

Romneya coulteri

Tree Poppy (UK)
Californian Tree Poppy (UK and USA)
Matilija Poppy (USA)

This shrubby, Californian herbaceous perennial produces eye-catching, 10-13cm (4-5in) wide, white flowers with bright golden bosses of stamens at their centres from mid-summer to autumn. It grows best in warm areas, where its underground runners can sometimes be too invasive. Therefore, reserve it for planting alongside a path or for setting in a shrub border. In an herbaceous border it sometimes becomes too vigorous.

Height: 1.2-1.8m (4-6ft)
Spread: 1.2-1.5m (4-5ft)
Cultivation: Deeply-cultivated, fertile soil and a sunny and southerly position suit it best. It dislikes root disturbance and therefore is best planted from pots in late spring or early summer. In autumn, cut down the stems to just above soil-level. Young plants need a covering of bracken or straw during their early life.
Propagation: Sow seeds in well-drained seed compost, in seedboxes during late winter or early spring. Place in 13°C (55°F). Germination is not rapid. When the seedlings are large enough to handle, prick them off into small pots. Overwinter them in pots in a cold frame and plant into a garden in spring.

Left: Romneya coulteri *Large white flowers with bright, golden centres are borne amid bluish-green, deeply-lobed leaves from mid-summer to autumn. Its beautiful flowers compensate for its invasive and spreading nature.*

Romneya coulteri looks superb when planted at the bottom of a flight of garden steps. Its invasive and spreading nature softens the sides of the steps with foliage and white flowers.

**Above: Santolina
chamaecyparissus** *This hardy
evergreen shrub is superb in hot,
sunny borders. It is grown for its
attractive leaves.*

Santolina chamaecyparissus

(*Santolina incana*)
Cotton Lavender (UK)
Lavender Cotton (USA)

A beautiful dwarf hardy evergreen
shrub with finely-divided, silvery,
woolly leaves. It forms a neat
hummock, and during mid-summer
bears bright lemon-yellow, button-
like flowers.
Height: 45-60cm (1½-2ft)
Spread: 45-60cm (1½-2ft)
Cultivation: Well-drained soil in
full sun assures success with this
warmth-loving plant. If the plant
becomes straggly, lightly trim back
in spring or after the flowers fade.
Propagation: From mid to late
summer take 5-7.5cm (2-3in) long
half-ripe cuttings from sideshoots.
Insert them in equal parts moist
peat and sharp sand. Place in a cold
frame. Overwinter in a cold frame.

Senecio bicolor

(*Cineraria bicolor/Cineraria
maritima/Senecio maritimus/
Senecio cineraria*)

This half-hardy perennial from
Mediterranean regions is usually
grown as a half-hardy annual for
planting in summer-bedding
schemes. In warm, southerly areas
it will survive outdoors most winters
and can be seen in many gardens
as a left-over from summer
bedding arrangements. However, it
looks best when combined with
other plants, so that its attractive
silvery appearance acts as a colour
and texture contrast. The leaves
are covered with white, woolly hairs
which give this plant its distinctive
appearance.
From mid-summer to autumn it
bears 2.5cm (1in) wide flowers, but
these are not as attractive as the
foliage and are best removed.
Several attractive varieties are
available, such as 'Diamond' with
deeply-divided, almost white
leaves, and 'Silver Dust' with fern-
like, deeply-dissected and intensely
silvery-white foliage. These are
small and lower-growing than the
normal type.
Height: 45-60cm (1½-2ft)
Spread: 30-38cm (12-15in)
Cultivation: Any ordinary garden
soil and a sunny position suits it.
Set new plants in the garden in late
spring.
Propagation: From late winter to
mid-spring sow seeds 3mm (⅛in)
deep in loam-based seed compost.
Place in 15°C (59°F). Germination
takes about ten days. When the
seedlings are large enough to
handle, prick them off into boxes of
loam-based compost. Slowly
accustom the young plants to
outdoor life and plant into the
garden when all risk of frost has
passed.

Below: Stachys byzantina *A
beautiful ground covering plant that
forms a sea of leaves densely
covered with silvery hairs, creating
a soft and woolly texture.*

Santolina chamaecyparissus creates a superb
backcloth for many border plants, but they should not
be strongly coloured. Instead, choose those with
flowers that reveal delicate and demure pastel shades.

Senecio bicolor harmonizes with many other plants,
including Cherry Pie (*Heliotropium x hybrida*), *Salvia
farinacea* 'Victoria', the brightly and dominantly-
flowered *Salvia splendens,* and China Asters.

CHAPTER TWO

Above: Senecio bicolor 'Silver Dust' *The silvery, fern-like carpet created by this summer-bedding plant is ideal for highlighting other plants.*

Stachys byzantina

Lamb's Tongue (UK)
Woolly Betony · Lamb's Ears (USA)

This herbaceous perennial, native from the Caucasuses to Iran is now correctly known as *Stachys byzantina* but is much better known as *S. olympica*, or even by the earlier name *S. lanata*. It is grown for its beautiful, oval, mid-green leaves which are so densely covered with white, silvery hairs that they assume a woolly appearance. The stems spread and root freely, creating a superb ground-cover plant. Upright stems develop small, purple flowers during mid-summer. The form 'Silver Carpet' is excellent for covering the soil with silvery leaves, and is a non-flowering type. It is only half-hardy and in severe winters can be damaged, especially by a combination of water and frost.
Height: 30-45cm (1-1½ft)
Spread: 30-45cm (1-1½ft)
Cultivation: Well-drained soil in light shade or full sun suits it. In autumn, cut down to soil-level those long stems that have borne flowers.
Propagation: It is easily increased by lifting and dividing congested plants in spring. Replant the young parts from around the outside of the clump.

Further plants to consider

Colchicum speciosum 'Album'
Height: 10-15cm (4-6in)   Spread: 15cm (6in)
Hardy bulb with glistening white, lax and goblet-shaped flowers during late summer and into early autumn. The leaves, which grow 30-38cm (12-15in) long, appear in spring.

Dictamnus albus
Burning Bush (UK and USA) · Gas Plant · Dittany · Fraxinella (USA)
Height: 60cm (2ft)   Spread: 45cm (1½ft)
A short-lived hardy herbaceous perennial with white, spider-like flowers borne in spikes up to 30cm (12in) long during mid-summer. During warm evenings a highly volatile oil emitted by the plant can sometimes be ignited, without causing damage to the foliage or flowers.

Euphorbia marginata
Snow on the Mountain (UK and USA) · Ghostweed (USA)
Height: 60cm (2ft)   Spread: 30-38cm (12-15in)
A hardy bushy annual grown for its soft green leaves which as the plant matures become veined and widely edged in white.

Galtonia candicans
Summer Hyacinth (UK and USA)
Height: 1.2m (4ft)   Spread: 20-25cm (8-10in)
A hardy bulbous border plant with slightly glaucous leaves. Upright stems bear many white, pendulous, bell-shaped flowers.

Lilium candidum
Madonna Lily (UK and USA)
Height: 1.2-1.5m (4-5ft)   Spread: 25-38cm (10-15in)
Well-known hardy basal-rooting lily which during mid-summer bears white trumpet-shaped fragrant flowers about 7.5cm (3in) long.

Narcissus 'Actaea'
Height: 38cm (15in)   Spread: 10-15cm (4-6in)
A hardy spring-flowering bulbous plant, belonging to the *Poeticus* group, with white petals and a red-rimmed yellow cup.

Phlox paniculata 'Fujiyama'
Border Phlox (UK and USA) · Summer Phlox (USA)
Height: 75cm (2½ft)   Spread: 30-38cm (12-15in)
Hardy herbaceous perennial with upright stems bearing pure-white flowers in cylindrical heads from mid to late summer.

Tiarella cordifolia
Foam Flower (UK and USA)
Height: 15-30cm (6-12in)   Spread: 30cm (12in)
Hardy herbaceous ground-covering plant with mid-green, maple-like leaves and creamy-white flowers.

Stachys byzantina is superb when grown with blue flowered plants such as Cat Mint (*Nepeta x faassenii*), Purple-leaved Sage (*Salvia officinalis* 'Purpurascens') *Salvia x superba* or *Ruta graveolens* 'Jackman's Blue'.

ROCK AND NATURALIZED GARDENS

Rock gardens usually receive more love and attention than any other part of the garden of equal size. The plants are diminutive, often early-flowering and frequently fussy about drainage. Though they need a certain amount of special care and attention, yard-for-yard rock gardens can support a greater range of plants than other sites.

Many people consider alpine and rock garden plants to be tender and fussy plants, but this is not necessarily correct. They are normally very hardy and will tolerate low temperatures, but are susceptible to a combination of excessively wet and freezing conditions. These conditions are made worse by poor drainage and leaves which fall on and around the plants in autumn.

An ideal location for a rock garden would be a raised site either on a slope or a well drained artificial mound where the plants get plenty of light. However, if this is not available, cracks in dry stone walls, gaps in natural paving or even stone sinks provide attractive homes for rock garden plants. Hybrids of *Lewisia cotyledon* are superb candidates for sink gardens, while the Cobweb Houseleek *Sempervivum arachnoideum*, with an attractive globular rosette of leaves and bright rose-red flowers, is another delight. There are many other suitable plants to be found in this chapter.

Naturalized gardens – perhaps helping a garden pond fuse into the overall garden scene, or on a warm grassy bank at the side of a rock garden, or perhaps a sheltered and lightly-shaded spot beneath a canopy of deciduous trees – can feature beautiful plants. In addition to cultivated plants, many native species are available and can be easily raised from seeds. If you have a small area which can be devoted to native plants you will be surprised by their rich colours.

Left: Grape Hyacinths (Muscari armeniacum) *with their tightly-clustered azure-blue flower heads, create a strong colour contrast with a mixed assortment of yellow, pink and red polyanthus.*

ROCK AND NATURALIZED GARDENS

Above: **Androsace primuloides 'Chumbyi'** *This is a delightful rock garden plant with beautiful clear pink flowers during mid-spring to mid-summer. It is essential that the rosettes are kept relatively dry during winter.*

Androsace primuloides

(*Androsace sarmentosa*)
Rock Jasmine (UK and USA)

A hardy rock garden perennial with silky white, woolly, narrow, lance-shaped, mid-green leaves. The rosettes of rose-pink flowers are borne on 5-10cm (2-4in) stems from mid-spring to mid-summer. The form 'Chumbyi' has clear pink flowers, while 'Watkinsii' bears highly attractive rosy-red flowers.
Height: 10-13cm (4-5in)
Spread: 38-60cm (15-24in)
Cultivation: Good drainage and a sunny position are essential. Preferably, the soil should contain coarse sand or limestone grit. Set the plants in position during spring. Wet soil encourages the leaves to rot, and in very wet areas protection with cloches may be necessary during winter.
Propagation: This is quite easily achieved by potting up rooted rosettes at the edges of the main clump in early autumn. Stand the pots in an open but sheltered part of the garden during winter. Protect them from excessive rain as necessary and plant out into the garden during spring.

Below: **Anthyllis montana** *This European alpine needs full sun and a well-drained gritty soil. Once established, it is best left alone, as its tap-root system resents any disturbance.*

Androsace lanuginosa, from the Himalayas, is a delightful trailing and mat-forming Rock Jasmine, with silver-green leaves and pinkish flowers in mid-summer and autumn. It is ideal for drystone walls.

Armeria juniperifolia

(*Armeria caespitosa*)
Thrift (UK and USA)

This hardy evergreen perennial from Spain is one of the best known rock garden plants, producing stiff grass-like, grey-green leaves in tufted clumps. The 12-18mm (½-¾in) wide, tightly packed, pink flower-heads are borne singly at the tops of 5-7.5cm (2-3in) long stems during late spring and early summer. The form 'Bevan's Variety' is widely grown and displays deep pink flowers on 2.5-5cm (1-2in) stems.
Height: 5-7.5cm (2-3in)
Spread: 20-25cm (8-10in)
Cultivation: Any good well-drained garden soil suits thrift, and it likes a position in full sun. Set the plants in position during spring or autumn. As soon as the flowers fade, clip them off to make the plants neat for the rest of the year.
Propagation: This is easily done by lifting and dividing large clumps in spring. Replant them immediately. Alternatively, 5cm (2in) basal cuttings can be taken in late summer and inserted in equal parts peat and sharp sand.

Anthyllis montana

Mountain Kidney Vetch (UK)

An unusual rock garden plant that forms a low woody bush with hairy foliage, giving it a silvery appearance. During mid-summer it bears red or red-purple flowers at the stem ends.
Height: 20-30cm (8-12in)
Spread: 38-45cm (15-18in)
Cultivation: Anthyllis prefers a well-drained gritty soil and a sunny site. It will tolerate a limestone soil.
Propagation: During summer, take 5-7.5cm (2-3in) long cuttings with heels. Insert them in pots containing a sandy compost and put them in a cold frame. It is difficult to raise from seeds, but these can be sown in early spring and placed in a cold frame. Once planted, it is best left alone as it resents disturbance.

Above: **Armeria juniperifolia** **'Bevan's Variety'** *A reliable and neat tufted rock garden plant that flowers in early summer, armeria also grows well in a stone sink. The flowers and foliage can be enhanced by covering the soil with clean shingle.*

Below: **Armeria maritima** **'Bloodstone'** *This species is related to the slightly smaller Armeria juniperifolia and rises to 15-25cm (6-10in). Again it is ideal for rock gardens or for setting at the edges of a border. This variety produces glowing crimson flowers.*

Armeria pseudarmeria, often better known as *A. plantaginea*, grows much larger than *A. lanuginosa*, to a height of 60cm (2ft) and a spread of 38cm (15in). The variety 'Bees Ruby' has bright ruby red flowers.

Astilbe x arendsii

False Goat's Beard (UK)
Perennial Spiraea (USA)

This beautiful hardy herbaceous hybrid perennial has *Astilbe chinensis davidii* in its parentage and comes in a colour range from purple-red to nearly white. Many pink and red forms are available, flowering from mid to late summer. Varieties to look for include 'Bressingham Beauty' (rich pink and free-flowering), 'Fanal' (intense deep red), 'Red Sentinel' (intense brick red), 'Rheinland' (rich pink) and 'Federsee' (rose-red).

Height: 60-90cm (2-3ft)
Spread: 38-50cm (15-20in)
Cultivation: Astilbes prefer fertile, moisture-retentive soil in full sun or light shade. In dry seasons it may be necessary to water the plants. Applying a mulch helps to conserve moisture in the soil. In autumn, cut the foliage down to soil-level.
Propagation: Lifting and dividing established clumps every three or four years in spring is the easiest method. Do not let the roots dry out when dividing them. Replant them immediately so that the roots do not become dry.

Above left: Astilbe x arendsii
This beautiful hardy herbaceous plant has feathery spires of flowers from mid to late summer. It is ideal for a moist area in the garden. It is best planted in large drifts where it creates a dominant display for much of the summer.

Above: Astilbe chinensis
'Pumila' *Most astilbes like to grow by the side of a pool, but this diminutive form does well in drier conditions. During summer it develops fluffy pink spires that display themselves above the foliage, never failing to produce an exciting spectacle.*

Astilbes are an ideal choice for the moist surrounds of informal garden pools. The red and pink forms blend well with yellow hemerocallis and the large blue heads of *Hydrangea macrophylla*.

Astilbe chinensis 'Pumila'

Without a doubt, this miniature astilbe is a treasure in a rock garden. Its herbaceous perennial nature ensures fresh, mid-green, fern-like foliage each year, with 23cm (9in) long spires of fluffy pink flowers flushed purple appearing from mid-summer to autumn.

Height: 23-30cm (9-12in)
Spread: 30-38cm (12-15in)
Cultivation: Relatively moist and fertile soil in full sun or light shade suit this plant. The roots like a cool position, for example by the side of a rock that affords a shady and cool root run. In autumn cut the plants down to soil-level.
Propagation: It is most easily increased by lifting and dividing clumps every three or four years and replanting them 25-30cm (10-12in) apart. Do this in mid-spring and water well until the plants are established.

Cornus alba

Red-barked Dogwood (UK)
Tartarian Dogwood · Tatarian Dogwood (USA)

This hardy, vigorous, wide-spreading, deciduous shrub belongs to a group loosely known as Dogwoods or Cornels. This particular species has a suckering habit and produces masses of upright stems. The current year's stems are bright red in winter. All these are suitable for a wild or naturalized garden.

Height: 2.1-2.7m (7-9ft)
Spread: 1.8-3m (6-10ft)
Cultivation: Rich, moist soil and full sun suit these shrubs best. During spring, cut down the stems to within a few inches of the soil to encourage the development of shoots that will display good rich colour in late summer and winter.
Propagation: It is easily increased by layering long shoots in autumn. Alternatively, take hardwood cuttings in autumn, inserting them in trenches with sand along their bases to prevent waterlogging.

Above: **Cornus alba 'Sibirica'** *This distinctively bright-stemmed shrub makes an impressive picture during winter. To obtain highly-coloured shoots, the previous season's growth must be cut down nearly to soil-level in spring.*

Astilbe chinensis 'Pumila' with its upright spires can create the effect of sudden height in a rock garden. It often looks good by a drystone wall, whose colour and texture complement the flowers.

Cornus alba 'Sibirica' looks best in a site where low-angled winter sun will catch the stems. It makes an ideal companion for daffodils, which will provide colour to hide its stems when cut down in spring.

Left: **Daphne cneorum** *One of the most beautiful and pleasantly-scented of all garden plants, this daphne will spread up to 1.3m (4½ft) wide. The four-petalled rose-pink flowers appear during early summer.*

Dianthus pavonius

(*Dianthus neglectus · Dianthus alpinus*)

This attractive but variable hardy rock garden plant forms neat hummocks of narrow grey-green leaves. During mid to late summer these are smothered with pale pink to deep crimson 3cm (1¼in) wide flowers on short stems 2.5cm (1in) long.
Height: 10-20cm (4-8in)
Spread: 15-20cm (6-8in)
Cultivation: Ordinary well-drained garden soil and a sunny position assure success. Sprinkling stone chippings over the surface helps to prevent heavy rain storms splashing soil on to the plants. The chippings also improve surface drainage.
Propagation: During mid-summer take 7.5-10cm (3-4in) long cuttings and insert them in pots containing equal parts peat and sharp sand. Place these in a cold frame. When rooted, pot the plants up into loam-based compost in small pots and replace in the frame. When established, plant out into the garden.

Daphne cneorum

Garland Flower (UK and USA)

This is a beautiful and highly scented ground-hugging and spreading evergreen shrub from Central and Southern Europe, ideal for a rock garden. The wiry stems are well clothed with narrow, deep green leaves, and the 12mm (½in) wide rose-pink flowers appear during early summer. The form 'Eximia' boasts deeper pink flowers and is slightly larger.
Height: 16cm (6in)
Spread: 75cm-1.3m (2½-4½ft)
Cultivation: Daphnes like a well-drained but moisture-retentive garden soil in full sun or slight shade. They tolerate lime in the soil. As the roots need to be kept cool, mulch with well-rotted compost in spring. If the plants spread too much in one direction, prune them back carefully after flowering.
Propagation: The easiest way for a home gardener to increase this plant is by layering shoots in autumn. Alternatively, take 5-10cm (2-4in) long heel cuttings in mid to late summer and insert them in pots containing equal parts peat and sharp sand, placed in a cold frame. When the plants are rooted, pot them up into loam-based compost, setting them out in the garden about eighteen months later into their final positions.

Below: **Dianthus pavonius** *This dainty rock garden plant is often better known as* Dianthus neglectus. *During summer it displays fringed pale pink to deep crimson flowers.*

Daphne cneorum is very adaptable and mixes well with many other plants. Try growing tall St Bernard's Lily (*Anthericum liliago*) behind, with silver-leaved *Europs acraeus* on one side.

Left: **Erinus alpinus** *This beautiful and highly adaptable plant lives happily in a rock garden or on a dry stone wall. It seeds itself readily, rapidly producing a supply of fresh plants.*

Right: **Fritillaria imperialis** *This distinctive and eye-catching spring-flowering bulb produces an impressive stem bearing bell-shaped flowers. The tuft of leaves at the top of the stem creates the impression of a crown.*

Erinus alpinus

A hardy though relatively short-lived dwarf evergreen perennial for rock gardens or drystone walls. It also does well between natural paving slabs. The spoon-shaped, mid-green leaves are deeply toothed and borne in low, tufted mounds with bright pink 6mm (¼in) wide, star-shaped flowers from early spring to late summer. The form 'Mrs Charles Boyle' has deep pink flowers, while 'Dr Hanele' produces attractive carmine blooms.

Height: 7.5cm (3in)
Spread: 15-20cm (6-8in)
Cultivation: Well-drained soil is essential, as is a sunny position.
Propagation: Erinus seeds itself quite readily, and even the cultivated forms come true when grown from seed.

Fritillaria imperialis

Crown Imperial (UK and USA)

This familiar, vigorous and distinctive plant from the Himalayas produces stiff, upright stems with wavy lance-shaped glossy green leaves partly clasping them. During spring, it bears dense clusters of bell-shaped 5cm (2in) long flowers at the tops of the stems. These range from yellow to rich red. Above the flowers is a cluster of partially erect leaves, resembling a crown. It is just as attractive in large drifts in a naturalized or woodland garden as in a formal setting, perhaps alongside a path.

Height: 60-90cm (2-3ft)
Spread: 30-38cm (12-15in)
Cultivation: Fritillarias require fertile, well-drained soil in full or light shade. As the fleshy bulbs are easily damaged, they are best planted 20cm (8in) deep during autumn and left in one position for several years. Setting the bulbs on their sides prevents water rotting their tops. In heavy soils, put a handful of sharp sand under each bulb. During autumn, cut down the stems to soil-level.
Propagation: Fritillarias can be grown from seed, but this method takes up to six years to produce flowering-sized bulbs, so it is better to propagate from offsets taken from the parent bulb in late summer. Plant them in a nursery bed for two years before transferring them to their final flowering positions.

Erinus alpinus is a delight when allowed to fill the gaps in natural stone paths, in harmony with antennarias, *Helichrysum bellidioides*, *Mazus repens*, *Mentha requienii* and *Valeriana montana*.

Fritillaria imperialis is ideal for naturalizing with other plants, like miniature tulips and violas, in a wild garden. However, it also does well in narrow beds in small, more formal gardens.

Geranium dalmaticum

This neat Yugoslavian and Albanian Crane's-bill is a densely foliaged herbaceous perennial with deeply-lobed, rather palm-like, mid-green, flossy leaves that take on gorgeous tints in autumn. During mid to late summer it bears 2.5cm (1in) wide, demure pink, five-petalled, saucer-shaped flowers on stems 10-13cm (4-5in) long.
Height: 15cm (6in)
Spread: 25-30cm (10-12in)
Cultivation: Any well-drained garden soil in full sun or partial shade is suitable. In autumn, cut down the plant to soil-level.
Propagation: It is easily increased by lifting and dividing clumps in spring or autumn. It is quite easy to split up the plants. If some of them are rather small, pot them up into small pots and allow them to establish themselves properly before setting them out in the rock garden in their permanent positions.

Left: Geranium dalmaticum
A dainty Crane's-bill for a rock garden, this species has mid-green leaves that take on lovely red and orange tints in autumn. These form a bonus to the soft pink flowers.

Gypsophila repens

(*Gypsophila prostrata*)

This pretty mat-forming, wiry-stemmed, trailing alpine gypsophila with narrow grey-green leaves looks superb when clothed with 9mm ($\frac{1}{3}$in) wide pink or white flowers throughout the summer. The form 'Letchworth Rose' is a delightful pink, while 'Dorothy Teacher' bears bluish-grey leaves and clear pink flowers.
Height: 10-15cm (4-6in)
Spread: 45-60cm (1$\frac{1}{2}$-2ft)
Cultivation: Well-drained, slightly alkaline soil is best, although gypsophilas also do well in acid conditions. They are best positioned to trail over the top of a drystone wall or large rocks.

Geranium dalmaticum has a flattened-dome shape, making it an ideal choice for the junction of two paths in a rock garden. It is also superb for a terrace or dry stone wall where it can spill over.

Gypsophila aretioides is another alpine species worth growing, with a tight, cushion-forming growth 5cm (2in) high. *G. cerastioides*, 7.5cm (3in) high, has grey leaves and clusters of white flowers.

Propagation: During spring, take 5cm (2in) long cuttings and insert them in pots containing equal parts of peat and sharp sand. Place these in a cold frame. When rooted, pot up the plants into 7.5cm (3in) pots of loam-based compost. They can be planted out in autumn or spring.

Right: Helianthemum nummularium 'Ben Dearg'
Few mid-summer-flowering rock plants are as impressive as this lowgrowing, somewhat sprawling perennial. And even if it does exceed its position, it can easily be trimmed back after flowering.

Below: Gypsophila repens 'Letchworth Rose' *This distinctive pink-flowered alpine gypsophila produces a frothy mass of flowers well suited for tumbling over walls and large rocks. Its loose and lax nature when trailing over walls allows the attractive nature of the stone to be seen.*

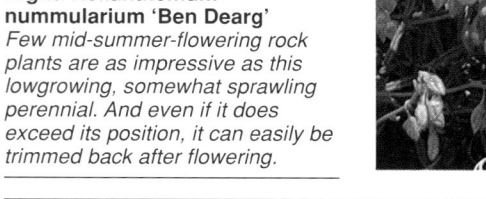

Helianthemum nummularium

(*Helianthemum chamaecistus H. vulgare*)
Rock Rose (UK) ·
Sun Rose · Rock Rose (USA)

This shrubby, low-growing and spreading plant is invaluable in a rock garden. The deep green, narrow, elliptical leaves are borne sparsely on trailing stems, with 12-25mm (1/2in-1in) wide, saucer-shaped flowers appearing during mid-summer. The colour range includes 'Beech Park Scarlet' (crimson-scarlet), 'Wisley Pink' (pink), 'Ben Dearg' (deep copper-orange) and 'Cerise Queen' (rosy-red).
Height: 10-15cm (4-6in)
Spread: 45-60cm (1½-2ft)
Cultivation: Well-drained garden soil and a sunny position assure success. Do not hesitate to deal with over-rampant plants; they will withstand quite severe pruning after flowering.
Propagation: During mid to late summer take 5-7.5cm (2-3in) long cuttings with 'heels'. Insert them in pots of equal parts peat and sharp sand and place these in a cold frame. Pot up the plants when rooted into small pots of loam-based compost and replace in a cold frame. Plant out into the rock garden in late spring.

Helianthemum nummularium is extremely impressive when trailing over a low wall, so the plant can be seen from above as well as the sides. It is useful for breaking up the stark outline of a wall.

Oxalis adenophylla

This delightful, dainty, low-growing hardy perennial has a fibre-coated bulb-like rootstock, greyish leaves and long-stemmed, solitary, cup-shaped, satiny-pink flowers in early summer.

Height: 6.5-7.5cm (2½-3in)
Spread: 15cm (6in)
Cultivation: A well-drained, light, peat-enriched soil and a sunny position are essential. A light soil covering of well-washed shingle helps to ensure good drainage and an attractive background for the flowers and foliage. The foliage dies down during winter.
Propagation: This can be easily done by separating the bulb offsets in early spring. These can be replanted directly into the rock garden or potted into a gritty compost until healthy young plants become properly established. Another beautiful South American oxalis, but this time for an alpine house, is *O. enneaphylla* 'Rosea'. It is bulbous-rooted, with partially folded grey leaves and pale rose-pink flowers which appear during mid-summer.

Below: **Oxalis adenophylla**
The delicate appearance of this Chilean hardy perennial never fails to add an element of interest to rock gardens.

Parahebe catarractae

This dainty-flowered sub-shrub delights in cascading over and between rocks, displaying its massed terminal heads of flowers, featuring rose-purple lines set on a background of white, during summer. The mid to dark green, lance-shaped to oval leaves with serrated edges are an attractive bonus.

Height: 25-30cm (10-12in)
Spread: 38-45cm (15-18in)
Cultivation: Parahebes delight in a well-drained neutral soil, preferably covered with well-washed shingle and in a sunny position. Set them at the top of the rock garden so

Oxalis adenophylla has delicate colouring, and needs subtly coloured neighbours if it is not to be dominated. It looks at its best when given plenty of space, rather than being hemmed in.

Left: **Penstemon newberryi**
This sprawling and scrambling penstemon produces pink to rose-pink flowers, and there are many other superb penstemons suitable for rock gardens.

Penstemon newberryi

This is a useful bushy semi-evergreen sub-shrub for trailing over rocks and dry stone walls, where its sprawling nature helps to merge the structural elements. Its elongated, 3-4cm (1¼-1½in) long, snapdragon-like, pink to rose-pink flowers appear against a carpet of small, mid-green leaves during mid-summer.

Height: 20cm (8in)

Spread: 30-38cm (12-15in)

Cultivation: A well-drained soil is essential. Penstemons flourish in full sun, though a sheltered site may be needed, as the plants will suffer during exceptionally cold winters, despite being generally hardy. Badly drained soils contribute to failure during cold spells. If possible, it is wise to have a stock of small plants ready to replace any that are damaged.

Propagation: Although they can be increased from seed sown during early spring in boxes of loam-based seed compost, the resulting seedlings can be variable. Instead, take 5-7.5cm (2-3in) long cuttings from non-flowering shoots during late summer or early autumn. Insert them in pots containing equal parts peat and sharp sand and put these in a cold frame. When the young plants are rooted, pot them up into loam-based compost and place in a cold frame during winter. Plant out into the garden in late spring. Another attractive alpine species is *P. davidsonii*, a low sub-shrub which grows up to 10cm (4in) high and produces ruby-red flowers in mid-summer.

they can tumble between rocks and benefit from better drainage at the top of a slope.

Propagation: It is easily increased by taking soft cuttings 5-7.5cm (2-3in) long, from mid to late summer. Insert them in pots of sandy compost and place these in a cold frame. When the plants are properly rooted, nip out their growing tips to encourage dense bushy growth. This species is related to the hebes and veronicas, and very frequently there is some confusion about the identity of plants. To ensure you have the right plants buy only those listed as *Parahebe catarractae*, not *Hebe catarractae*.

Left: **Parahebe catarractae**
This beautiful shrubby plant delights in well-drained soil and a sunny position.

Parahebe catarractae blends well with dainty bright yellow flowers, but beware of overdoing such a combination as the contrast can be overpowering. A good companion is *Sedum acre* 'Aureum'.

Penstemon roezlii, which grows to 15cm (6in) high, is another candidate for the edge of a rock ledge where it can cascade freely. *P. scouleri* with lavender-blue flowers, is upright and slightly taller.

ROCK AND NATURALIZED GARDENS

Saponaria ocymoides

Soapwort · Rock Soapwort (UK)
Soapwort (USA)

This delightful, vigorous, trailing rock-garden perennial is invaluable for creating prostrate mats of colour flowing over rocks or cascading from dry stone walls. It produces long, lance-shaped, mid-green leaves, with five-petalled, 12mm (½in) wide, bright rose-pink flowers from mid to late summer. Several excellent forms are available, such as 'Rubra Compact' (rich carmine), 'Splendens' (dark pink) and 'Compacta' which is like the ordinary type but more compact.
Height: 7.5cm (3in)
Spread: 30cm (1ft)
Cultivation: Soapworts appreciate a well-drained fertile garden soil in full sun or light shade.
Propagation: Plants can be lifted and divided in autumn or spring. Alternatively, soft stem cuttings can be taken in summer from non-flowering shoots and inserted in pots of sandy compost, placed in a cold frame. Pot plants up into loam-based compost when rooted.

Above: Saponaria ocymoides
This delightful rock garden plant cascades in a spectacular manner over stone walls and rocks. In such positions the bright rose-pink flowers are a delight, appearing from mid to late summer.

Below: Saponaria officinalis
This is the original single-flowered form, with fragrant rose-pink flowers borne on erect stems. A superb double-flowered pink form is now available, too. It is best positioned in a wild garden where its invasive nature does not interfere with neighbouring plants.

Saponaria officinalis

Soapwort Bouncing Bet (UK and USA)

This hardy herbaceous perennial is a native of Europe and parts of Asia, and is often found naturalized in areas in Britain that are or have been inhabited by humans. The common name Soapwort refers to the leaves which, when bruised in water, create a lather. At one time, Soapwort was known as Fuller's Herb; a fuller was a person whose trade was to cleanse cloth. In the past it was used to clean old curtains, although why it was relegated to such a job is not clear when it was perfectiy efficient on other cloths.

The 2.5-4cm (1-1½in) wide flowers are pink and single and borne in mid to late summer in terminal clusters on stiff, upright stems, clasped by pale-green leaves. Several attractive forms are available, such as 'Roseoplena', with double pink flowers.
Height: 45-90cm (1½-2ft)
Spread: 60cm (2ft)
Cultivation: Soapwort prefers a well-drained fertile soil and a position in full sun or light shade. In exposed areas it will require support from twiggy sticks that the foliage can grow through and hide. In autumn, cut down the stems to soil-level.
Propagation: You can take cuttings in summer, but it is much easier to increase by lifting and dividing established clumps in autumn or spring.

Saponaria ocymoides is such a spectacular plant when in bloom that the pink flowers can be dominated by stronger coloured plants nearby, so take care when planting it in a group.

Saponaria officinalis is known as Bouncing Bet in North America. In this context, 'bouncing' refers to the good health and vitality this medicinal herb may bring; 'Bet' is an abbreviation for Elizabeth.

Above: **Thymus drucei** *This delightful European and British native prostrate sub-shrub is a delight with its fragrant summer flowers, and is invaluable for covering bare soil with colour.*

Thymus drucei

(*Thymus serpyllum*)
Wild Thyme (UK)
Wild Thyme · Lemon Thyme (USA)

Few gardeners do not know this prostrate hardy sub-shrub with narrow, rather spoon-shaped grey-green leaves. The variably coloured flowers – from red to pink and white – appear in small clustered heads from mid to late summer. Several superb forms are available, including 'Annie Hall' (pale pink) and 'Coccineus' (rich crimson).
Height: 4-7.5cm (1½-3in)
Spread: 60-90cm (2-3ft)
Cultivation: Any good, well-drained garden soil in a sunny position suits thyme. To keep the plants neat, use a pair of garden shears to clip off dead flower heads.
Propagation: The easiest way to increase this plant is by lifting and dividing congested clumps in spring or early autumn.

Further plants to consider

Antennaria dioica
Height: 5-30cm (2-12in)   Spread: 30-45cm (1-1½ft)
A hardy evergreen perennial with a creeping habit and white, pink-tipped flowers during early summer. The form 'Nyewood' boasts crimson flowers, while 'Rosea' has deep pink blooms.

Dianthus deltoides 'Flashing Light'
Maiden Pink (UK and USA)
Height: 15-23cm (6-9in)   Spread: 15cm (6in)
A beautiful rock-garden plant for crevices and between natural paving slabs. From mid-summer to autumn it reveals bright crimson flowers. Other forms include 'Wisley Variety' (carmine-red) and 'Brilliant' (bright rose-pink).

Diascia x 'Ruby Field'
Height: 25-30cm (10-12in)   Spread: 30-38cm (12-15in)
A spreading and somewhat mat-forming hardy rock garden plant with small toothed leaves and warm glowing pink flowers during much of summer.

Phlox douglasii 'Eva'
Height: 5-10cm (2-4in)   Spread: 30-45cm (1-1½ft)
A low-growing shrubby rock-garden plant forming a mat of mid-green leaves and small pink flowers during early summer.

Saxifraga aizoon rosea
(*Saxifraga paniculata rosea*)
Height: 15-20cm (6-8in)   Spread: 15-25cm (6-10in)
A beautiful euaizoonia saxifraga with wide lance-shaped silver-green leaves and sprays of deep pink early summer flowers. It is also suitable for growing in containers.

Sempervivum arachnoideum
Cobweb Houseleek (UK)
Cobweb Houseleek · Spiderweb Houseleek (USA)
Height: 10cm (4in)   Spread: 23-30cm (9-12in)
A widely-grown succulent plant with rosettes of green leaves, often flushed with red, and bright red, 18mm (¾in) wide flowers during mid-summer.

Phlox subulata
Moss Phlox (UK)
Moss Pink · Moss Phlox · Mountain Phlox (USA)
Height: 5-10cm (2-4in)   Spread: 30-45cm (1-1½ft)
A beautiful sub-shrub forming a mat of mid-green, narrow leaves with pink or purple flowers in spring. Forms to look for include 'Alexander's Surprise' (salmon-pink), 'Scarlet Flame' (brilliant scarlet), 'Star Glow' (bright red) and 'Temiscaming' (brilliant magenta-red).

Thymus drucei is the parent of several unusual and exciting forms, such as 'Lanuginosa' with greyish woolly leaves and lilac flowers, and 'Silver Queen' with silver and green variegated leaves.

ROCK AND NATURALIZED GARDENS

Anemone blanda

Blue Windflower (UK)
Windflower (USA)

This welcome and reliable spring flowering plant has rather fern-like deeply-cut dark green leaves and 2.5-4cm (1-1½in) wide daisy-like flowers in pale blue, pink, lavender or white.

Height: 13-15cm (5-6in)
Spread: 10-13cm (4-5in)
Cultivation: Well-drained fertile soil neutral or slighty acid, in light dappled shade, suits it best. The corms are best planted in autumn 5cm (2in) deep and 13-15cm (5-6in) apart.
Propagation: Lift and divide congested clumps in late summer. Alternatively, sow seeds when ripe in pots or boxes of loam-based compost, placing them in a cold frame. Prick off the seedlings into boxes when they are large enough to handle.

Right: Anemone blanda 'Blue Pearl' *Anemones are always welcome in spring, with their neat, daisy-like flowers with bright centres. There is a range of colours, including this striking blue variety. They can be naturalized beneath trees or set in neat clumps in a rock garden.*

Aubrieta deltoidea

This is one of the best-known rock garden plants, well suited for covering large areas and for trailing over walls. It is also useful as an edging to paths and for combining with herbaceous plants. There are many forms, originated from selected seedlings of this hardy, spreading and low-growing evergreen perennial. These include 'Barker's Double' (rose-purple), 'Dr. Mules' (violet-purple), 'Henslow Purple' (bright purple), 'Triumphant (blue) and 'Tauricola' (deep purple-blue).

Height: 7.5-10cm (3-4in)
Spread: 45-60cm (1½-2ft)
Cultivation: Well-drained, slightly limy garden soil and a sunny position suit it best. Trim the plants after flowering.
Propagation: The plants can be easily increased by lifting and dividing them during early autumn.

Far right: Aubrieta deltoidea 'Ballawley Amethyst'
This handsome, spreading and trailing evergreen perennial is ideal for cascading over walls, as an edging to paths and even for growing with herbaceous plants. There are many forms to choose from, with colours ranging from pink through to blue and violet-blue.

Right: Anemone coronaria *This is the well-known florist's anemone, popular in both borders and in rock gardens, as well as being extensively grown for cut-flowers.*

Anemone blanda is striking when naturalized among the dappled light filtering through silver-barked trees. Also, try a mixture of anemones, polyanthus, Grape Hyacinths and Drumstick Primulas.

Aubrietia deltoidea harmonizes with many others including the hardy pink or white perennial *Arabis caucasica*, the yellow-flowered bulb *Tulipa tarda*, and the hardy perennial yellow *Alyssum saxatile*.

Above: **Campanula cochleariifolia**
*This hardy dwarf perennial with its
nodding thimble-like flowers is a
delight in a rock garden. It is one of
the most amenable and rewarding
of all campanulas.*

Campanula cochleariifolia

(*Campanula pusilla*)
Fairies' Thimbles (UK)

A dainty, undemanding easily-
grown hardy dwarf perennial, this is
ideal for a rock garden. It displays
mid-green, shallow-toothed leaves
and 12mm (½in) long, nodding,
bell-shaped, sky-blue flowers
during mid to late summer. A white
form is also available.
Height: 10-15cm (4-6in)
Spread: 30-38cm (12-15in)
Cultivation: Well-drained soil and
full sun suit it. Set the plants in
position in autumn or spring.
Propagation: It is easily increased
by lifting and dividing large clumps
in autumn or spring. Alternatively,
take soft cuttings 5cm (2in) long in
spring, insert them in pots of equal
parts peat and sharp sand and
place these in a cold frame. When
the cuttings are rooted, pot them
up into small pots until they are
large enough to be planted in the
garden. In well drained soil, it soon
spreads to form large mats of
flowers and foliage.

Campanula cochleariifolia is ideal for trailing and
cascading over rocks. It also delights in growing
between natural stone paving slabs, and is superb
for planting at the sides of paths in large rock gardens.

ROCK AND NATURALIZED GARDENS

Above: Chionodoxa luciliae gigantea *The dominant colour of these delicate flowers will brighten any garden in late winter. It is not a fussy plant, and grows well in any well-drained soil in full sun. All chionodoxas are superb for bringing colour during late winter.*

Chionodoxa luciliae

Glory of the Snow (UK and USA)

This bright hardy bulb from Asia Minor produces brilliant sky-blue, 2.5cm (1in) wide flowers during late winter and early spring. Each flower has a white centre. The form *Chionodoxa luciliae gigantea,* often called *C. gigantea,* is larger, and has pale violet-blue 4cm (1½in) wide flowers with small white centres. Chionodoxas are ideal for rock gardens, for naturalizing in short, fine grass and for placing at the front of borders.
Height: 18-20cm (7-8in)
Spread: 7.5-10cm (3-4in)
Cultivation: Ordinary well-drained garden soil and full sun assure success.Plant the bulbs 6.5cm (2½in) deep.
Propagation: Lift and divide large clumps as soon as the leaves have died down. Replant the bulbs immediately.

Colchicum autumnale

Autumn Crocus (UK)
Autumn Crocus · Fall Crocus · Meadow Saffron · Mysteria · Wonder Bulb (USA)

This hardy corm-bearing plant bears large mid to dark green leaves up to 25cm (10in) long in spring and early summer, which later die back. In autumn, it produces 15cm (6in) high, goblet-shaped, rosy-lilac flowers, often with a chequered pattern. There are also some lovely purplish forms, as well as white varieties and 'Roseum-plenum', with double rose-pink flowers.
Height: 25-30cm (10-12in)
Spread: 20-25cm (8-10in)
Cultivation: It delights in well-drained soil in full sun or light shade. Plant the corms during autumn, 7.5cm (3in) deep in small groups.
Propagation: It can be raised from seed, but the production of flowering-sized corms takes up to seven years.

Above: Colchicum speciosum
This unusual corm-bearing plant flowers in autumn after its foliage has died down. It thrives in sun or partial shade and is superb for bringing colour to the garden.

It is easier to lift congested clumps when the leaves have died down and remove the offsets. Plant them out in a nursery bed for a couple of years until ready for their final positions, and replant the parent corms too.

Colchicum speciosum

Autumn Crocus (UK)

This distinctive hardy corm-bearing plant from Asia Minor displays 30cm (1ft) long, 10cm (4in) wide leaves in spring and early summer. In autumn, when the leaves have died back, its 15cm (6in) high stems bear flowers in a wide range of colours, from white to pinkish-lilac

---

Chionodoxa luciliae is superb for planting under the golden-yellow flowers of the Chinese Witch Hazel (*Hamamelis mollis*). It also blends perfectly with *Narcissus cyclamineus* 'February Gold'.

Colchicum autumnale, the Autumn Crocus or Meadow Saffron, has nothing to do with crocuses or with saffron which comes from *Crocus sativus*. However, its dried corms are a valuable ingredient of medicines.

Right: Colchicum autumnale
Another corm-bearing plant, it produces leaves in spring and early summer that die back afterwards. In autumn, it bears crocus-like flowers that provide welcome colour.

and reddish-purple. It has been crossed with other species to create many superb hybrids.
Height: 30-38cm (12-15in)
Spread: 25-30cm (10-12in)
Cultivation: Well-drained soil in full sun or light shade suits it. During autumn, plant the corms 7.5-10cm (3-4in) deep in small clumps.
Propagation: It can be raised from seed, but the production of flowering sized corms takes up to seven years. It is easier to lift congested clumps when the leaves have died down and remove the offsets, planting them out in a nursery bed for a couple of years until ready for their final positions. Replant the large, parent corms, too.

Colchicum speciosum is useful for planting under shrubs and trees, where its spring and early summer leaves cannot swamp nearby plants. It is superb for planting under species roses.

131

Convolvulus sabatius

(Convolvulus mauritanicus)

This handsome North American trailing and mat-forming perennial is not fully hardy, so it is ideal for warm, sunny rock gardens or even in hanging-baskets. The 2.5-4cm (1-1½in) long, almost round, mid-green leaves are surmounted by 2.5cm (1in) wide, purple-blue trumpet-shaped flowers with small white throats borne singly from mid to late summer.

Height: 5-7.5cm (2-3in)
Spread: 45-60cm (1½-2ft)
Cultivation: Light, well-drained sandy soil in a warm area and a sheltered position suit it best. It is only really successful in warmer areas.
Propagation: During mid-summer, take 5cm (2in) long cuttings, inserting them in pots of equal parts peat and sharp sand, placing these in a cold frame. When the cuttings are rooted, pot them up singly into small pots of loam-based compost and over-winter them in a frost-proof greenhouse. Wait until late spring before planting them out into the garden or in containers.

Below: Convolvulus sabatius *This delightful member of the bindweed family is often better known as* Convolvulus mauritanicus. *It is not fully hardy but well worth growing for its beautiful blue flowers from mid-summer onwards.*

Above: Crocus tomasinianus
This is one of the earliest crocuses to flower, in late winter. It needs protection from cold winds but, once established, it will thrive in most gardens.

Crocus tomasinianus

An attractive late-winter flowering bulb, this crocus displays narrow dark green leaves with pronounced white midribs. The flowers range in colour from pale lavender to reddish-purple and are borne during late winter and into early spring. Good varieties include 'Barr's Purple' and 'Whitewell Purple', both purple.

Convolvulus sabatius can be used in a rock garden to cover large, bare areas or to trail over rocks where it helps to fuse the various elements of the rock garden together.

Crocus tomasinianus mixes well with many other late-winter flowering plants, such as *Cyclamen coum* and the Winter Aconite *(Eranthis hyemalis)* or with early-flowering shrubs like *Mahonia japonica*.

Crocus vernus

(*Crocus neapolitanus*)
Dutch Crocus (UK and USA)

The species is the parent of the many varieties of Dutch Crocus with large goblet-shaped flowers in a range of colours including lilac, purple and white, often with striking veining. Flowering is during early spring. There are many varieties to choose from and blue or purple ones include 'Queen of the Blues' (lavender-blue), 'Striped Beauty' (dark purple-blue stripes on a silver-white background and with a violet-purple base to the petals) and 'Purpureus Grandiflorus' (purple-blue).

Height: 7.5-13cm (3-5in)
Spread: 4-5cm (1½-2in)
Cultivation: Well-drained soil and a sheltered and sunny position suit it. It can be grown in rock gardens or naturalized in the short, fine grass of an alpine meadow.
Propagation: Lift and divide the corms when the foliage has died down after flowering. Remove the small cormlets and replant them.

Below: **Crocus vernus 'Striped Beauty'** *This Dutch crocus has delicate veining on its large goblet-shaped flowers. The bulbs increase naturally until large drifts are formed if given free-draining soil and a positon where they get plenty of sun.*

Height: 7.5-10cm (3-4in)
Spread: 5-6.5cm (2-2½in)
Cultivation: Ordinary well-drained soil and a sunny, sheltered place free from cold winds are suitable. It is often recommended for naturalizing in short grass, but it does not always do well in such a position and is best planted in the bare soil of rock gardens or under deciduous trees and shrubs. Set the corms 6.5-7.5cm (2½-3in) deep.
Propagation: It will seed and naturalize itself quite readily, especially in bare soil. Alternatively, remove cormlets from around the corms. When replanted, these take two or three years to produce good plants.

Crocus vernus is a perfect match for *Narcissus cyclamineus* 'February Gold', with bright yellow spring flowers, and *Crocus aureus* 'Dutch Gold' which has deep yellow blooms.

ROCK AND NATURALIZED GARDENS

Left: **Cyclamen hederifolium**
This is one of the hardiest and most free-flowering of all cyclamens. The flowers appear from late summer to early winter, growing best under trees where the plant gains shelter and shade.

Edraianthus pumilio

Grassy Bells (USA)

This hardy herbaceous perennial from Yugoslavia is an excellent rock garden plant. It produces clumps of narrow grey-green leaves, and clusters of upturned lavender-blue funnel-shaped flowers during early summer. It is ideal for planting in troughs and stone sinks.
Height 5-7.5cm (2-3in)
Spread: 15-25cm (6-10in)

Cultivation: Well-drained deep soil and a sunny position suit it best.
Propagation: During late winter, sow seeds in small pots of loam-based seed compost and place them in a cold frame. Prick out the seedlings into bigger pots when they are large enough to handle. Alternatively, in late summer, take 5cm (2in) long cuttings and insert them in pots of equal parts peat and sharp sand, placing them in a cold frame. When they are rooted, pot up the cuttings. Plant them in the garden in spring.

Below: **Edraianthus pumilio**
This is an excellent choice for a well-drained scree bed in a rock garden, or for a trough or stone sink. The lavender-blue, funnel-shaped flowers appear in summer.

Cyclamen hederifolium

(*Cyclamen neapolitanum*)
Baby Cyclamen (USA)

An easily-grown, long-lived, free flowering and extremely hardy corm-bearing plant, this cyclamen has deep green leaves, red beneath and with silvery markings above. The variable, mauve to pink, 2.5cm (1in) long flowers appear from late summer to early winter. There is also a white form.
Height: 10cm (4in)
Spread: 10-15cm (4-6in)
Cultivation: Humus-rich, well-drained soil in light, dappled shade suits it best. Plant the corms in late summer, where they can be left undisturbed for many years. It is a long-lived plant and even old corms produce flowers.
Propagation: The corms do not produce offsets, so they must be increased by sowing seeds in late summer, thinly and in pots of loam-based compost. Place the pots in a cold frame or against a wall. When the seedlings are large enough to handle, prick them off into individual pots of a loam-based compost. When they are strong and well-grown, plant them into their final positions.

Cyclamen hederifolium is ideal for naturalizing in bare soil beneath trees, planting on banks, or in a rock garden. If left undisturbed, the plants eventually create large drifts of colour.

Edraianthus pumilio is ideal for a scree bed, where its foliage blends with small stone chippings. Even when grown in a stone sink, it can be given a similar background.

Endymion hispanicus

(*Scilla campanulata · Scilla hispanica*)
Spanish Bluebell (UK)
Spanish Bluebell · Spanish Jacinth · Bell-flowered Squill (USA)

A dominating plant, this bluebell has broad strap-like leaves and blue, pink or white bell-shaped flowers, suspended from upright stems, which appear from spring to mid-summer. Several varieties are available, including 'Excelsior' (deep blue) and 'Myosotis' (clear blue).
Height: 30cm (1ft)
Spread: 15-30cm (6-8in)
Cultivation: Fertile, moist but not boggy soil and an open or slightly shaded position are best.
Propagation: Self-sown seedlings appear if the seeds are allowed to

fall on surrounding soil. Alternatively, lift and divide clumps annually, replanting them immediately as the bulbs do not have outer skins and soon become dry and damaged. The bulbs do not store well, shrivelling if kept too dry.

Right: Erythronium dens-canis
This is a beautiful corm-bearing plant for a moist naturalized garden or the side of an informal pool. It needs shade and a north-facing slope, which help to prevent the soil drying out during summer.

Below Endymion hispanicus *This striking bluebell forms large clumps in moist soil under light shade. When set in light woodland in a wild garden, it creates a carpet of colour from spring to mid-summer.*

Erythronium dens-canis

Dog's-tooth Violet (UK and USA)

This hardy corm-bearing plant for wild gardens has broad lance-shaped leaves blotched with brown or grey. During spring, it displays pink-purple nodding six-petalled 5-7.5cm (2-3in) wide flowers with reflexed petals, resembling those of the Turk's Cap Lily, *Lilium martagon*. Several forms are available, including 'Lilac Wonder' (pale purple) and 'Purple King' (rich purple). White and pink forms are also available.
Height: 15cm (6in)
Spread: 10-15cm (4-6in)
Cultivation: Moisture-retentive but not totally saturated soil is needed. Semi-shade and a north-facing slope are desirable. Set the corms in position in late summer, where they can be left undisturbed for several years to produce a lovely display.
Propagation: The quickest way to increase this plant is by removing offsets in late summer, when the leaves have died down. Place them in a nursery bed for three or four years to develop into plants large enough to be set in the garden. Growing from seed takes five or more years to produce sizeable plants. During this period, keep the nursery bed free from weeds and well watered.

Endymion hispanicus can be planted with a wide range of plants, such as polyanthus, or underneath *Magnolia x soulangiana* with its white chalice-shaped flowers in spring. It also looks good with other bulbous flowers.

Erythroniums are a delight in a moist, naturalized area. Other species useful for creating colour contrast are the American Trout Lily (*E revolutum*), with pink flowers, and *E. tuolumnense,* with bright yellow flowers.

ROCK AND NATURALIZED GARDENS

Gentiana acaulis

(*Gentiana kochiana · G. alpina · G. clusii*)
Trumpet Gentian (UK)
Stemless Gentian (USA)

This is a beautiful hardy perennial for a rock garden, creating early summer colour. The brilliant blue, 5-7.5cm (2-3in) long, trumpet-shaped flowers are near stemless and borne amid mats of glossy, mid-green leaves.
Height: 7.5cm (3in)
Spread: 38-45cm (15-18in)
Cultivation: Heavy, gritty, moisture-retentive but well-drained loam and a sunny position suit it. Set the plants in position during spring.
Propagation: It is easily increased by division of the plants in late spring or early summer.
Alternatively, take 5cm (2in) long cuttings from basal shoots in mid to late spring. Insert them in pots of equal parts peat and sharp sand and place these in a cold frame. Pot up the cuttings, when rooted, into small pots of loam-based. compost and replace in the cold frame. Plant out into the garden during spring of the following year.

Right: Gentiana acaulis
A beautiful but often variable plant for a rock garden, this gentian displays its brilliant blue trumpets in early summer.

Gentiana septemfida

Crested Gentian (USA)

This hardy, reliable and undemanding gentian from Iran and Asia Minor has lance-shaped, mid-green leaves and a profusion of terminal, deep blue flowers from mid to late summer. Each flower is about 4cm (1½in) long and resembles an upturned trumpet.
Height: 20-30cm (8-12in)
Spread: 25-30cm (10-12in)
Cultivation: Any good, rich, moisture-retentive garden soil suits it. Grow it in either full sun or light shade. Fortunately, it is one of the easiest gentians to grow.

Propagation: Good forms are best raised from 5cm (2in) long cuttings taken in spring and inserted in pots of equal parts peat and sharp sand, placed in a cold frame. When the cuttings are rooted, pot them up into small pots and replace in the cold frame until spring of the following year. It can also be increased by sowing seeds in autumn and placing them in a cold frame.

Right: Gentiana septemfida
This is one of the easiest gentians to grow, with an abundance of deep blue upturned trumpet-like flowers from mid to late summer. It is ideal for nestling in a rock garden.

Gentiana acaulis blends with several other rock garden plants, including saxifragas, *Violas cornuta,* the Pasque Flower (*Pulsatilla vulgaris*), *Aster alpinus, Thymus drucei* and *Geranium dalmaticum.*

Gentiana septemfida is superb on its own in a rock-garden pocket, but also combines well with alpine species of gypsophila, such as *Gypsophila cerastioides* and *G. repens,* both with white or pink flowers.

Gentiana sino-ornata

This is an outstanding autumn flowering gentian with 5cm (2in) long, brilliant blue, trumpet-shaped flowers. These are striped with a deeper blue, as well as greenish-yellow. The leaves are narrow, mid-green and rather grass-like, producing a pleasant backcloth for the flowers. This beautiful gentian was discovered by the world-famous plant hunter George Forrest (1873-1932) in 1910-11 in South-west China. On the same expedition Forrest collected seeds of the beautiful shrub *Pieris formosa forrestii*, which was named in his honour.

Height: 15cm (6in)
Spread: 30-34cm (12-18in)
Cultivation: Fertile, deep, peaty acid soil and a shaded position suit it best. Take care that the soil does not dry out during hot summers. Set the plants out in the garden during spring when the soil is warm.
Propagation: The easiest way to increase this plant is by lifting and dividing large clumps in spring.

Ipheion uniflorum

(*Brodiaea uniflora · Milla uniflora Triteleia uniflora*)
Spring Starflower (UK and USA)

This beautiful and reliable bulbous plant forms a hummock of grass-like leaves and 5cm (2in) wide, six-petalled, star-shaped, scented flowers during spring. They range from white to deep lavender-blue in colour. There are several good varieties, including 'Caeruleum' (pale-blue), 'Wisley Blue' (violet-blue) and 'Violaceum' (violet).

Height: 15-20cm (6-8in)
Spread: 7.5-10cm (3-4in), but plants grow together to form a large clump.
Cultivation: Ordinary well-drained garden soil in full sun suits it. A sheltered position is also needed. Plant the bulbs 5cm (2in) deep in autumn.
Propagation: During autumn, lift and divide large clumps, replanting the bulbs immediately so that they do not dry out. You can also do this immediately after flowering.

Right: Gentiana sino-ornata
This beautiful and well-known Chinese and Tibetan gentian is a true delight in autumn, and when seen in a large drift is highly memorable. It needs a soil rich in leafmould. The narrow mid-green leaves provide a perfect foil for the dominantly-coloured, brilliant blue, trumpet-shaped flowers.

Below: Ipheion uniflorum
'Violaceum' *This beautiful form of the Spring Starflower bears lovely six-petalled flowers during spring. It is ideal for creating low hummocks of colour alongside paths, and looks especially attractive at the sides of crazy-paving and gravel paths.*

Gentiana sino-ornata is often difficult to combine with other plants and is therefore best seen on its own, planted as a large, bold splash of colour against a wall or foliage plants.

Ipheion uniflorum makes a welcome early splash of colour in rock gardens or as an edging to paths. In borders it can be combined with deciduous azaleas and *Rhododendron luteum*.

Iris cristata

Dwarf Crested · Iris Crested Iris · Crested Dwarf Iris (USA)

This is a beautiful North American dwarf crested iris for a rock garden. During late spring, it bears 5-6.5cm (2-2½in) wide, lilac-purple flowers, whose white crests are tipped with orange.

Height: 15cm (6in)
Spread: 15-20cm (6-8in)
Cultivation: Slightly moist, fertile soil enriched with leafmould is needed, either slightly acid or neutral. A sheltered position in light shade is desirable.
Propagation: After flowering, lift and divide the plants, replanting the rhizomes immediately.

Below: **Iris cristata** *This dwarf crested iris from the southern states of North America needs slightly acid or neutral soil in light shade. It is well suited to planting in a peat bed.*

Iris gracilipes

This crested iris belongs to the group of irises which have orchid-like flowers with cock's-comb crests instead of beards. This species is hardy, with slender, dark green leaves, and 2.5-5cm (1-2in) wide, lavender-pink flowers, which appear during mid and late spring.
Height: 20-25cm (8-10in)
Spread: 20-25cm (8-10in)
Cultivation: Fertile, moisture-retentive lime-free soil is essential, in a

sheltered and slightly shaded position. To ensure that the soil is rich in humus, top-dress it with well-decomposed compost in spring. Plant the rhizomes in the soil during late spring, just below the surface.
Propagation: It is easily increased by lifting and dividing the rhizomes in late spring. Other crested irises are best lifted, divided and replanted immediately after the flowers have faded, but this beautiful species is the exception to the rule.

Below: **Iris gracilipes**
This small crested iris displays pretty flowers in spring. It is ideal for planting in moist, acid soil, in a sheltered, slightly shaded position.

Iris kaempferi

Japanese Iris (USA)

This beardless iris belongs to a group that delights in moist soil. It displays deeply ribbed, deciduous, deep green leaves, and 10-20cm (4-8in) wide flowers in early summer. Many varieties and strains of this iris have been developed, with colours including blue, reddish-purple, pink and white. Some are completely one colour, while others have a mixture and a few reveal a netting of white or coloured veins.
Height: 60-90cm (2-3ft)
Spread: 45-60cm (1½-2ft)
Cultivation: Moist soil at the edge of an informal pool is best, but the roots

Iris gracilipes is a dwarf iris that is ideal for a sheltered pocket in a rock garden. Alternatively, plant it among small acid-loving shrubs that offer shade and protection for the delicate flowers.

Iris kaempferi forms a bold display at the side of a pool, ideal as a backcloth for the pool itself and for bringing height to the pool surrounds. The large, bright flowers are best grown on their own.

should not be set in the water. Rich soil and an annual mulch of well-rotted compost are aids to success. Plant the rhizomes just below the surface during the spring or autumn.

Propagation: It is easily increased by lifting and dividing the rhizomes immediately flowering is over. At this time the plants can be easily lifted, even from very boggy soil. They must be replanted immediately.

Below: Iris kaempferi *This handsome beardless iris for moist soil at the edges of a pond has been bred in Japan to produce a wide range of flower forms and colours during early summer.*

Above: Iris reticulata 'Jeanine' *This is a reliable bulbous iris for a rock garden or front of a border, flowering in late winter and early spring. It is suitable for chalky soil.*

Iris reticulata

This well-known, small, bulbous iris is ideal for a rock garden or the front of a border. It is now available in a range of colours, but the true species is blue and violet, with or without orange blazes on the falls (the lower, drooping petals). Flowers appear during late winter and early summer. Good forms include 'Cantab' (light blue), 'Clairette' (sky-blue), 'Royal Blue' (deep blue) and 'Jeanine' (violet blue).

Cultivation: Light, well-drained chalky soil in full sun or light shade suits it. Plant fresh bulbs in autumn, covering them with a 5-7.5cm (2-3in) layer of soil. This attractive bulb can also be grown indoors, but the plants should not be taken inside until the flower buds show colour. They are better grown in a cold greenhouse or conservatory.

Propagation: It is easily increased by lifting and dividing large clumps in late summer or early autumn. Large bulbs can be replanted, while smaller ones should be planted in a nursery bed and grown on for a few years until large enough to set out in their final, flowering positions.

Iris reticulata blends with many early spring-flowering plants, such as the Snowdrop (*Galanthus nivalis*), the yellow-flowered shrub *Mahonia japonica* and the Corsican Hellebore (*Helleborus lividus corsicus*).

ROCK AND NATURALIZED GARDENS

Above: Lithodora diffusa 'Grace Ward' *This is a beautiful prostrate plant for a rock garden, cascading over rocks to form a large mat of colour. This form produces intense blue flowers from mid-summer to early autumn.*

Right: Muscari armeniacum
This stunningly attractive blue bulbous plant for spring colour, ideal for naturalizing under deciduous shrubs or as a path edging, is a native of Turkey and the Caucasus.

Below: Pontederia cordata
This eye-catching North American water plant brings height and colour late in summer. Eventually it forms a large clump, with purple-blue flowers.

Lithodora diffusa

(*Lithospermum diffusum*)

This superb hardy, spreading, mat-forming perennial for a rock garden, is often better known by its previous botanical name, even though this has been superseded. The creeping stems are covered with small, oval dark green leaves, and the five-lobed,12mm(1/2in) wide, deep-blue flowers appear from mid-summer to early autumn. Two varieties are widely available: 'Heavenly Blue' (deep blue) and 'Grace Ward' (a beautiful intense blue).
Height: 7.5-10cm (3-4in)
Spread: 45-60cm (1½-2ft)
Cultivation: Light, well-drained, slightly acid soil rich in leafmould or peat suits it best, and a position in full sun will ensure success.
Propagation: It is not easy to increase, the exact time for taking the cuttings being critical. Take 4-6.5cm (1½-2½in) long heel cuttings after the first week in mid-summer. Insert them in boxes of equal parts peat and sharp sand and place in a cold frame. Ensure the compost does not dry out.

Lithodora diffusa can be used with other prostrate plants, such as *Helianthemum nummularium* 'Beech Park Scarlet' and the blue-purple *Campanula portenschlagiana*.

Muscari armeniacum

Grape Hyacinth (UK and USA)

In spring, this well-known hardy bulb has the heads of its stems tightly clustered with bell-like azure-blue to deep purple-blue flowers, which have whitish rims to their mouths. The narrow dark green leaves tend to spread and separate as the flowers appear. Several forms are available, such as 'Cantab' (pale sky blue), 'Heavenly Blue' (bright blue) and 'Blue Spike' (double and mid-blue). It is ideal for planting in large drifts under shrubs or in fine grass. When planted in a rock garden, it needs careful watching as it can soon spread and dominate choice plants.

Height: 18-23cm (7-9in)
Spread: 10-13cm (4-5in)
Cultivation: Any well-drained garden soil in full sun suits it. During late summer or early autumn, plant new bulbs 7.5cm (3in) deep.
Propagation: It often spreads quite easily by self-sown seedlings. Alternatively, large clumps can be lifted and divided when the leaves are yellowing. Replant them immediately.

Pontederia cordata

Pickerel Weed (UK and USA)

This is a hardy and vigorous herbaceous perennial for the edge of a garden pool, in water up to 23cm (9in) deep. The glossy, deep green heart-shaped leaves are borne on stiff, long, upright stems, with 5-10cm (2-4in) long heads of purple-blue flowers during late summer and into early autumn.

Height: 45-75cm (1½-2½ft)
Spread: 30-45cm (1-1½ft)
Cultivation: Rich, fibrous loam and a sunny position are needed, with the rhizomes covered by several inches of water. Planting is best done during late spring or early summer.
Propagation: It is best increased by lifting and dividing the rhizomes in late spring. Take care that they do not dry out. Also, make sure that the roots are submerged deeply until the plants are established.

Muscari armeniacum is a superb companion for Primroses and polyanthus. *Anemone blanda* can be added to this trio, and they can all be set like a multi-coloured ruff around a spring-flowering tree.

Pontederia cordata is ideal for the side of a formal pool, where its foliage spills out over the edges, softening and blending the structured elements with the pool and creating a bright splash of colour.

Primula vialii

A distinctive outdoor primula, this species has a rosette of large pale green narrow lance-shaped leaves and 7.5-13cm (3-5in) long, poker-like, dense spikes of slightly scented lavender-blue flowers during mid-summer.
Height: 20-30cm (8-12in)
Spread: 23-30cm (9-12in)
Cultivation: Moisture-retentive fertile soil and light shade suit it. The soil must not dry out during summer, but at the same time should never be waterlogged.
Propagation: Established plants can be divided and replanted directly after the flowers have faded. However it is often better to sow seeds in summer in loam-based compost and place them in a cold frame. Shade the boxes and subsequent seedlings from strong sunlight. When they are large enough to handle, prick off the seedlings into boxes and replace them in the cold frame. Plant them out into the garden in spring.

Right: Primula vialii This beautiful Chinese primula bears poker-like spikes of slightly-scented lavender-blue flowers in mid-summer. When planted in a large drift, perhaps at the side of an informal garden pool, it is a stunning sight in flower.

Primula denticulata

Drumstick Primula · Drumstick Primrose (UK)

This popular hardy primula produces a dramatic garden display. The pale-green lance-shaped leaves form a compact rosette at its base while during spring and into early summer the stems bear 5-7.5cm (2-3in) wide globular flower heads in colours ranging from deep purple to deep lilac and carmine. A white form 'Alba' is also available, while 'Ruby' is rose-purple.
Height: 23-30cm (9-12in)
Spread: 20-25cm (8-10in)
Cultivation: Moisture-retentive

Above: Primula denticulata This is the well-known Drumstick Primula, with globular heads of flowers during spring and into early summer. It is an excellent and reliable plant for beginners to gardening and seldom fails to attract attention.

loam, enriched with leafmould, and a lightly shaded site are ideal.
Propagation: Sow seeds in mid-summer in pots of loam-based compost and place them in a cold frame. When they are large enough to handle, prick out the seedlings into boxes of compost and plant them out into the garden in autumn.

Puschkinia scilloides

(*Puschkinia libanotica · P. sicula · Adamsia scilloides*)
Striped Squill (UK)

This exceptionally attractive small hardy bulb suits many sites in the garden, from naturalizing in low, fine grass to planting in rock gardens or alongside narrow borders at the bases of walls. The mid-green, strap-like leaves are surmounted by arching stems, bearing up to six, silvery-blue, bell-shaped, 12mm (1/2in) long flowers during spring.
Height: 13-20cm (5-8in)
Spread: 7.5-10cm (3-4in)
Cultivation: Any light garden soil and a position in sun or partial shade

Primula denticulata is an amenable plant that mingles happily with many other spring-flowering types, such as *Anemone blanda*, the Grape Hyacinth (*Muscari armeniacum*), Daffodils and Primroses.

Primula vialii needs careful positioning in a garden, as its distinctive flowers are best not forced to compete with other low-growing plants. It is best given a bed or corner to itself.

Above: Ramonda myconi *A distinctive alpine plant that prefers not to have moisture covering its leaves, Ramonda is therefore happier planted at a slight angle on a slope or between rocks, where it will freely produce its blue flowers.*

Ramonda myconi

(*Ramonda pyrenaica*)

A hardy, dainty-flowered, rosette-forming rock-garden plant with evergreen, deep green, crinkled and rusty-haired leaves. The 2.5-4cm (1-1½in) wide, lavender-blue flowers with golden stamens are borne in late spring, several to a stem.
Height: 10-15cm (4-6in)
Spread: 20-25cm (8-10in)
Cultivation: Well-drained leafmould enriched garden soil and a cool position on the north side of a slope suit it best. Do not allow the soil to dry out. It is also good for planting in rock crevices or between peat blocks.
Propagation: During autumn or early spring, sow seeds in a tray of a loam-based compost and place it in a cold frame. When they are large enough to handle, prick out the seedlings into small pots and replace them in the frame. Plant them out into the garden when they are well established. Alternatively, take leaf-cuttings in mid-summer. They take about six weeks to produce roots. Pot up immediately.

assure success. Plant the bulbs in autumn, 5cm (2in) deep, and leave them where they are for many years.
Propagation: After flowering and when the foliage has died down, lift and divide congested clumps. Remove and dry the bulbs, replanting them in autumn.

Right: Puschkinia scilloides *This attractive bulbous plant produces silvery-blue flowers in spring on arching stems. It tolerates sun or partial shade, and, once planted, can be left undisturbed for many years.*

Puschkinia scilloides displays such soft-coloured flowers that they can be blended with many other rock garden plants. The vivid mauve flowers of *Viola labradorica* are highlighted by puschkinia's flowers.

Ramonda myconi, with its wrinkled rusty-coloured leaves and blue flowers, is so distinctive that it is best given plenty of space to reveal itself. A background of washed shingle helps to show it off even better

ROCK AND NATURALIZED GARDENS

Above: Rhododendron 'Blue Tit'
This dwarf dome-shaped evergreen shrub has funnel-shaped lavender-blue flowers that darken with age. It is ideal for a rock garden creating height and dramatic colour in late spring and early summer.

Rhododendron 'Blue Tit'

A hardy and reliable small-leaved evergreen dwarf rhododendron for a rock garden, peat bank or heather garden. It forms a dense, rounded shrub with small funnel-shaped lavender-blue flowers at the tips of the branches during late spring and into early summer As the flowers age, they become dark blue.
Height: 90cm (3ft)
Spread: 90cm-1.2m (3-4ft)
Cultivation: Moisture-retentive acid soil in light shade under trees is best. To keep the soil moist, mulch the surface with well-decomposed compost in spring.
Propagation: After flowering, take cuttings of young shoots with heels and insert them in pots of peaty compost. Place them in a cold frame and grow on until ready for planting out in the garden.

Scilla sibirica

Siberian Squill (UK and USA)

This popular, hardy, spring-flowering bulbous plant has wide, dark green, strap-shaped leaves, which appear in spring. These are followed by

Above: Scilla sibirica 'Spring Beauty' *These vivid-blue flowers appear in spring, delighting in moist but well-drained soil in a wild garden or boggy area around a pond.*

several stems, each bearing two to five brilliant blue, nodding, bell-shaped flowers. The blue is so dominant that if often appears to overwhelm other plants. It is the form 'Spring Beauty' (often known as 'Atrocaerulea'), with deep blue flowers, that is most often seen.
Height: 13-15cm (5-6in)
Spread: 7.5-10cm (3-4in)
Cultivation: Well-drained but moist soil in full sun or slight shade suits it. Set the bulbs 5-7.5cm (2-3in) deep in late summer.
Propagation: Established clumps can be lifted and divided in autumn; otherwise they are best left alone.

Right: Rhododendron 'Blue Star'
This dominantly coloured dwarf rhododendron creates a bold display. Several other varieties are noted for their flowers, too, including 'Blue Diamond' with clusters of rich lavender-purple flowers in spring. It is slow-growing and only 1m [3-2ft] high.

Right: Scilla tubergeniana
Although its colouring is not so striking as Scilla sibirica *it does form a soil-covering mass of colour and is ideal for planting in rock gardens or under deciduous shrubs, where it brings early colour.*

Many other **blue-flowered rhododendrons** can be used in small gardens, such as 'Blue Diamond' (lavender-blue), 'Blue Chip' (brilliant blue), 'Praecox' (rose-purple) and 'Saint Merryn' (intense blue).

Scilla sibirica is superb for planting under *Daphne mezereum* 'Alba' or among the lilac-flowered carpet provided by a mass planting of the diminutive Violet Cress (*Ionopsidum acaule*).

Above: **Sisyrinchium bermudianum**
This is a beautiful plant for a rock garden, where it readily increases itself by self-sown seedlings which grow in the gaps between paving stones, as well as other inhospitable places in the garden.

Scilla tubergeniana

This attractive hardy bulbous plant from North-west Iran displays its pale blue or white flowers in early spring. At first, the flowers are bell-like, but later they flatten amid wide strap-like glossy bright green leaves. In addition to this species and *Scilla sibirica*, the 23-30cm (9-12in) high Cuban Lily (*Scilla peruviana*) is well worth growing in the border. During early summer, this scilla bears crowded heads of attractive, star-shaped blue flowers.
Height: 7.5-10cm (3-4in)
Spread: 7.5-10cm (3-4in)
Cultivation: Moist but well-drained soil in full sun or light shade suits it best. Plant the bulbs 7.5cm (3in) deep in late summer.
Propagation: Congested clumps can be lifted and divided in autumn. Alternatively, it can be raised from seed, but this takes up to five years to produce flowering-sized plants.

Sisyrinchium bermudianum

Blue-eyed Grass (UK and USA)

A hardy member of the iris family, with stiff and erect narrow grey-green leaves and branched stems. At their tips, the stems bear 12mm (½in) wide, star-shaped, satin-blue, yellow-centred flowers from early summer until late autumn. It is best grown in a rock garden.
Height: 20-25cm (8-10in)
Spread: 15-23cm (6-9in)
Cultivation: Well-drained, humus-enriched garden soil and a sunny position ensure success. In autumn, cut off dead leaves and flowered stems.
Propagation: It tends to readily increase itself by seed, and these seeds can be gathered and potted up for planting out at a later stage when better developed. Bring them on in a cold frame and set them out in the garden when they are growing strongly.

Scilla tubergiana has subtly coloured flowers, and can be mixed with other small bulbs, like the Winter Aconite (*Eranthis hyemalis*) and Snowdrop (*Galanthus nivalis*), without being dominated by or overwhelming them.

Sisyrinchium brachypus is another delightful species, with 18mm (¾in) wide, star-shaped, yellow flowers, borne from early summer onwards on relatively low plants, only 15cm (6in) high.

Tecophilaea cyanocrocus

Chilean Crocus (UK and USA)

This beatiful crocus-like, South American bulbous plant is not fully hardy in temperate regions, but is well worth growing for its gorgeous 4cm (1½in) long flowers, with deep blue to purple petals and white throats, which appear in spring.
Height: 10-13cm (4-5in)
Spread: 13-15cm (5-6in)
Cultivation: In its native Chile, it grows on stony, well-drained slopes. In the garden, therefore, it needs well-drained sandy soil, and a warm and sunny position. It grows outdoors only in mild areas, free from severe frost. In wet climates it needs protection with cloches during winter. Plant the corms in mid-autumn.
Propagation: It is not easily increased and usually the plants produce few cormlets. When grown in a cool greenhouse, the plants can be removed from the pots in autumn and the cormlets potted up.

Veronica teucrium

This hardy alpine veronica forms a clump of upright stems bearing mid to dark green,toothed lance-shaped leaves, with 5-7.5cm (2-3in) long spikes of sky blue flowers during most of summer. Several cultivated varieties are available, which are lower growing than the original species: these include 'Trehane' (golden-yellow leaves and pale blue flowers), 'Shirley Blue' (deep blue flowers) and 'Rosea' (rose-pink flowers and only 15cm (6in) high).
Height: 23-38cm (9-15in)
Spread: 45-60cm (1½-2ft)
Cultivation: Ordinary well-drained garden soil and a sunny position are essential for continued success.
Propagation: During spring, lift and divide large clumps. Alternatively, take cuttings from mid to late summer and insert them in pots of equal parts peat and sharp sand. When they are rooted, pot up the cuttings and overwinter them in a cold frame before planting them out in the garden.

Above: Tecophilaea cyanocrocus
A low-growing rock garden plant that thrives in a well-drained, sheltered and warm position. Excessive moisture in winter will harm it. The richly-coloured, crocus like flowers appear in spring.

Below: Veronica teucrium 'Trehane'
This beautiful rock garden plant has golden-yellow leaves, and bears spires of pale blue flowers during most of summer. Its foliage blends well with rocks, harmonizing with the colour of the stone.

Tecophilaea cyanocrocus is a warmth-loving bulb that does well in situations similar to those needed by the tender South African nerines and the beautiful Algerian Iris *(Iris unguicularis)*, also known as *Iris stylosa*.

Veronica teucrium is ideal for planting at the front of borders as well as rock gardens, especially mixed with yellow and white flowers. In a rock garden it blends well with the lemon-yellow *Hypenicum olympicum* 'Citrinum'.

Above: **Viola cornuta** *This beautiful hardy viola is ideal for well-drained but moist and fertile soil in sun or slight shade. It is perfect for bringing colour to path edges or in rock gardens. There is also a white-flowered form.*

Viola cornuta

Horned Violet (UK and USA)

A reliable, lusty and robust violet from the Pyrenees, the Horned Violet bears lavender or violet-coloured flowers that provide early or mid-summer colour. The 2.5cm (1 in) wide, spurred flowers are borne above the mid-green, oval leaves, which have rounded teeth. Several forms are available, including 'Minor' (lavender-blue), 'Jersey Gem' (blue-purple) and 'Alba' (white).

Height: 10-30cm (4-12in)
Spread: 30-38cm (12-15in)
Cultivation: Fertile, well-drained but moist soil in full sun or slight shade suits it best. Pick off dead flowers to encourage the development of further blooms.
Propagation: During spring or summer, sow seeds 6mm (¼in) deep in a prepared seedbed outdoors. When large enough to handle, thin the seedlings to 25-30cm (10-12in) apart. In autumn, transfer to flowering positions.

Further plants to consider

Meconopsis betonicifolia
(*Meconopsis baileyi*)
Himalayan Blue Poppy (UK) Blue Poppy (USA)
Height: 90cm-1.5m (3-5ft)   Spread: 45cm (1½ft)
A distinctive hardy herbaceous perennial for a moist, shaded area, producing 6.5-7.5cm (2½-3in) wide, sky blue flowers during mid-summer.

Meconopsis grandis
Height: 45-60cm (1½-2ft)   Spread: 45cm (1½ft)
A hardy herbaceous perennial for a moist and lightly-shaded area, bearing 10-13cm (4-5in) wide, rich blue to purple flowers during early summer.

Meconopsis quintuplinervia
Harebell Poppy (UK and USA)
Height: 23-30cm (9-12in)   Spread: 30-38cm (12-15in)
A spreading dwarf perennial, with mid-green leaves and 5cm (2in) wide, nodding, lavender-blue or purple flowers during early summer.

Mertensia virginica
Virginian Cowslip (UK)
Bluebells · Virginia Bluebell · Virginia Cowslip · Roanoke-bells (USA)
Height: 30-60cm (1-2ft)   Spread: 45cm (1½ft)
A hardy herbaceous perennial with blue-grey, lance-shaped leaves and pendulous clusters of purple-blue flowers in early summer.

Omphalodes verna
Blue-eyed Mary (UK) Creeping Forget-me-not (USA)
Height: 13-15cm (5-6in)   Spread: 30-38cm (12-15in)
A spreading herbaceous perennial for a rock garden or woodland. From early spring to early summer, it bears white-throated, bright blue flowers, 12mm (½in) wide.

Primula juliae
Height: 7 5-10cm (3-4in)   Spread: 25-30cm (10-12in)
A delightful mat-forming primula with yellow-eyed, 18mm (¾in) wide, reddish-purple flowers in spring and early summer.

Primula marginata
Height: 10-13cm (4-5in)   Spread: 20-25cm (8-10in)
A beautiful alpine primula with grey-green, silver-edged leaves and numerous heads of 18-25mm (¾-1in) wide, fragrant, lavender-blue flowers in spring. The form 'Linda Pope' has deep lavender-blue flowers.

Pulsatilla vulgaris
(*Anemone pulsatilla*)
Pasque Flower (UK and USA)
Height: 25-30cm (10-12in)   Spread: 30-38cm (12-15in)
A beautiful and highly memorable hardy herbaceous perennial with mid-green, fern-like leaves and 5-7.5cm (2-3in) wide, cup-shaped, purple flowers with bright centres during spring and early summer.

Viola cornuta is robust enough to be set at the front of border with a backing of white flowers. Alternatively, position it in a rock garden, where it can trail over the rocks and merge with other plants.

ROCK AND NATURALIZED GARDENS

Right: Achillea tomentosa
This delightful herbaceous perennial has mats of fern-like leaves and tightly-packed flower heads during mid to late summer. It needs well-drained soil and a sunny position.

Achillea tomentosa

This is a bright, dwarf herbaceous perennial for the rock garden, crevices between natural stone paths and in dry stone walls. It displays long, softly hairy and fern-like grey-green leaves which form prostrate mats. Densely-packed heads of bright yellow flowers, 7.5cm (3in) wide, appear on 15cm (6in) long stems during mid to late summer.
Height: 15-18cm (6-7in)
Spread: 25-30cm (10-12in)
Cultivation: Achilleas need a well-drained soil and a sunny position. Avoid damp conditions which encourage slugs to graze on the foliage.
Propagation: The easiest way to increase this plant is by division of the roots in autumn or spring. Spring is the best time, as autumn-divided plants need to be overwintered in a cold frame. Alternatively, take soft cuttings in mid-summer and place in sandy compost in pots in a cold frame.

Alyssum saxatile

Gold Dust · Golden Tuft · Rock Madwort (UK)

This well-known shrubby evergreen perennial has a tumbling and cascading growth habit, making it ideal for covering dry stone walls. Its grey-green leaves are lance-shaped, with 10-15cm (4-6in) wide heads of golden-yellow flowers in early summer. Several superb forms are widely available, including 'Dudley Neville', with biscuit-yellow flowers, and 'Citrinum', with bright lemon-yellow flowers.
Height: 23-30cm (9-12in)
Spread: 30-45cm (1-1½ft)
Cultivation: Ordinary garden soil,

Achillea tomentosa is ideal for setting between natural paving slabs or in crevices at the top of dry stone walls. In a rock garden, sprinkle stone chippings around the plant for an attractive background and good drainage.

Alyssum saxatile can be used in combination with many other plants, from the biennial Forget-me-not Polyanthus, the bulbous *Chionodoxa luciliae* and Grape Hyacinth to the rock-garden Aubrietia.

well-drained, and a position in full sun are needed. After flowering, cut the plants back to encourage the development of young growths.
Propagation: Named types do not come true from seed and are therefore best raised by taking 5-7.5cm (2-3in) long cuttings in summer. Insert them into equal parts peat and sharp sand. When the plants are rooted, pot them up into loam-based compost and replace in a cold frame. Plant out into the garden in spring. The young plants are best set out in their new positions in spring, though this can be done in late summer in mild areas.

Left: Alyssum saxatile **'Dudley Neville'** *This beautiful shrubby perennial has biscuit-yellow flowers which cascade down walls in early summer like a coloured waterfall. Other forms are brighter.*

Cedrus deodara 'Golden Horizon'

This semi-prostrate slow-growing evergreen conifer is often twice as wide as it is high. It has graceful, pendulous, golden-leaved branches, and as the dwarf tree matures, it resembles a golden cascade.
Height: 60-75cm (2-2½ft)
Spread: 75-1.2m (2½-4ft)
Cultivation: Well-drained garden soil suits it – it will do well even in coastal areas.
Propagation: It is a grafted form, so its propagation is best left to expert nurserymen.

Below: Cedrus deodara 'Golden Horizon' *This beautiful slow-growing evergreen conifer produces a cascading array of golden foliage. Its spread is frequently up to twice its height.*

Above: Chamaecyparis lawsoniana 'Aurea Densa' *This dense, slow-growing dwarf conifer is ideal for rock gardens, containers and stone sinks. It can also be planted among small ericas and heathers.*

Chamaecyparis lawsoniana 'Aurea Densa'

A densely-foliaged slow-growing dwarf evergreen conifer, this tree is ideal for rock gardens and containers. It has a dome-shaped habit, with bright golden-yellow foliage. After ten years, it reaches about 30-50cm (12-20in) high and 25-38cm (10-15in) wide.
Height: 90cm-1m (3-3½ft)
Spread: 75-90cm (2½-3ft)
Cultivation: Well-drained garden soil is essential for success, and a position in full sun to help maintain the golden-yellow foliage.
Propagation: Take 10cm (4in) long heel cuttings in spring, inserting them into equal parts peat and sharp sand. Place them in a cold frame and, when rooted, pot up into small pots. Plunge them into soil in a nursery bed and plant them out into a sheltered bed in autumn for a few years.

Cedrus deodara 'Golden Horizon' is ideal in a heather garden, surrounded by prostrate colour-contrasting conifers. Alternatively, place it between blue-foliaged upright conifers, such as *Picea pungens* 'Hoopsii' or *Picea pungens* 'Koster'.

Chamaecyparis lawsoniana 'Aurea Densa' is ideal for a small collection of dwarf and slow-growing conifers, and looks attractive when positioned among prostrate blue-foliaged junipers such as *Juniperus horizontalis* 'Blue Moon'.

ROCK AND NATURALIZED GARDENS

and plunge these into soil in a nursery bed. During autumn, put the young plants into a nursery bed for three or four years before setting them out in their permanent positions. It is often confused with *C.l.* 'Aurea Densa', which has a compact habit and golden-yellow foliage arranged in short, densely-packed and flattened sprays. In *C.l.* 'Minima Aurea' the sprays of foliage are mainly arranged vertically. Both, however, are ideal conifers for a rock garden.

Left: **Chamaecyparis lawsoniana 'Minima Aurea'** *A beautifully-foliaged dwarf conifer, it also has an attractive shape. The golden-yellow foliage remains bright throughout the year and grows in a distinctive vertical pattern.*

Below: **Chamaecyparis pisifera 'Filifera Aurea'** *A slow-growing conifer, this variety is prized for its thread-like golden foliage which droops at its tips and gives a weeping appearance. Eventually, it will develop into a pretty large tree.*

Chamaecyparis lawsoniana 'Minima Aurea'

An attractive, slow-growing, evergreen conifer with a rounded form and vertically-arranged, scale-like, golden-yellow leaves, it reaches 50cm (20in) high and 40cm (16in) wide. It is ideal for planting in a rock garden.
Height: 1m (3½ft)
Spread: 80cm (32in)
Cultivation: This conifer needs ordinary well-drained garden soil and a position in the open. It does best in full sun, which helps to maintain the golden foliage.
Propagation: During spring, take 10cm (4in) long heel cuttings, inserting them into equal parts peat and sharp sand and placing them in a cold frame. When rooted, pot them up into small pots

Chamaecyparis lawsoniana 'Minima Aurea' looks superb on its own in a rock garden, or in a heather garden where it can be set in threes in a sea of white-flowered ericas. Set them several feet apart so that their shapes are not impaired.

Chamaecyparis pisifera 'Filifera Aurea'

This distinctive slow-growing evergreen conifer has thread-like golden foliage which trails at its tips, giving it a weeping appearance. It has a mop-head, somewhat conical shape. It is ideal for setting in a large rock garden or in a heather garden. After ten years it will reach 1m (3½ft) high, with a spread of 1.2m (4ft). Several other forms of this species are a delight in the rock garden. These include the conical *C.p.* 'Plumosa Aurea Nana' with a height of 90cm (3ft) and a 60cm (2ft) spread. It retains its golden colour throughout the year. *C.p.* 'Nana Aureovariegata' is another lovely form, with golden variegated foliage. Other golden forms include *C.p.* 'Squarrosa Sulphurea' with a rounded form and bright sulphur-yellow foliage, and *C.p.* 'Gold Spangle' with an open but rounded form and bright golden foliage. It is especially attractive in winter.
Height: 4.5m (15ft)
Spread: 4.5-5.4m (15-18ft)

Cultivation: Well-drained garden soil, and a position in full sun are needed.
Propagatlon: During spring, take 7.5-10cm (3-4in) long cuttings from side-shoots, insert them into pots of equal parts of peat and sharp sand and place these in a cold frame. Pot up the cuttings when rooted, and eventually set them in a nursery bed for three or four years, until they are large enough to be planted in the garden.

Above: Cytisus x beanii
This dwarf broom is ideal where it can tumble over rocks or dry stone walls and display its pea-shaped yellow flowers in late spring and early summer. It delights in a sunny position and well-drained but not very rich soil.

Cytisus x beanii
Broom (UK and USA)

A beautiful hybrid broom, this is a semi-prostrate deciduous shrub. During late spring and early summer, its yellow pea-like flowers are produced in ones, twos or threes on the previous year's shoots. The leaves are narrow, hairy and mid-green.
Height: 45-60cm (1½-2ft)
Spread: 75-90cm (2½-3ft)
Cultivation: Well-drained garden soil in full sun is best. Do not plant this cytisus in rich soil. Always use pot-grown plants, because it dislikes root disturbance. No regular pruning is needed.
Propagation: During late summer, take 5-9cm (2-3½in) long heel cuttings, inserting them into equal parts peat and sharp sand. Place the pots in a cold frame and, when the cuttings are rooted, pot them up into a sandy loam-based compost. Plunge the pots into a sheltered part of the garden and plant them out either in late spring or early autumn.

Chamaecyparis pisifera 'Filifera Aurea' is suitable for a prime position in a heather garden. Its strong colour, attractive foliage shape and eventual size make it an ideal focal point.

Cytisus x beanii is ideal for bringing colour and height to a rock garden. When trailing over a drystone wall, it relieves the flatness of its top. Retaining walls alongside paths often present the.best sites.

Eranthis hyemalis

Winter Aconite (UK and USA)

This distinctively-flowered, tuberous-rooted plant blooms late in winter, often amid snow. The 2.5cm (1in) wide, buttercup-like, lemon-yellow flowers appear with a ruff of pale green leaves. They are borne on stiff, near upright stems which rise from pale green and deeply-cut leaves.

Height: 10cm (4in)
Spread: 7.5-10cm (3-4in)
Cultivation: Winter Aconite needs a well-drained but moisture-retentive soil in full sun or partial shade. Heavy loams often provide the best conditions. Set the tubers 2.5cm (1in) deep in late summer.
Propagation: Lift the tubers as soon as the plant dies down and cut them into sections. Replant 7.5cm (3in) apart. Alternatively, sow fresh seed in seed compost. It also produces self-sown seedlings that can be replanted.

Erythronium tuolumnense

This beautiful corm-bearing plant has nodding, yellow, turk's-cap flowers during late spring. Each flower has six-pointed petals. The bright green, glossy, spatula-shaped leaves arise from soil-level, and provide a superb background for the yellow flowers.

Height: 15-30cm (6-12in)
Spread: 13-15cm (5-6in)
Cultivation: Fertile, moisture-retentive soil with a north-facing slope is best. Plant the corms in late summer. It is essential that the soil does not dry out. To ensure this, add peat, leafmould or garden compost before planting.
Propagation: It can be raised from seed, but this method often takes several years to produce flowering plants. The best way for home gardeners to increase this plant is by removing offsets in summer as the leaves die down. Put the offsets in a nursery bed for a few years until they reach flowering size, then plant them out.

Eranthis hyemalis is ideal for a corner in the rock garden, perhaps among stone chippings which help to prevent soil being splashed on them during heavy rain storms. Eranthis mixes well with Snowdrops (*Galanthus hyemalis*).

Erythronium tuolumnense is a wild garden plant, blending well with Wake Robin (Trillium grandiflorum) and the *Rhododendron* 'Blue Tit' which has lovely funnel-shaped lavender-blue flowers.

Left: **Eranthis hyemalis**
This ground-hugging tuberous plant has distinctive large, buttercup-like flowers with ruffs of pale green leaves. It grows best in heavy loams which do not dry out in spring or summer.

Euryops acraeus

A beautiful miniature evergreen shrub from the Drakensberg Mountains in Lesotho, southern Africa, euryops is an upright plant, densely clothed in summer in bright silver leaves and pure gold daisy-like flowers on short grey stems. It is often wrongly called *Euryops evansii*. It was once thought to be tender and was restricted to alpine houses. However, it will grow perfectly well in a well-drained site in a rock garden.
Height: 25-30cm (10-12in)
Spread: 45-60cm (1½-2ft)
Cultivation: Euryops likes ordinary well-drained garden soil and a position in full sun.
Propagation: Cuttings of non-flowering shoots can be taken in summer and inserted in sandy compost. However, it is easier and quicker to detach suckers from around the base of the plant. Pot them up in a well-drained sandy compost and place the pots in a cold frame until the plants are large enough to be set out in the garden.

Far-left: **Erythronium tuolumnense** *This corm-bearing plant delights in moist soil and shade, producing yellow flowers in late spring. It likes to be left undisturbed, so a wild garden setting is best. It can be planted in an informal group with other erythroniums.*

Left: **Euryops acraeus**
This beautiful low-growing evergreen shrub for the rock garden has silvery foliage. The large, pure-gold, daisy-like flowers appear during summer, forming a handsome combination with the striking leaves.

Euryops acraeus grows well in hot places: a scree-bed on a hot, dry slope suits it well, and its silvery foliage is highlighted by the stone chippings. The foliage is also attractive when set with dark-green-leaved plants.

ROCK AND NATURALIZED GARDENS

Genista lydia

Bulgarian Broom (UK)

A hummock-forming dwarf deciduous shrub. During late spring and early summer, it has bright golden-yellow, pea-shaped flowers on arching or prostrate, slender, five-angled, glabrous green shoots. The grey-green leaves are very narrow. It is ideal for a large rock garden, or for trailing over banks and low walls.

Height: 60-90cm (2-3ft)

Spread: 1.2-1.8m (4-6ft)

Cultivation: Genista does well in well-drained light soil in full sun, but it even succeeds in poor soils.

Propagation: During late summer, take 5-7.5cm (2-3in) long heel cuttings and insert them into pots of equal parts peat and sharp sand. Place these in a cold frame. When the plants are rooted, pot them up into free-draining sandy compost and plunge the pot in soil in a well-drained corner of the garden. Plant into the garden in autumn or spring.

Right: **Genista lydia** *The beautiful pea-shaped, golden-yellow flowers appear in late spring and early summer on this low-growing deciduous shrub. It is well suited to a large rock garden.*

Left: **Genista pilosa prostrata** *This useful prostrate deciduous shrub has ground-hugging shoots, and small broom-like yellow flowers in late spring and early summer. It is essential to provide free-draining soil and a sunny position.*

Genista pilosa

This distinguished, ground-hugging, deciduous shrub has procumbent shoots when young, later becoming an attractive tangled mass of slender twiggy shoots. During late spring and early summer, it reveals small pea-shaped yellow flowers. A prostrate, ground-hugging form is also available which grows no more

---

Genista lydia looks best when cascading over a low wall, perhaps from a high position on a rock garden. Set colourful and low growing plants, such as helianthemums and campanulas, beneath its waterfall-like shoots.

Genista pilosa is a delight when set at the top of a low wall where its shoots can trail over the top. Plant small dry-wall plants below it to continue the interest and colour for a longer period.

Genista sagittalis
(Chamaespartium sagittale)

This curious and unusual hardy shrub acquires the character of an evergreen plant from its unusual winged branches. The leaves themselves are scattered and few. Small, yellow, pea-like flowers appear in summer. It is an excellent ground-cover plant.

Height: 10-15cm (4-6in)
Spread: 45-60cm (1½-2ft)
Cultivation: Most garden soils suit it, as long as they are well-drained, light and in a sunny position, but it will even grow in poor soils. No pruning is needed, other than the occasional cutting back of intrusive shoots.
Propagation: During summer, take soft cuttings, inserting them around the edge of a 13-15cm (5-6in) clay pot containing a mixture of four parts sharp sand and one part peat. Next spring, when they are rooted, pot them up and plant out the following autumn.

Below: **Genista sagittalis**
This excellent prostrate shrub produces pea-like yellow flowers in summer. Its winged shoots are an attractive bonus, with the true leaves scattered and few, and small and hairy when young.

than 7.5cm (3in) high, and 90cm-1.2m (3-4ft) wide. Both types are ideal for a rock garden.
Height: 38-45cm (15-18in)
Spread: 60-90cm (2-3ft)
Cultivation: Any ordinary garden soil that is not too rich and has good drainage is suitable. Choose a sunny position. Cut out congested shoots after flowering.
Propagation: During late summer take 5-7.5cm (2-3in) long heel cuttings and insert them into pots of equal parts peat and sharp sand. Place these in a cold frame. When the cuttings are rooted, pot them up into free-draining sandy compost and plunge the pots in soil in a well-drained corner of the garden. During autumn or spring, set the plants in the garden.

Genista sagittalis is ideal as a ground-cover shrub filling large spaces between rocks. Another ground-hugging shrub is *Genista delphinensis*, the most prostrate of all brooms, only 2.5-5cm (1-2in) high, with bright yellow flowers in mid-summer.

ROCK AND NATURALIZED GARDENS

Juniperus communis 'Depressa Aurea'

This is a dwarf, wide-spreading and prostrate evergreen conifer with needle-like foliage. In spring, the leaves are bright butter-yellow, remaining golden all summer and dulling to bronze in autumn. In ten years it will grow 30cm (1ft) high and 1.2m (3ft) wide.
Height: 30-45cm (1-1½ft)
Spread: 2.4-3m (8-10ft)
Cultivation: This juniper needs good, well-drained soil in full sun. Like all golden-leaved conifers, it requires good light to ensure that the foliage remains bright.
Propagation: During late summer, take heel cuttings 5-10cm (2-4in)

Above: Iris innominata
This rhizome-bearing perennial iris prefers humus-rich soil, it dislikes lime. Flower colour can vary from plant to plant. Selected forms are best increased by division of the underground rhizomes.

Iris innominata

This rhizome-bearing iris comes originally from North America. Its long, narrow, dark green leaves are evergreen, and the stems bear one or two beardless flowers during early and mid-summer. They are 5-6.5cm (2-2½ in) wide and in a range of colours, including cream, buff, yellow and orange. The plant forms a wide-spread clump.
Height: 15-25cm (6-10in)
Spread: 25-38cm (10-15in)
Cultivation: This plants delights in neutral or slightly acid soil, thriving in a peat bed. It also grows well in a pocket of fertile and humus-rich soil in a rock garden. It will do well in full sun or light shade.
Propagation: Sow seeds in autumn or spring in a loam-based seed compost, keeping them at 7°C (45°F). Prick out the seedlings into small pots. Use small plants, because large ones do not transplant easily. Good forms can be increased by detaching pieces of the rhizomes in autumn.

Iris innominata needs a roomy site in the rock garden. Setting stone chippings around the plant shows off the attractive dark green and narrow leaves. Do not set other plants too close, or they may spoil its rounded shape.

Juniperus communis 'Depressa Aurea' is well suited to a rock garden. If positioned at the bottom of a slight slope, its beautiful foliage can be admired from above; planted by the side of a pond, it is a delight.

long, inserting them into pots of equal parts peat and sharp sand. Place these in a cold frame until the plants are rooted, then set them out in a nursery bed for a couple of years before planting them in the garden. When setting them out, remember that ultimately they will have a wide spread. Do not position them where they will eventually have to be pruned severely and their shape ruined.

Below: **Juniperus communis 'Depressa Aurea'** *A prostrate juniper with golden foliage, its shoots spread out just above soil-level, forming a dense shrub. In time it forms a golden carpet up to 3m (10ft) wide.*

Above: **Juniperus x media 'Old Gold'** *A well-known, wide-spreading slow-growing conifer, this variety retains its golden foliage throughout the year. Its ascending branches give it the appearance of a golden explosion.*

Juniperus x media 'Old Gold'

This is an old and trusted semi-prostrate compact evergreen conifer. It has golden scale-like leaves which remain bright throughout the year. In ten years, it should reach 70cm (28in) high and 1.5m (5ft) wide.
Height: 1.8m (6ft)
Spread: 2.4m (8ft)
Cultivation: Well-drained garden soil and a position in full sun or slight shade are required. Good light ensures continuity of golden foliage throughout the year. It is a distinctive conifer and should not be cramped by other plants.
Propagation: During late summer, take heel cuttings 5-10cm (2-4in) long, inserting them into pots of equal parts peat and sharp sand. Place these in a cold frame until the cuttings are rooted, then set them out in nursery beds for a couple of years before planting them in their final positions.

Juniperus x media 'Old Gold' is superb for a junction between two paths or for creating a focal point in a heather garden. Its foliage also contrasts handsomely with paving slabs on a patio.

ROCK AND NATURALIZED GARDENS

Narcissus bulbocodium

Hoop Petticoat Daffodil (UK and USA)

This is a delicate bulbous plant with funnel-shaped, crinoline-like yellow flower trumpets, 2.5cm (1in) wide. These have tapering and slightly spiky petals. These appear during late winter and early spring. It is especially useful for naturalizing in an alpine meadow among fine grasses. Alternatively, it can be grown in soil pockets in a rock garden.
Height: 10-15cm (4-6in)
Spread: 10-13cm (4-5in)
Cultivation: Free-draining but moisture-retentive soil and slight shade are needed. Avoid soils which dry out in spring. Set the bulbs in holes three times their own depth in late summer. If setting them in grass, first spread out the bulbs irregularly on the grass and plant them where they lie. This helps to create a natural arrangement.
Propagation: Congested clumps can be lifted and replanted every three or four years.

Narcissus cyclamineus

This eye-catching miniature narcissus has bright, rich-yellow, tube-like trumpets, and petals completely swept back. It flowers in late winter and early spring. Like *Narcissus bulbocodium*, it can be naturalized in short, fine grass, or planted in sheltered corners in a rock garden.
Height: 15-20cm (6-8in)
Spread: 10cm (4in)
Cultivation: This narcissus prefers a moist, but not waterlogged, soil in slight shade. Plant the bulbs in late summer, setting them in holes three times their own depth.
Propagation: Lift, divide and replant congested clumps in summer, but do not thin out the bulbs too much; dominant clumps look best.

Narcissus bulbocodium can be harmonized with other spring-flowering plants, such as the Winter-flowering Jasmine (*Jasminium nudiflorum*) and the early spring purplish-pink *Rhododendron* 'Tessa'.

Narcissus cyclamineus is attractive when planted in short grass, with random clumps of a pink winter-flowering heather set behind it. Varieties of *Erica herbacea* (*E. carnea*) are ideal choices for this purpose.

Left: Narcissus bulbocodium
This is the Hoop Petticoat Daffodil, a small, delicate bulb with late winter and early spring flowers which resemble crinolines. It is excellent for naturalizing in areas covered by short, fine grass.

Right: Portulaca grandiflora
This beautiful rock garden or border flower is ideal for poor, dry soils. During summer, it displays saucer-shaped flowers in a range of colours, including yellow.

Below: Narcissus cyclamineus
A distinctive early, spring-flowering dwarf narcissus, ideal for naturalizing in short grass. It also does well alongside streams.

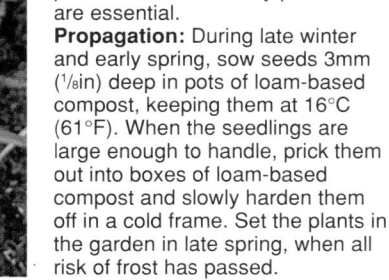

Portulaca grandiflora

Sun Plant (UK) · Rose Moss · Sun Plant · Eleven-O'Clock (USA)

An unusual, half-hardy succulent annual, the Sun Plant has narrow, fleshy, cylindrical bright green leaves and semi-prostrate, sprawling reddish stems. From early to late summer, it bears 2.5cm (1in) wide saucer-shaped red, purple or yellow flowers with bright yellow stamens. There are several varieties, extending the colour range to pink, crimson orange and white. The F1 forms display double, rose-like flowers. It is ideal for a rock garden or border, and is also useful for filling gaps in any sunny position.
Height: 15-23cm (6-9in)
Spread: 6-20cm (6-8in)
Cultivation: Well-drained – even poor – soil and a sunny position are essential.
Propagation: During late winter and early spring, sow seeds 3mm (1/8in) deep in pots of loam-based compost, keeping them at 16°C (61°F). When the seedlings are large enough to handle, prick them out into boxes of loam-based compost and slowly harden them off in a cold frame. Set the plants in the garden in late spring, when all risk of frost has passed.

Above: Solidago brachystachys
This unusual miniature Golden Rod, rarely exceeds 15cm (6in) high, with golden-yellow flowers held in clusters during late summer and early autumn.

Alternatively, sow seeds 6mm (1/4in) deep in late spring where the plants are to flower. Thin out the seedlings to 15cm (6in) apart.

Solidago brachystachys

(*Solidago cutleri*)
Dwarf Golden Rod (UK)

This unusual, hardy herbaceous Golden Rod has mid green, lance-shaped leaves and golden-yellow flowers borne in clusters during late summer and into early autumn. Its low, slightly sprawling nature makes it ideal for a rock garden.
Height: 15cm (6in)
Spread: 30-38cm (12-15in)
Cultivation: Any good garden soil will do, but it must be well drained and in sun or slight shade.
Propagation: During spring lift and divide established clumps. Replant the young pieces from around the outside, discarding old parts. They will produce self-sown seedlings, but avoid growing these as they do not resemble the parents.

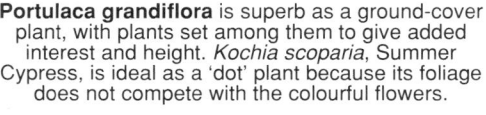

Portulaca grandiflora is superb as a ground-cover plant, with plants set among them to give added interest and height. *Kochia scoparia*, Summer Cypress, is ideal as a 'dot' plant because its foliage does not compete with the colourful flowers.

Solidago brachystachys does well with a sprinkling of stone chippings around it. This helps to prevent soil splashing on to the foliage during heavy rain storms, as well as creating an attractive and interesting background.

ROCK AND NATURALIZED GARDENS

Sternbergia lutea

Yellow Star Flower · Winter Daffodil · Lily of the Field (UK)
Winter Daffodil · Lily of the Field (USA)

This well-known bulb-bearing rock garden plant bears goblet-shaped, shining waxy-yellow flowers up to 5cm (2in) long, in late summer and into early autumn. The strap-shaped, deep green leaves remain small and immature until the following spring.
Height: 10-15cm (4-6in)
Spread: 10-13cm (4-5in)
Cultivation: Well-drained soil and a sunny position are needed. Leave the bulbs undisturbed for as long as possible. Set new bulbs 10-15cm (4-6in) deep in late summer.
Propagation: Lift congested clumps in late summer, dividing and replanting them as soon as possible. Offset bulbs often take two years before producing flowers.

Taxus baccata 'Repens Aurea'

This is a low, prostrate, slow-growing evergreen conifer with dense foliage. Each leaf is green, with gold edges. The gold is pale in spring, gradually deepening during summer. The spreading branches have attractive drooping tips. In ten years, it will have grown about 35cm (4ft) high and 1m (3¹/₂ft) wide.
Height: 90cm (3ft)
Spread: 3m (10ft)
Cultivation: Well-drained soil in full sun suits it best. Indeed, if grown in shade, it soon loses its beautiful colour, so ensure it gets plenty of light.
Propagation: During late summer or early autumn, take 7.5-10cm (3-4in) long heel cuttings. Insert them into equal parts peat and sharp sand and place these in a cold frame. When the cuttings are rooted, plant them out in a nursery bed for a couple of years before setting them in the garden.

Above: Sternbergia lutea
A distinctive late-flowering bulb which looks like a crocus and produces a welcome display of brilliant yellow flowers, it is ideal for bringing late colour to the corner of a rock garden.

Below: Taxus baccata 'Repens Aurea' *It is essential that this attractive prostrate yew with bright green and gold foliage is planted in full sun if it is to keep its bright variegated colouring.*

Sternbergia lutea, with its dominantly-coloured flowers, needs to be set in a passive, non-conflicting setting. A backcloth of green or grey foliage will provide the right setting.

Taxus baccata 'Repens Aurea' needs a neighbour of contrasting colour and shape. Blue or dark-green foliaged conifers are best; if you want this golden yew to have a domed appearance, trim it with shears.

Thuja orientalis 'Aurea Nana'

This attractively rounded, slow-growing, evergreen dwarf conifer has vertical plates of yellow-green, scale-like leaves which turn gold in winter. In ten years it will reach 60cm (2ft) high, with a spread of 50cm (20in).
Height: 1m (3½ft)
Spread: 75-90cm (2½-3ft)
Cultivation: Deep, moist but not continually saturated garden soil, and a position in full sun assure success. In shady areas it will be a disappointment, with dull green foliage instead of yellow.
Propagation: During late summer or early autumn, take 5-10cm (2-4in) long cuttings, inserting them into pots of equal parts peat and sharp sand. Place these in a cold frame and, when the cuttings are rooted, plant them out in a nursery bed for a couple of years before transferring them to the garden.

Above: **Thuja orientalis 'Aurea Nana'** *This beautifully-shaped, slow-growing compact conifer has yellow-green scale-like leaves which turn gold in winter. It needs full sun to keep its colouring.*

Below: **Thuja plicata 'Rogersii'** *This beautiful dwarf conifer has dense foliage, green with golden edges. In winter, this turns bronze and remains attractive throughout that too often dull period.*

Thuja plicata 'Rogersii'

This dwarf slow-growing conical evergreen conifer has a lovely yellow glow. The fine foliage is packed in tight green clusters, with the edges of the scale-like leaves a rich golden-yellow. In winter the leaves become bronze. It is ideal for rock gardens, scree beds and for mixing in heather collections. It is so slow-growing that in ten years it will reach only 70cm (28in) high and 40cm (16in) wide.
Height: 1m (3½ft)
Spread: 90cm (3ft)
Cultivation: Ordinary garden soil is suitable, but it must not become dry during summer. A sheltered position in full sun also suits it.
Propagation: During late summer or early autumn, take 5-10cm (2-4in) long cuttings and put them into pots of equal parts peat and sharp sand. Place these in a cold frame and, when the cuttings are rooted, plant them out into a nursery bed for a couple of years before you set them in the garden.

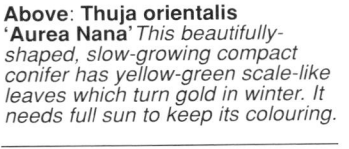

Thuja orientalis 'Aurea Nana' is excellent for a rock garden or small heather collection. Prostrate conifers with colour-contrasting colours can be set near it. In a rock garden, small spring bulbs give added interest.

Thuja plicata 'Rogersii' looks especially good when set with stone chippings around it. The changing light patterns of the chippings pick up the colours in the thuja. This is especially effective in full sun.

ROCK AND NATURALIZED GARDENS

Above: **Tropaeolum polyphyllum**
This spectacular, tuberous-rooted rock garden plant from South America has long stems clothed in grey leaves and yellow flowers during mid-summer. It tends to die down when flowering is over.

Tropaeolum polyphyllum

This distinctive tuberous-rooted, ground-hugging herbaceous perennial has lobed grey-green leaves on arching stems. The large, rich yellow flowers, 12mm (½in) wide, appear on stems arising from the leaf joints during early and mid-summer. The whole plant often dies down after flowering, and is likely to come up in a different position the following year.
Height: 7.5-10cm (3-4in)
Spread: 90cm-1.2m (3-4ft)
Cultivation: Plant the tubers during spring, in friable soil, at a depth of 25-30cm (10-12in). Position them so that the plants will trail naturally, preferably over a large rock. It delights in a warm and sunny position, although it also grows in light shade.
Propagation: Once established, propagation is very easy. Just dig up the tubers in spring, replanting them before they dry out.

Tulipa sylvestris

This bulbous, easily grown tulip species has narrow grey-green leaves and scented yellow flowers, 5cm (2in) wide. The reflexed petals make the flowers appear even larger than they are. Flowering is during mid-spring. These tulips are suitable for rock gardens and borders, and for naturalizing in woodland and grass.
Height: 30-38cm (12-15in)
Spread: 10-15cm (4-6in)
Cultivation: Well-drained soil, a sheltered site and a sunny south-facing position are ideal. Plant the bulbs in late summer or early autumn .
Propagation: You can raise plants from seed, but it is easier to increase from offsets.

Tulipa tarda

(Tulipa dasystemon)
This eye-catching species tulip has narrow mid-green leaves, developing in a rosette from soil level. It bears up to five flowers on each stem. They have star-shaped, pointed yellow petals with white edges, up to 4cm (1½in) long. This tulip is ideal at the front of a border or in a rock garden.
Height: 15cm (6in)
Spread: 7.5cm (3in)
Cultivation: Well-drained soil and a sheltered position, preferably in good light and facing south, are most suitable. The bulbs can be left in the soil, but remember to remove the leaves as soon as they have died down.
Propagation: Congested clumps can be lifted and divided in autumn, replanting the bulbs 15cm (6in) deep and 7.5-10cm (3-4in) apart.

Left: **Tulipa sylvestris**
An easily-grown species with beautiful scented yellow flowers, this tulip is ideal for rock gardens and borders as well as for naturalizing in woodland and grass.

Below: **Tulipa tarda**
This small tulip is ideal for a rock garden. It needs an open and sunny position, where the flowers will open wide in good light. Up to five are produced on each stem.

Tropaeolum polyphyllum comes into its own when allowed to creep over large rocks and eventually tumble into space. It is ideal for covering wide-topped walls, especially soil-retaining types.

Tulipa tarda associates well with many plants: in the rock garden with the Pasque Flower (*Pulsatilla vulgaris*), and in the border with Crown Imperial (*Fritillaria imperialis*) and mauve-flowered violas.

Verbascum x 'Letitia'

A pretty hybrid between
V. dumulosum and *V. spinosum*, with a twiggy but compact habit, it has velvety, grey-green lance-shaped leaves and numerous clear yellow flowers, 2.5cm (1in) wide, from mid-summer onwards.
Height: 25-38cm (10-15in)
Spread: 38-45cm (15-18in)
Cultivation: This lovely plant needs a sandy, well-drained soil in full sun. It dislikes continual dampness during winter and may require protection with panes of glass. It is ideal for scree beds and dry stone walls. It is also suitable for growing in an alpine house where it will thrive in a pot on a gravel-covered bench.
Propagation: The easiest way to increase it is by taking 5cm (2in) long heel cuttings during early summer, inserting them in pots of equal parts peat and sharp sand. Place them in a cold frame.

Further plants to consider

Draba bryoides imbricata
Height: 5-6.5cm (2-2½in)   Spread: 4-5cm (1½-2in)
An attractive, compact, hardy herbaceous perennial for the rock garden, with small cross-shaped golden-yellow flowers in spring.

Fritillaria pallidiflora
Height: 25-30cm (10-12in)   Spread: 10-15cm (4-6in)
An unusual fritillaria, with 4cm (1½in) long bell-shaped yellow flowers during spring.

Halimium ocymoides
(*Helianthemum algarvense*)
Height: 60-90cm (2-3ft)   Spread: 90cm-1.2m (3-4ft)
A beautiful compact shrub suitable for large rock gardens, where it reveals 2.5cm (1in) wide, bright yellow flowers with chocolate blotches in mid-summer.

Hypericum polyphyllum
Height: 15cm (6in)   Spread: 25-30cm (10-30in)
A low-growing shrubby perennial, with 4cm (1½in) wide golden flowers from mid to late summer. The form 'Sulphureum' bears pale yellow flowers.

Morisia monanthos
Height: 2.5cm (1in)   Spread: 10-15cm (4-6in)
A beautiful, low herbaceous perennial, with cross-shaped golden-yellow flowers, 12mm (½in) wide, forming clusters during spring and early summer.

Ranunculus gramineus
Height: 25-30cm (10-12in)   Spread: 20-25cm (8-10in)
A pretty member of the buttercup family, ideal for damp corners in a wild garden. From early to mid-summer it bears citron-yellow flowers. The foliage is narrow and glaucous-blue.

Roscoea cautleoides
Height: 30-38cm (12-15in)   Spread: 25-30cm (10-12in)
A hardy herbaceous perennial, with pale yellow, orchid-like flowers, 4-5cm (1½-2in) long, in mid-summer.

Uvularia perfoliata
Throat-wort (UK)
Height: 20-25cm (8-10in)   Spread: 15-20cm (6-8in)
A pretty rhizome-bearing perennial for a rock garden or peat bed. In late spring it produces many bell-shaped, pendant, pale-yellow flowers, singly or in pairs.

Waldsteinia fragarioides
Height: 13-20cm (5-8in)   Spread: 25-30cm (10-12in)
A strawberry-like North American plant, ideal for a large rock garden. During early summer it bears small, five-petalled, golden-yellow flowers above three-lobed, strawberry-like leaves.

Verbascum x 'Letitia' delights in a sunny position, especially one with good drainage such as the top of a dry stone wall. Its compact nature helps to interrupt the flatness of many such walls, and provides colour.

Above: Arabis ferdinandi-coburgi 'Variegata' *has a low, somewhat sprawling nature, ideal for planting between rocks. It bears white flowers in spring.*

Arabis ferdinandi-coburgi 'Variegata'

This very attractive evergreen rock garden plant has mid- to dark-green leaves with whitish edges, and a mat-forming habit. It is ideal for planting between rocks. During spring it develops white, cross-shaped flowers.

Height: 8-10cm (3½-4in)
Spread: 30-45cm (12-18in)
Cultivation: Plant in well-drained soil in light shade. Remove the dead flowers.
Propagation: Lift and divide congested plants in spring or autumn.

Arundinaria japonica

(Pseudosasa japonlca · Bambusa metake)

This widely-grown bamboo is hardy and vigorous and superb for creating a screen or hedge. It develops upright, olive-green canes, later arching slightly under the weight of foliage, which mature to a dull matt-green. The dark, glossy-green leaves are 15-30cm (6-12in) long and 2.5-5cm (1-2in) wide. It is a bamboo that does not become too invasive, seldom spreading rapidly or far.

Height: 3-4.5m (10-15ft)
Spread: Forms a large, dense clump and eventually the roots became entwined, forming a near solid mass.
Cultivation: Set new clumps in position only when the soil has warmed up, often as late as early

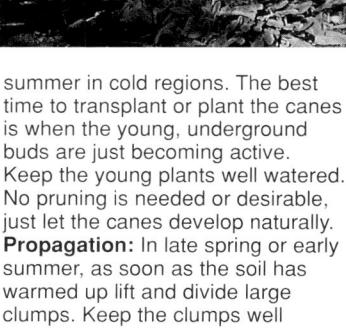

summer in cold regions. The best time to transplant or plant the canes is when the young, underground buds are just becoming active. Keep the young plants well watered. No pruning is needed or desirable, just let the canes develop naturally.
Propagation: In late spring or early summer, as soon as the soil has warmed up lift and divide large clumps. Keep the clumps well

---

Arabis ferdinandi-coburgi 'Variegata' harmonizes well with dwarf conifers, such as *Juniperus communis* 'Compacta'. The spring-flowering, yellow-flowered *Potentilla tabernaemontani*, brings further interest.

Arundinaria japonica a member of the grass family, flowers sporadically but not frequently. Suggestions that clumps die after flowering are untrue, most continue to grow normally.

Epimedium perralderianum

Barrenwort . Bishop's Hat (UK)

An attractive low-growing and ground-covering evergreen perennial, ideal for a naturalized garden in light shade. When young the leaves are bright green with bronze-red tints. In autumn these assume rich coppery hues. During early to mid-summer, plants bear bright yellow flowers.
Height: 23-30cm (9-12in)
Spread: 30-38cm (12-15in)

Cultivation: Plant in light, sandy, well-drained but moisture-retentive soil in light shade.
Propagation: In spring, lift and divide congested plants, replanting them 30cm (12in) apart.

Below: Epimedium perralderianum *This ground-covering evergreen plant has bright green leaves that assume rich tints in autumn. The bright yellow flowers are borne on arching stems during early and mid-summer.*

Above: Arundinaria japonica *This handsome and widely-grown bamboo forms a wonderful screen or hedge as well as developing into a beautiful clump in a grass surrounding. Do not set it in formal lawns.*

watered until established, especially if the weather is dry and the soil is sandy.

Epimedium x rubrum is a hybrid, widely grown as ground cover. When young the mid-green leaves are tinted red, becoming first orange and later yellow in autumn. Additional crimson fowers are borne in early summer.

Glyceria maxima 'Variegata'

Manna Grass · Reed Sweetgrass (UK)

This grass-like herbaceous perennial delights in having its roots in water or moist soil around a pond. In spring, the young green shoots have pinkish-white stripes, but as the season progresses the pink fades. It is a strong-growing plant, and may become too invasive for small ponds.
Height: 0.9-1.2m (3-4ft)
Spread: 0.9-1.2m (3-4ft)
Cultivation: If grown in a pond, plant it in a container so that its top is 5-7.5cm (2-3in) below the surface of the water. Do not plant directly into the soil in a pond, as the roots can be invasive and pierce plastic lining materials. If planted in surrounding moist soil, again set in a container. In autumn the leaves die down and these need to be removed.
Propagation: Divide congested plants in spring.

Above: Glyceria maxima 'Variegata' *When planted in a garden pond surrounded by concrete it helps to soften the harsh edges. Ensure that it is planted in a container, as the roots can damage plastic pool liners.*

Below: Gunnera manicata *A gravel-surfaced path near to a large clump of this giant-leaved plant creates an harmonious association, as well as allowing the leaves to be seen close-up. They are most attractive in spring.*

Glyceria maxima 'Variegata' is eye-catching and creates a dominant feature in the soil around a pond or in the shallow edges. Do not crowd other variegated plants around it, as they will fight for attention.

Gunnera manicata

This distinctive, eye-catching, large-leaved, rhubarb-like herbaceous perennial is superb in a naturalized garden. It forms a large clump of thick, stiff, prickly, upright stems with large, dark green, kidney-shaped leaves. Leaves up to 1.8m (6ft) wide are frequently seen. An added facet is the green flowers, which are borne in cone-shaped heads up to 30cm (12in) wide and 60cm (2ft) high.

This eye-catching plant is not suitable for small gardens, but where it can be accommodated it is certain to attract attention – garden visitors will want to be photographed next to it!
Height: 1.5-2.7m (5-9ft)
Spread: 3-4.5m (10-15ft)
Cultivation: Plant in moisture-retentive peaty soil in full sun or light shade. Shelter from hot, strong, summer winds is beneficial. The crown of the plant can be protected from severe frost by allowing the leaves as they die down in autumn to rest on the plant's centre. A thin layer of soil over the leaves adds further protection. In spring, draw the old leaves and soil away from the plant's centre.
Propagation: Plants can be raised from seeds sown in spring and placed in 16°C (61°F), but division is quicker and easier. In late spring, remove small clumps from around the outside of the main plant. Transfer into pots and place in a frost-free place until established.

Hosta fortunei 'Albopicta'

Plantain Lily (UK and USA)

Hostas are widely-grown border plants with a hardy, herbaceous, perennial nature. Many species have leaves totally of one colour, but many are variegated and bring additional colour to gardens. *Hosta fortunei* 'Albopicta', often sold as 'Picta', is superb when planted in a wild garden, alongside an informal garden pond or near to small pools in a series of waterfalls. The young leaves are pale green, broadly variegated with buff-yellow. As a bonus, mauve flowers are borne in mid-summer on stiff, upright stems. Another attractive variegated hosta within this species is 'Aureomarginata', displaying leaves edged with light yellow.
Height: 45-60cm (1½-2ft)
Spread: 50-60cm (20-24in)
Cultivation: Plant in well-drained but moisture-retentive fertile soil in light, dappled shade. Variegated hostas retain their variegations best in light shade, but not in dark and gloomy positions.
Propagation: Divide and replant congested plants in spring.

Left: Hosta fortunei 'Albopicta'
This attractively foliaged plant is superb when planted around the edges of a water garden. It likes moisture-retentive soil.

Gunnera manicata provides a focal point in a water or bog garden. Its large rhubarb-like leaves create a superb contrast with spiky, upright plants such as moisture-loving irises.

Hosta fortunei 'Albopicta' is such a handsome and distinctive plant that its shape is spoilt if planted too close to others, as well as its colour impact being diminished.

ROCK AND NATURALIZED GARDENS

Hosta rectifolia 'Tall Boy'

Plantan Lily (UK and USA)

In addition to the many variegated leaved hostas there are some superb single-colour types. The above variety is tall, with beautiful green leaves and high spires of violet-mauve flowers in mid-summer. Other single-coloured species include *Hosta sieboldiana* 'Elegans', *Hosta* 'Halcyon' which forms a mound of bright silvery-grey leaves, *Hosta* 'Blue Skies' with vivid-blue foliage and *Hosta lancifolia* with mid-green leaves. The leaves of hostas help to soften the edges of borders, in flower borders as well as wild and naturalized gardens.
Height: 1-1.3m (3½-4½ft)
Spread: 75-90cm (2½-3ft)
Cultivation: Plant in well-drained but moisture-retentive soil in light, dappled shade.
Propagation: Divide and replant congested plants in spring.

Right: Hosta rectifolia 'Tall Boy'
is a dominant plant creating a backcloth for other plants as well as producing its own flowers in eye-catching spires in mid-summer.

Iris pseudacorus 'Variegatus'

This water-loving tall iris is ideal for planting alongside the margins of ponds where its upright, sword-like, bluish-green leaves with yellow stripes create a distinctive feature. It has the bonus of producing yellow flowers, up to 7.5cm (3in) wide, during early summer.
Height: 75-90cm (2½-3ft)
Spread: 45cm (1½ft)
Cultivation: During spring, set new plants in water up to 15cm (6in) deep.
Propagation: Every three or four years lift and divide congested clumps immediately after the flowers fade.

Hosta rectifolia 'Tall Boy', as well as other hostas, harmonizes well in a naturalized garden with azaleas. They provide interesting shapes and colours when the azaleas are not in flower.

Above: Iris pseudacorus
'Variegatus' *This water-loving plant is ideal for planting alongside paths surrounding ponds. The stiff, upright leaves create height and visually help to establish colour next to path edges.*

Lamium galeobdolon 'Variegatum'

Variegated Yellow Archangel (UK and USA)

A superb ground-covering hardy perennial with upright stems bearing silvery-flushed evergreen leaves that assume bronze tints in autumn and winter. It has the bonus of developing whorls of yellow, nettle-like flowers during early and mid-summer. Botanically, this plant is correctly known as *Lamiastrum galeobdolon* 'Variegatum'.
Height: 15-30cm (6-12in)
Spread: 30-45cm (1-1½ft)

Cultivation: Ordinary soil suits it, but avoid those which are dry, and plant in light to medium shade. To encourage the development of total ground cover, use garden shears to cut over the plants as soon as the flowers fade.
Propagation: Lift and divide congested plants in autumn or spring.

Above: Lamium galeobdolon
'Variegatum' *has attractive leaves that create a superb foil for other plants, as well as preventing the growth of weeds.*

Iris pseudacorus 'Variegatus' harmonizes with the well-known Double Kingcup *(Caltha palustris* 'Flore Pleno'), with golden-yellow flowers in late spring and early summer. They like the same water depth, 15cm (6in).

Lamium galeobdolon 'Variegatum' is a dominant plant both when in flower, during early and mid-summer, and just when the variegated leaves are present. They create a superb backcloth for other plants.

ROCK AND NATURALIZED GARDENS

Above: Lamium maculatum *is ideal for planting in a wild garden where it soon carpets the soil with attractive foliage.*

Lamium maculatum

Spotted Dead Nettle (UK and USA)

An excellent hardy perennial with mid-green leaves displaying central silver stripes. It has the bonus of developing pinkish-purple flowers during early summer. It is ideal for creating colour in a wild garden, in an herbaceous border or one formed of a medley of plants.
Height: 25-30cm (10-12in)
Spread: 30-45cm (1-1½ft)
Cultivation: Plant in moisture-retentive, fertile soil in full sun or light to medium shade.
Propagation: Lift and divide plants in autumn or spring.

Right: Osmunda regalis *In late summer and autumm, when the sun's rays are low, the russet-tinted foliage looks especially eye-catching. The colours are clearly reflected in the surface of still water.*

Lamium maculatum creates a superb weed-smothering backcloth for other plants, especially all-green leaved types and forms. These range from large-leaved hostas to phormiums and ferns

Osmunda regalis

Royal Fern · Flowering Fern (UK and USA)

This superb, large, hardy fern is ideal for planting around the edge of an informal pond. Large clumps of it often grow 2.4-3m (8-10ft) high, but in gardens is less vigorous and therefore more manageable. The fresh-green fronds assume rich tints in autumn. As plants grow they develop a mass of black roots at their bases, often 60-75cm (2-2½ft) high in old plants.The variety 'Purpurescens' is attractive, with bright coppery-pink fronds in spring, becoming glaucous-green as the season progresses and assuming rich tints in autumn.

Height: 1.2-1.5m (4-5ft)
Spread: 1.8-2.4m (6-8ft)
Cultivation: Plant in moisture-retentive, fertile soil in full sun or light shade. A position at the edge of an informal pond is best, where some roots can grow into water.
Propagation: In spring divide congested plants.

Above: Pachysandra terminalis 'Variegata' *This variegated, ground-hugging, sub-shrub, with white-edged green leaves, creates a complete carpet of weed-smothering leaves. It is ideal for planting among shrubs and trees.*

Pachysandra terminalis 'Variegatus'

This hardy, evergreen, low-growing and ground-covering sub-shrub has mid-to deep-green leaves with white edges. During late winter and spring it bears greenish-white flowers.

Height: 23-30cm (9-12in)
Spread: 38-45cm (15-18in)
Cultivation: Plant in any good soil, preferably moisture-retentive, in sun or light shade. It is an ideal plant for creating attractive ground-cover under trees. If the shade is dense however, the ordinary all-green form is best. It is not necessary to prune the plant.
Propagation: In spring lift and divide congested plants.

Osmunda regalis creates a dominant splash of colour around ponds. It also harmonizes well with other moisture-loving plants such as the Giant Cowslip and large-leaved *Peltiphyllum peltatum.*

Pachysandra terminalis 'Variegata' creates an attractive ground covering in a naturalized setting. It is especially suitable for creating ground cover around deciduous, summer-flowering shrubs.

Sasa veitchii

Kuma Bamboo Grass (USA)

This eye-catching bamboo develops large thickets of deep purplish-green stems later becoming dull purple. These are headed by oblong dark green leaves up to 20cm (8in) long and about 5cm (2in) wide. They are attractively variegated – at first they tend to wither at their edges, before becoming pale straw or whitish along their edges in autumn.

Height: 0.9-1.2m (3-4ft)

Spread: Eventually forms a large clump.

Cultivation: Plant in moisture-retentive but not waterlogged soil, in full sun or light shade. Avoid positions exposed to cold, drying winds. No pruning is needed.

Propagation: Lift and divide congested plants in early summer.

Do not divide bamboos early in the year, before the soil has become warm. Keep new plants moist until established, especially if the weather is dry and hot.

Below: Sasa veitchii *This thicket-forming bamboo develops very attractive leaves. It does not grow excessively high and therefore can be planted in moderately-sized gardens. It is a trouble-free plant.*

Sasa veitchii is ideal for planting on a bank alongside streams and paths. When covered with a light dusting of snow it is very attractive and it will eventually recover even after a thick layer.

Above: Vinca major 'Variegata'
This sprawling ground-hugging plant is very tolerant and amenable, creating colour in poor soil as well as diffused shade. It flowers mainly in late spring and early summer.

Vinca major 'Variegata'

Variegated Greater Periwinkle (UK and USA)

This well-known and widely-grown evergreen mat-forming sub-shrub is normally grown in its all-green form. However, for extra colour and interest, the variegated type with pale green and white leaves is worth growing. Also known as 'Elegantissima', it has pale purple-blue flowers during late spring and early summer, and often a further burst of colour in late summer and into autumn. It is ideal for creating colour under trees and around shrubs in a wild garden setting.
Height: 15-38cm (6-15in)
Spread: 0.9-1.2m (3-4ft)
Cultivation: Well-drained, but not parched soil, in light shade.
Propagation: Divide congested plants in late summer or spring, replanting healthy young parts.

Further plants to consider

Adiantum pedatum
American Maidenhair · Five-finger Fern . Northern Maidenhair Fern (USA)
Height: 15-45cm (6-18in)   Spread: 30-60cm (1-2ft)
A hardy fern with a graceful, cascading outline. The fronds die down in autumn, fresh ones appearing in spring. Plant in moisture-retentive, fertile soil in light shade. It is best planted where it can cascade freely.

Ajuga reptans 'Variegata'
Variegated Bugle (UK)
Height: 10-25cm (4-10in)   Spread: 38-45cm (15-18in)
A beautiful carpet-forming herbaceous perennial with grey-green leaves variegated with cream. Other variegated forms include 'Multicolor' (sometimes known as 'Rainbow') with pink, yellow and bronze leaves. Additionally, these varieties develop erect spires of blue flowers during mid-summer.

Athyrium filix-femina
Lady Fern (UK and USA)
Height: 45-90cm (1$\frac{1}{2}$-3ft)   Spread: 45-90cm (1$\frac{1}{2}$-3ft)
A hardy, dainty fern with fresh green, finely-divided fronds. Plant it in fertile, moist soil in light shade. The fronds die down in autumn, fresh ones appearing in spring. It is ideal for planting in a naturalized garden. Avoid cold and windy positions.

Chamaecyparis pisifera 'Filifera Aureovariegata'
Height: 0.75-1m (2$\frac{1}{2}$-3$\frac{1}{2}$ft)   Spread: 60-90cm (2-3ft)
A slow-growing conifer, ideal for a large rock garden, with thread-like foliage bearing green leaves splashed with golden-yellow.

Matteuccia struthiopteris
(Onoclea germanica/Struthiopteris germanica)
Ostrich Feather Fern . Shuttlecock Fern (UK)
Height: 0.9-1.5m (3-5ft)   Spread: 60-90cm (2-3ft)
This hardy, moisture-loving fern is ideal for planting in damp, but not waterlogged soil. The graceful, pale green fronds are borne in a shuttlecock-like formation.

Phlox amoena 'Variegata'
Height: 23cm (9in)   Spread: 25-38cm (10-15in)
A beautiful rock garden plant with salmon-pink flowers during mid-summer and silvery-variegated leaves throughout the year.

Sedum spurium 'Variegatum'
Height: 7.5-10cm (3-4in)   Spread: 30-40cm (12-18in)
A pretty, mat-forming, rock garden evergreen perennial with pale pink flowers during mid and late summer. Additionally, the variegated leaves form an attractive carpet.

Vinca major 'Variegata' is ideal in a wild naturalized garden, creating colour around the bases of shrubs, smothering weeds and softening the edges of paths.

ROCK AND NATURALIZED GARDENS

Aponogeton distachyos

Water Hawthorn (UK and USA)
Cape Pondweed · Cape Asparagus
(USA)

A beautiful hardy perennial, aquatic
plant with light green, elongated
leaves and heavily-scented, pure
white flowers with black anthers
from mid to late summer, and often
into autumn.
Height: Surface of water.
Spread: 45-60cm (1½-2ft) or more.

Cultivation: It is a true aquatic and
needs a water depth of 23-60cm
(9-24in). Plant in neutral or slightly
acid compost in a plastic-frame
container. Full sun is needed,
although it will flower in slight
shade. New plants are best set in
position in late spring or early
summer.
Propagation: New plants can be
raised from seed, but for home
gardeners it is easier to lift and
divide congested plants with
several crowns in late spring or
early summer. Young plants are
slow to become established.

Above: Aponogeton distachyos
*The pure-white flowers with black
anthers are borne in forked clusters
just above the surface of the water.*

Galanthus nivalis

Common Snowdrop (UK and USA)
Fair Maids of February ·
Candlemas Bells (UK)

Snowdrops are frequently confused
with Snowflakes, but can be easily
identified. Snowdrops have three
short inner petals and three long
outer petals, whereas Snowflakes
have six petals all the same size.

Aponogeton distachyos is outstandingly eye-catching,
especially in full sun. Do not plant it close to vigorous
waterlilies, as these tend to suffocate and distract
attention from this scented aquatic plant.

The Common Snowdrop flowers during late winter and into spring, with nodding heads of white flowers amid glaucous, strap-like leaves. There are several superb varieties, such as 'Flore-plena' with double flowers, and 'S. Arnott' with larger flowers, up to 36mm (1½in) long. The sub-species *G. n. reginae-olgae* flowers in autumn, before the development of its leaves.

Height: 7.5-20cm (3-8in)

Spread: 7.5-13cm (3-5in)

Cultivation: Moisture-retentive, slightly heavy soil suits it best, although this bulb will survive in most soils. Good light is needed, so avoid heavily shaded sites. If the soil is rich and moist, plants grow much larger than when in poor, slightly drier positions.

Propagation: Lift and divide large clusters just after the flowers fade. Do not allow the bulbs to dry out, replanting them immediately into new positions and setting them 10-15cm (4-5in) deep.

Below: Galanthus nivalis
Snowdrops are particularly welcome in mid-winter, with their bright, white flowers. They are superb in a rock garden when clustered around rocks, which create an attractive background for the flowers.

Above: Houttuynia cordata *A moisture-loving hardy herbaceous perennial, ideal for planting around an informal pond. It also grows well in shallow water. However, it spreads rapidly and can become too invasive for small gardens.*

Houttuynia cordata

A hardy herbaceous perennial from China and Japan that thrives in moist soil in a cool, shaded position. It also grows well in shallow water, up to 5cm (2in) deep. Unfortunately, it can be invasive, spreading by underground stems. These grow direct from soil-level and bear near heart-shaped blue-green leaves with a metallic sheen. During mid summer it displays terminal heads of pure white flowers. The best form is 'Plena', with double flowers.

Height: 30-45cm (1-1½ft)

Spread: 30-38cm (12-15in) or more

Cultivation: Moisture-retentive soil and cool, light shade suit it best. Keep alert to its rapid spread.

Propagation: During autumn or spring lift congested clumps and break up into small pieces, each with a stem and root. Pot them up individually and grow in a sheltered corner until established and large enough to plant into the garden.

Galanthus nivalis can be left to form large clusters. It harmonizes superbly with colour and shape-contrasting bulbous plants such as purple and blue varieties of *Iris reticulata*, which flower in late winter and early spring.

Houttuynia cordata has a tangy aroma that some people find unpleasant. In Vietnam it is cultivated as a salad plant, as well as for treating eye diseases, while in Nepal the leaves are eaten in soups.

ROCK AND NATURALIZED GARDENS

Left: Iberis sempervirens *This neat, small plant is ideal for planting in a rock garden, where it develops masses of beacons of white flowers during early to mid-summer. The variety 'Little Gem' is slightly smaller.*

Iberis sempervirens

Evergreen Candytuft · Edging Candytuft (USA)

A reliable hardy evergreen perennial with narrow, dark green leaves. From early to mid-summer it creates a wealth of clear white flowers in heads 4cm (1½in) wide. There are several superb forms, such as 'Little Gem' at 10cm (4in) high and spreading to 23cm (9in), and 'Snowflake' at 15-23cm (6-9in) high and spreading to form a mat of foliage and pure-white flowers. The ordinary form of this plant is best reserved for border edges and banks, but 'Little Gem' is ideal for rock gardens.
Height: 20-25cm (8-10in)
Spread: 45-60cm (1½-2ft)
Cultivation: Well-drained soil and full sun suit it. Remove dead flower heads to extend the flower period – after they fade use shears to lightly cut off the old heads.
Propagation: It is easily increased during mid and late-summer by taking 5cm (2in) long softwood cuttings from non-flowering shoots. Insert them in a mixture of equal parts moist peat and sharp sand. Place in a cold frame. When rooted, pot individually into small pots and overwinter in a cold frame.

Ipheion uniflorum

Spring Starflower (UK and USA)

A dainty, hardy bulbous plant, ideal for planting alongside a path in a naturalized area or in a rock garden. The long, narrow, pale green leaves have a slightly garlic-like aroma. However, the star-like whlte flowers, which appear from mid- to late spring, are sweetly–scented. Flower colour is variable, ranging from white to violet-blue.
Height: 15-20cm (6-8in)
Spread: Forms a clump.
Cultivation: Plant in well-drained soil in full sun or light shade. Plant the bulbs 5cm (2in) deep in late summer or early autumn. The only routine job is to remove dead leaves and old flower stems in late summer.
Propagation: Lift and divide congested plants, every two or three years, in autumn.

Iberis sempervirens is an evergreen perennial which has some well-known relatives. *Iberis umbellata*, Candytuft, is a hardy annual, while *Iberis amara* is another hardy annual and known as the Wild Candytuft.

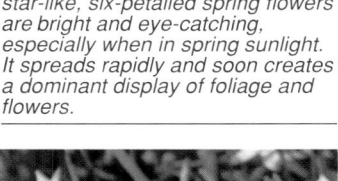

Above: Juniperus 'Grey Owl' *The elegant, silvery-grey foliage has slightly cascading tips, which enhance the plant. The yellowish stems create an additional feature. Plants which intrude on their neighbours can be pruned in spring. It cohabits well with callunas and ericas.*

Juniperus 'Grey Owl'

This vigorous, spreading conifer is often known as *Juniperus virginiana* 'Grey Owl'. It is too large for planting in small rock gardens, but can create a superb backcloth in large ones or even to form a break between a wild area and a rock garden. It is an elegant, spreading conifer, with slender sprays of soft, silvery-grey foliage.
Height: 0.9-1.2m (3-4ft)
Spread: 1.5-1.8m (5-6ft)
Cultivation: Ordinary well-drained soil and a position in light shade or full sun suits it. Avoid heavily shaded positions, as this does not encourage the best colouring in the foliage.
Propagation: During late summer and into early autumn take 7.5-10cm (3-4in) long heel-cuttings from lateral shoots. Insert them in equal parts moist peat and sharp sand. Place in a cold frame.

Ipheion uniflorum is often seen in its blue forms, such as 'Caeruleum' and 'Wisely Blue', but the white form is just as attractive. It is ideal as an edging to a path, and harmonizes well with logs used as a rustic path edging.

Juniperus 'Grey Owl' is superb for covering the soil with silvery-grey foliage, and looks especially attractive when seen against a dark background. But beware of positioning it in heavy shade.

ROCK AND NATURALIZED GARDENS

Polygonatum x hybridum

Solomon's Seal (UK and USA)
David's Harp · Lady's Seal (UK)

Well-known hardy herbaceous perennial, a cross between *Polygonatum multiflorum* and *P. odoratum*, the Angular Solomon's Seal. Both of these plants are native to the British Isles, as well as in Europe and temperate parts of Asia. Each year the fat, rhizomatous roots develop long, upright but arching, stems clothed with lance-shaped mid-green and ribbed leaves that clasp the stems. The slightly waisted, white, mid-

Leucojum aestivum 'Gravetye Giant'

Snowflake (UK)
Giant Snowflake · Summer Snowflake (USA)

This small, late spring-flowering bulbous plant develops nodding, cup-shaped, white flowers. The tips of the petals are delicately lined in green. Unlike Snowdrops, all of its six petals are the same size.
Height: 50cm (20in)
Spread: 15-20cm (6-8in)
Cultivation: Moisture-retentive soil

Above: Leucojum aestivum 'Gravetye Giant' *The late spring flowers create an attractive feature in a rock garden, lightly shaded wild garden or around the bases of deciduous shrubs. Once established it needs little attention and is quite hardy.*

and light shade are needed. Plant the bulbs 7.5-10cm (3-4in) deep during late summer and early autumn.
Propagation: Divide congested clumps as the leaves die down.

Leucojum aestivum 'Gravetye Giant' is ideal in a rock garden, where it co-habits well with the single, anemone-like flowers of *Hepatica nobilis*. These are in white, red and purple, and appear from late winter to spring.

Polygonatum x hybridum, with its arching stems of white flowers, harmonizes with variegated hostas such as *Hosta crispula*. A backdrop of the yellow *Rhododendron* 'Goldsworth Yellow' creates extra colour and interest.

summer flowers, up to 2.5cm (1in) long, hang in clusters of two to five from the leaf-joints during mid-summer. When cut, and while still in bud and taken indoors, the flowers soon fill a room with a delicious scent.

Height: 0.6-1m (2-3½ft)
Spread: 38-45cm (15-18in)
Cultivation: It is so successful that it grows in most soils, but is happiest in moisture-retentive rich soil in light shade under trees. It delights in leafmould and welcomes an annual mulch of leafmould or peat in late spring. This prevents the roots becoming dry during hot summers. During late autumn, cut down stems to soil level.

Propagation: During autumn or spring lift and divide congested clumps. Take care not to damage the roots or to allow them to become dry. Replant them just below the surface.

Below: Polygonatum x hybridum
This easily-grown and undemanding herbaceous perennial is superb at the fringe of a wild garden, or perhaps near to the edge of a patio. It has the bonus of sweetly-scented flowers. Unfortunately, it can be invasive, spreading into neighbouring plants.

Sanguinaria canadensis 'Flore pleno'

Bloodroot (UK and USA)
Red Puccoon (USA)

This hardy herbaceous perennial from North America is ideal for a rock garden or planting at the edge of a border. During spring and early summer it produces white flowers that open to about 4cm (1½in) wide. These are followed by greyish-green, hand-like and lobed leaves that die down by late summer.

Height: 13-15cm (5-6in)
Spread: 30-38cm (12-15in)
Cultivation: Well-drained but moisture-retentive peaty soil is needed, in full sun or slight shade. Once established plants are best left undisturbed. Set new plants in position in autumn or spring, or immediately after the flowers fade.
Propagation: Lift and divide congested plants immediately after flowering.

Above: Sanguinaria canadensis 'Flore Pleno' *The pure white double flowers are highlighted by the greyish-green, lobed leaves. It is ideal in a rock garden. Once established leave undisturbed.*

Sanguinaria canadensis 'Flore Pleno' gains its common name from the red sap that exudes from the thick, fleshy roots. North American Indians used the juices to colour their bodies and to stain domestic articles.

ROCK AND NATURALIZED GARDENS

Saxifraga cotyledon

This graceful, hardy evergreen rock garden plant seldom fails to create interest with its mid to late summer plume-like sprays of pure white, 12mm (½in) wide, flowers. The sprays can be up to 60cm (2ft) long. The form 'Southside Seedling' has strap-like leaves and arching sprays, up to 30cm (12in) long, of white flowers speckled red.
Height: 45-60cm (1½-2ft)
Spread: 30-38cm (12-15in)
Cultivation: Good drainage is essential on a scree bed or when

summer it develops 10cm (4in) long heads of creamy-white, frothy-looking flowers at the tops of arching stems. These are clothed with glossy, lance-shaped, light green leaves.
Height: 75-90cm (2½-3ft)
Spread: 0.9-1.2m (3-4ft)

Right: Smilacina racemosa
During late spring and early summer, fluffy, white flowers appear at the tops of arching stems. Eventually, this North American hardy herbaceous plant forms a dominant feature in a woodland setting.

planted between rocks.
Propagation: After the flowers fade in late summer, lift and divide congested clumps. Large pieces can be planted straight into a rock garden, but small pieces are best potted-up and placed in a cold frame during winter to give them protection.

Smilacina racemosa

False Solomon's Seal (UK)
False Spikenard (UK and USA)
Solomon's Zigzag · Treacleberry (USA)

This North American hardy herbaceous perennial is superb when naturalized in a wild garden. During late spring and early

Above: Saxifraga cotyledon 'Southside Seedling' *This superb plant never fails to capture attention. It is an excellent crevice plant, creating a dominant display of colour from quite small rooting areas. In summers it bears white flowers.*

Cultivation: Deeply cultivated, rich, moisture-retentive soil in light shade is needed. Eventually, it spreads to form a large clump. In early winter, cut the stems down to soil level.
Propagation: Lift and divide large clumps of plants in the autumn, replanting the young parts from around the outside of the clump.

Zantedeschia aethiopica

(*Calla aethiopica*)
Arum Lily (UK and USA)
Florist's Calla · Garden Calla · Calla Lily · Pig Lily · Trumpet Lily · Common Lily (USA)

This unusual South African, rhizomatous and deciduous perennial is not hardy outside in all areas. During spring and early summer it displays 13-23cm (5-9in) long, white, fleshy, flower heads that resemble those of Arum Lilies. Botanically, these are spathes (modified leaves), and are borne at the tops of long, fleshy, stiff stems. The proper flowers are yellow and borne in the insides of the white spathes. The hardiest variety is 'Crowborough', and this is the one mainly grown outdoors.
Height: 45-90cm (1½-3ft)
Spread: 60-90cm (2-3ft)
Cultivation: Because this plant is not fully hardy, select a warm, sheltered, south-facing position, in the lee of a wall or where it can gain protection from other plants. Moisture-retentive soil is best, although 'Crowborough' once established grows well in dry soils. Set the plants in position in late spring, covering them with 10cm (4in) of soil. In areas with very cold winters, lift the roots in autumn and overwinter them in large pots in a

---

Saxifraga cotyledon 'Southside Seedling' has long stems of cascading flowers which look at their best when highlighted against large rocks. Don't cramp them with other plants - it spoils their display.

Smilacina racemosa is ideal in a lightly-shaded woodland setting, but take care not to crowd it with large plants. A backcloth of the yellow-flowered and sweetly scented *Rhododendron luteum* creates a pleasing combination.

greenhouse. Alternatively, cover the roots in winter with a thick mulch of leafmould or peat.

Propagation: During spring, lift plants and remove offsets from around their bases. Divide large plants at the same time.

Above: Zantedeschia aethiopica 'Crowborough' *A fairly hardy Arum Lily, with beautiful heads of white flowers during summer. It harmonizes superbly with astilbes and moisture loving primulas.*

Further plants to consider

Anemone nemorosa
Wood Anemone (UK) · European Wood Anemone (USA)
Height: 15-20cm (6-8in)　Spread: 15cm (6in)
This hardy herbaceous perennial is ideal for naturalizing in lightly shaded woodland or in a wild garden. The 2.5cm (1in) wide white flowers are borne in mid to late spring.

Cardiocrinum gigantea
Giant Lily (UK)
Height: 1.8-2.4m (6-8ft)　Spread: 75-90cm (2½-3ft)
This beautiful hardy bulbous plant was earlier classified as a lily. During mid-summer it bears tall, upright spires packed with slightly pendent creamy-white or greenish-white flowers up to 15cm (6in) long. It is ideal for planting in a wild garden setting.

Convallaria majalis
Lily of the Valley (UK and USA)
Height: 15-20cm (6-8in)　Spread: 30-45cm (12-18in)
A hardy invasive herbaceous perennial with elliptic, mid-green leaves and white, waxy flowers during late spring and into early summer.

Daboecia cantabrica 'Alba'
Height: 60-75cm (2-2½ft)　Spread: 60-75cm (2-2½ft)
A small lime-hating hardy evergreen shrub usually grown in a heather garden, but also suitable for creating ground-cover. This is a white-flowered form of the purplish-pink-flowered St. Dabeoc's Heath. The pitcher-shaped flowers are borne from mid-summer to early winter.

Erica tetralix 'Alba Mollis'
Height: 23-30cm (9-12in)　Spread: 23-30cm (9-12in)
This is a white-flowered form of the Cross-leaved Heath. Also known as 'Mollis', this variety has beautiful grey foliage and white flowers.

Helichrysum bellidioides
Height: 7.5cm (3in)　Spread: 25-30cm (10-12in)
A beautiful half-hardy alpine plant, ideal for a rock garden, with clusters of white flowers up to 18mm (¾in) wide during early and mid-summer.

Lysichiton camtschatcensis
Height: 60-75cm (2-2½ft)　Spread: 45-60cm (1½-2ft)
A superb eye-catching, hardy herbaceous plant that revels in moist ground around ponds and streams. During late spring and early summer it develops white, arum-like flowers above green leaves.

Primula denticulata 'Alba'
Drumstick Primula (UK)
Height: 20-25cm (8-10in)　Spread: 15-20cm (6-8in)
This white-flowered form of the moisture-loving border primula is ideal for a woodland or wild garden. The globular flower heads, often up to 7.5cm (3in) wlde, of white flowers appear from mid-spring to early summer.

Zantedeschia aethiopica 'Crowborough' is attractive when planted within the protection of a small hedge formed of Box (*Buxus sempervirens* 'Suffruticosa'). The small, pale green leaves of the Box harmonize with the white spathes.

CHAPTER THREE

CONTAINER GARDENING

Houses and patios with flowers growing in window-boxes, in tubs, hanging-baskets and other containers are rather like cakes with large glossy cherries on top; they are the first features to capture attention. They sparkle and show off their colours. Few containers are successfully planted solely with single-colour flowers; usually, a colourful, bright mixture looks best and creates colour over a longer period. However, some colours can be the key to an impressive display and benefit from being displayed against certain background colours. For instance, strong yellows look extra bright and distinguished against white backgrounds. Zinnias and marigolds interplanted with red geraniums are a delight against white walls. Dark backgrounds also show off yellow flowers to advantage, but the containers are best painted white to give extra contrast. Red-flowered plants look vibrant against a white wall – scarlet flowers in particular – can look very dramatic. Pink-flowered container plants look superb against a grey background and in such a position, plants with deep red flowers can also be used to effect.

White walls provide colour-contrasts for blue flowers. Try a mixed planting of deep blue Grape Hyacinths and yellow-flowered polyanthus in a large tub positioned against a white wall. White-flowered plants are not candidates for display against a white wall. Instead, red walls offer the greatest colour-contrast, but can be too dominant.

A wall-basket is similar in appearance to a hanging basket which has been cut vertically in half and secured to a wall. Position the basket so that its top is about 90cm (3ft) above the ground. These baskets are admirable for displaying plants, but remember that they need regular watering during summer and that some water will trickle down the wall. On brick-surfaced walls this is not a problem, but if it is colour-washed then the water may eventually create stains. However, this can be prevented by lining the basket with polythene and piercing holes in its base and towards the front.

Left: Flowers *in troughs, tubs and hanging-baskets are especially welcome on patios and terraces. They are a delight in small gardens.*

Above: **Amaranthus caudatus** *This half-hardy annual is worthy of a place in any garden. The long tassels of crimson flowers are borne from mid-summer to autumn. It looks superb when planted in large containers.*

Amaranthus caudatus

Love-lies-bleeding (UK)
Love-lies-bleeding · Tassel Flower (USA)

A beautiful tropical half-hardy annual with large light green leaves and drooping 38-45cm (15-18in) long tassels of crimson flowers from mid-summer to autumn. In late summer and autumn the leaves and stems take on a bronze or crimson appearance. It is ideal for mixed borders and beds of annuals, or for planting in large containers such as tubs.
Height: 90cm-1.2m (3-4ft)
Spread: 38-45cm (15-18in)
Cultivation: Fertile, moisture-retentive and well-cultivated soil in a sunny position assures success. When grown in containers, use loam-based compost.
Propagation: During mid-spring, sow seeds 3mm (⅛ in) deep in loam-based compost in 15°C (59°F). When they are large enough to handle, prick off the seedlings into pots or boxes of loam-based compost and place them in a cold frame to harden off. Plant them out in the garden or in containers when all risk of frost has passed. When grown in a bed of annuals, the seeds can be sown in situ during late spring. Thin the seedlings to 38-45cm (15-18in) apart when big enough to handle.

Camellia japonica

Of all tub-grown plants this hardy evergreen shrub is one of the most spectacular. The dark green, leathery leaves taper to a point, while the 7.5-15cm (3-6in) wide flowers appear from late winter to late spring, in a colour range from white to pink, red and purple. At one time this plant was thought to be quite tender, but it has since proved to be relatively hardy, although the flowers are easily damaged by early-morning sun glancing on those covered with a layer of frost.
Height: 1.8-2.4m (6-8ft) in tubs

Camellia japonica has lovely red and pink forms, including 'Donation' (large semi-double clear pink), 'Adolph Audusson' (blood-red with yellow stamens) and 'Laura Walker' (semi-double and bright red).

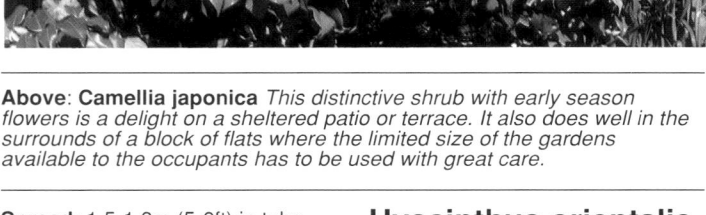

Above: **Camellia japonica** *This distinctive shrub with early season flowers is a delight on a sheltered patio or terrace. It also does well in the surrounds of a block of flats where the limited size of the gardens available to the occupants has to be used with great care.*

Spread: 1.5-1.8m (5-6ft) in tubs.
Cultivation: Camellias in containers need to be planted in large tubs. Use a well-drained compost, such as three parts peat, two of loam and one of sharp sand. Ensure the base of the tub is pierced with several holes and a thick layer of coarse drainage material placed over them. Position the tub out of cold winds and direct early morning sunshine. During late spring after flowering cut back any straggly shoots.
Propagation: During mid to late summer, take 7.5-10cm (3-4in) long cuttings, inserting them in pots containing equal parts peat and sharp sand. Keep at 13°C (15°F). When the cuttings are rooted, pot them up into lime-free compost. Then gradually pot up into large pots until the plants can be set in a tub. Although it is normally easier to increase this plant by layering low shoots, this is nearly impossible when it is grown in a tub.

Hyacinthus orientalis

Common Hyacinth · Garden Hyacinth (UK)
Hyacinth · Dutch Hyacinth · Common Hyacinth (USA)

Most gardeners and houseplant enthusiasts are familiar with these beautifully-scented bulbs that are equally at home in raised beds, tubs, troughs and window-boxes, as well as in spring-bedding schemes in borders. They can also be induced to flower during winter and early spring indoors, but specially prepared bulbs are needed. The true species is no longer generally grown and it is the larger-flowered Dutch hyacinths that are commonly seen. These have elegant, scented, 10-15cm (4-6in) high spires of wax-like flowers in a wide colour range. Pink and red forms include 'Amsterdam' (salmon-pink), 'Jan Bois' (cerise-pink), 'La Victoire' (red) and 'Pink Pearl' (pink).
Height: 15-23cm (6-9in)

Spread: 10-15cm (4-6in)
Cultivation: Light, well-drained but moisture-retentive soil suits it. When grown in the garden, the bulbs should be set in position, 13-15cm (5-6in) deep, in autumn. This is usually best done after summer-flowering plants have been removed. Set the bulbs about 15cm (6in) apart. Leave them in position until after they flower, then lift and replant them in an out-of-the-way position where they can be left undisturbed to bloom during the following and successive years in a naturalized display.
When grown in containers, use loam-based compost, setting the bulbs 13-15cm (5-6in) deep and the same distance apart. Plant the bulbs during autumn. When grown in small-area containers take care to ensure that the compost does not become alternately waterlogged and then frozen for long periods during winter. After flowering, replant among shrubs.
Propagation: Buy fresh, healthy bulbs each year for replanting.

Below: **Hyacinthus orientalis**
Many of these bulbs are suitable for growing indoors, while some are ideal for planting in containers on patios and terraces, or for using in formal spring-bedding displays.

Hyaclnthus orientalis does well in a large tub, cohabiting with other spring-flowering bulbs. Pink hyacinths mix well in tubs and window-boxes with red species tulips, Grape Hyacinths and yellow crocuses.

CONTAINER GARDENING

Petunia x hybrida

Common Garden Petunia (USA)

A half-hardy perennial best grown as a half-hardy annual, and used in containers as well as for bedding schemes in the garden. The large trumpet-shaped flowers appear from mid to late summer and often into autumn, and are available in a wide colour range. The *Single Multiflora* types (height 15-23cm/6-9in) include 'Gypsy' (coral salmon-red) and 'Resisto' (rose-pink). *Single Grandiflora* types (height 23-30cm/9-12in) include 'Pink Cascade' (pink, and ideal for hanging baskets) and 'Sparkler' (large bright scarlet).

Cultivation: Light, well-drained and moderately-rich compost is best for containers. Excessively rich compost encourages lush growth at the expense of flowers.

Propagation: During late winter and early spring, sow seeds lightly and thinly in loam-based compost in 15°C (59°F). After germination, and when large enough to handle, prick off the seedlings into boxes or pots of loam-based compost. Slowly harden off the plants and set them in containers or the garden when all risk of frost has passed.

Top: **Petunia x hybrida** *The large trumpet-shaped heads of this Argentinean half-hardy annual are a delight in all types of containers, from window boxes and troughs to hanging-baskets.*

Above: **Zinnia eiegans**
Large-flowered and tall varieties can be grown in big tubs, but it is the small types that are better for troughs and window-boxes. Also, these smaller types are easier to blend with other container plants.

Left: **Salvia splendens**
'Flarepath' *The bright scarlet flower spikes of this half-hardy annual contrast well with its dark foliage. It is ideal for summer-bedding schemes, as well as for planting in containers and window-boxes.*

Salvia splendens

Scarlet Sage (UK)
Scarlet Salvia (USA)

A well-known Mexican half-hardy perennial usually grown as a half-hardy annual for use in summer-bedding schemes and containers, from tubs to window-boxes. It is a plant with bright-green tooth-edged foliage and 4-5cm (1½-2in) long scarlet flowers which are themselves surrounded by scarlet bracts. Flowering is over a long period, from mid-summer to the frosts of autumn. Forms include white, scarlet, purple and salmon flowers, such as 'Flarepath' (bright scarlet),'Blaze of Fire' (bright scarlet) and 'Carabiniere' (intense scarlet).

Height: 30-38cm (12-15in)
Spread: 30-38cm (12-15in)

The name **petunia** is derived from the Brazilian *petun*, meaning tobacco, and refers to the petunia's affinity with the tobacco plant. Both belong to the same plant family, the Solanaceae.

Salvia splendens, with its scarlet flowers, is an obvious colour-contrasting candidate for summer bedding schemes. Whites, light blues and silver-leaved plants are excellent companions.

Cultivation: Ordinary well-drained garden soil and a sunny position assure success. Nipping out the tips of the growing shoots when the plants are 7.5cm (3in) high encourages bushiness.

Propagation: During late winter and early spring sow seeds 6mm ($^1/_4$in) deep in loam-based compost at 20°C (68°F). When they are large enough to handle, prick out the seedlings into boxes of loam-based compost and slowly harden off in a cold frame. Plant out into the garden after all risk of frost has passed.

Zinnia elegans

Youth and Age (UK)
Common Zinnia · Youth-and-old Age (USA)

This well known half-hardy Mexican annual normally grows to 60-75cm (2-2$^1/_2$ft). It is therefore the lower growing types, at 15-38cm (6-15in) high, that are better for troughs and window-boxes. The taller types can also be grown, but are best reserved for large tubs, and then in a massed display. The lower forms are often in mixed colours as well as single types. Those in pink and red include 'Pink Buttons' (salmon-pink) and 'Red Riding Hood' (scarlet).

Cultivation: Well-drained loam-based compost is needed, and to ensure that the relatively small quantities of soil in troughs and window-boxes do not dry out during summer, water your zinnias regularly. A sunny and sheltered position suits them, and pinching out the tips of young plants encourages bushiness. Also, remove dead flowers to encourage the development of further ones.

Propagation: During early spring sow seeds 6mm ($^1/_4$in) deep in trays of loam-based compost, kept at 15°C (59°F). When they are large enough to handle, prick out the seedlings into boxes or pots and slowly harden them off in a cold frame. Plant them out into containers as soon as all risk of frost has passed.

Further plants to consider

Begonia semperflorens
Height: 15-23cm (6-9in)   Spread: 15-23cm (6-9in)
This well-known summer-bedding begonia is really a greenhouse perennial, but is usually grown as a half-hardy annual. It can also be used in containers on patios and terraces. It is a bushy, much-branched plant with glossy bright-green leaves and pink, red and white flowers from mid to late summer and often into autumn. Red and pink forms include 'Sheila' (vivid orange-scarlet), 'Rosanova' (cerise pink), 'Pink Avalanche' (pink, and ideal for window-boxes, hanging baskets and tubs), 'Pandy' (blood red), 'Carmine' (rose-pink) and 'Indian Maid' (deep scarlet).

Impatiens: Hybrid Varieties
These abundantly flowering half-hardy perennials are often treated as half-hardy annuals for bedding schemes and for growing in containers. A single-colour form, 'Blitz' (15cm/6in) has orange-scarlet flowers and is a good choice for planting in tubs and window-boxes, while 'Rosette' (15cm/65in) has a mixture of colours including scarlet, rose, salmon, pink and white.

Mimulus 'Malibu'
Height: 10-15cm (4-6in)   Spread: 15cm (6in)
This is one of the most outstanding forms of this half-hardy annual, with a compact but vigorous habit and very deep orange flowers during summer. It is ideal for hanging baskets as well as troughs and window-boxes.

Pelargonium peltatum
Ivy-leaved Geranium (UK)
Ivy Geranium · Hanging Geranium (USA)
Trailing stems up to 90cm (3ft) long.
A superb pelargonium for hanging baskets or the fronts of window-boxes or troughs. Red and pink forms include 'Madame Crouse' (double, bright pink), 'Mexican Beauty' (single, crimson), 'Galilee' (double, rose), 'Lilac Gem' (double, pale pink), 'Mrs W.A.R. Clifton' (double, scarlet), 'Sir Percy Blakeney' (double, rich crimson-scarlet) and 'Ville de Paris' (deep salmon to pink).

Roses – Miniature Types
These are just like normal roses, but a great deal smaller. The almost thornless branches bear double or semi-double flowers 18-40mm ($^3/_4$-1$^1/_2$ in) wide in clusters during mid-summer. Many continue to flower intermittently for much of summer. These miniatures are suitable for deep window-boxes or troughs. Even within this group there is a wide range of sizes, from those at 23cm (9in) to types at 30-38cm (12-15in). The colour range is wide and includes white, yellow, orange and purple. Pink and red forms include 'Cinderella' (15-23cm/6-9in: double and shell-pink, merging to white at the edges) 'Darling Flame' (30-38cm/12-15in: fragrant, and bright orange-red), 'Maid Marion' (20-25cm/8-10in: deep red), 'New Penny' (20cm/8in: semi-double salmon-pink and orange), 'Peria de Monserrat' (30-38cm/12-15in: double and rose-pink) and 'Rouletti' (23-30cm/9-12in: double and rose-pink).

Zinnias are named after the German botanist Johann Gotfried Zinn (1727-1759). *Zinnia elegans,* originally native to Mexico, comes in a wide colour range, including striking red and pink forms.

CONTAINER GARDENING

Above: Agapanthus campanulatus
This is a beautiful plant for the garden as well as in large containers, where it quickly forms a strongly coloured focal point.

Agapanthus campanulatus

African Lily (UK)

This fleshy-rooted nearly hardy herbaceous plant from Natal has mid-green, sword-like leaves that arise from its base. During late summer, it reveals pale blue flowers in crowded, rounded heads, borne at the tops of long, stiff stems above the foliage. Several varieties extend the colour range from white to amethyst. 'Isis' has large heads of lavender-blue flowers. Although not fully hardy, it is ideal for a large tub on a warm and sheltered patio, preferably facing south or west.
Height: 60-75cm (2-2¹/₂ft)
Spread: 38-45cm (15-18in)

Cultivation: Well-drained, fertile soil and a sheltered sunny position suit it. Spring is the best time to set the plants out in the open soil. You should cover the crowns with 5cm (2in) of soil. In containers, use a free-draining, loam-based compost. After flowering, cut the stems down to soil-level and cover the base of the plant with straw, bracken or peaty compost. Plants in containers are best placed in a cold, frost-free greenhouse during winter, both to protect the crowns from frost and to prevent the compost from becoming too wet.
Propagation: The easiest method is to lift and divide congested clumps in mid to late spring. Take care not to damage the roots.

Convolvulus tricolor

(*Convolvulus minor*)

This beautiful hardy bushy annual from Southern Europe has dark green wide lance-shaped leaves and rich blue trumpet-shaped 4cm (1¹/₂in) wide flowers with yellow or white throats from mid to late summer. Several superb varieties are available, including 'Blue Flash' at 23cm (9in) high with brilliant blue flowers with star-like white and yellow centres, and 'Royal Ensign' with a trailing habit and deep blue flowers displaying yellow and white centres. The shorter varieties include 'Rainbow Flash' at 15cm (6in) high. This is a new dwarf hybrid in a wide range of colours including blue, purple, pink and rose.
Height: 30-38cm (12-15in)
Spread: 20-25cm (8-10in)
Cultivation: Ordinary well-drained fertile garden soil and a sunny position suits them. Select a sheltered position, and the taller-growing types may require support from twiggy sticks. These delightful plants are ideal for window-boxes and troughs, or at the fronts of borders. And of course they can also be grown in annual borders.
Propagation: When growing for window-boxes or the fronts of borders, sow seeds in early spring in pots of loam-based compost at

---

Agapanthus campanulatus needs a large container all to itself – do not try mixing it with bulbous plants. These are best planted in separate containers and stood around the agapanthus.

Convolvulus tricolor brings a distinctive brightness to borders, happily blending with many annuals such as French and African Marigolds (*Tagetes erecta* and *T. patula*).

15°C (59°F). When they are large enough to handle, prick out the seedlings into boxes of loam-based compost and harden them off in a cold frame. Plant them out when all risk of frost has passed.

Alternatively, sow seeds in late spring where the plants are to flower, 12mm (1/2in) deep. When large enough to handle, thin the seedlings to 23cm (9in) apart. For larger plants, sow seeds under cloches during late summer.

Right: **Convolvulus tricolor 'Rainbow Flash'** *This dwarf hybrid produces bright new flowers each morning, and is ideal for window-boxes, tubs and troughs. Other varieties are a good choice for annual and mixed borders.*

Felicia bergeriana

Kingfisher Daisy (UK and USA)

This stunningly attractive half-hardy annual has a mat-forming habit and grey, hairy, lance-shaped leaves. The 18mm (3/4in) wide, steel-blue flowers with gold centres appear from mid to late summer. It is ideal for growing in containers, such as tubs, troughs and window-boxes, as well as for positioning as an edging to paths or in a rock garden.
Height: 15cm (6in)
Spread: 15-20cm (6-8in)
Cultivation: Well-drained garden soil and a sheltered position in full sun suits it. When grown in containers use a well-drained loam-based compost.
Propagation: From early to mid-spring sow seeds thinly in pots of loam-based seed compost at 15°C (59°F). Prick out the seedlings into boxes of loam-based compost and harden them off in a cold frame. Set the plants out in the garden or in containers during late spring, after all risk of frost has passed.

Right: **Felicia bergeriana** *This is an eye-catching half-hardy annual ideal for growing in containers, as a path edging or in a rock garden. It is a South African plant that requires a sheltered and warm position.*

Felicia bergeriana is neat and dwarf, making it suitable for inclusion in a potpourri of bright annuals in containers. These plants look best when viewed from above, so do not plant them in high window-boxes.

CONTAINER GARDENING

Hyacinthus orientalis

Common Hyacinth · Garden
Hyacinth (UK)
Hyacinth · Dutch Hyacinth
Common Hyacinth (USA)

These beautifully-scented bulbs are
equally at home whether in spring-
bedding schemes or in raised beds,
tubs, troughs and window-boxes.
The true species is no longer
generally grown and therefore it is
the larger-flowered Dutch Hyacinths
that are commonly seen. These
have elegant, scented, 10-15cm
(4-6in) high spires of wax-like
flowers in a wide range of colours,
including blue.

Height: 15-23cm (6-9in)
Spread: 10-15cm (4-6in)
Cultivation: Light, well-drained but
moisture-retentive soil suits it, and
when grown in a garden the bulbs
can be set in position, 13-15cm (5-
6in) deep, in autumn. This is
usually done after summer-
flowering plants have been
removed from the border or
container. The bulbs are left in
position until after they flower, then
lifted and re-planted in an out-of-
the-way position where they can be
left undisturbed to flower during the
following and successive years.
When grown in containers, use a
loam-based compost, setting the
bulbs 13-15cm (5-6in) deep and the
same distance apart. Plant the
bulbs during autumn. When grown
in small-area containers – window
boxes and troughs – take care to
ensure that the compost does not
become totally saturated with water
and then freeze for long periods
during winter. Large tubs usually
need less care and attention. After
flowering, the bulbs can be lifted
and planted among shrubs.
Propagation: Although hyacinths
can be raised from seeds, they take
up to six years to produce flowering
sized bulbs by this method and
even then large-flowered types do
not always come true. It is therefore
much easier to buy flowering-sized
bulbs each year. Make sure you buy
your bulbs from a reputable supplier
who can guarantee their quality.

Above: **Hyacinthus orientalis** *The
fragrance and colours of these
flowers can be better appreciated
when they are grown in containers
or raised beds. Such beds are easily
maintained by gardeners who are in
wheelchairs or have infirmities that
prevent them from bending. But take
care not to make the beds too wide
or the wrong height.*

Left: **Hyacinthus orientalis
'Ostara'** *This is a deep purple-blue
hyacinth that produces a dense
sea of colour in borders or
containers. It also gives off a
wonderful scent.*

Hyacinthus orientalis can be mixed with many
bulbs, such as Grape Hyacinths, species tulips and
yellow crocuses. Another combination is blue
crocuses, Grape Hyacinths, species tulips and
Narcissus cyclamineus 'February Gold'.

Lobelia erinus

Edging Lobelia (USA)

This well-known reliable border edging and container plant is a half-hardy perennial invariably grown as a half-hardy annual. It has light green leaves, with masses of 6mm (¼in) wide pale blue or white flowers from early summer to the frosts of autumn. There are both trailing and compact border edging varieties, in a range of colours. The border-edging compact types include 'Cambridge Blue' (pale blue), 'Crystal Palace' (dark blue) and ' Mrs Clibran' (brilliant blue). Trailing types include 'Blue Cascade' (Cambridge blue) and 'Sapphire' (brilliant blue). Some varieties, such as 'Colour Cascade Mixed', reveal flowers in shades of blue, mauve, red and rose.

Height: 10-23cm (4-9in)
Spread: 10-15cm (4-6in)
Cultivation: Fertile, moist garden soil in a sheltered and sunny position in light shade suits it. In containers use well-drained loam-based compost.
Propagation: During late winter and early spring, sow seeds thinly and shallowly in pots of loam-based compost at 15°C (59°F). As soon as the seedlings can be handled, prick

Above: **Lobelia erinus** *These are indispensable half-hardy annuals for both containers and the garden. When growing them in containers, take care that the compost does not dry out during summer, especially when in shallow urns that hold relatively small amounts of compost.*

them out into boxes of loam-based compost and harden them off in a cold frame. Move the plants to the garden when all risk of frost is over To create an instant display of colour, plant lobelias in pots in a greenhouse.

Lobelia erinus blends with a wealth of other plants. A happy combination for containers is the pink-flowered fibrous-rooted *Begonia semperflorens* 'Pink Avalanche' and *Lobelia erinus* 'Cambridge Blue'.

Lobelia erinus is a good bed-fellow for geraniums in both containers and borders. Try pink pelargoniums with dark blue lobelia, or light or dark blue lobelia with French Marigolds (*Tagetes patula*) that display strong, rich colours.

CONTAINER GARDENING

Above: **Myosotis alpestris**
'Ultramarine' *The deep blue
flowers of this Forget-me-not form
a dense, low carpet. It is ideal for
bringing colour to a rock garden or
for planting in combination with
spring-flowering yellow or orange
bulbs.*

Myosotis alpestris

(*Myosotis rupicola/Myosotis
sylvatica alpestris*)
Forget-me-not (UK)
Forget-me-not · Scorpion Grass
(USA)

This well-known hardy perennial
best treated as a hardy biennial, is
ideal for planting in a container, a
rock garden or a bed with spring-
flowering bulbs where it forms a
dense blanket of fragrant azure-
blue flowers from late spring to
mid-summer. Several exciting
forms are available, including
'Ultramarine' (deep blue) and 'Blue
Ball' (rich indigo-blue).
Height: 10-20cm (4-8in)
Spread: 15-23cm (6-9in)
Cultivation: Moderately fertile
well-drained but moisture-retentive
soil in light shade is best.
Propagation: During mid-summer
sow seeds 6mm (¼in) deep in a
well-prepared seedbed. When they
are large enough to handle, plant
out the seedlings 15cm (6in) apart
in nursery rows. If originally sown
thinly they can just be thinned to
15cm (6in) apart. Keep the rows
weeded and in autumn plant out
into their flowering positions.

Right: **Myosotis alpestris**
*This half-hardy annual is just as
good in containers as in a border
perhaps as an edging. Even on its
own it creates a dense splash of
colour early in the year.*

Myosotis alpestris can form an ideal low edging to
beds, with a centre planting of the higher-growing
(30cm/1ft) *Myosotis sylvatica* 'Blue Bird' and yellow or
light orange tulips.

Further plants to consider

Campanula isophylla
Italian Bellflower · Star of Italy (UK)
Italian Bellflower · Falling Stars · Star of Bethlehem (USA)
Height: 15cm (6in)   Spread: 45-60cm (1½-2ft)
A trailing dwarf perennial, often used indoors as a house plant but hardy outside in hanging baskets in milder, sunny gardens. The heart-shaped mid-green leaves are borne amid a mass of tangled trailing stems, with 2.5cm (1in) wide star-shaped blue flowers appearing in late summer and into autumn.

Crocus chrysanthus
Height: 7.5cm (3in)   Spread: 6.5cm (2½in)
This delightful spring-flowering bulb brings colour to containers as well as to rock gardens. The species type is golden-yellow, but there
are several blue or mauve forms, such as 'Blue Pearl' (pale blue on the outside, white within), 'Lady Killer' (purple-blue, edged white) and 'Princess Beatrix' (clear blue with a yellow base).

Crocus vernus
(*Crocus neapolitanus*)
Dutch Crocus (USA)
Height: 10-13cm (4-5in)   Spread: 7.5cm (3in)
This spring-flowering bulb is the parent of the large Dutch crocuses widely seen in gardens and containers. Blue, mauve and purple forms include 'Queen of the Blues' (lavender-blue), 'Negro Boy' (deep reddish-purple) and 'Purpureus Grandiflorus' (purplish-blue).

Exacum affine
Persian Violet (UK) · German Violet/Persian Violet (USA)
Height: 23-30cm (9-12in)   Spread: 20-25cm (8-10in)
Although usually grown as a plant for the home, in milder areas it can be used in containers on warm patios and terraces. From mid to late summer it displays fragrant, saucer-shaped 12-18mm (½-¾in) wide purple flowers with yellow stamens.

Fuchsia magellanica 'Pumila'
Height: 15-20cm (6-8in)   Spread: 25-30cm (10-12in)
This dwarf but spreading form of the hardy fuchsia is dainty and small enough for tubs, where it reveals red and purple flowers from mid to late summer and often into autumn.

Petunia x hybrida
Common Garden Petunia (USA)
Height: 25-38cm (10-15in)   Spread: 30-38cm (12-15in)
A half-hardy perennial best grown as a half-hardy annual, and used in containers as well as for bedding schemes in the garden. The large trumpet-shaped flowers from mid to late summer and often into autumn, are available in a wide colour range, including mauve and blue. Among these are 'Resisto Blue' (mid-blue), 'Polaris' (deep blue with a white star), 'Blue Frost' (deep violet-blue with a pure white edge) and 'Blue Bedder' (blue). There are also many varieties with mixed colours including blue violet and mauve.

Myosotis alpestris also looks splendid when planted in a spring-flowering bedding display with creamy-yellow tulips and an occasional edging tuft of the lemon-gold *Alyssum saxatile* 'Citrinum'.

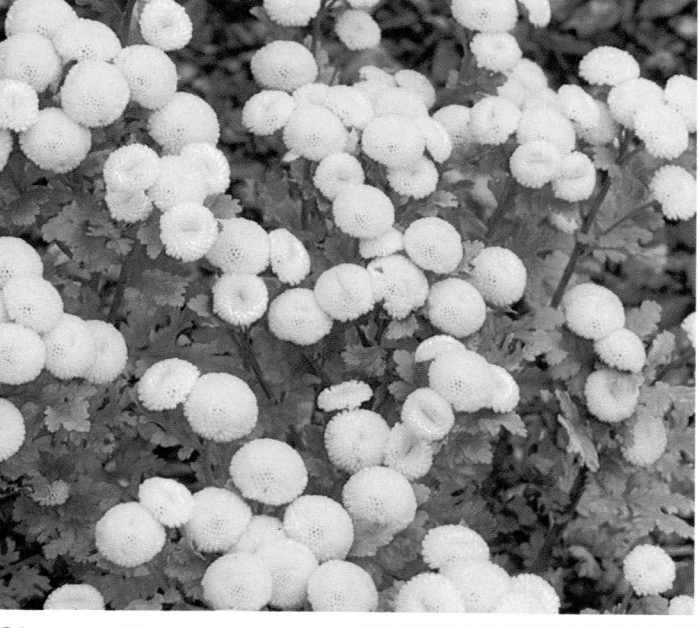

Coreopsis tinctoria

(Coreopsis bicolor)

This is one of the best known hardy annuals, bringing a profusion of colour to the garden from mid to late summer. The 5cm (2in) wide, daisy-shaped, bright yellow flowers are borne on stiff stems. The plant is just as good in containers on a patio as in the garden with other annuals. However, the dwarf varieties, at 23-30cm (9-12in), are better in containers than the taller types, at 60-90cm (2-3ft). 'Dwarf Dazzler' at 30cm (1ft) and 'Dwarf Mixed' at 23cm (9in) are best in containers, while 'All Double Mixed' and 'Single Mixed' at 75-90cm (2½-3ft) are best in a border. The lower ones can be used in borders, but towards the front.
Height: 23-90cm (9in-3ft) range
Spread: 15-25cm (6-10in) range
Cultivation: Well-drained fertile soil in a sunny position ensures success; this is a particularly good plant for town gardens.
Propagation: When grown in a hardy annual border, sow seeds thinly in drills during spring and early summer in the positions where the plants are to flower. When they are large enough to handle, thin out the seedlings. However, when grown for use in containers, sow seeds in early

Chrysanthemum parthenium

(• :atricaria eximia)
Feverfew (UK and USA)

This hardy herbaceous perennial is grown as an annual, with pungent light green leaves and small white flowers, 18mm (¾in) wide, from mid to late summer. Several old and trusted varieties are available, such as 'Golden Ball' which grows to 25cm (10in) and has golden-yellow double flowers on compact plants. 'Snow Ball' is another good variety, up to 30cm (1ft) high, with masses of ivory-white double flowers. 'Gold Star' at 20cm (8in) has yellow-centred flowers, surrounded by white petals. Other varieties reach 75cm (2½ft), but it is the low-growing types that are best for border edging and containers such as tubs, troughs and window-boxes.
Height: 23-75cm (9in-2½ft)
Spread: 23-60cm (9in-2ft)
Cultivation: Feverfew likes well drained, fertile, light soil in full sun

Above: Chrysanthemum parthenium 'Golden Ball'
This is a useful compact annual for the edges of borders and tubs, as well as window-boxes and troughs. The bright button-like flowers bring life to the garden.

or slight shade. In containers, use a good loam-based compost and, to encourage bushiness, nip out the initial flower buds.
Propagation: To produce plants for growing in containers, sow seeds 3mm (1⅛in) deep in trays of loam-based seed compost in late winter or early spring. Keep the trays at 15°C (59°F). As soon as the seedlings are large enough to handle, prick them off into boxes of loam-based compost and harden them off in a cold frame. Plant them out into the garden in late spring. Alternatively, sow seeds directly into the border where the plants are to flower. Make shallow drills in the soil during late spring, lightly covering the seeds. When large enough to handle, thin the seedlings to 25cm (10in) apart.

Chrysanthemum parthenium 'Golden Ball' suits formal bedding schemes, set as an edging to *Pelargonium* 'Masterpiece', with its double orange flowers and tricoloured foliage. For added height use *Senecio maritima* as a 'dot' plant.

Coreopsis tinctoria is available in a wide range of heights, suitable for a variety of positions: front and middle of borders, edging to paths and borders, and in containers. For a quick display, rapidly covering the soil, set the plants closer together.

spring in loam-based compost kept at 16°C (61°F). When the seedlings are large enough to handle, prick them out into pots five to a 15cm (6in) container, and harden them off in a cold frame. Plant them into containers in the garden during late spring and early summer.

Left: **Coreopsis tinctoria 'Dwarf Dazzler'** *A beautiful and reliable dwarf form with golden and crimson flowers through much of summer, this is a useful plant for towns and cities with pollution problems.*

Hypericum olympicum 'Citrinum'

This low-growing, deciduous, mound-like St. John's Wort develops 23-30cm (9-12in) high stems clothed with small, grey-green, narrowly oval or oblong stalkless leaves. The bright lemon-yellow five-petalled summer flowers, 5cm (2in) wide, have central bosses of long, spiky stamens. It is ideal for the corner of a stone sink, or in a rock garden. It is often wider-spreading than the figures given below; instead of being 45cm (1½ft) in breadth, it may after several years reach 90cm (3ft) wide. At the same time it forms a slightly higher mound. If plants in sink gardens do become too large, swamping other plants, transplant them to the border in mid to late spring when the soil is warming up.

Height: 23-30cm (9-12in)
Spread: 30-45cm (1-1½ft)
Cultivation: Well-drained fertile soil and a sunny position suit this plant.
Propagation: During early and mid-summer, take 5cm (2in) long cuttings, inserting them into pots of equal parts peat and sharp sand. Place these in a cold frame. When the cuttings have rooted, pot them up into pots of loam-based compost and overwinter in a cold frame. Transplant them into the garden during spring.

Above: **Hypericum olympicum** 'Citrinum' *The bright lemon-yellow flowers, 5cm (2in) wide, with large central bosses of spiky stamens, are a delight in summer. The flowers appear at the tops of leaf-clad stems.*

Hypericum olympicum '**Citrinum**' with its strong yellow flowers, blends with the blue-flowered *Veronica prostrata*. Position it so that the blue flowers are next to the yellow ones of the hypericum.

CONTAINER GARDENING

Mesembryanthemum oculatus 'Lunette'

This beautiful early-flowering, low-growing, half-hardy annual boasts bright yellow daisy-like flowers with darker centres. The flowers appear earlier than those of *criniflorum* types, and under duller conditions. It is ideal for the front of window-boxes and in hanging-baskets.

Height: 7.5-10cm (3-4in)
Spread: 15-25cm (6-10in)
Cultivation: Well-drained light soil is best, and a position in full sun. In containers, use a sandy loam-based compost.
Propagation: During spring, sow seeds in trays of loam-based

Above: **Mesembryanthemum oculatus 'Lunette'** *A new, early-flowering, half-hardy annual, this variety is ideal for the edge of window-boxes and hanging-baskets. It is a bright and reliable plant.*

compost kept at 18°C (65°F). After germination, prick off the seedlings into boxes or pots, and harden them off in a cold frame. Set the plants 20-23cm (8-9in) apart in the containers. Alternatively, if no heat is available, sow seeds in the open soil where they are to flower during late spring, thinning the seedlings later. However, germination may not be rapid.

Mesembryanthemum oculatus 'Lunette' is ideal for filling bare patches in rock gardens, creating colour before the permanent plants are fully established. It gives good ground cover, and brings colour right up to the edges of rocks and paths.

Sedum spathulifolium

This North-west American perennial succulent plant will soon form a dense mat of foliage. The grey-green leaves, borne in fleshy rosettes, are covered during mid-summer with 5cm (2in) wide heads of bright yellow flowers on 10cm (4in) stems. The form 'Cape Blanco' displays silvery-grey foliage, while 'Purpureum' has large purple leaves. 'Aurea' has leaves tinted yellow. These plants can be used in sink gardens as well as rock gardens. *Sedum acre* 'Aureum', a form of the Biting Stonecrop, native to Western Europe, including Britain, is an invasive and mat-forming plant and is best grown in crevices in dry stone walls, where it produces a mass of small mid to yellow-green leaves. During mid-summer, it bears flattened 2.5-4cm (1-1½in) wide heads of golden-yellow star-like flowers. Its spreading and mat-forming growth habit can be used to create an attractive feature by planting it where it can spread − away from choice rock garden subjects − and underplanting it with miniature bulbs. *Sedum acre* is also known as the Wall-pepper, an indication of its natural home.

Height: 5-10cm (24in)
Spread: 23-30cm (9-12in)
Cultivation: Well-drained garden soil in full sun is best, and although all sedums are relatively drought-resistant, do not allow the soil to become rock hard.
Propagation: The easiest way to increase this plant is to divide congested clumps. This can be done at almost any time, but spring is best. Alternatively, small pieces which break off soon produce roots when pushed into compost.

Left: **Sedum spathulifollum 'Cape Blanco'** *A distinctive stonecrop, this has silvery-grey leaves and bright yellow flowers during mid-summer. Several other forms are available, with purple or yellow-tinted leaves.*

Sedum spathulifolium 'Cape Blanco' can be used in a stone sink with several other plants, such as *Lithodora diffusa* with blue flowers, *Sedum cauticolum* with rosy-blush blooms, and *Sedum* 'Vera Jameson'.

Ursinia anethoides

This half-hardy perennial is usually grown as a half-hardy annual. It has daisy-like, brilliant orange-yellow flowers, 5cm (2in) wide, with central purple discs from early to late summer. Several superb varieties are available, including 'Sunstar' with deep orange flowers and dark red central discs, and 'Sunshine', with bright golden-yellow flowers and maroon discs. It does well in borders and containers.

Height: 38-45cm (15-18in)
Spread: 25-30cm (10-12in)
Cultivation: Light, relatively poor soil suits it best, and a position in full sun.
Propagation: During early spring, sow seeds 3mm (⅛in) deep in trays of loam-based compost kept at 15°C (59°C). When the seedlings are large enough to handle, prick them out into boxes and place them in a cold frame to harden off. In late spring, after all risk of frost has passed, plant them out into a container.

Above: **Ursinia anethoides** *This bright, half-hardy annual with golden-yellow flowers needs plenty of sunshine. It is admirable for bringing colour to hot, sunny patios and terraces, where its flowers create interest over a long period. Ursinias make excellent pot plants.*

Venidium fastuosum

Monarch of the Veldt (UK)
Cape Daisy (USA)

This superb half-hardy annual from South Africa brings colour to all gardens, whether in containers or in a border. It has deeply-lobed leaves and stems with a silvery-white texture, and large, rich orange daisy-like flowers, 10cm (4in) wide, from early to late summer. The inner edges of the petals are banded purple-brown, with a central black cone. They are ideal as cut flowers. Another species, *Venidium decurrens*, also native to South Africa, boasts beautiful, large-faced, daisy-like, dark-centred, golden-yellow flowers up to 6.5cm (2½in) wide. It is really a half-hardy perennial but is invariably grown as an annual. Its flowers appear from mid-summer to early autumn on plants 25-30cm (10-12in) high and with a similar spread, with deeply-lobed greyish-

Ursinia anethoides is worth planting on its own in a large tub or low urn: its boldly-coloured and long-lasting flowers would dominate and subjugate plants set with it. However, in a border it can be planted in small groupings, with bold blues around it.

Above: **Tagetes patula** *Popularly known as French Marigolds, these favourite border flowers make a bold display of bright yellow.*

green leaves. Like *Venidium fastuosum*, it is ideal as a cut-flower for home decoration.
Height: 50-60cm (20-24in)
Spread: 30-38cm (12-15in)
Cultivation: Well-drained, fertile, light compost in containers or borders is essential, and a sunny position.
Propagation: Sow seeds thinly in boxes of loam-based compost during early spring. Keep them at 16°C (61°F). When the seedlings are large enough to handle, prick them out into boxes or pots of loam-based compost and harden them off in a cold frame before planting them in containers or a border in late spring.

Left: **Venidium fastuosum**
The stunningly attractive 10cm (4in) wide flowers make an ideal feature for a container on a sunny patio. The flowers are also excellent for cutting for the house.

Further plants to consider

Calceolaria 'Fothergillii'
Slipper flower (UK) Slipperwort · Slipper Flower · Pocketbook Flower (USA)
Height: 15cm (6in)   Spread: 15-20cm (6-8in)
A hardy perennial, well suited to rock gardens or window-boxes, with yellow pouch-shaped flowers revealing purple-flecked throats. Two other low-growing forms are available: 'Golden Bunch' at 20cm (8in) with yellow flowers, and 'Midas' at 20cm (8in) with pure yellow flowers.

Erysimum alpinum
(*Cheiranthus alpinus*)
Alpine Wallflower · Fairy Wallflower (UK)
Height: 15cm (6in)   Spread: 10-15cm (4-6in)
A beautiful, diminutive hardy biennial that can be set at the edge of a stone sink to create extra 'instant' colour during early summer. The sulphur-yellow 12mm (¹/₂in) wide flowers are beautifully fragrant.

Petunia 'Summer Sun'
Height: 30-38cm (12-15in)   Spread: 30-38cm (12-15in)
Ideal for flowering in large containers on patios, displaying 5-6.5cm (2-2¹/₂in) wide yellow flowers.

Tagetes erecta 'Aztec Fire Mixed'
African Marigold
Height: 20-25cm (8-10in)   Spread: 25-30cm (10-12in)
A half-hardy annual, with flowers in shades of hot gold and grapefruit yellow from early summer onwards.

Tagetes patula 'Fireflame'
French Marigold
Height: 20-25cm (8-10in)   Spread: 25-30cm (10-12in)
An exceptionally beautiful, half-hardy, dwarf double French Marigold, with golden-yellow and red flowers. An even smaller variety is 'Gypsy Sunshine' at 15-20cm (6-8in) high, with warm butter-yellow flowers. An ultra dwarf single form is Teeny Weeny' at 13cm (5in), with red and yellow flowers.

Tagetes tenuifolia 'Lemon Gem'
(*Tagetes signata*)
Height: 23cm (9in)   Spread: 23-30cm (9-12in)
A beautiful, small, half-hardy annual with a neat, mound-like habit, clothed with lemon-yellow flowers from early summer onwards. 'Golden Gem', 15cm (6in) has golden flowers.

Zinnia 'Short Stuff'
Height: 15-18cm (6-7in)   Spread: 15-20cm (6-8in)
This hybrid is available in six different colours, including yellow. Its blooms are double, disease-resistant and ideal for containers.

Venidium fastuosum needs white or blue colour around it to show off its beautiful flowers. But remember to choose flowers that do not rise above and hide the rich orange blooms.

CONTAINER GARDENING

Above: Arundinaria viridistriata
With its tufted nature and green leaves striped rich yellow, this dwarf bamboo has plenty of eye-appeal. It can be used on even the smallest of patios.

Arundinaria viridistriata

This superb bamboo, often sold as *Arundinaria auricoma* or *Pleioblastus viridistriatus*, is ideal for growing in a container on a patio. It is a hardy, erect, tufted plant with purplish-green stems and green leaves striped rich yellow. Usually, the whole plant assumes a yellowish and light green nature.

Height: 1-1.2m (3½-4ft)
Spread: 38-60cm (15-24in)
Cultivation: Plant in moisture-retentive soil in a large pot, or eventually, a tub. When placed in good light it reaches the suggested height, but when in shade is not so vigorous. To encourage the development of new canes cut out the old ones in autumn.
Propagation: Divide congested plants in early summer, but never when the compost or soil is cold.

Above: Arundinaria nitida *This superb bamboo is eye-catching when planted in either a garden or a tub on a patio. Large wooden tubs are the best containers. Ensure that the compost is kept moist.*

Arundinaria nitida

(*Sinoarundinaria nitida*)

A graceful, fast-growing, hardy bamboo that creates a thicket of greenish-purple canes that mature to deep purple. The brilliant mid-green leaves, about 8cm (3½in) long and 12mm (½in) wide, are glaucous on their undersides, with finely-bristled edges. As well as being grown in a garden, it makes an excellent plant for a large tub on a patio.

Height: 2.4-3.6m (8-12ft)
Spread: Forms a large clump
Cultivation: Plant in moisture-retentive soil in light shade. When grown in full sun, the leaves are occasionally damaged. Also, the leaves may be singed by cold winds during winter.
Set new clumps in position only when the soil has warmed up in spring, which may be as late as early summer in cold regions. Keep the young canes well watered. If they are allowed to become dry they soon suffer. No pruning is needed or even desirable, just allow them to grow naturally.
Propagation: In late spring or early summer, as soon as the soil is warm, lift and divide large clumps. Keep them well watered until established.

Arundinaria nitida is such a graceful plant that it is known as Queen of the Arundinaria. As well as being attractive, it produces a gentle rustling sound even in the slightest breeze.

Arundinaria viridistriata is one of the most attractive bamboos. It is eye-catching when planted in a white container and positioned on a patio. Select a sunny position and keep the compost moist in summer.

Aucuba japonica 'Variegata'

Spotted Laurel (UK)
Japanese Aucuba · Japanese
Laurel (USA)

This well-known evergreen shrub (sometimes known as 'Maculata') has an attractive dome-shaped outline, with leathery, somewhat oval, shiny green leaves spotted yellow. During spring it bears olive-green, star-shaped flowers, followed in autumn and through to the following spring with clusters of bright red berries.

Height: 1.2-1.5m (4-5ft) in a tub

Spread: 1-1.2m (3½-4ft) in a tub
Cultivation: When grown in a border it often reaches 1.8-3m (6-10ft) high and 1.8-2.4m (6-8ft) wide, but in a tub on a patio is reserved in growth. It is such a useful shrub that when young and very small it is grown in cool rooms indoors. Outdoors it thrives in coastal areas, surviving salt spray. No regular pruning is needed, although occasionally a misplaced shoot may need to be removed in spring. ·
Propagation: In late summer and early autumn take 10-13cm (4-5in) long cuttings. Insert them in equal

parts moist peat and sharp sand, and place in a cold frame. When rooted, during the following spring, plant into a nursery bed until well established and large enough to be planted into a tub on a patio. Keep the compost evenly moist to enable the plant to become established in the container.

Below: Aucuba japonica 'Variegata' *The leathery, shiny green leaves, attractively spotted in yellow, seldom fail to attract attention. It is undemanding and can be grown with little trouble - a very 'gardenworthy' shrub.*

Aucuba japonica 'Variegata' is an evergreen shrub that brings colour to patios and gardens throughout the year. In spring place pots of bright yellow daffodils around it.

Buxus sempervirens

Common Box (UK and USA)

This slow-growing evergreen shrub is seldom grown in its normal form. More often, it is the less vigorous, lower-growing forms that are mainly seen in gardens, such as 'Elegantissima' (dome-shaped and densely clothed in small, dark green leaves with irregular creamy-white edges) and 'Suffruticosa' (known as the Edging Box and widely planted alongside beds, as well as in tubs).

Height: 1.8-2.4m (6-8ft)
Spread: 1.2-1.8m (4-6ft)
Cultivation: Plant in any good soil, in full sun or light shade. No regular pruning is needed for the species other than occasionally cutting out misplaced shoots. However, the dwarf types grown as dwarf hedges or in containers need trimming with shears in late summer.
Propagation: During late summer, take 7.5cm (3in) long cuttings. Insert them in equal parts moist peat and sharp sand, and place in

Below: Buxus sempervirens 'Suffruticosa' *This evergreen shrub with small, dark green leaves, creates a superb background for other plants on a patio.*

a cold frame. When rooted, plant into a nursery bed for two or three years before setting in the garden or a tub.

Euonymus fortunei 'Emerald and Gold'

This evergreen, dwarf and bushy shrub (often sold as 'Emerald 'n' Gold') is superb for creating year-round colour in a tub, as well as softening the edges of a patio. The small, oval, mid-green leaves are variegated in bright gold and in winter become tinged bronzy-pink. Other beautiful evergreen varieties, differing in height slightly from the above variety, include 'Emerald Charm' with deep green leaves and white veins; 'Silver Queen' with green leaves variegated creamy-white; 'Emerald Gaiety' with a spreading and upright habit and green leaves edged in white; 'Golden Prince' (sometimes known as 'Gold Tip') with new foliage tipped in bright gold; 'Sheridan Gold' with bright green leaves suffused rich golden-yellow and 'Sunspot' with dark green leaves splashed at their centres with golden-yellow.

Height: 30cm (1ft)
Spread: 38-60cm (15-24in)
Cultivation: Well-drained compost and a slightly sheltered position suit it, and a position in full sun or light shade. No regular pruning is needed, other than cutting out in spring misplaced and straggly stems.
Propagation: In late summer take 7.5-10cm (3-4in) long heel-cuttings, inserting them in equal parts moist peat and sharp sand. Place in a cold frame. In sprlng, pot up the rooted cuttings and when established plant into a tub or into the garden.

Left: Euonymus fortunei 'Emerald and Gold' *This hardy, bushy, variegated shrub creates colour throughout the year. It is at its best when positioned in full sun, preferably in a corner position where the stems can sprawl.*

Buxus sempervirens 'Suffruticosa' is the parent of more than fifteen attractive forms, including variegated, pendulous and prostrate types. The dwarf type 'Suffruticosa' has been grown as a border edging for several centuries.

Fatsia japonica

Japanese Aralia · False Castor Oil
Plant (UK)
Japanese Fatsia · Formosa Rice
Tree · Glossy-leaved Paper Plant ·
Paper Plant (USA)

This slightly tender evergreen
shrub (often grown as a
houseplant, as well as in
conservatories and sunrooms)
benefits from the protection of a
south or west-facing wall or fence.
The glossy-green leaves have
seven to nine large lobes with
coarsely-toothed edges. During
autumn, milky-white flowers are
borne in large, branching heads.
Height: 1.8-4.5m (6-15ft)
Spread: 1.8-3.6m (6-12ft)
Cultivation: Plant in well-drained
but moisture-retentive soil in a
sheltered position. No regular
pruning is needed, other than
cutting out misplaced and straggly
shoots in spring.
Propagation: Although plants can
be raised by sowing seeds in

Above: Fatsia japonica *This
distinctive slightly tender evergreen
shrub has large leaves that create
dignity and quiet in a garden. For
success it needs a slightly
sheltered position.*

compost in spring and placing
them in 10-13°C (50-55°F), it is
easier to detach sucker-like shoots
in spring and to pot them into a
loam-based compost. Place them
in a cold frame. When established
plant into the garden.

Euonymus fortunei 'Emerald and Gold' is a
sprawling, evergreen, variegated shrub that is ideal for
planting in a tub or in a border around a patio. Its lax
nature helps to soften the edges of patios.

Fatsia japonica, known as the False Castor Oil
Plant, is often erroneously known as the Castor Oil
Plant, which correctly is *Ricinus communis,* a plant
with highly poisonous parts.

CONTAINER GARDENING

Hebe x andersonii 'Variegata'

This slightly tender, evergreen shrub has soft, light-green leaves edged in cream. It has the bonus of developing 7.5-13cm (3-5in) long, stiffish, tassel-like heads of lavender flowers from mid to late summer, and even into early autumn. It grows well in a sheltered corner on a patio.

Height: 60-90cm (2-3ft)
Spread: 60-75cm (2-2½ft)
Cultivation: Plant in well-drained compost in a large pot or small tub, and place in a sheltered, sunny position. It grows well in chalky compost. No regular pruning is needed, other than cutting out misplaced shoots in spring. In cold areas it needs the protection of a conservatory or greenhouse in winter, as it will not withstand severe frosts.

Propagation: In late summer take 7.5-10cm (3-4in) long cuttings from non-flowering shoots. Insert them in equal parts moist peat and sharp sand, and place in a cold frame until rooted.

Below: Hebe x andersonii 'Variegata' *Either displayed on its own in a pot on a patio, or in a low grouping with other plants, this slightly-tender variegated evergreen plant is well worth growing for its year-through colour.*

Pieris japonica 'Variegata'

A beautiful slow-growing, bushy, evergreen shrub with mid-green leaves, attractively edged yellowish-white. When young they are tinged pink. It has the bonus of developing terminal clusters of drooping Lily-of-the-Valley-like, white waxy flowers during spring.
Height: 60-75cm (2-2½ft)
Spread: 75-90cm (2½-3ft)
Cultivation: Plant in moisture-retentive, lime-free compost in a medium to large-sized tub. Position in light shade, with protection from cold winds. No regular pruning is

Hebe x andersonii 'Variegata' is superb in a container on a patio, as well as in a small border perhaps alongside a paved area. Choose a pot that harmonizes with the plant.

Above: Pieris japonica 'Variegata'
This slow-growing, variegated, evergreen shrub has mid-green leaves with attractive yellow-white edges. When in a tub do not allow the soil to dry out, especially in summer. And ensure that the compost is acid, not alkaline.

needed, other than cutting out straggly and misplaced shoots in spring. Also, pick off faded flowers.
Propagation: In late summer take 7.5-10cm (3-4in) long cuttings and insert in pots of sandy compost. Place in a cold frame. In spring, pot up the rooted cuttings singly into small pots.

Further plants to consider

Hebe x franciscana 'Variegata'
Height: 45-60cm (1¹/₂-2ft)   Spread: 45-60cm (1¹/₂-2ft)
This slightly tender compact evergreen shrub creates a mound of rich green leaves with creamy edges. Additionally, it bears mauve-blue flowers. When young and smaller than the size suggested above, it can be planted in a window-box. Ensure that it is given a sheltered position on a sunny patio.

Hedera helix
Trailing and cascading
This well-known small-leaved ivy has many varieties that are ideal as climbers, but others, especially when young, are superb for planting in window-boxes to create colour during summer. When planted at the edges of containers they help to soften sharp outlines, as well as providing colour from late spring to the frosts of autumn. Many of these variegated forms are hardy, especially when grown outside during summer, but are best placed in a frost-proof conservatory or greenhouse during winter.

Salvia officinalis 'Tricolor'
Height: 38-45cm (15-18in)   Spread: 38-45cm (15-18in)
When in a tub, this hardy aromatic shrub reaches the above size, but in a border is slightly larger. This variegated plant, related to the common sage, has greyish-green leaves splashed creamy-white and suffused pink. There are many other forms of *Salvia officinalis* – both ornamental and cullinary, such as the Common Sage, that can be planted in containers on patios.

Trachycarpus fortunei
Chusan Palm · Fan Palm (UK) Windmill Palm · Hemp Palm · Chinese Windmill Palm (USA)
Height: 2.4-6m (8-20ft)   Spread: 1.8-3m (6-10ft)
This slow-growing near-hardy palm needs a warm, south or south-west position in a warm climate. Its height and spread are variable, depending on the climate and its age. The fan-like leaves, up to 90cm (3ft) wide, are formed of shiny, mid-green segments. During mid-summer, small yellow flowers are borne in dense clusters. When young it can be grown in a large tub on a sheltered patio, but it is much better when grown at the edge of a paved area, where it will then have a much longer life span.

Vinca major
Periwinkle · Greater Periwinkle (UK and USA) · Blue Buttons · Band Plant (USA)
Height: 15-38cm (6-15in)   Spread: 0.9-1.2m (3-4ft)
This well-known trailing and sprawling plant can be planted around edges of large tubs, helping to soften their often harsh sides, as well as creating a background of shiny, mid to dark green leaves. From spring to mid-summer, and sometimes continuously throughout summer, it bears blue flowers about 2.5cm (1in) wide.

Pieris japonica 'Variegata' is ideal in a woodland setting or in a large tub on a sheltered, lightly-shaded patio. It is best on its own, or merged with all-green plants.

Alyssum maritimum

(*Lobularia maritima*)
Sweet Alyssum (UK and USA)

This popular annual is widely grown as a border edging. It creates a mass of white, lilac or purple flowers from early to late summer. For white flowers, select varieties such as 'Little Dorrit', 'Snow Crystals', 'Carpet of Snow' and 'Minimum'. Correctly, this plant is now known as *Lobularia maritima* but invariably sold as *Alyssum maritimum*.

Height: 7.5-15cm (3-6in)
Spread: 20-30cm (8-12in)
Cultivation: Ordinary well-drained soil and a position in full sun suit it.
Propagation: Plants are usually raised as half-hardy annuals. During late winter or early spring sow seeds 6mm (¼in) deep in seed compost in seedboxes and place in 10-15°C (50-59°F). When the seedlings are large enough to handle prick them off into seedboxes. Slowly harden off the young plants and set into the garden as soon as all risk of frost has passed. Alternatively, in mid-spring sow seeds 6mm (¼in) deep *in situ*.

Alyssum maritimum, when grown in one of its many white forms, creates a pleasing contrast with blue lobelia. Remember that alyssum is more vigorous than the lobelia, so plant them in the ratio of two to one.

Left: Anthemis cupaniana *This bright-faced perennial creates a pleasing partnership with an old container. It is superb when positioned in a lawn, as well as on a patio.*

position.

Propagation: Lift and divide congested plants in spring. Alternatively, in mid-summer take 6.5-7.5cm (2½-3in) long cuttings. Insert them in equal parts moist peat and sharp sand, and place in a cold frame.

Anthemis nobilis

(*Chamaemelum nobile*)
Chamomile · Common Chamomile (UK and USA)
Russian Chamomile (USA)

A well-known mat-forming perennial wlth moss-like, finely-dissected, aromatic, deep green leaves that form a carpet. From mid to late summer it bears white, daisy-like flowers up to 4cm (1½in) wide. As well as creating a sea of attractive foliage, it can be planted in a container, but ensure that its colour creates an harmonious relationship with the foliage.
Height: 10-15cm (4-6in)
Spread: Mat-forming and spreading.
Cultivation: Plant in well-drained soil in full sun. In a container, set the plant 10-13cm (4-5in) apart, but 15cm (6in) when used to create a mat of growth.
Propagation: If only a few plants are needed, lift and divide congested plants in early spring. Alternatively, take 5-7.5cm (2-3in) long basal cuttings in late spring. Insert them in a sandy compost and place in a cold frame. When rooted, pot up into a light, sandy compost.

Left: Anthemis nobilis *Ensure that the colour of the container harmonizes with the deep green foliage. Terracotta containers create the most harmonious combination; avoid garish colours.*

Left: Alyssum maritimum *creates a sea of white flowers throughout summer. Do not let the compost become dry as this quickly reduces the display.*

Anthemis cupaniana

An attractive spreading perennial that can be planted in containers as well as flower borders. It also looks good when planted to trail and tumble over a dry stone wall. The finely-dissected, aromatic, greyish leaves create a superb foil for the bright-faced white flowers which appear from mid to late summer.
Height: 15-25cm (6-10in)
Spread: 30-38cm (12-15in)
Cultivation: Plant in well-drained soil or compost, in a bright sunny

Anthemis cupaniana, when in a flower border should not be planted close to strongly-coloured flowers, as these soon distract attention. Lavender and the Sun Rose (*Cistus x purpureus*) are good companions.

Anthemis nobilis, better known as Chamomile, can be used to create an unusual, but not hard-wearing, lawn. For this purpose, use the variety 'Treneague', a non-flowering variety.

Dimorphotheca ecklonis 'Prostrata'

(*Osteospermum ecklonis 'Prostrata'*)
African Daisy (UK)

This low-growing, bushy and spreading perennial creates a dominant display of white, 7.5cm (3in) wide flowers with mustard-yellow centres during mid and late summer. These are borne amid mid-green, lance-shaped leaves.

Height: 15-20cm (6-8in)
Spread: 30-38cm (12-15in)
Cultivation: Light, well-drained compost and a warm, sunny position suit it best. In autumn, cut down the old stems. During winter, keep excess water off the plants by placing cloches over them.
Propagation: During mid-summer, take 7.5cm (3in) long half-ripe cuttings. Insert them in equal parts

Above: Dimorphotheca ecklonis 'Prostrata' *The white, mustard-yellow centred flowers glisten and sparkle when in sunlight, creating a dominant feature. The old stone sink adds further interest to the display.*

moist peat and sharp sand. Overwinter the plants in a cold frame and plant out into containers in the garden in late spring.

Dimorphotheca ecklonis 'Prostrata' creates a stunningly attractive display when planted in an old stone sink. It is enhanced with a backcloth of the Chilean Potato Tree, (*Solanum crispum*), with aquilegias at the front.

Above: Helichrysum petiolatum
This silver-leaved, tender perennial is ideal for planting in a hanging-basket, where it creates interest throughout summer.

Helichrysum petiolatum

An attractive, sprawling and cascading, tender perennial, ideal for planting in a hanging-basket or in a large pot, where it happily mingles with the other plants. The silver stems and leaves create a superb foil for both yellow-flowered and dark-foliage plants. When planted in a border, it grows up to 38cm (15in) high and creates a mound of attractive foliage. In a pot or hanging-basket it is more reserved. *Helichrysum microphyllum* is another superb plant, with silvery-grey, small leaves.
Height: 20-38cm (8-15in)
Spread: 38-60cm (15-24in)
Cultivation: Plant in light, well-drained compost and position in full sun. Occasionally, trim back long stems to encourage the development of sideshoots and a neater, less sprawling appearance.
Propagation: During mid-summer, take 5cm (2in) long cuttings from sideshoots. Insert in a sandy compost. When rooted, pot up into small pots and overwinter in a frost-proof frame. Avoid high temperatures during winter. Plant into a container in spring.

Further plants to consider

Agapanthus 'Bressingham White'
African Lily (UK and USA)
Height: 75-90cm (2½-3ft)   Spread: 45-60cm (1½-2ft)
A beautiful, fleshy-rooted plant with large, white flower heads borne at the tops of upright stems. Many African Lilies are not fully hardy outside, but this superb plant is ideal for growing in tubs on a patio. It looks especially attractive when planted in a square-sided tub.

Begonia semperflorens 'Olympia White'
Wax Plant (UK and USA)
Height: 15cm (6in)   Spread: 15-20cm (6-8in)
A compact half-hardy annual which is planted into window-boxes, troughs and tubs in early summer, after all risk of frost has passed. It is just as attractive when planted in the garden. Pure-white flowers appear above glossy, dark green leaves during summer. For colour contrast grow it with an orange-scarlet variety such as 'Sheila'.

Crocus chrysanthus 'Snow Bunting'
Height: 7.5-13cm (3-5in)   Spread: 6.5-7.5cm (2½-3in)
This small bulbous plant has white petals and a deep yellow throat. The outsides of the petals are marked with deep purple. The flowers appear during late winter and are ideal for brightening containers, as well as the edges of patios.

Echeverias
Height: 7.5-15cm (3-6in) - wide range   Spread: 7.5-13cm (3-5in)
These are usually thought to be houseplants, but during summer they can be placed outdoors on a sunny patio. The range of echeverias is wide. Many have attractive, succulent leaves, which are borne in rosettes and have a white, waxy sheen.

Geranium 'White Orbit'
Height: 30cm (12in)   Spread: 30-38cm (12-15in)
A beautiful geranium raised from seed sown during mid to late winter in 21-24°C (70-75°F). Maintain an even temperature and when the seedlings are large enough to handle prick out into seedboxes. Slowly harden off and plant into containers, or the garden, after all risk of frost has passed. This superb variety has short flowering stems and compact heads full of white flowers.

Santolina chamaecyparissus corsica
Height: 30-38cm (12-15in)   Spread: 30-38cm (12-15in)
This is a slightly smaller and more compact form of *Santolina chamaecyparissus*, also known as Cotton Lavender and Lavender Cotton. This smaller type is ideal for a small container or planting in a rock garden, where its dome shape and finely-dissected silvery and woolly leaves soon capture attention. During summer it becomes covered with bright lemon-yellow, button-like flowers. Plant it in a small, round tub and position in full sun.

Helichrysum petiolatum, like many other silver-foliaged plants, thrives in sunny places and in a well-drained light soil. These plants are usually also relatively tolerant of dry soils.

CHAPTER FOUR

WALLS AND TRELLISES

T here are few gardens that do not have space for several climbers. Even the most modest bungalow has growing space that is not usually exploited, and a rear garden is likely to have an area of close-boarded or other fencing available for growing plants. If garden fencing cannot be used, pergolas, rustic poles or trellises can be erected. All too often vertical space is ignored, and the smaller the garden, the more valuable this area of space becomes.

There are climbers and wall shrubs to suit all walls, from those with a warm and southerly aspect to those which face east or north. Wall shrubs for southerly or westerly aspects include the Moroccan Broom (*Cytisus battandieri*), with golden-yellow flowers during mid-summer, and the Evergreen Laburnum (*Piptanthus laburnifolius*), with pea-shaped, bright-yellow flowers in late spring and early summer. Wall shrubs for cold walls include the Firethorn (*Pyracantha* 'Watereri') with foamy-white flowers in summer, followed by bright red berries which last well into the winter months.

Several climbers and wall shrubs also bloom in winter. One of the best known of the winter-brighteners is the Winter-flowering Jasmine (*Jasminum nudiflorum*). It is one of nature's leaners, needing a framework to which it can be tied. From early winter and often to early spring it bears yellow, star-shaped flowers along shoots bare of leaves.

Climbers with coloured foliage, such as the soft–yellow leaved *Humulus lupulus aureus* bring further vertical colour to a garden, while those with leaves that become richly-coloured in autumn are a further attraction. Perhaps the best known one is the Boston Ivy (*Parthenocissus tricuspidata*), which has rich crimson and scarlet leaves in autumn.

Heights and spreads given for the plants in this chapter should only be taken as guides. If more space is available in one direction, the plant will adapt its growth accordingly.

Left: Wisteria sinensis 'Alba' *soon clothes a wall with large, pendulous bunches of white, pea-like and sweetly-scented flowers.*

Abutilon megapotamicum

Trailing Abutilon (USA)

A distinctive, somewhat tender wall shrub with slender stems bearing three-lobed, slender-pointed bright green leaves. During early to late summer, it reveals pendulous, bell-shaped, red and yellow flowers.
Height: 1.5-1.8m (5-6ft)
Spread: 1.8-2.4m (6-8ft)
Cultivation: Good, well-drained garden soil in a sheltered and sunny position is essential. It is not hardy outside in all areas. In cold areas it is best grown in a greenhouse. This plant does not need regular pruning.

A greenhouse border abutilon, somewhat similar to *A. megapotamicum*, is *A. x milleri*. It is a garden hybrid between *A. megapotamicum* and *A. pictum*. In a greenhouse border it rises to 1.8m (6ft) high and 2.4 (8ft) wide, although in a large pot it reaches only about half this size. It is a plant which is well worth growing in a pot in a conservatory. It has the same slender habit as *A. megapotamicum*, with 4cm (1½in) long yellow flowers striped red from late spring to late autumn. Another abutilon for a greenhouse border is *A. x hybridum* 'Ashford Red', with similar growth measurements as *A. x milleri* when grown in a greenhouse border or in a pot. The mid-green three to five-lobed leaves present a perfect foil for the 4cm (1½in) long pendant salmon-red flowers borne from late spring.
Propagation: During mid-summer take 7.5-10cm (3-4in) long half-ripe cuttings. Insert in pots containing equal parts peat and sharp sand and keep at 15°C (58°F). When the plants are rooted, pot them up into loam-based compost.

Right: **Abutilon megapotamicum**
This fairly tender wall shrub soon attracts attention with its red and yellow flowers, borne from early to late summer. A sunny position against a wall is essential.

Abutilon megapotamicum is an adaptable plant. Its slender stems allow it to be trained to suit many positions – in corners, under windows or between large windows. It needs wire for support.

Above: **Camellia x williamsii 'Donation'** *This lovely shrub thrives in an.
acid soil and a sheltered position, producing a wealth of semi-double
orchid-pink flowers from late winter to spring. Avoid places where the
early-morning sun will shine on frost-covered flowers.*

Camellia x williamsii

This well-known hardy evergreen
shrub is a hybrid between *Camellia
japonica,* the Common Camellia,
and *Camellia salvenensis,* the
Salwin River Camellia from
Western China. The flowers, which
appear even on small plants, are
either single or semi-double and
range from white and pink to rose-
purple, all displaying distinctive
yellow stamens. They are 5-7.5cm
(2-3in) wide and appear from early
winter to spring. Pink forms include
'Citation' (semi-double and pale
pink), 'Coppelia' (single and
carmine-rose), 'Donation' (semi-
double and silvery-pink), 'J.C.
Williams' (single and blush-pink),
'November Pink' (single, early and
bright pink) and 'St. Ewe' (single,
funnel-shaped and rose-pink).
Height: 1.8-2.4m (6-8ft)
Spread: 1.2-1.8m (4-6ft)

Cultivation: Fertile, light, acid
moisture-retentive soil and a
position in sun or partial shade suit
this beautiful shrub. Light shade
from trees is ideal, giving protection
from frost and strong sun in the
early morning. A south-facing
position should be avoided
because these plants need a cool
root-run. No pruning is needed,
except in the initial shaping of the
shrub and the annual removal of
misplaced and straggling shoots.
Propagation: During mid-summer,
take 7.5-10cm (3-4in) long cuttings
and insert them in pots containing
equal parts peat and sharp sand,
kept at 13°C (55°F). Pot up the
rooted cuttings into an acid loam-
based compost and slowly
acclimatize them to a lower
temperature. Alternatively, layer
low-growing shoots in early
autumn, although it takes about 18
months to produce roots.

Camellia japonica, the Common Camellia, is a
splendid shrub with some beautiful red varieties, such
as 'Chandleri' (semi-double), 'Donckelarii' (semi-
double flowers) and 'Mathotiana' (double).

WALLS AND TRELLISES

Above: **Cotoneaster horizontalis** *A reliable shrub that brings colour to any garden in autumn with its beautiful red berries. It is excellent for planting against walls, on banks or as ground-cover.*

Cotoneaster horizontalis

Herringbone Cotoneaster ·
Fishbone Cotoneaster (UK)
Rock Cotoneaster (USA)

This popular semi-evergreen or deciduous hardy shrub has small, dark glossy green leaves borne on stiff frameworks of branches that spread out in a herringbone fashion. The 8-12mm (1/3-1/2in) wide pink flowers appear in mid-summer and are followed in autumn by round red berries borne in profusion along the branches. This is an adaptable shrub with many roles in the garden, from covering banks, where it will rise to 60cm (2ft) with a spread up to 1.8m (6ft), to sprawling over low walls or planting against a wall, where it will grow to 1.8-2.4m (6-8ft) tall with a spread of 1.5-2.1m (5-7ft). It is an

ideal shrub for east and north-facing walls.
Cultivation: Any good garden soil and a sunny position suit it, although it is hardy enough for a cold wall.
Propagation: Although it can be increased by seeds sown in autumn or early winter in pots of loam-based compost, placed in a cold frame or a sheltered position in a corner of the garden, this method takes a long time to produce sizeable plants. As an alternative, take heel cuttings 7.5-10cm (3-4in) long in late summer and insert them in pots of equal parts peat and sand, placed in a cold frame. Plant out the cuttings in a nursery bed when they are rooted and established. A further method is to layer low-growing shoots in late autumn or early winter.

Parthenocissus tricuspidata

(*Vitis inconstans*)
Boston Ivy (UK)
Boston Ivy · Japanese Ivy (USA)

This is a hardy and vigorous self-clinging deciduous climber from China, Japan, Korea and Taiwan. The shape of the leaves is variable, but usually toothed and trifoliate in young leaves and three-lobed in older ones. In autumn they turn a gloriously rich crimson and scarlet. The form 'Veitchii' (previously known as *Ampelopsis veitchii*) bears small leaves tinged purple when young.
Height: 7.5-15m (20-50ft)
Spread: 4.5-7.5m (15-25ft)
Cultivation: Fertile soil and a large wall or tree up which it can climb are the essential elements for success with this beautiful and popular climber; given these, it flourishes with little or no assistance.
Propagation: During late summer take 10-13cm (4-5in) long cuttings. Insert them in sandy compost and keep at 13°C (55°F). Pot up when rooted. Alternatively, long shoots can be layered in late autumn.

Robinia hispida

Rose Acacia (UK)
Moss Locust · Rose Acacia ·
Bristly Locust · Mossy Locust (USA)

This is an open, rather gaunt hardy deciduous shrub from South-east North America, ideal for growing against a south or west-facing wall. The dark green leaves, up to 25cm (10in) long, are formed of seven to thirteen leaflets each 4-6.5cm (1½-2½in) long. The distinctive pea-like rose-pink flowers are about 3cm (1¼in) long and borne in drooping bunches of five to ten flowers, in early to mid-summer.
Height: 1.8-2.4m (6-8ft)
Spread: 2.1-2.7m (7-9ft)
Cultivation: Any well-drained moderately-rich soil in a sunny position suits a robinia. Avoid excessively rich soil. No regular pruning is needed.

Cotoneaster horizontalis planted against a high wall at the back of a border provides a useful foil for many shrubs, including azaleas. When grown as ground-cover in a border it merges with other shrubs, especially grey-leaved ones.

Propagation: It is best raised by grafting onto its relative *Robinia pseudoacacia,* although suckers can be detached from the bases of non-grafted plants.

Above: Parthenocissus tricuspidata *This hardy deciduous climber produces a generous covering of rich crimson and scarlet leaves in autumn. The only drawback is that it needs a large wall up which to climb. Alternatively, it is at home climbing a large, old tree that would be enhanced by a dash of colour and glamour in autumn.*

Right: Robinia hispida
The pea-like rose-pink flowers of this early-summer-flowering wall shrub are especially appealing against an old brick wall. A sunny position is essential for success.

Parthenocissus henryana, the Chinese Virginia Creeper, is best suited to a small garden, and it requires a sheltered position. The leaves, formed of three or five leaflets, turn shades of red in autumn.

Robinia hispida was first seen and collected by an Englishman, Mark Catesby, in the foothills of the Appalachian Mountains in 1714. Before he was able to collect seeds the region was burnt by Indians.

Right: **Tropaeolum speciosum**
Bright scarlet flowers appear on the scrambling stems during summer, with a backcloth provided by mid-green six-lobed leaves. The plant is seen at its best when it is growing through and over other shrubs.

Tropaeolum majus

Nasturtium · Great Indian Cress (UK)

A well-known and widely-grown climbing and trailing hardy annual from South America, ideal for covering fences, trelliswork and for scrambling over banks. The highly distinctive smooth and mid-green leaves are circular, and the early to late summer 5cm (2in) wide orange or yellow flowers are faintly scented. Also, the leaves have a strong, pungent smell. The colour range has been extended to include red, pink and maroon flowers.
Height: 1.7-2.4m (6-8ft) climbing type
Spread: 60cm-1.2m (2-4ft) climbing type
Cultivation: This is an ideal plant for poor soils and a sunny position. If the soil is rich, the growth of the plants is excessive and at the expense of the flowers. Initially, the young plants need twiggy sticks up which to climb, but once established on a trellis or wire framework, they need no extra support.
Propagation: During spring, seeds can be sown 18mm (³⁄₄in) deep where the plants are to flower. If the seedlings are crowded, thin them out to 10-15cm (4-6in) apart. However, for early-flowering plants, especially those for hanging baskets, sow seeds in early spring in trays of loam-based seed compost at 13°C (55°F). When they are large enough to handle, put the seedlings singly in 7.5cm (3in) pots and slowly harden them off in a cold frame until they can be planted outside during late spring or early summer when they are growing strongly.

Left: **Tropaeolum majus** *The original form of this hardy trailing and climbing annual is yellow and orange, but seedsmen have extended the colour range to include red, pink and maroon. It is an ideal climber for poor soil.*

Tropaeolum speciosum

Flame Creeper · Flame Nasturtium · Scotch Flame Flower (UK)

An exotic-looking Chilean deciduous perennial climber, the Flame Creeper has a creeping rhizome-producing rootstock that dies down to soil-level in autumn. It has a sprawling growth habit, with downy and hairy stems bearing six-lobed mid-green leaves, which have downy undersides. During

Tropaeolum majus has long been used by cooks as well as gardeners. The flowers and young leaves can be added to salads, and have a warm taste not unlike that of common cress.

mid-summer to autumn it reveals 4cm (1½in) wide long-stemmed trumpet-like scarlet flowers formed of five rounded and waved petals.
Height: 3-4.5m (10-15ft)
Spread: 75cm-1m (2½-3½ft)
Cultivation: Acid or neutral soil enriched with leafmould and peat suits this plant. It does best when planted in association with a shrub through which its stems can clamber. The flowers are then able to reach the light, while the roots remain cool.
Propagation: It is easily increased by lifting and dividing the roots in early spring, setting them 15-20cm (6-8in) deep. Take care not to damage the fleshy roots. It can also be increased by sowing seeds in a cold frame in spring, but it is difficult to establish.

Further plants to consider

Akebia quinata
Five-leaf Akebia · Chocolate Vine (USA)
Height: 1.5-2.4m (5-8ft)   Spread: 1.2-1.5m (4-5ft)
A sprawling and lax semi-evergreen climber with leaves formed of five leaflets. The fragrant red-purple flowers appear in spring.

Berberidopsis coraliina
Coral Plant (UK)
Height: 4.5m (15ft)   Spread: 2.4-3.5m (8-12ft)
A distinctive evergreen climber, well suited to a shaded and sheltered wall. During mid to late summer, it bears clusters of deep coral-crimson flowers.

Campsis radicans
Trumpet Vine (UK)
Cow-itch · Trumpet Honeysuckle (USA)
A superb self-clinging hardy deciduous climber with light green leaves formed of seven to eleven leaflets. During late summer, it displays rich scarlet and orange trumpet-shaped flowers.

Clematis montana 'Rubens'
Mountain Clematis (UK)
Height: 7.5-10.5m (25-35ft)   Spread: 4.5-6m (15-20ft)
A beautiful vigorous deciduous climber with bronze-green leaves and pale pink flowers.

Clematis – Large-flowered
Several of these magnificent shrubs have red and pink forms including 'Ernest Markham' (petunia-red), 'Hagley Hybrid' (shell-pink), 'Nelly Moser' (mauve-pink with a carmine bar) and 'Ville de Lyon' (bright carmine-red).

Lapageria rosea
Chilean Bell Flower (UK)   Chile-bells · Copihue (USA)
Height: 3-4.5m (10-15ft)   Spread: 1.8-2.4m (6-8ft)
A semi-hardy tender, evergreen climber that needs a sheltered and relatively frost free position. From mid-summer to autumn it displays rose-crimson bell-shaped flowers, singly or in clusters.

Parthenocissus quinquefolia
(*Vitis quinquefolia* · *Vitis hederacea*)
True Virginia Creeper · Virginia Creeper (UK)
American Ivy · Five-leaved Ivy · Virginia Creeper (USA)
Height: 12-18m (40-60ft)   Spread: 6-10.5m (20-35ft)
A vigorous and spreading hardy deciduous climber with matt-green leaves, formed of three or five leaflets, which turn brilliant scarlet and orange in autumn.

Tropaeolum speciosum is useful for growing through shrubs, but it can also be planted in conjunction with a climber, such as the variegated small-leaved ivy *Hedera helix* 'Goldheart'.

WALLS AND TRELLISES

Above: **Abutilon vitifolium** *This nearly-hardy shrub is a delight when set against a warm wall, where it will produce pale to deep mauve flowers in early and mid-summer. It likes the shade and protection afforded by nearby plants.*

Abutilon vitifolium

Flowering Maple · Parlor Maple · Indian Maple (USA)

This beautiful deciduous shrub needs the protection of a warm wall, and grows best in milder climates. It develops downy, grey, three or five-lobed, palm-like leaves, and 5cm (2in) wide, pale to deep mauve flowers that open flat during early and mid-summer. The form 'Veronica Tennant' produces large flowers.
Height: 2.4-5m (8-15ft)
Spread: 1.5-2.1m (5-7ft)
Cultivation: Well-drained ordinary garden soil suits it; choose a position in slight shade and against a warm south or west-facing wall. No regular pruning is needed.
Propagation: It is best raised from seeds sown in mid-spring in loam-based compost at 16°C (61°F). When they are large enough to handle, prick out the seedlings into pots of loam-based compost and place them in a cold frame. Once the young plants are established, plant them out into a nursery bed for a couple of years.

Ceanothus impressus

Californian Lilac (UK)
Santa Barbara Ceanothus (USA)

This impressive evergreen shrub with a bushy habit is best grown against a warm wall. In the open it is not fully hardy. During spring, it reveals clusters of deep blue flowers amid small deep green leaves with deeply impressed veins.
Height: 2.4-3m (8-10ft).
Spread: 1.8-2.4m (6-8ft)
Cultivation: Light, fertile soil and a south or west-facing wall suit it best. It tolerates lime in the soil. No regular pruning is needed, other than initially shaping it when young.
Propagation: During late summer take half-ripe cuttings 6.5-7.5cm (2½-3in) long, inserting them in pots of equal parts peat and sharp sand. Place them in a propagation frame at 16°C (61°F). When the cuttings are rooted, pot them up into small pots of loam-based compost, setting them out in the garden when they are well grown.

Above: **Ceanothus impressus**
This beautiful evergreen Californian Lilac with small deep blue flowers in spring is not fully hardy and requires the protection of a south or west-facing wall. Ceanothus plants are native to North America, and come mostly from California.

Ceanothus rigidus

Californian Lilac (UK)
Monterey Ceanothus (USA)

This beautiful half-hardy evergreen wall shrub has distinctive wedge-shaped dark green leaves and 18-25mm (³/₄-1in) long clusters of purple-blue flowers during spring. It has a stiff, upright, compact growth habit, ideal for narrow or restricted areas.
Height: 1.8-3m (6-10ft)
Spread: 1.2-1.5m (4-5ft)
Cultivation: Light, fertile soil and a warm wall facing south or west ensure success. No regular pruning is needed, other than shaping during formative years.

Abutilon vitifolium is superb with yellow-flowered shrubs and trees, such as the glorious bright yellow daisy-like flowers of *Senecio* 'Sunshine' and the sweetly-scented yellow broom *Genista cinerea*.

Ceanothus impressus is superb when positioned under a high window or at the side of a lower one. Because of its neat, tight growth small late-winter and spring-flowering bulbs can be set at its base.

Propagation: During late summer, take half-ripe cuttings 6.5-7.5cm (2½-3in) long, inserting them in pots of equal parts peat and sharp sand. Place them in a propagation frame at 16°C (61°F). When the cuttings are rooted, pot them up into small pots of loam-based compost, planting them out in the garden when they are well grown.

Left: **Ceanothus rigidus** *This half-hardy evergreen shrub is ideal for a narrow, restricted area against a wall. It is a native of North America and was first introduced into England in 1847.*

Ceanothus thrysiflorus repens

Californian Lilac (UK)
Creeping Blueblossom (USA)

This hardy, vigorous, mound-forming evergreen shrub is ideal for planting against a wall, where it creates a dense screen of small shiny green leaves and light blue flowers in 7.5cm (3in) long clusters during early summer. This versatile shrub is also suitable for a large rock garden.
Height: 1.2-1.5m (4-5ft)
Spread: 1.5-1.8m (5-6ft)
Cultivation: Light, fertile soil and a south or west-facing position are best. No regular pruning is needed, other than an initial pruning during its formative years.
Propagation: During late summer, take half-ripe cuttings 6.5-7.5cm (2½-3in) long, inserting them in pots of equal parts peat and sharp sand. Place them in a propagation frame at 16°C (61°F). When they are rooted, pot up the cuttings into small pots of loam-based compost, and plant them in the garden when they are well grown. Ensure the young plants are well established.

Left: **Ceanothus thrysiflorus repens** *This hardy evergreen shrub is ideal for covering walls, especially under windows. It is lower growing than* Ceanothus thrysiflorus, *which often reaches 3m (10ft) or more.*

Ceanothus rigidus is an excellent partner for low growing yellow-flowered shrubs that will continue the display into summer. Potentillas, with their long flowering period, are ideal for this purpose.

Ceanothus thrysiflorus repens creates a display of flowers at an earlier stage in its life than most ceanothus species – often when only two years old – so it is useful in new gardens or re-planned ones.

WALLS AND TRELLISES

Clematis – Large-flowered Types

These are some of the most spectacular and well-known of all climbers, producing a stunning display of large flowers during summer. They are derived from several forms, such as *florida, Jackmanii, lanuginosa, patens, texensis* and *viticella*. They are superb for training over pergolas, trellises or along wires tensioned against a wall. Most are single forms, but a few have double flowers. They include a wide range of colours, among which blue, mauve and purple can be found in the following types: 'Alice Fisk' (mauve), 'Barbara Dibley' (pansy-violet, with a carmine stripe), 'Belle of Woking' (pale mauve, and double), 'Gipsy Queen' (rich velvety violet-purple), 'Jackmanii Superba' (rich violet-purple), 'Marcel Moser' (mauve, with a deep carmine bar), 'Mrs Cholmondely' (pale blue), 'Percy Picton' (intense mauve with a pink eye), 'President' – also called 'The President' – (deep purple-blue), 'Vyvyan Pennell' – (deep violet-blue) and 'William Kennet' (lavender-blue).

Height: 1.2-3m (4-10ft)

Spread: 75cm-1.8m (2½-6ft)

Cultivation: Slightly alkaline, fertile, well-drained soil and an open and sunny position suit it, but the roots must be shaded from strong sunlight and you must not allow the soil to become dry during summer. Low-growing plants, as well as shrubs, can be positioned to keep the roots shaded and cool.

Propagation: They root readily from 10-13cm (4-5in) long stem cuttings taken in mid-summer and inserted in pots of equal parts peat and sharp sand, kept at 16°C (61°F). When the cuttings are rooted, pot them up singly into 7.5cm (3in) pots of loam-based compost and place them in a cold frame during winter. Transfer the cuttings to larger pots in spring or summer and plant them out into the garden in autumn. Alternatively, new plants can be obtained by layering low shoots in spring; they will root within a year or so.

Above: **Clematis 'Alice Fisk'**
This eye-catching clematis, which produces an abundance of large blooms, is a delight in a flower border when given a rustic pole for support. It does well in combination with other plants, which give its roots welcome shade.

Left: **Clematis 'Percy Picton'**
This is a relatively weak-growing type, but is ideal when planted in a small area. It is especially attractive when planted against a well-weathered wall.

Right: **Cobaea scandens**
This vigorous climber is grown as a half-hardy annual, and needs a sheltered and sunny position. The large bell-shaped purple flowers have distinctive green calyces (their outer protective parts).

Clematis are easily trained up supports, as they hang by their leaves. Each leaf is formed of several leaflets held on long stalks, and it is these that secure the shoots in position.

Clematis are exciting when planted in association with roses, perhaps either side of an entrance. Blue clematis are eye-catching with yellow, creamy-white or pink roses, and low growing plants at the base to keep their roots cool.

Cobea scandens

Cathedral Bells · Cup and Saucer Vine (UK)
Mexican Ivy · Monastery Bells · Cup and Saucer Vine (USA)

This spectacular Mexican half-hardy perennial climber is best grown as a half-hardy annual. Fast-growing, it is ideal for trellis work and pergolas, displaying mid to dark green leaves formed of three pairs of leaflets, and 6.5-7.5cm (2½-3in) long, bell-shaped, purple flowers with green, saucer-like calyces (outer, protective parts) from early to late summer. In a greenhouse it soon reaches 6m (20ft).

Height: 3-4.5m (10-15ft)
Spread: 1.8m (6ft)
Cultivation: Ordinary well-drained garden soil and a sunny, sheltered position are needed. If the soil is too rich, excessive growth is produced at the expense of flowers. Nip out the tips of young plants to encourage the development of sideshoots. Wire supports or wooden trelliswork are needed for support.
Propagation: During late winter and early spring, sow seeds singly 12mm (½in) deep in 7.5cm (3in) pots containing loam-based compost and kept at 16°C (61°F). When young plants are established move them to a cold frame to harden off. Plant into the garden after all risk of frost has passed.

Further plants to consider

Clematis alpina
(*Atragene alpina*)
Height: 1.5-1.8m (5-6ft)   Spread: 90cm-1.2m (3-4ft)
An attractive, but weak-growing deciduous climber, with 2.5-3cm (1-1½in) wide, cup-shaped, violet-blue, late spring and early summer flowers that hang with their faces downwards. The form 'Frances Rivis' is free-flowering, with larger flowers.

Clematis macropetala
Height: 2.4-3.6m (8-12ft)   Spread: 1.2-1.5m (4-5ft)
A hardy, bushy, deciduous climber, related and quite similar to *C. alpina*. It produces 5-7.5cm (2-3in) wide, pendulous, light and dark blue flowers in early to mid-summer. The form 'Maidwell Hall' has deep blue flowers.

Clematis viticella
Height: 2.4-3.5m (8-12ft)   Spread: 1.5-1.8m (5-6ft)
A slender though bushy deciduous climber, with bell-shaped 5-6.5 cm (2-2½in) wide blue, violet or reddish-purple flowers during mid to late summer and in to early autumn. The form 'Abundance' has soft purple flowers and 'Royal Velours' has deep velvety-purple ones.

Passiflora caerulea
Common Passion Flower · Blue Passion Flower (UK) · Blue Passion Flower (USA)
Height: 6-7.5m (20-25ft)   Spread: 4.5-6m (15-20ft)
A vigorous evergreen climber, not fully hardy in cold, exposed areas. During summer, it has 7.5cm (3in) wide white-petalled flowers with blue-purple centres.

Solanum crispum
Chilean Potato Tree (UK)
Height: 4.5-6m (15-20ft)   Spread: 3.5-4.5m (12-15ft)
A hardy semi-evergreen bushy and scrambling climber, producing star-shaped purple-blue flowers with yellow anthers from mid-summer into autumn. The form 'Glasnevin' (syn. 'Autumnale') is hardier than the original type species.

Solanum jasminoides
Jasmine Nightshade (UK) · Potato Vine (USA)
Height: 3-4.5m (10-15ft)   Spread: 1.8-2.4m (6-8ft)
A rapid-growing, twining, evergreen climber, which has star-shaped pale blue flowers, with golden anthers in their centres, from mid-summer to autumn.

Wisteria floribunda 'Macrobotry'
Japanese Wisteria (UK and USA)
Height: 7.5-9m (25-30ft)   Spread: 6-7.5m (20-25ft)
A spectacular hardy deciduous climber, displaying fragrant lilac-blue and purple flowers in drooping clusters up to 90cm (3ft) long in early to mid-summer. Arguably, it is the last word in climbers, and is certain to catch the eye.

Annual climbers have the advantage of quickly clothing trelliswork or pergolas and of producing variety each year – important in small gardens where change is needed to create continuing interest.

Above: **Cytisus battandieri** *This wall shrub is a spectacular plant from Morocco, with pineapple-scented flowers displayed in cone-like heads during mid-summer. The silvery leaves are a further delight.*

Cytisus battandieri

Moroccan Broom (UK)

This startlingly attractive deciduous or semi-evergreen shrub from the Atlas Mountains in Morocco is often grown as a free-standing shrub, and is ideal for south or west-facing walls. The pineapple-scented, golden-yellow mid-summer flowers are borne in 10cm (4in) long cone-like clusters during mid-summer. The large, grey, laburnum-like leaves are covered with silky-white hairs which give them a silvery appearance.
Height: 2.4-3.5m (8-12ft)
Spread: 2.4-3m (8-10ft)
Cultivation: Well-drained, deeply-cultivated neutral or slightly acid soil is best. Soils which are alkaline tend to make the plant short-lived. A south or west-facing wall is best. The shrub flowers on wood formed the previous season, so cut back the shoots after flowering to within a few inches of their bases. Do not cut into the old wood, as it may then not break into new growth.
Propagation: You can sow seeds in spring and raise the seedlings in a cold frame. Alternatively, take 7.5-10cm (3-4in) long heel cuttings in late summer. Insert them into pots containing equal parts of peat and sharp sand, and transfer to a cold frame. Pot up the cuttings, when rooted, into small pots of a peat-based compost and plant out into the garden in late summer.

Humulus lupulus aureus

This is an unusual herbaceous perennial climber with soft yellow three to five-lobed coarsely-toothed leaves, 10-15cm (4-6in) wide. It has stems which twine clockwise. It is especially useful for clothing garden features such as arches and pergolas, or perhaps trailing over a path and forming a tunnel of soft yellow leaves.
Height: 3-6cm (10-20ft)
Spread: 2.4-3.5m (8-12ft)
Cultivation: Fertile, moist but not waterlogged soil suits it best, and a position in full sun. In autumn, remove all dead foliage and cut the stems down to soil-level.

Cytisus battandieri, with its bright-yellow flowers, contrasts perfectly with the strong blue flowers of agapanthus set below it. Both these plants appreciate a warm, sunny position.

Humulus lupulus aureus soon takes to a trellis or pergola, but will also trail and climb through a neglected, sparse hedge, filling the gaps with its attractive yellow leaves.

Jasminum nudiflorum

Winter-flowering Jasmine · Winter Jasmine (UK)

This hardy deciduous shrub with long, whip-like stems is perhaps one of the best known winter-flowering shrubs, blooming from early winter often through to early spring. It has lustrous dark green leaves, each made up of three leaflets, and 18-25mm (³/₄-1in) wide, bright yellow star-shaped flowers, borne singly or in small clusters on shoots developed since the previous spring. During flowering, the shoots are bare of leaves. It is not strictly a climber, but a 'leaner' that needs support.

Height: 1.8-3m (6-10ft)
Spread: 1.8-2.4m (6-8ft)
Cultivation: This jasmine needs moderately fertile well-drained soil, preferably against an east or north-facing wall. The dainty flowers do not appear to be damaged by frost alone, but when frost is combined with early-morning sun, it causes damage. Because the flowers are produced on shoots developed since the previous spring, it can be pruned back hard in spring. Leave all the main shoots alone and just cut back the flowered shoots to two or three buds of their origin. This pruning encourages the development of side-shoots which will bear flowers the following winter. The new shoots will need tying-in to supports throughout the summer months.

Propagation: During late summer, take 7.5-10cm (3-4in) long semi-ripe cuttings; cut the lower ends just below a leaf-joint. Insert them into pots containing equal parts of peat and sharp sand, and keep at 7°C (45°F). When the cuttings are rooted, pot them up into 7.5cm (3in) pots of loam-based compost and put them in a cold frame. Alternatively, layer low-growing shoots in autumn. Rooting usually takes about a year.

Above: **Humulus lupulus aureus**
The soft yellow, three to five-lobed leaves of this herbaceous perennial form a dense screen ideal for covering unsightly objects. In fertile, moist soil it soon becomes an eye-catching display.

Right: **Jasminum nudiflorum**
This winter-flowering shrub can be trained against a wall or allowed to sprawl up and over a low wall. The bright yellow, star-shaped flowers are borne singly or in small clusters along bare shoots.

Propagation: It can be increased from seed, but division of the rootstock in early autumn or spring is an easier method of propagation.

Jasminum nudiflorum looks good with another winter flowering plant, *Mahonia aquifolium*, which has terminal clusters of golden-yellow flowers. It also mixes with the violet and yellow *Iris histrioides*.

WALLS AND TRELLISES

Lonicera nitida 'Baggesen's Gold'

A densely-leaved evergreen shrub
with 6mm (¼in) long, golden-yellow
leaves which turn yellow-green in
autumn. It can be grown as a
specimen shrub in a border, where
its foliage has year-round interest.
But it is best positioned against a
sunny wall or unsightly shed or
garage, where it soon forms an
attractive screen.
Height: 1.5-1.8m (5-6ft)
Spread: 90cm-1.5m (3-5ft)
Cultivation: Lonicera likes a well-
drained fertile soil in full sun. Good
light enhances the attractive leaves
and maintains their gold colouring.
No regular pruning is needed, other
than trimming it in spring to fill the
space allotted to it. Although, like
its parent form, it can be trimmed
with shears, it is far better left with
a more informal shape.
Propagation: An easy way is to
layer low-growing shoots in late
summer or early winter. They
usually take about a year to
develop roots. Also, hardwood
cuttings, 20-25cm (8-10in) long,
can be taken in late summer and
inserted in a sheltered corner.
These also take about a year to
produce roots. Another way is to
take 10cm (4in) long cuttings
during mid to late summer,
inserting them in pots containing
equal parts of peat and sharp sand
and placing them in a cold frame.
Pot up the cuttings, when they are
rooted, into a loam-based compost,
and replace in the cold frame. Plant
out in a nursery bed in spring until
established, when they can be
planted in their final sites in autumn
or in the following spring. Choose a
sunny position.

Lonicera tragophylla

Chinese Woodbine (UK)

A beautiful, vigorous, deciduous
climber, ideal for fences, archways,
pergolas and walls, this plant was
introduced into cultivation in 1900
from its native Western China.
During mid-summer, it displays
large terminal clusters of scentless,
bright golden-yellow flowers with
trumpets up to 4cm (1½in) wide
and tubes up to 7.5cm (3in) long.
Height: 4.5-6m (15-20ft)
Spread: 3-4.5m (10-15ft)
Cultivation: It delights in a position
with a cool root-run. Well-drained
relatively fertile soil is needed, with
the foliage and flowers in full sun.
No regular pruning is needed, other
than cutting out dead wood after
flowering.
Propagation: Seeds can be sown
in loam-based compost when ripe
in early autumn, and placed in a
cold frame. Alternatively, take 7.5-
10cm (3-4in) long cuttings in mid-
summer. Insert them into pots
containing equal parts of peat and
sharp sand and place them in a
cold frame. When rooted, pot up
the cuttings and replace them in
the cold frame.

Lonicera nitida 'Baggesen's Gold' is ideal for
covering unsightly sheds or garages. Bulbs with
strong blue flowers make a superb colour contrast
set close to its base; Grape Hyacinths are ideal.

Piptanthus laburnifolius

(Piptanthus nepalensis)
Evergreen Laburnum

This is an unusual, slightly tender, almost evergreen shrub with dark green leaves formed of three lance-shaped leaflets, 7.5-15cm (3-6in) long. The pea-shaped, bright-yellow laburnum-like flowers, 4cm (1½in) long, appear in late spring and early summer. It can be grown in the open, but does better against a south or west-facing wall.
Height: 2.4-3.5m (8-12ft)
Spread: 1.8-3m (6-10ft)
Cultivation: Light, well-drained soil in a sheltered, warm position is essential. No regular pruning is needed, other than cutting out dead branches in spring. If the foliage has been badly damaged by frost, cut it back in spring.
Propagation: It is easily increased from seeds sown in early spring in peaty compost and placed in a cold frame. When large enough to handle, prick off the seedlings into small pots of loam-based compost. The plants can be set in a nursery bed in autumn, for a year or so. Alternatively, take 7.5-10cm (3-4in) long, half-ripe heel cuttings in late summer. When they are rooted, pot them up into small pots.

Above: Lonicera tragophylla
This vigorous climber is well suited to a large wall, in a position which gives it a cool root-run and plenty of sun for the foliage. Flowering is during mid-summer. It is best positioned where its roots are in shade, perhaps from a shrub.

Right: Piptanthus laburnifolius
This unusual, almost evergreen shrub bears pea-shaped, bright-yellow flowers in late summer. It can be grown as a specimen shrub, but is better against a warm wall. It will not live long in cold or very windy areas.

Lonicera tragophylla is ideal for trailing over a sparsely foliaged tree, a trellis or a pergola. The roots soon find the cool side of the tree, while the flowers climb into the sunlight.

Rosa ecae 'Helen Knight'

A dainty, hardy, deciduous shrub rose, well-branched and prickly with slender, pliable, arching reddish-brown stems. The small, fern-like leaves are formed of five to nine oval leaflets, with the clear yellow, saucer-shaped flowers, 5cm (2in) wide, borne freely during mid-summer.

Height: 1.5-2.1m (5-7ft)
Spread: 1.2-1.5m (4-5ft)
Cultivation: Ordinary well-drained garden soil, not too light is suitable. A position in full sun is essential, facing south or west. Little pruning is needed, other than thinning out congested wood and bare shoots during early spring – or late winter in mild areas.
Propagation: During late summer and early autumn, take 23cm (9in) long heel cuttings, or take cuttings just below a bud. Insert them in a sand-lined, straight-sided trench, so that two-thirds of each cutting is buried. Remove the lower leaves from the cuttings.

Right: Rosa ecae
'Helen Knight' *Few species roses for training against a wall are as attractive as this shrub, with 5cm (2in) wide, clear yellow flowers during mid-summer. It must have a sunny position to ensure success.*

Left: **Thunbergia alata** *This bright half-hardy annual is ideal for a cool greenhouse but also excellent in a warm, sheltered and sunny position outdoors. The orange-yellow flowers, with dark purple-brown centres, appear from mid-summer to autumn.*

Thunbergia alata

Clock Vine · Black-eyed Susan (UK)
Black-eyed Susan Vine (USA)

This extremely bright-flowered, half-hardy annual climber has stems which twine around its supports. It bears ovate light green leaves and orange-yellow flowers with dark purple-brown centres, 5cm (2in) wide, from mid-summer to autumn. It is ideal for a cool greenhouse, but also thrives outdoors if given a warm position.
Height: 1.2-1.8m (4-6ft)
Spread: 60-90cm (2-3ft)
Cultivation: Ordinary well-drained soil and a sunny, sheltered position are essential.
Propagation: In spring, sow seeds 6mm (¼in) deep, three seeds to a 7.5cm (3in) wide pot. Use loam-based compost and keep at 16°C (61°F). When the seedlings are growing well, slowly harden them off, setting the plants outside as soon as all risk of frost is over.

Rosa ecae 'Helen Knight' can be planted with *Clematis montana.* They flower at the same time when the pure white clematis flowers mingle attractively with the yellow rose blooms.

Thunbergia alata can be grown on its own, but it is more attractive when allowed to climb among a blue-flowered clematis. If you grow it in a pot, make a tripod from bamboo canes for a support.

Above: **Tropaeolum peregrinum**
This beautiful half-hardy annual bears interestingly shaped canary-yellow flowers from mid-summer to autumn. The light green, five-lobed leaves provide an attractive foil for the dramatic flowers.

Tropaeolum peregrinum

(Tropaeolum canariense)
Canary Creeper (UK)
Canary-bird Flower · Canary-bird Vine · Canary Creeper (USA)

This rapid-growing, twining, half-hardy perennial is frequently grown as a half-hardy annual. It bears five-lobed blue-green leaves and canary-yellow, elegantly-fringed flowers, 1.8-2.5cm (³/₄-1in) wide and adorned with graceful green spurs, from mid-summer to autumn. It looks superb when planted in bold drifts in a border, or in hanging baskets or window-boxes, where it can trail.
Height: 2.4-3.5m (8-12ft)
Spread: 75-90cm (2¹/₂-3ft)
Cultivation: Fertile, but not excessively rich soil in a warm and sunny position is best. The Canary Creeper also needs support from trelliswork or canes.
Propagation: During late winter and early spring, sow two seeds 12mm (¹/₂in) deep in a 7.5cm (3in) wide pot of loam-based compost. Keep the pot at 16°C (61°F). After germination, thin to one seedling per pot. Harden them off and plant them out into the garden in early summer, after all risk of frost damage has passed.

Further plants to consider

Clematis cirrhosa balearica
Fern-leaf Clematis (UK)
Height: 3.5-4.5m (12-15ft)
A daintily, evergreen, slender-stemmed climber with prettily divided leaves, tinged bronze in winter. The pale yellow flowers, 5cm (2in) wide, and spotted reddish-purple inside, appear throughout winter.

Clematis orientalis
Orange-peel Clematis (UK)
Height: 3-5.4m (10-18ft)
A vigorous, deciduous climber with a mass of tangled shoots, bearing slightly fragrant, bell-shaped, nodding yellow flowers, 5cm (2in) wide, during late summer and into autumn.

Clematis rehderana
Height: 4.5-6m (15-20ft)
A deciduous climber with coarsely-toothed leaflets and nodding, bell-shaped flowers during late summer and autumn. The flowers are a soft primrose yellow and are cowslip-scented.

Clematis tangutica
Height: 3-4.5m (10-15ft)
An attractive, deciduous, slender, vigorous climber with a rambling nature. It bears lantern-shaped, rich-yellow flowers in late summer and into autumn.

Hedera helix 'Goldheart'
Ivy
Height: 1.8-4.5m (6-15ft)   Spread: 1.8-2.4m (6-8ft)
A hardy, self-clinging climber with dark green leaves displaying dominant yellow central splashes. It produces its best colouring on south or west-facing walls, but will nevertheless survive the coldest of northerly aspects if required to.

Jasminum mesnyi
Primrose Jasmine (UK) Japanese Jasmine · Primrose Jasmine · Yellow Jasmine (USA)
Height: 1.8-3m (6-10ft)
An evergreen climber, best suited to a south or west-facing wall in a warm area. During spring and into early summer, it bears 5cm (2in) wide, semi-double yellow flowers.

Pittosporum tobira
Japanese Pittosporum · Australian Laurel · Mock Orange · House-blooming Mock Orange (USA)
Height: 2.4-3.5m (8-12ft)
A slow-growing evergreen for sheltered, warm areas. From spring to mid-summer, it displays orange-blossom-scented, creamy-white flowers in terminal clusters. It needs the protection of a south or west-facing wall.

Tropaeolum peregrinum blends well in cottage-style gardens, but it also suits modern gardens, especially as a cloak for hiding ugly objects. For example, it will soon clothe a pole supporting a car-port.

WALLS AND TRELLISES

Actinidia chinensis

Chinese Gooseberry (UK and USA) Kiwi Berry · Yang-toa (USA)

This hardy deciduous climber soon clothes a wall or pergola with large, heart-shaped dark green leaves up to 20cm (8in) long and 18cm (7in) wide. It also has fragrant, creamy-white flowers which turn to buff-yellow, during late summer. They are followed by gooseberry-like fruits, first green then brown.
Height: 5.4-10.5m (18-30ft)
Spread: 3.6-7.5m (12-25ft)
Cultivation: Grow in any good soil, but avoid those which are chalky or badly drained. Pinch out the growing tips of young plants to encourage bushiness. Preferably, plant it against a south or west-facing wall, in full sun or light shade. Male and female flowers are usually borne on separate plants. It is therefore necessary to have plants of both sexes if fruits are to be produced.
Propagation: During mid-summer, take 7.5-10cm (3-4in) long half-ripe cuttings and insert in equal parts moist peat and sharp sand. Well-drained compost is essential. Place in a closed propagation frame with slight bottom heat.

Actinidia kolomikta

Kolomikta Vine (UK)

This superb hardy twining deciduous climber has heart-shaped, dark green leaves with white or pink tips. Sometimes, this variegation spreads to cover the whole lower half of the leaf. The attractive colouring is encouraged when the plant is in full sun, against a south or west-facing wall. During early summer it bears slightly fragrant white flowers.
Height: 2.4-3.6m (8-12ft)
Spread: 1.8-3m (6-10ft)
Cultivation: Plant in well-drained but moisture-retentive, fertile, acid soil. Avoid chalky soils. Full sun or light shade suits it. The only pruning that is needed is to thin out shoots on those plants that have

Right: Actinidia chinensis *The large, heart-shaped leaves of this deciduous Chinese climber create an impressive display during summer. It is a vigorous plant and can soon swamp its supports, and other plants, with large leaves.*

filled their allotted space and are becoming very congested. This is best carried out in late winter or early spring.
Propagation: In mid to late summer take 7.5-10cm (3-4in) long cuttings and insert in a sandy compost. Place in a frame with slight bottom heat. When rooted, transfer into small pots and place in a cold frame.

Below: Actinidia kolomikta *When planted to grow up an old house wall this superbly variegated deciduous climber is exceptionally attractive. It can be easily trained around the windows without spoiling the plant's slightly lax nature.*

Actinidia chinensis is well-known in China for its fruits, the size of a large plum, which are eaten as a dessert. Selected forms are grown in New Zealand, where they are known as Kiwi berries.

Actinidia kolomikta, the Kolomikta Vine, is a superb climber even when planted on its own. When co-habited with the orange-scarlet flowered Chilean Glory Flower (*Eccremocarpus scaber*) both highlight each other.

Cotoneaster horizontalis

Fish-bone Cotoneaster ·
Herringbone Cotoneaster (UK)
Rock Cotoneaster (USA)

This well known and widely grown hardy deciduous shrub is ideal for covering north and east-facing walls with small, glossy, dark-green leaves. These are borne on a framework of shoots that resemble the bones of a herring. It is also ideal for clothing banks or large unsightly rocks with attractive foliage. It has the bonus of producing 2.5cm (½in) wide pink flowers during early to mid-summer, followed by round, red, shiny berries.
Height: 1.5-2.1m (5-7ft) when grown against a wall.
Spread: 1.5-1.8m (5-6ft) when grown against a wall.
Cultivation: When planted to

Above: Cotoneaster horizontalis
A low-wall can be made more attractive by planting this shrub close to it and allowing the fans of foliage to gently spill over the top. Use secateurs in spring to remove unwanted growth.

cover a bank it often has a 1.5-2.1m (5-7ft) spread, rising 45-60cm (1½-2ft) high. Plant it in any good soil in full sun or shade. No regular pruning is needed, other than cutting out misplaced shoots in early spring.
Propagation: In mid-summer, take 7.5-10cm (3-4in) long heel-cuttings, inserting them in equal parts moist peat and sharp sand. Place in a cold frame. When rooted, plant into a nursery bed for two or three years before moving into a garden. Alternatively, layer low-growing shoots in autumn. These take about a year to develop roots.

Cotoneaster horizontalis merges well with many plants, including hydrangeas, low-growing evergreen azaleas, hostas, and *Euonymus fortunei*. All grow under a light canopy of deciduous trees, such as Silver Birches.

Hedera canariensis 'Variegata'

Canary Island Ivy (UK)
Variegated Ivy · Gloire de Marengo
· Hagenburger's Ivy (USA)

This evergreen climber is also known as *Hedera canariensis* 'Gloire de Marengo'. Although not as hardy as *Hedera colchica* 'Dentata Variegata', and frequently grown indoors as a climbing houseplant, it is well worth growing against a warm wall in areas not subject to severe frosts. The dark green leaves are broadly heart-shaped, merging to silvery-grey then whitish-yellow at their edges.
Height: 4.5-6m (15-20ft)
Spread: 1.8-3.6m (6-15ft)
Cultivation: It is impossible to give the exact size of this climber, as it will quickly adapt its growth if given more support in one direction than another. Plant it in any good well-drained but moisture-retentive soil,

in a sunny position. Good light is vital to encourage the attractive variegations, and therefore select a sheltered, warm, south or west-facing position. No regular pruning is needed. In spring cut back those plants that have exceeded their positions.
Propagation: In mid to late summer take 7.5-13cm (3-5in) long cuttings from the tips of shoots, inserting them in equal parts moist peat and sharp sand. Place in a propagation frame until rooted, then pot up individually and replace in a cold frame until well established.

Below: Hedera canariensis 'Variegata' *This variegated climber is ideal for planting on the warm, sunny side of a wall. Eventually it scales the wall and is very attractive when peeping over its top. It blends well with the bricks.*

Hedera colchica 'Dentata Variegtata'

Persian Ivy (UK and USA)
Colchis Ivy · Fragrant Ivy (USA)

This well-known hardy evergreen climber has large, broadly oval, bright green leaves conspicuously variegated with irregular creamy-yellow edges. As the leaf ages these become creamy-white.
Height: 6-9m (20-30ft)
Spread: 1.8-4.5m (6-15ft)
Cultivation: It is impossible to give the exact size of this vigorous climber as, if given more support in one direction, it will take advantage of it. Plant it in any good well-drained but moisture-retentive soil, in a sunny position. Good light is vital to encourage the attractive variegations, so therefore select a south or west-facing position. No regular pruning is needed, other than cutting back in spring those plants which have exceeded their positions.
Propagation: In mid to late summer take 7.5-13cm (3-5in) long cuttings from the tips of shoots, inserting them in equal parts moist

Hedera canariensis 'Variegata' is not so hardy as *Hedera colchica* 'Dentata Variegata', but usually recovers after being damaged by frost during severe winters. Preferably grow against a warm sheltered wall.

Hedera colchica 'Dentata Variegata' eventually creates a large evergreen screen of brightly variegated leaves. It is widely used to cover porches, and forms an attractive combination with tubs of hydrangeas.

peat and sharp sand. Place in a propagation frame until rooted, then pot up individually and place in a cold frame until well established.

Left: Hedera colchica 'Dentata Variegata' *The variegated leaves create welcome colour throughout the year. Each leaf has a drooping nature with bright, broad, yellow edges. Spray the leaves with clean water during summer. This helps to keep them clean and to prevent an infestation of red spider mites.*

Hedera helix 'Goldheart'

This hardy, evergreen, variegated form of the Common Ivy, also known as the English Ivy, creates an eye-catching climber for walls. It is self-clinging (and not too vigorous for small walls) revealing bright, dark green leaves with conspicuous yellow splashes at their centres.

Height: 1.5-4.5m (5-15ft)
Spread: 1.5-2.4m (5-8ft)
Cultivation: It is impossible to predict the exact spread and height of this climber. Plant it in any good well-drained but moisture-retentive soil in a sunny position. Good light is vital to encourage the attractive variegations. No regular pruning is needed, other than cutting back in spring those plants that have exceeded their positions.
Propagation: In mid to late summer take 7.5-10cm (3-4in) long cuttings from the tips of shoots, inserting them in equal parts moist peat and sharp sand. Place in a propagation frame until rooted, then pot up individually and place in a cold frame until well established.

Right: Hedera helix 'Goldheart' *creates a dominant eye-catching display throughout the year, but especially in spring when the new leaves are borne. The centre of each leaf is conspicuously splashed bright yellow.*

Hedera helix 'Goldheart' is a small-leaved, variegated climber that is ideal for climbing brick walls. It also forms a harmonious partnership with the red-flowered climber *Tropaeolum speciosum*, the Flame Creeper.

Lonicera japonica 'Aureoreticulata'

This variegated, evergreen or semi-evergreen climber is superb when climbing a trellis on a sheltered patio. Its bright green leaves, conspicuously veined in golden-yellow, always attract attention. In cold areas this form of the well-known Japanese Honeysuckle may lose many of its leaves, but the plant itself is seldom killed. Dry soil also encourages the leaves to fall off.
Height: 1.8-3m (6-10ft)
Spread: 1.8-2.4m (6-8ft)

Cultivation: It is impossible to be precise about the height and spread of this climber. Well-drained but moisture-retentive fertile soil in full sun or light shade suits it. Preferably select a warm south or west-facing position. No regular pruning is needed, other than thinning congested plants In spring.

Below: Lonicera japonica 'Aureoreticulata' *This eye-catching climber with small, brightly variegated leaves is ideal for bringing colour to a trellis in a warm part of a garden, perhaps close to a patio.*

Propagation: In mid and late summer take 7.5-10cm (3-4in) long cuttings and insert them in equal parts moist peat and sharp sand. Place in a cold frame. When rooted, pot up individually and later plant into their growing positions preferably in spring or early summer.

Trachelospermum jasminoides

Star Jasmine · Confederate Jasmine (USA)

This slow-growing, evergreen climber is ideal for clothing walls with leathery, shiny, somewhat lance-shaped dark green leaves. During mid to late summer it bears fragrant, 2.5cm (1in) wide, white flowers in lax heads.
Height: 2.4-3.6m (8-12ft)
Spread: 2.4-3m (8-10ft)

Lonicera japonica 'Aureoreticulata' is an attractively variegated form of the Japanese Honeysuckle. However, it is not so vigorous as the all-green type, and needs the protection of a warm wall.

Below: Trachelospermum jasminoides *The fragrant, 2.5cm (1in) wide white flowers appear during summer. They are highlighted by the glossy, dark-green leaves. It is hardy in most areas, but avoid excessively cold positions and regions.*

Cultivation: Plant in well-drained, slightly acid, peaty soil against a warm west or south-facing wall. Remove dead flowers and thin out congested shoots in late spring.
Propagation: During mid-summer take 7.5-10cm (3-4in) long cuttings from sideshoots. Insert them in equal parts moist peat and sharp sand and place in a propagation frame. When rooted, pot up into a loam-based compost and overwinter in a cold frame.

Further plants to consider

Aristolochia durior
(*Aristolochia macrophyla/Aristolochia sipho*)
Dutchman's Pipe (UK and USA) · Pipe Vine (USA)
Height: 3.6-6m (12-20ft)   Spread: 2.4-4.5m (8-15ft)
This is a fast-growing, vigorous and twining, hardy, deciduous climber that needs support. When grown against a wall trelliswork is necessary, but occasionally it is allowed to sprawl over other plants or dead trees. It becomes clothed with broadly heart-shaped, large, mid-green leaves up to 25cm (10in) long and slightly less in width. During mid-summer it bears pipe-shaped, 2.5-4cm (1-1½in) long, yellow, brown and green flowers.

Hedera colchica 'Sulphur Heart'
Height: 6-9m (20-30ft)   Spread: 1.8-4.5m (6-15ft)
This evergreen, large-leaved ivy is impressively variegated, and often sold as 'Paddy's Pride'. The leaf colour is varied; occasionally some are nearly all yellow, but most are irregularly splashed yellow, changing to pale then deep green.

Hedera helix 'Silver Queen'
Height: 1.5-4.5m (5-15ft)   Spread: 1.5-2.4m (5-8ft)
A colourful, small-leaved ivy with leaves variegated grey, white and silver, with the added attraction of being tinged pink in winter. There are many other attractively variegated varieties, including 'Buttercup' with rich yellow leaves that become yellow-green then pale green as they age, and 'Glacier' with small, silvery-grey leaves with white edges.

Jasminum officinale 'Aureovariegatum'
Height: 1.8-3m (6-10ft)   Spread: 1.8-2.4m (6-8ft)
This variegated form of the twining and deciduous Common White Jasmine has grey-green leaves with seven or nine leaflets. These have highly attractive creamy-yellow blotches and variegations. It is also known as *J.O.* 'Aureum'.

Parthenocissus henryana
Chinese Virginia Creeper (UK)
Height: 3-6m (10-20ft)   Spread: 3-4.5m (10-15ft)
An exceptionally beautiful deciduous branching and bushy, self-clinging climber, with dark green leaves formed of three or five leaflets. The mid-rib and main veins are attractively variegated in pink and white. Towards the end of summer, and especially in autumn, the variegations become more pronounced as the green changes to brilliant red.

Tropaeolum speciosum
Flame Creeper (UK)
Height: 2.4-4.5m (8-15ft)   Spread: 60-90cm (2-3ft)
This deciduous, herbaceous, perennial climber has a creeping, rhizomatous rootstock that creates a wealth of six-lobed, mid-green leaves on twining stems. It it not self-supporting, and needs a supporting framework or another plant to climb up. These range from Yew and holly hedges to ceanothus trained against a wall.

Trachelospermum jasminoides clothes walls throughout the year with beautiful leaves. Although plants cannot be planted in front of it, it does benefit from a narrow border of bulbs and bedding-plants at its base.

WALLS AND TRELLISES

![Carpenteria californica flowers against foliage]

Carpenteria californica

Tree Anemone (USA)

This near hardy evergreen shrub from California grows well in the shelter of a south or west-facing wall. It looks especially attractive when planted against a wall with an old and weathered appearance. It has rich, glossy-green leaves and terminal clusters of up to seven, 5-7.5cm (2-3in) wide, white flowers during mid-summer.
Height: 3-3.6m (10-12ft)
Spread: 1.8-2.4m (6-8ft)
Cultivation: Good soil, even slightly alkaline, suits it, and the shelter of a warm wall. New plants are best set in position in late spring, rather than in autumn. No regular pruning is needed, other than cutting out straggly and misplaced shoots after the flowers fade.
Propagation: During late spring, sow seeds in loam-based seed compost in seedboxes. Place in 16°C (61°F). When large enough to handle, prick off the seedlings into small pots and place in a cold frame.

Clematis montana

Mountain Clematis (UK)

This is a popular and easily-grown clematis, creating a mass of pure white flowers up to 5cm (2in) wide during early summer. It is a deciduous climber, with dark green leaves. When initially planted it tends to grow straight up, but at about 3m (10ft) branches out and forms a large, tangled head of shoots and flowers. This growth habit makes it ideal for trailing over the top of a wall, across an arch or over a porch.

Right: Carpenteria californica
This Californian evergreen shrub creates a wealth of 5-7.5cm (2-3in) wide white flowers at the tips of shoots during mid-summer. These appear among a foil of rich, glossy-green leaves.

Carpenteria californica looks at its best when peeping over an old wall and highlighted by clear blue sky. Try growing it over an old brick arch which crosses a path - it is superb.

234

Left: Clematis montana *Clouds of white, four-petalled and scented flowers appear during early summer. It looks especially attractive when leaning over the top of an old wall.*

Height: 6-9m (20-30ft)
Spread: 4.5-6m (15-20ft)
Cultivation: Fertile, moisture-retentive, deeply-cultivated, slightly chalky soil suits it. It enjoys warmth and sunlight, but ensure that the roots are cool and moist. Initially it needs a cane to lead the young shoots to a supporting framework. Little pruning is needed, other than cutting back old plants in spring to fit their allotted areas.
Propagation: The easiest way for a home gardener to increase this plant is by layering low-growing shoots in early spring. Alternatively, take 10-13cm (4-5in) long cuttings during mid-summer, formed of half-ripe wood. Insert in equal parts moist peat and sharp sand, and place in 16°C (61°F). When rooted, pot up individually and overwinter in a frost-proof greenhouse.

Lonicera japonica

Japanese Honeysuckle (UK)
Gold-and-Silver Flower (USA)

This well-known, evergreen or semi-evergreen rampant climber creates masses of white, fragrant flowers which change to yellow with age. These are borne from mid-summer to early autumn. The form 'Halliana' is especially attractive, with highly fragrant, white flowers. It is widely-grown in the form 'Aureoreticulata', which has bright green leaves with conspicuous golden veins. It flowers well when grown against a warm wall.
Height: 4-5-7.5m (15-25ft)
Spread: 3-4..5m (10-15ft)
Cultivation: Fertile, well-drained soil in full sun or partial shade suit it. Little pruning is needed, other than cutting out straggly shoots in spring when the plant becomes overgrown.
Propagation: During mid to late

summer take 10cm (4in) long cuttings, inserting them in equal parts moist peat and sharp sand. Place in a cold frame. When rooted, plant into a nursery bed until large enough to be transferred into the garden.

Above: Lonicera japonica *Few climbers are as pleasing on the eye and the nose as this well-known and widely-grown climber. With age, the tubular, fragrant flowers, up to 4cm (1½in) long, slowly change from white to light yellow.*

Clematis montana creates a spectacular display when planted alongside the yellow-flowered *Rosa ecae* 'Helen Knight'. This rose has the bonus of having a wealth of light green, fern-like leaves on arching stems.

Lonicera japonica is superb for creating a romantic arbour or screen, decked with sweetly-scented white flowers for much of summer. These are borne amid a tangled mass of slender shoots.

WALLS AND TRELLISES

Wisteria sinensis 'Alba'

White Chinese Wisteria (UK and USA)

The normal form of this vigorous, hardy deciduous eye-catching Chinese climber has mauve flowers, but this variety has beautiful white ones. These are pea-shaped and borne in cascading bunches up to 30cm (12in) long during early summer, often before the foliage is fully developed. After the flowers have faded, the dark to mid-green leaves, formed of up to eleven leaflets, are an attractive feature.
Height: 6-7.5m (20-25ft) or more.
Spread: 7.5-9m (25-30ft) or more.
Cultivation: Fertile, deeply-cultivated soil and a warm position in the protection of a south or west-facing wall suit it best. Avoid poor, shallow soils. When grown against a wall a supporting framework is needed, either from tensioned

Above: Polygonum baldschuanicum *The fleecy-white flowers of this rampant climber swamp it during mid and late summer, creating a sea of colour. When trailing over the top of a high wall it is especially attractive.*

Polygonum baldshuanicum

Mile-a-minute Vine · Russian Vine (UK)
Bukhara Fleece Flower (USA)

Correctly, this twining, deciduous, rampant climber is known as *Fallopia baldschuanica*, as well as *Bilderdykia baldschuanica*. Whatever its name, it is not a climber for small fences or walls, as it will grow up to 4.5m (15ft) a year and soon swamp a limited area. From mid to late summer it produces white or pale-pink flowers amid bright green leaves.
Height: 6m (20ft)
Spread: 6-12m (20-40ft)
Cultivation: It grows well in all soils, even those with a chalk content. Plants need a little shelter so that they become established quickly, but after then it tolerates any aspect. No pruning is needed, other than a trim when it exceeds its allotted space.
Propagation: During mid-summer take 7.5-10cm (3-4in) long heel-cuttings and insert in equal parts moist peat and sharp sand. Place in a cold frame. When rooted, pot up individually.

Polygonum baldschuanicum is probably the fastest-growing climber. It requires firm support, such as a wall, rather than rustic poles which, when old, may become strained by strong winds blowing on the foliage.

wires or a lattice-work of wood. Wisterias also grow well on pergolas, enabling bunches of flowers to hang freely. Prune established wisterias during mid-summer by cutting back the current season's young shoots to within five or six buds of its base. Those plants which are becoming too large can be pruned back in late winter to keep them within bounds.

Propagation: During mid to late summer take 10cm (4in) long cuttings, cutting their bases just below a joint. Insert them in a heated propagation frame. Pot up when rooted and overwinter in a cold frame.

Below: Wisteria sinensis 'Alba'
The beautiful pea-shaped flowers in long, cascading bunches, are especially attractive when grown against a dark background. It is a vigorous climber that requires plenty of room.

Further plants to consider

Abeliophyllum distichum
Height: 1.2-1.8m (4-6ft)   Spread: 1.5-1.8m (5-6ft)
Slightly tender deciduous wall shrub best grown against a south or west-facing wall. During late winter and into spring it bears almond-scented white flowers with bright gold stamens. Sometimes, the flowers are faintly tinged pink when opening.

Clematis armandii 'Snowdrift'
Height: 4.5-6m (15-20ft)   Spread: 4.5-6m (15-20ft)
A vigorous evergreen climber, often exceeding the sizes suggested above. During spring it bears saucer-shaped, 5cm (2½in) wide, pure-white flowers.

Clematis flammula
Height: 2.4-3m (8-10ft)   Spread: 1.8-2.4m (6-8ft)
A bushy deciduous climber that creates a tangled mass of bright green leaves and sweetly-scented white flowers in large clusters during late summer and into early autumn.

Clematis 'Marie Boisselot'
Height: 3-5.4m (10-18ft)   Spread: 3-3.6m (10-12ft)
A superb large-flowered hybrid clematis with large, pure-white flowers with cream stamens from mid to late summer.

Jasminum officinale
Common White Jasmine (UK) · Poet's Jessamine (USA)
Height: 1.8-7.5m (6-25ft)   Spread: 3-4.5m (10-15ft)
Vigorous, deciduous, twining and clambering climber with fragrant, pure-white flowers from mid to late summer.
Jasminum polyanthum is not fully hardy and only survives outside in warm areas. Outside it blooms from late spring to mid-summer, with fragrant white flowers flushed pink. It is also grown indoors, in greenhouses and conservatories, when it flowers from early winter to spring.

Magnolia grandiflora
Southern Magnolia · Bull Bay Magnolia (USA)
Height: 3-4.5m (10-15ft)   Spread: 2.4-3m (8-10ft)
Slightly tender evergreen tree best grown against a west or south-facing wall. From mid to late summer it bears fragrant, bowl-shaped, creamy-white flowers up to 20cm (8in) wide.

Wisteria sinensis 'Alba' looks especially attractive when clambering along the top of an old wall, with bunches of white flowers cascading from the woody stems. Ensure that the stems are trained near to the tops of walls.

CHAPTER FIVE

TREES AND SHRUBS

Trees and shrubs are the plants that provide permanency and continuity in a garden, establishing a framework around which other garden brighteners can be set. Some can also be used to form hedges, create boundaries or separate small sections and areas within the main garden.

Many trees and shrubs bear richly-coloured berries in autumn and often through much of the winter season. Red-berried trees include many species of Malus and Sorbus, while sources of blue berries are *Callicarpa bodinieri giraldii, Clerodendrum trichotomum* and *Viburnum davidii.*

Yellow and golden-leaved shrubs and trees are especially welcome in spring and early summer, when their fresh rich colours are accentuated by the increasing intensity of the sunlight. The golden-leaved *Acer japonicum* 'Aureum' makes a splendid small specimen tree, with the bonus of leaves that turn reddish-crimson in autumn before falling.

As well as yellow-leaved trees and shrubs, there is a wealth of trees and shrubs that produce reds and scarlets in their leaves during autumn. These include many members of the Maple family, a group seen at their best in the New England region of North America during autumn. Other trees and shrubs with autumn colour include the North American Sweet Gum *(Liquidambar styraciflua), Parrotia persica* and the Paperbark Maple *(Acer griseum)*, with trifoliate leaves coloured red and scarlet in autumn. The Paperbark Maple has the bonus of peeling, light orange-brown underbark.

The heights and spreads given for plants in this chapter are those twenty years after being planted in good soil. Where a plant continues to grow after this period of time, ultimate heights are also given.

Left: Genista cinerea *creates a dazzling dense splash of colour. Here, this deciduous shrub is seen framed by stone walls and a gravel path, which help to soften the impact of the intense yellow flowers and allow it to blend in with its surroundings.*

TREES AND SHRUBS

Acer palmatum 'Dissectum Atropurpureum'

This hardy and reliable deciduous shrub is a delight in any garden, producing a dome-like canopy of finely cut bronze-red leaves throughout summer.

Height: 1.2-1.5m (4-5ft)
Spread: 2.1-2.7m (7-9ft)
Cultivation: Well-drained but moisture-retentive cool soil in full sun or light shade suits this shrub. A sheltered position is also useful.
Propagation: It is usually grafted, so its propagation is best left to expert nurserymen.

Left: **Acer palmatum 'Dissectum Atropurpureum'**
When set amid a light green ground-cover plant, this hardy deciduous shrub is superb. It looks just as good planted in the well-manicured lawn of a formal garden.

Below: **Azalea 'Kirin'**
This hardy evergreen azalea, with its magnificent display of deep rose flowers in spring, is ideal for a woodland setting in light shade. Acid soil is essential.

Acer palmatum 'Dissectum' is a similarly shaped and sized form, but with finely-cut light green leaves. In a large garden, plant it to contrast with the bronze-red form, but don't crowd them together.

Azalea 'Kirin'

This is one of the hardy evergreen Kurume azaleas, with a relatively low and spreading habit. In spring it is covered with masses of deep rose flowers. Other superb Kurume types include 'Addy Wery' (vermilion-red), 'Benigirl' (bright crimson), 'Blaauw's Pink' (salmon-pink), 'Hinodegiri' (bright crimson), 'Hinomayo' (clear pink) and 'Rosebud' (rose-pink).

Height: 90cm-1.2m (3-4ft)
Spread: 1.2-1.5m (4-5ft)
Cultivation: Well-drained light acid soil in partial shade and a sheltered position suit it best. Keep the soil well mulched. It grows well in a lightly-shaded woodland setting.
Propagation: It can be increased by cuttings, but it is easier for home gardeners to propagate it by layering low-growing shoots in spring. Rooting of these shoots may take up to two years.

Right:Crataegus laevigata 'Rosea Flore Plena' *This superb form of this deciduous tree produces double pink flowers in spring that completely cover the attractive foliage.*

Crataegus laevigata

(*Crataegus oxyacantha*)
Hawthorn · May (UK)
English Hawthorn · Quick-set Thorn · White Thorn (USA)

This well-known European native deciduous tree has rounded, shallowly three or five-lobed, mid-green leaves. During late spring and early summer, it reveals 5-7.5cm (2-3in) wide, highly scented, white flowers. But many forms of crataegus create pink or red displays, such as 'Paul's Scarlet' (double and scarlet), 'Rosea' (single and pink) and 'Rosea Flore Plena' (double and pink). *Crataegus monogyna*, the Common May, May or Quick, known in North America as the English Hawthorn, is a densely-branched and thorny tree often used for hedging and bears heavily-scented white flowers in early summer. In contrast, *C.m.* 'Pendula Rosea' is a pink-flowered form with pendulous and graceful branches. Many crataegus species are known for their attractive fruits. *Crataegus x grignonensis,* a small hybrid, is a late flowering form with long-lasting, large, bright-red fruits. It also has the bonus of leaves that remain green up until winter. *Crataegus x lavallei,* also known as *C. x carrierei,* is densely branched with orange-red haws that persist throughout winter. During early summer it reveals large clusters of white flowers. *Crataegus x prunifolia* is another hybrid, with spiny branches and a compact head. The early summer white flowers are followed in autumn by large red fruits that persist well into winter.

Height: 4.5-6m (15-20ft)
Spread: 4.5-5.4m (15-18ft)
Cultivation: Any good garden soil and a position in an open and sunny position suit this tree. No regular pruning is needed, other than training the plant during its formative years.
Propagation: Named forms are budded or grafted, and this is best left to specialist nurserymen.

Crataegus laevigata does well as a specimen tree in a lawn or in a mixed border, where it creates a blanket background of colour in spring. Its wide-spreading nature makes it suitable for deep borders.

Deutzia x elegantissima 'Fasciculata'

A widely-grown hardy hybrid deciduous shrub with an upright and busy growth habit. The matt-green, slender-pointed, lance-shaped leaves provide an attractive foil for the sweetly-scented, star-shaped, bright rose-pink, 5-7.5cm (2-3in) wide flowers, borne on arching branches in late spring and early summer.
Height: 1.2-1.5m (4-5ft)
Spread: 1.2-1.5m (4-5ft)
Cultivation: Ordinary well-drained garden soil in full sun or light shade suits it well. Flower colours tend not to fade rapidly when a deutzia is positioned in light shade. During summer, after flowering, cut out old flowered stems to soil-level. This encourages the development of fresh shoots from the shrub's base.
Propagation: Although half-ripe 7.5-10cm (3-4in) long cuttings can be taken in mid-summer and inserted in equal parts peat and sharp sand, it is easier for the home gardener to take 25-30cm (10-12in) long hardwood cuttings in autumn. Insert them in a trench in a nursery bed. Line the base of the trench with sand.

Embothrium coccineum

Chilean Fire Bush (UK)
Chilean Fire Tree · Chilean Firebush (USA)

This eye-catching ornamental evergreen tree has an upright growth habit, and produces suckers. The leaves, which are scattered along the branches, are leathery, lance-shaped and mid-green. During early to mid-summer, it produces brilliant orange-scarlet flowers, tubular when they first appear. It is not fully hardy in all areas, and in cold places is severely damaged by frosts. The form 'Norquinco Valley' is a hardier type.
Height: 4.5-6m (15-20ft)

Spread: 2.4-3m (8-10ft)
Cultivation: Well-drained but moisture-retentive neutral or acid deep woodland soil suits it best. In most gardens a position facing south or west and against a high wall is perfect. In winter, protect young plants with a covering of straw. No regular pruning is needed, other than initially removing misplaced shoots and later shortening straggly growths after flowering.
Propagation: Although seeds can be sown in spring in loam-based compost at 13°C (55°F), it is far easier for home gardeners to remove sucker growths from around the base of the tree and then pot them up. Plant the young trees in late spring.

Above: **Deutzia x elegantissima 'Fasciculata'** *This hardy deciduous shrub is a delight in late spring and early summer, with its bright rose-pink flowers backed by a foil of matt-green leaves. It is ideal for a small garden.*

Right: Embothrium coccineum *This is one of the most spectacular and desirable of all garden trees, although it is really hardy only in milder areas. The superb fiery flowers appear in late spring.*

Top right: Gaultheria procumbens *This beautiful carpeting sub-shrub has glorious berries in autumn. This is the plant from which Wintergreen Oil is obtained, a volatile pale-green substance.*

Deutzia scabra, which bears clusters of white flushed pink cup-shaped flowers, was at one time prized in Japan by polishers. Its leaves, with their rigid, star-shaped hairs, could be used as natural rougheners.

Embothrium coccineum does well when set in woodland among other trees and shrubs that give it some protection. It blends well with azaleas and heathers, which create interest at a lower level.

Gaultheria procumbens

Partridge Berry · Winter Green · Checkerberry (UK)
Wintergreen · Checkerberry · Teaberry · Mountain Tea · Ivry-leaves (USA)

A creeping, prostrate, hardy evergreen sub-shrub from North America with shiny dark green slightly-toothed leaves. During late summer, it produces small white or pink bell-shaped flowers, followed in autumn by bright red berries.

Height: 10-15cm (4-6in)
Spread: 75cm-1.2m (2½-4ft)
Cultivation: Acid, moist soil is essential, and a position in the open, or in light shade. Beware of sites where water drips from trees casting shade on the plants.
Propagation: During mid-summer take 5-7.5cm (2-3in) long cuttings with heels and insert them in equal parts peat and sharp sand. Place them in a cold frame. When rooted, pot up the plants into small pots of lime-free compost with a high proportion of peat, and place them outside. Preferably, plunge the pots in soil in a nursery bed, so that the compost remains cool and moist.

Gaultheria procumbens was an invaluable plant for early North American settlers. The berries provided winter food for partridge and deer, while the leaves were used as a substitute for tea.

Hibiscus syriacus

(*Althaea frutex*)
Shrubby Mallow (UK)
Rose-of-Sharon·Althaea· Shrub
Althaea (USA)

A native of Syria, this hardy
deciduous shrub provides colour in
mid to late summer and even into
autumn. The 7.5cm (3in) wide flowers
appear in a colour range from white
to pink, purple and red. Superb pink
and red forms include 'Red Heart'
(white flowers with conspicuous red
centres), 'Woodbridge' (rose-pink
with a carmine eye) and 'Violaceus
Plenus' (double and wine-red).
Height: 1.8-2.4m (6-8ft)
Spread: 1.2-1.8m (4-6ft)
Cultivation: Well-drained fertile
garden soil and a position in full sun
but sheltered from buffeting winds
suit this lovely shrub. Regular
pruning is not needed, but long
shoots can be cut back immediately
after flowering.
Propagation: During mid-summer,
take 7.5-10cm (3-4in) long heel
cuttings and insert them in pots of
equal parts peat and sharp sand.
Place them in a heated frame at
16°C (61°F) and when the plants are
rooted, pot them up into loam-based
compost and overwinter in a cold
frame. When the plants fill their pots,
transfer them to larger ones and
place outdoors until autumn, when
they can be planted out into the
garden.

**Top left: Hibiscus syriacus
'Woodbridge'** *This highly
distinctive shrub has large rose-
pink flowers with carmine eyes. A
sheltered but sunny position is
essential.*

Kalmia latifolia

Calico Bush·Mountain Laurel (UK)
Mountain Laurel·Calico Bush·
Ivybush·Spoonwood (USA)

This outstandingly beautiful
evergreen shrub has leathery,
lance-shaped, mid to dark green
leaves. During mid-summer it
displays 7.5-10cm (3-4in) wide
clusters of bowl-shaped, bright pink
flowers. 'Clematine Churchill' is an
attractive form with rich red flowers.
It gains the name Spoonwood from
its use in the manufacture of
household items such as spoons

**Above: Hibiscus syriacus 'Red
Heart'** *This outstandingly attractive
shrub has white flowers with
conspicuous red centres. It grows
best in a sheltered position in the
garden.*

and ladles.
Height: 1.8-3m (6-10ft)
Spread: 1.8-2.4m (6-8ft)
Cultivation: Moist, slightly acid
fertile soil in light shade suits it
best. No regular pruning is needed,
other than removing faded flowers.
Propagation: The easiest way for
a home gardener to increase this
plant is by layering low shoots in
late summer. Rooting takes about a
year, when the new plants can be
severed from the parent and
planted in a nursery bed for a year
or so before finally being set out
into the open garden.

Hibiscus rosa-sinensis, a closely-related
greenhouse plant from China, was much favoured by
Chinese ladies. When bruised, the flowers turn black
or purple and were used to dye hair and eyebrows.

Above: **Kalmia latifolia** *This beautiful evergreen mid-summer flowering North American shrub produces clusters of bowl-shaped bright pink flowers. When out of flower, the plant has the appearance of a rhododendron. Position it in acid soil and light shade.*

Below: **Kolkwitzia amabilis 'Pink Beauty'** *This is a real eye-catcher, with its clear pink flowers from late spring to early summer. In winter the brown peeling bark is attractive in the low rays of winter sun.*

Kolkwitzia amabilis

Beauty Bush (UK and USA)

This hardy deciduous shrub from Western China has an upright stance and arching branches displaying dull dark green leaves. The stems have attractive peeling brown bark. During late spring to early summer, it is profusely covered with pink foxglove-like flowers with yellow throats. The best form is 'Pink Cloud' with clear pink flowers.

Height: 1.8-3m (6-10ft)
Spread: 1.5-3m (5-10ft)
Cultivation: Ordinary well-drained garden soil and a position in full sun suit it best. During mid-summer, after the flowers have faded, cut out a few of the older flowering stems at soil-level. This will encourage the development of further shoots.
Propagation: During mid to late summer, take 10-15cm (4-6in) long cuttings from non-flowering shoots. Insert them in pots of equal parts peat and sharp sand and place in a cold frame. When rooted, set the cuttings in a nursery bed for a year. Plant them out into the garden when established.

Kolkwitzia amabilis is ideal for a shrub or mixed border. It looks superb with Foxgloves set in front of it. The thimble-like flowers arranged in long spires form an attractive shape contrast.

TREES AND SHRUBS

Leycesteria formosa

Flowering Nutmeg · Granny's Curls
Pheasant Berry (UK)
Himalaya Honeysuckle (USA)

This handsome and unusual deciduous hardy shrub from the Himalayas has mid-green, heart-shaped leaves and, in late summer, funnel-shaped flower-heads, formed of small white flowers surrounded by highly conspicuous dark claret bracts. These are followed by round, shiny purplish-red berries in autumn.
Height: 1.5-2.1 m (5-7ft)
Spread: 1.2-1.5m (4-5ft)
Cultivation: Any well-drained

Above: **Lavatera olbia 'Rosea'**
This shrubby perennial produces a wealth of leaves surmounted by pink-red flowers from mid to late summer, often into early autumn. It grows well in warm, coastal areas.

Lavatera olbia 'Rosea'

Tree Mallow (UK and USA)

This rough-stemmed, vigorous, somewhat tender, sub-shrub is native to the Western Mediterranean region. The three to five-lobed soft and woolly grey leaves provide a foil for the large pinkish red flowers borne on short stalks from mid to late summer.
Height: 1.5-2.1m (5-7ft)
Spread: 1.5-1.8m (5-6ft)
Cultivation: Rich well-drained garden soil suits the Tree Mallow, preferably in a warm site in full sun against a wall. Keep the soil moist during summer, and in spring cut back the foliage to soil-level. Leaving the foliage on the plant during winter helps to protect the roots of the plant from severe cold, as well as appearing attractive when covered with frost.
Propagation: During spring, take half-ripe cuttings.

Lavatera arborea is also known as the Tree Mallow, but this is a biennial with an erect growth habit, which has soft mid green leaves and 5cm (2in) wide pale purple flowers during mid to late summer.

garden soil, preferably in full sun, suits this shrub. It does well in coastal areas. During spring, cut out at soil-level the shoots that bore flowers the previous year.
Propagation: In autumn, take 23-25cm (9-10in) long hardwood cuttings. Insert them in a nursery bed, where they will take about a year to produce roots. They should then be left for a further year.

Below: Leycesteria formosa *The eye-catching flowers of this hardy deciduous shrub appear during late summer. In autumn, the flowers are followed by purplish-red berries.*

Magnolia liliiflora 'Nigra'

(*Magnolia soulangiana 'Nigra'*)

A spectacular hardy deciduous shrub with rather straggly growth, this magnolia bears mid to dark green leaves up to 20cm (8in) long. During late spring to early summer, it produces handsome 7.5cm (3in) long deep reddish-purple flowers.
Height: 1.7-2.4m (6-8ft)
Spread: 1.5-2.1m (5-7m)
Cultivation: Well-drained loamy garden soil and a sheltered site are essential. During spring, top-dress the soil with well-rotted compost. No regular pruning is needed, other than

Above: Magnolia liliiflora 'Nigra' *Few shrubs are as stunningly attractive as this hardy deciduous species with its large, upright, reddish-purple flowers. It is ideal for planting as a specimen in a large lawn.*

---

shaping the shrub during its formative years.
Propagation: Although cuttings 10cm (4in) long can be taken in mid-summer and inserted in pots containing a sandy compost and kept at 21°C (70°F), it is much easier for a home gardener to layer low shoots in spring. However, these often take up to two years to form roots.

Leycesteria formosa produces its flowers along shoots several feet above soil-level, so lower growing plants such as bergenias and hellebores are best positioned around it.

Magnolias are named in honour of Pierre Magnol, a professor of botany and medicine at Montpelier, Southern France. Most species are said to have aromatic tonic qualities.

TREES AND SHRUBS

Pieris floribunda 'Forest Flame' is ideal if you like
brilliant red early spring foliage. Slowly the leaves
turn pink, then creamy-white and later green. A bonus
is the clusters of drooping white flowers.

Pieris japonica 'Blush'

An outstanding compact, hardy, evergreen shrub with mid-green leaves, which are coppery when young, and clustered spring heads of pale blush-pink flowers, rose-pink when in bud. The form *P. japonica* 'Christmas Cheer' is especially hardy and develops flowers flushed deep rose at their tips during winter. This Japanese form bears its flowers even on young and small plants. For added interest *P. japonica* 'Variegata' has leaves edged creamy-white, as well as creamy-white flowers flushed pink when young. While the form 'Bert Chandler', raised in Australia, has young salmon-pink foliage before turning green.
Height: 1.8-2.4m (6-8ft)
Spread: 1.5-2.1m (5-7ft)
Cultivation: Moisture-retentive acid soil and light shade suit it well. A sheltered site is also desirable. During spring mulch the plants with well-rotted compost, and in dry summers water the soil.
Propagation: The easiest way for a home gardener to increase it is by layering low shoots in late summer. However rooting is not rapid, often taking up to two years. Alternatively, take 10cm (4in) long cuttings in mid to late summer and insert them in pots of equal parts peat and sharp sand. Place these in a cold frame. In spring, pot up the rooted cuttings into 7.5cm (3in) pots of acid loam-based compost.

Left: **Pieris japonica 'Blush'**
The rose-pink pitcher-like spring flowers never fail to create interest. This shrub has a delicate appearance, like many early-season plants. It needs acid soil.

Prunus – Japanese Cherries

This is the group of cherries so well-known for their beautiful spring and early summer flowers. The origin of most of them is obscure, but some are hybrids, while others are derived from *Prunus speciosa* and *Prunus serrulata spontanea*. Their colours range from pink to white. Pink forms include 'Cheal's Weeping Cherry' (also known as 'Kiku-shidare Sakura' with double pink flowers in early spring); 'Amanogawa' (a small columnar tree, with erect branches bearing fragrant semi-double shell-pink flowers in mid to late spring); 'Kanzan' (a well-known form, eventually making a large tree, which is one of the finest spring-flowering trees when it displays large and showy double purplish-pink flowers in mid-spring); 'Shimidsu Sakura' (a flat-topped wide-spreading tree with fringed double flowers, pink in bud and opening to white in late spring); and 'Taoyama Zakura' (a small, slow-growing, free-flowering tree with semi-double shell-pink flowers in mid-spring).
Cultivation: Well-drained ordinary garden soil in a sunny position suit Japanese Cherries best. These trees are shallow rooting, so take care not to damage them when cultivating the soil. The wide-spreading types need staking from their earliest years if they are not to fall over later. Pruning is not usually necessary, but if it is required do it in late summer.
Propagation: This involves budding or grafting, so it is best left to expert nurserymen who have the correct rootstocks.

Prunus cerasifera 'Atropurpurea' – often called 'Pissardii' – is known as the Cherry Plum and displays distinctive dark red leaves when young that eventually turn purple.

TREES AND SHRUBS

Above: Prunus sargentii
This is one of the most attractive cherries, displaying beautiful foliage when unfurling in spring and again in autumn when assuming red and orange tints. The clear pink flowers are borne in spring.

Prunus sargentii

Sargent Cherry (UK)
Sargent Cherry · North Japanese Hill Cherry (USA)

This is one of the most attractive of all cherries, forming a rounded head with bronze-red foliage when young. In autumn, the leaves take on shades of red and orange before falling. It is one of the first trees to show autumn colour. During spring, it produces clusters of clear pink single flowers. The only drawback to this species is that it eventually forms a tree too large for the average small garden.
Height: 7.5-9m (25-30ft)
Spread: 5.4-7.5m (18-25ft)
Cultivation: Ordinary, well-drained garden soil suits the Sargent Cherry. It does well in smoky and polluted areas. Cherries are shallow-rooted, so take care not to damage the roots. No regular pruning is needed, but should the removal of a large branch be necessary, do this in late summer, not during winter.
Propagation: It is increased by budding or grafting, and this is best left to a nurseryman.

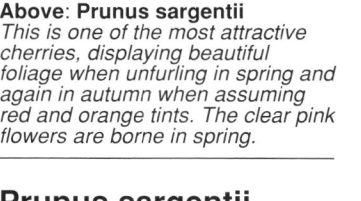

Prunus subhirtella 'Pendula'

This lovely hardy deciduous spring-flowering tree creates a weeping mound of pendulous shoots that bear delicate pale pink flowers during spring. There are several other exciting forms, such as *Prunus subhirtella* 'Pendula Rosea', the Weeping Spring Cherry, with pale pink flowers on a mushroom-shaped tree. This is the form often sold by nurseries as *P. subhirtella* 'Pendula', causing confusion between the two species. The form *P. subhirtella* 'Pendula Plena Rosea' is another weeping tree, with semi-double rose-pink spring flowers.
Height: 3-4.5m (10-15ft)
Spread: 3-6m (10-20ft)
Cultivation: Ordinary, well-drained, fertile, neutral soil and a relatively sheltered position suit this tree. Cherry trees are not deeply rooted, so soil cultivation must be shallow. No regular pruning is needed, but any shaping or large branch removal must be done in late summer, not winter.
Propagation: This is by grafting and budding on to selected stocks and is best left to expert nurserymen.

Left: Prunus subhirtella 'Pendula Rosea' *This stunningly attractive spring-flowering cherry tree forms a distinctive mushroom shape covered with pale pink flowers. It is an excellent choice for small gardens.*

Ribes sanguineum

Flowering Currant (UK)

This reliable and popular deciduous garden shrub from North America seldom fails to create interest. Its currant-like, mid to deep green, three- to five-lobed leaves provide an attractive foil for the 5-10cm (2-4in) long, deep rose-pink, spring flowers. Several excellent forms are available, including 'Pulborough Scarlet' (rich deep red) and 'King

Prunus subhirtella 'Pendula Rosea' produces a screen of colour right down to soil-level and looks best planted as a specimen tree on a lawn. If crowded with other trees, its distinctive form is lost.

Rosa rugosa

Ramanas Rose · Japanese Rose (UK)
Turkestan Rose · Japanese Rose (USA)

This hardy and sturdy deciduous shrub comes from Eastern Asia and has established itself as one of the best-known species roses. It is handsome, with hairy and prickly shoots and wrinkled dark green leaves, glossy above but downy beneath. During mid-summer it develops moderately-scented solitary flowers up to 7.5cm (3in) wide. Flowering often continues intermittently into autumn. It is then that the bright red tomato-shaped fruits, or 'hips', appear. Several red and pink-flowered forms are available, such as 'Frau Dagmar Hastrup' (single, pale rose-pink flowers, vivid pink in bud, with cream stamens); 'Rubra' (single and magenta-red); 'Roseraie de L'Hay' (often sold as 'Plena', bearing large, double, crimson-purple flowers with cream stamens); and 'Scabrosa' (large, single, violet-crimson flowers).
Height: 1.5-2.1m (5-7ft)
Spread: 1.2-1.3m (4-4¹/₂ft)
Cultivation: Ordinary well-drained garden soil is ideal, beware of sandy, chalky or very heavy clay soils. An open position in full sun or light shade is suitable, but avoid heavily shaded areas. Very little pruning is needed. If bushes do become overcrowded, cut them back in spring.
Propagation: Detach sucker-like growths in autumn, planting in a nursery bed. Alternatively, take hardwood cuttings 23cm (9in) long in autumn and insert them in sand-lined trenches in a nursery border.

Above: Ribes sanguineum
In spring this flowering currant produces a dominant display of deep rose-pink flowers. Several superb forms are available including a golden-yellow-leaved one that blends with dark leaves.

Edward VII' (deep crimson). The form 'Brocklebankii' is an attractive pink-flowered form, with the bonus of golden-yellow foliage.
Height: 1.7-2.4m (6-8ft)
Spread: 1.5-2.1m (5-7ft)
Cultivation: Any good well-drained soil in full sun or light shade is suitable. Pruning consists of cutting out old or congested wood at soil-level after flowering.
Propagation: During late autumn or early winter, take hardwood cuttings 25-30cm (10-12in) long and insert them in a nursery bed. They root quite easily and after only one season can be moved to their permanent positions in the garden.

Left: Rosa rugosa 'Frau Dagmar Hastrup' *This reliable species rose develops single, pale rose-pink flowers with cream stamens during mid-summer and intermittently through to autumn. These are followed by bright red, tomato-shaped fruits, commonly called 'hips' or 'heps'.*

Ribes sanguineum **'Brocklebankii'** with its golden-yellow foliage is a useful slow-growing and smaller form. It contrasts perfectly with the purple-leaved Smoke Tree *Cotinus coggygria* 'Foliis Purpureis'

Rosa rugosa is superb as a hedge, especially when peeping over a low brick wall. The wall also helps to prevent rubbish from the road collecting around the hedge's base. Set the plants 75-90cm (2¹/₂-3ft) apart.

Right: Viburnum x bodnantense
This impressive, sweetly-scented winter-flowering deciduous shrub is a welcome addition to any garden. Several shrub forms are available, with flowers appearing on naked branches during winter.

Viburnum x bodnantense

A well-known, slow-growing deciduous shrub with dull green, toothed leaves, tinged bronze when young. The sweetly-scented densely-packed, 2.5-5cm (1-2in) long clusters of rose-flushed white flowers appear on naked branches during mid-winter. It is available in several forms, including 'Dawn', with large clusters of richly-scented flowers, and 'Deben', with scented white flowers, delightfully pink when in bud and opening from late autumn to spring. Another winter-flowering viburnum is the deciduous *V. farreri,* often better known as *V. fragrans.* The highly scented nature of its pink-tinged white flowers is indicated by its synonym. From early winter to early spring it reveals its flowers in pendant clusters 2.5-4cm (1-1½in) long. For slightly later scented flowers *V. carlesii* 'Aurora' with pale pink flowers – but red in bud – and 'Diana' with red buds that open to reveal pink flowers are well worth considering.

Height: 2.7-3.5m (9-12ft)
Spread: 2.4-3m (8-10ft)
Cultivation: Well-drained but moisture-retentive soil is best; add well-decomposed compost, leafmould or peat if drainage is poor. A sunny position suits it best. Very little pruning is needed, other than the occasional removal of weak or old branches. Cutting back such shoots encourages the development of fresh shoots from the plant's base.
Propagation: During late summer, low-growing branches can be layered: this is the easiest method of increasing the plant for the home gardener.

Viburnum x bodnantense is best sited by a path or near the house if the highly-scented winter flowers are to be fully appreciated. Add an underplanting of spring bulbs to create extra and continuing colour.

Weigela Hybrids

These are some of the most beautiful of all hardy shrubs, with 2.5-3cm (1-1¼in) long, rather honeysuckle-shaped flowers during late spring and early summer. They are the result of crossing *Weigela florida* with other Asiatic types. Many named forms are available, such as 'Abel Carriere' (deep rose-carmine with a yellow throat), 'Ballet' (dark pinkish-red), 'Bristol Ruby' (bright ruby-red with near black buds), 'Eva Rathke' (bright red), 'Fairy' (soft rose-pink), 'Newport Red' (dark red) and 'Styriaca' (red buds opening to reveal pink flowers). Weigela was formerly known as Diervilla, when the genus was named in honour of the Frenchman Dierville. In many old books it is mentioned under this name.

Height: 1.5-1.8m (5-6ft)
Spread: 1.5-2.4m (5-8ft)
Cultivation: Well-drained but moisture-retentive rich soil and a position in full sun suit it best. It requires regular pruning, each year after flowering, cutting back one or two of the old stems to soil-level. This will encourage the development of fresh main shoots from ground-level.
Propagation: Take hardwood cuttings 25-30cm (10-12in) long in mid to late autumn and insert them in a nursery bed. Rooting takes about a year. Alternatively, during mid-summer, take 7.5-10cm (3-4in) long half-ripe cuttings from non-flowering shoots and insert them in pots of equal parts peat and sharp sand kept at 16°C (61°F). Pot up the cuttings when rooted and slowly harden them off. Place them in a cold frame during winter and plant them out into a nursery bed in spring. They will need to remain there for about a year before being set in their permanent positions.

Left: **Weigela 'Bristol Ruby'** *This is one of the many hybrid weigelas, previously often known as* Diervilla. *It does best when planted in rich, moist soil and given a sunny position.*

Further plants to consider

Aesculus x carnea
Red Horse Chestnut (UK and USA)
Height: 4.5-6m (15-20ft)   Spread: 2.4-3m (8-10ft)
A beautiful chestnut with mid-green leaves and 15-20cm (6-8in) high candles of rose pink flowers in early to mid-summer.

Erica herbacea
Erica carnea
A well-known hardy evergreen sub-shrub with several pink and red forms. These include 'Adrienne Duncan' (carmine-red), 'Eileen Porter' (carmine-red), 'Myretoun Ruby' (deep rose-pink), 'Praecox Rubra' (deep rose-red), 'Springwood Pink' (rose-pink) and 'Winter Beauty' (rose-pink).

Lilac – Garden Forms
These are the forms of the Common Lilac (*Syringa vulgaris*) with large heads of flowers. Many have pink or red flowers and include 'Congo' (scented, dark red in bud and becoming pink), 'Marechal Foch' (single carmine-rose), 'Mrs Edward Harding' (claret-red), 'Sensation' (purplish-red) and 'Souvenir de Louis Spaeth' (wine red).

Malus floribunda
Height: 3.5-4.5m (12-15ft)   Spread: 3-4.5m (10-15ft)
A well-known round-headed hardy deciduous tree with single bright carmine flowers fading to pink in early summer.

Malus x eleyi
Height: 6-7.5m (20-25ft)   Spread: 4.5-6m (15-20ft)
A hardy deciduous spring-flowering tree with single reddish-purple flowers. These are followed by similarly coloured fruits.

Prunus dulcis 'Rosea-plena'
Height: 5.4-7.5m (18-25ft)   Spread: 5.4-7.5m (18-25ft)
This double pink-flowered form of the Common Almond is a delight in late spring.

Tamarix tetrandra
Tamarisk (UK and USA)
Height: 3-4.5m (10-15ft)   Spread: 3-4.5m (10-15ft)
A large, feathery and wispy hardy deciduous flowering shrub with pale to mid-green leaves and bright pink flowers in early summer. It is an excellent plant for coastal areas.

Weigelas suit a mixed border or one filled by shrubs and small trees with underplantings of bulbs. The form 'Foliis Purpureis', with purple leaves and pink flowers, creates long-term interest.

TREES AND SHRUBS

Ceanothus 'Gloire de Versailles'

(*Ceanothus x delinianus 'Gloire de Versailles'*)

This hardy deciduous rather open shrub is one of the best known ceanothus plants for a border. The soft, fragrant, powder-blue flowers are borne in heads up to 20cm (8in) long from mid-summer until early autumn. It is best planted in a mixed border, where its long stems can splay out over lower-growing plants.
Height: 1.8-2.4m (6-8ft)
Spread: 1.5-2.1m (5-7ft)
Cultivation: Well-drained fertile soil in good light suits it. Because the flowers are borne on the new wood, the bush must be pruned hard in spring. Cut back the previous season's shoots almost to their points of origin. Follow this with an application of fertilizer to encourage the rapid growth of new shoots.
Propagation: During summer, take 7.5-10cm (3-4in) long half-ripe cuttings of the current season's growth, inserting them in pots of equal parts peat and sharp sand. Place them in a propagation frame at a temperature of 16°C (61°F). When they are rooted, pot up the cuttings into 7.5cm (3in) pots of loam-based compost and overwinter them in a cold frame. Plant them out in the garden in spring.

Cercis siliquastrum

Judas Tree (UK)
Judas Tree · Love Tree (USA)

A hardy, rounded, wide-spreading, deciduous tree from the Orient and Southern Europe, the Judas Tree is said to be the tree from which Judas Iscariot hanged himself after the betrayal of Jesus Christ. Whether or not this is true, there is no doubt that the tree is eye catching and distinctive. It bears clusters of rich rose-purple flowers on bare branches in early summer. After the flowers have faded it develops rounded, glaucous-green leaves with heart-shaped bases. Subsequently, it produces attractive flat, green, pea-like pods tinted red when fully ripe.

Abies concolor 'Glauca Compacta'

This beautiful dwarf and compact conifer (often sold as *Abis concolor* 'Compacta') has an irregular shape and greyish-blue foliage. It is so slow-growing that even after twenty five years it often reaches no more than 75cm (2½ft) high, with a 1m (3½ft) spread. It is ideal for a rock garden, or even in a large container.
Cultivation: Deep, well-drained, slightly acid soil suits it best. It prefers

Above: Abies concolor 'Glauca Compacta' *This is one of the best slow-growing dwarf conifers for a rock garden or container. Its greyish-blue foliage is very attractive and looks at its best when the tree is planted on its own or in a colour-contrasting group.*

a warm, dry position. It is essential to avoid chalky soils.
Propagation: It is raised by grafting, a technique best left to nursery experts.

Abies concolor 'Violacea Prostrata' is another blue conifer ideal for a small garden. It is semi or totally prostrate, with strongly-coloured silver-blue foliage. Another prostrate blue form is *Abies procera* 'Glauca Prostrata'.

Ceanothus 'Gloire de Versailles' originated in France. In 1830 a breeding programme was initiated to raise new hybrids and this shrub was one of the results. Most ceanothus shrubs with French-sounding names originated at that time.

Above: **Ceanothus 'Gloire de Versailles'** *This strikingly impressive deciduous shrub produces large heads of powdery-blue flowers on open stems from mid to late summer. It is best grown in a mixed border.*

Height: 4.5-6m (15-20ft)
Spread: 3.5-4.5m (10-15ft)
Cultivation: Any good garden soil and a sunny position away from late spring frosts suit it. No regular pruning is needed.
Propagation: During spring, sow seeds in pots of loam-based compost kept at 13°C (55°F). When they are large enough to handle, pot up the seedlings singly in loam-based compost and plunge the pots up to their rims in a sheltered corner. Once established, plant into the garden.

Right: **Cercis siliquastrum**
This is the well-known Judas Tree, which produces a wealth of colour along its bare branches in early summer. In colder areas it may require the protection of a south or west-facing wall.

Cercis siliquastrum is ideal for blending with late spring and early summer bulbs. Often, the tree becomes bare of low branches, and bright bulbs can create vital colour and interest around large and mature trees.

Corylus maxima 'Purpurea' produces its main burst of
foliage colour at eye height, and is useful for bringing
focal points to a shrub or mixed border. Its high stance
allows it to be underplanted with spring-flowering
bulbs – but not too close to its base.

Right: **Cotinus coggygria 'Notcutt's Variety'** *This superb hardy shrub with an imposing stature bears beautiful deep purple leaves. It produces its best colour when planted in poor soil.*

Corylus maxima 'Purpurea'

Purple-leaved Filbert (UK)

This is a rich-purple-leaved form of the Filbert, a native of Western Asia and Southern Europe. It is a deciduous shrub which has large, heart-shaped leaves. The whole shrub has an open, spreading growth habit, often becoming bare at its base. The parent form, *Corylus maxima,* was introduced into the British Isles in 1759 and soon became very popular for providing nuts. It also soon spread to North America and in 1833 several distinct varieties were known to be in cultivation. At one time it was widely grown in Europe, especially Italy and Spain. Early in the 1800s a plantation near Recus, Spain, yielded nuts that were shipped via Barcelona. They became known as Barcelona nuts.

Height: 2.4-3.5m (8-12ft)
Spread: 2.8-3m (8-10ft)
Cultivation: Any good well-drained garden soil and a sunny position, preferably sheltered from cold north and east winds, is suitable. During its early years, cut it back in late winter and early spring to encourage the development of shoots from around its base. Prune back by half the growth made the previous year. As the shrub develops, do not cut it back so severely. Throughout this period, cut out congested shoots from the centre of the shrub.
Propagation: Purple-leaved forms seldom come true from seeds and are therefore best increased by layering low growing shoots in autumn.

Left: **Corylus maxima 'Purpurea'** *This is a useful shrub for bringing colour-contrasting foliage to a garden throughout summer. It is a reliable plant, but is best given shelter from cold east and north winds.*

Cotinus coggygria 'Notcutt's Variety'

This hardy deciduous shrub has eye-catching deep purple leaves that never lose their freshness and are ultimately semi-translucent. It also bears feathery purple flowers during mid-summer.
Height: 3.5-4.5m (12-15ft)
Spread: 3-3.5m (10-12ft)
Cultivation: Any good well-drained garden soil and a position in full sun suit it. Avoid rich soils, as it produces the best colour when in poor conditions. No regular pruning is needed, other than initially shaping the plant when young.
Propagation: During late summer, take 10-13cm (4-5in) long heel cuttings, inserting them in pots of equal parts peat and sharp sand. Place the pots in a cold frame and during spring set out the young plants into a nursery bed until they are large enough to be planted out in the garden. Keep the nursery bed free from weeds.

Cotinus coggygria 'Notcutt's Variety' will produce a large specimen shrub on a lawn or as a backcloth for colour-contrasting plants. For small gardens, *C. c.* 'Royal Purple' is better, growing to 3m (10ft) in height and the same width.

Hydrangea macrophylla

Common Hydrangea (UK)
French Hydrangea ·Hortensia (USA)

This well-known deciduous and rounded shrub from Japan and China has oval, slightly pointed, coarsely-toothed light green leaves. The flower-heads appear from mid to late summer. There are two forms: *Hortensia* types and the

Lacecaps. The *Hortensia* forms have large globose heads, while the *Lacecaps* display flat flower heads formed almost entirely of sterile flowers with a flat disc-like corymb. In the centre there is an area of tiny fertile flowers, and this has a marginal ring of ray florets which are sterile. The form 'Blue Wave' is a good example of this type.
Height: 1.5-1.8m (5-6ft)
Spread: 1.5-1.8m (5-6ft)

Cultivation: Slightly acid, light, well-drained but moisture-retentive soil is best. Acid soil is essential to ensure that blue varieties remain blue. Pink varieties also produce blue colours when given an acid soil and an aluminium sulphate dressing.
Propagation: From late spring to mid-summer take cuttings 7.5cm (3in) long. Remove the lower leaves and cut the bases just below leaf joints. Insert them in pots of equal

Hydrangea macrophylla is ideal for forming a backcloth to a large lawn, where it provides colour .over a long period. In such a position, a *Hortensia* type is best. The *Lacecaps* perform better in a naturalized garden setting.

parts peat and sharp sand and place them in a cold frame. When the cuttings are rooted, pot them up into an acid compost and plunge the pots to their rims in a nursery bed until they are ready to plant out into the garden.

Left: Hydrangea macrophylla *Hortensia hydrangeas are reliable garden favourites, creating a dominant display of mop-like heads from mid to late summer.*

Right: Hydrangea macrophylla 'Blue Wave' *This vigorous Lacecap hydrangea provides flowers in shades of blue and pink throughout the summer months. It grows well in slight shade.*

Lavandula stoechas

French Lavender (UK)
French Lavender   Spanish Lavender (USA)

This hardy evergreen shrub is native to the Mediterranean region. It has narrow, grey-green leaves and distinctive, deep purple, tubular flowers borne on 2.5-5cm (1-2in) long four-angled spikes during early to mid-summer. It is characterized by tufted purple bracts (modified leaves) borne at the tops of the flower spikes.
Height: 30-45cm (1-1¹/₂ft)
Spread: 45-60cm (1¹/₂-2ft)
Cultivation: Light, well-drained soils and an open and sunny position suit it. It is not as hardy as the English Lavender and during severe winters can be seriously damaged in exposed areas.
Propagation: During late summer, take 7.5cm (3in) long cuttings and insert them in pots of equal parts peat and sharp sand. Place them in a cold frame. Pot them up when they are rooted and plant them out into the garden in spring.

Right: Lavandula stoechas *This pretty lavender has distinctive deep purple flowers topped by purple bracts (modified leaves) that persist long after the actual flowers have faded.*

Lavandula stoechas brings height and colour to a rock garden. Even after the flowers have faded, the grey-green leaves provide an attractive feature. Cover the soil with stone chippings to add extra interest and stop soil splashing on the leaves.

TREES AND SHRUBS

Above: Picea pungens 'Pendula'
With careful training and pruning, this often unpredictable conifer can be persuaded to develop a superb weeping shape and to create an exciting focal point in any garden.

Left: Picea pungens 'Koster'
This is one of the best blue spruces with a neat pyramidal habit. It looks especially attractive in spring.

Picea pungens 'Koster'

Koster's Blue Spruce (UK)

This distinctive form of the Colorado Spruce has intensely blue foliage and a neat growth habit, forming an upright and pyramidal shape up to 2.1m (7ft) high and 1m (3¹/₂ft) wide after ten years. During spring, it is further enhanced by pale blue tufts of new growth.
Height: 9m (30ft)
Spread: 3m (10ft)
Cultivation: Deep, moist soil – acid or neutral – is needed. A position in full sun or slight shade suits it best.
Propagation: It is grafted onto stocks of *Picea pungens* to produce a distinctive upright form. The cost to nurserymen of this time consuming technique accounts for the high price they will ask for young plants of this lovely variety.

Picea pungens 'Pendula'

This distinctive blue conifer – often known as *Picea pungens* 'Glauca Pendula' – sometimes has an erratic shape but can be recognized by its down-swept branches and glaucous-blue leaves. During spring, the young growths are tufted and pale blue. It often produces two leading shoots: one needs to be trained upright, while the other trails downwards.
Height: 3-5.4m (10-18ft)
Spread: 3-5.4m (10-18ft)
Cultivation: Moist, deep soil – acid or neutral – is best, and a position in slight shade or full sun.
Propagation: It needs to be grafted onto a stock of *Picea pungens,* so the plants are often expensive to buy, as with *P. pungens* 'Koster'.

Picea pungens 'Thomsen'

This eye-catching blue spruce has an upright, cone-like growth habit and branches packed with silvery-blue foliage. During spring, it develops a fresh growth of very pale silver-blue that contrasts with the older and darker foliage. It forms a small to medium-sized tree, reaching only 2.1m (7ft) high and 1m (3¹/₂ft) wide after ten years.
Height: 9m (30ft)
Spread: 3m (10ft)
Cultivation: Moist deep soil – acid or neutral – is best, and a position in slight shade or full sun.
Propagation: It is a grafted form and therefore plants tend to be expensive. Raising new plants is best left to nurserymen.

Right: Picea pungens 'Thomsen'
This is a beautiful blue spruce with a cone-shaped outline. The foliage is thick and the needles long. It grows steadily into a strong, upright shape.

Picea pungens 'Koster' brings height to a small planting of heathers or the edge of a small rock garden. Eventually it forms a large plant, but up to the age of 15-20 years, it is quite suitable for a small area.

Picea pungens 'Pendula' must be given space and an open situation where other plants do not compete for attention. For colour contrast, set it in a sea of Heather (*Calluna vulgaris*), selecting forms with gold-tinted foliage.

Further plants to consider

Hebe 'Autumn Glory'
Height: 60-90cm (2-3ft)   Spread: 75cm-1m (2½-3½ft)
A well-known evergreen hybrid shrub, with purple stems displaying dark green leaves. From mid-summer to autumn, it bears violet-purple flowers in spikes 4cm (1½in) long.

Hebe x andersonnii 'Variegata'
Height: 90cm (3ft)   Spread: 60-90cm (2-3ft)
A beautiful double-value somewhat tender evergreen shrub with mid-green and cream leaves. The soft mauve flowers borne in dense spikes 7.5-1.3cm (3-5in) long appear from mid-summer to autumn. It is ideal for setting in a mixed border, where it creates attention throughout the year.

Hibiscus syriacus 'Blue Bird'
Shrubby Mallow (UK) · Althaea · Rose of Sharon (USA)
Height: 1.8-2.4m (6-8ft)   Spread: 1.2-1.8m (4-6ft)
A hardy deciduous shrub, with rich green leaves and mid-blue, 7.5cm (3in) wide flowers from mid to late summer and often into autumn. The form 'Coeleste' has deep blue flowers, and 'Mauve Queen' has mauve flowers that reveal maroon centres.

Paulownia tomentosa
Princess Tree · Kari Tree (USA)
Height: 6-7.5m (20-25ft)   Spread: 3.5-4.5m (12-15ft)
A hardy deciduous tree, with mid-green heart-shaped leaves and lavender-blue flowers in early summer.

Teucrium fruticans
Shrubby Germander (UK)
Height: 1.2-1.5m (4-5ft)   Spread: 90cm-1.2m (3-4ft)
A somewhat tender evergreen shrub, only really suitable for warm areas. The greyish-green leaves are fragrant, with two-lipped, lavender-blue flowers appearing from mid to late summer.

Vinca major
Greater Periwinkle (UK)
Greater Periwinkle · Blue Buttons · Band Plant (USA)
Height: 15-30cm (6-12in)   Spread: 90cm-1.2m (3-4ft)
A well-known trailing and mat-forming evergreen sub-shrub, with glossy mid-green leaves. During spring and early summer, and often repeatedly into autumn, it produces 2.5-3cm (1-1¼in) wide, purple-blue flowers.

Vinca minor
Lesser Periwinkle (UK)
Lesser Periwinkle · Common Periwinkle · Myrtle · Running Myrtle (USA)
Height: 5-10cm (2-4in)   Spread: 90cm-1.2m (3-4ft)
A spreading, mat-forming evergreen sub-shrub, with 18-25mm (³/₄-1in) wide, blue flowers during spring and mid-summer, and often into autumn.

Picea pungens 'Thomsen' is superb when positioned several metres in front of yellow-foliaged conifers or in an open situation with clear sky behind. Take care not to cramp it with other conifers set too close, as this will spoil its shape.

Acer japonicum 'Aureum'

This beautiful, slow-growing, deciduous bushy tree has bright yellow, seven to eleven-lobed leaves. They are displayed in irregular layers, and in autumn turn rich crimson. It is an ideal tree for a small garden.

Height: 4.5-6m (15-20ft)
Spread: 3.5-4.5m (12-15ft)
Cultivation: Well-drained but moist soil in slight shade suits it best, as the foliage may be scorched in strong sunlight. It does well in chalky soils. No regular pruning is needed, other than initial shaping.
Propagation: It needs to be budded or grafted, and this is best left to expert nurserymen.

Left: **Acer japonicum 'Aureum'** *is a superb small maple for a lawn or in a mixed border. During autumn, the bright yellow leaves become rich crimson. Select a position sheltered from cold winds.*

Berberis darwinii
Darwin's Berberis (UK and USA)

This beautiful hardy evergreen shrub bears drooping bunches of flowers amid stalkless glossy, dark-green spiny leaves. From mid to late spring, it bears deep orange-yellow flowers. During late summer and early autumn there is a profusion of purplish-blue oval berries along the shoots.

Height: 1.7-3m (6-10ft)
Spread: 1.8-3m (6-10ft)
Cultivation: It succeeds in any good soil and in full light or slight shade, but position it away from drying winds. The only pruning required is to cut back straggly shoots after flowering.
Propagation: Although it can be increased from seed sown in April in the open soil, the plants do not always produce replicas of the parent. Therefore, take 7.5-10cm (3-4in) long cuttings with heels during late summer, inserting them into pots of equal parts of peat and sharp sand and place them in a

Below: **Berberis darwinii** *A widely-grown shrub, glowing with flowers in spring. It often forms a sprawling bush, with long shoots intermingled with neighbouring shrubs. When grown as a hedge, it requires regular pruning after flowering to keep it in shape.*

Acer japonicum 'Aureum' looks superb in a border, with underplantings of the spring-flowering *Crocus vernus* or variegated hostas. It also does well as a specimen in a lawn, or in a large tub on a patio.

Berberis darwinii although tall and spreading, can be set near the edge of a path if shoots are cut back after flowering. This allows both the spring flowers and the late summer berries to be admired.

cold frame. Set the rooted plants out into a nursery bed the following spring. Alternatively, pot up the rooted plants into large pots. This makes them easier to transplant into their permanent positions at a later date. This is a shrub frequently grown to form a spring-flowering hedge. If used as such, prune the plants by a quarter immediately after planting them, to encourage bushy growth.

Calceolaria integrifolia

(Calceolaria rugosa)

This half-hardy, upright, bushy, semi-shrubby evergreen perennial has bright yellow, pouch-like flowers, 12-25mm (1/2-1in) long, from mid to late summer. It grows outside only in warm areas, and even then requires the protection of a south or west-facing wall. The finely wrinkled, matt, mid-green leaves are lance-shaped.

Height. 1.2m (4ft)

Spread. 1.2-1.5m (4-5ft)

Cultivation: Light, well-drained fertile soil – neutral to acid – is best, and a position in full sun or partial shade. Usually the plants are discarded after flowering, but occasionally in warm and frost-free areas they may become perennial. Plants that do survive winter may still be cut back by cold weather, and are therefore best pruned in late spring to encourage new growth to develop.

Propagation: The plant is best increased from 7.5cm (3in) long heel cuttings in late summer, inserted into pots of equal parts peat and sharp sand. Keep these at 15°C (59°F) and when the cuttings have rooted, pot them up into peat-based compost. Plant into the garden in autumn.

Right: Calceolaria integrifolia
The vivid-yellow, pouch-like flowers of this half-hardy perennial are eye-catching. But grow it outside only in warm areas and with the protection of a south- or west-facing wall.

Calceolaria integrifolia, with its pouch-shaped flowers, gains its generic name because the flower parts resemble a shoe. In Latin, the word for shoemaker is *calceolarius.*

TREES AND SHRUBS

Catalpa bignonioides 'Aurea'

Golden Indian Bean Tree (UK)

Few trees with yellow foliage have more eye-catching leaves than this neatly-shaped, hardy deciduous tree for a small garden. The heart-shaped, rich yellow leaves, 10-25cm (4-10in) long and 7.5-20cm (3-8in) wide, remain attractive throughout summer. During mid-summer there are purple and yellow foxglove-like flowers.
Height: 6-7.5m (20-25ft)
Spread: 6-7.5m (20-25ft)
Cultivation: Catalpas appreciate any good garden soil and a position in full sun, slightly sheltered from cold winds. No regular pruning is needed, other than occasionally shaping the tree in early spring.
Propagation: During late summer, take 7.5-10cm (3-4in) long heel cuttings, inserting them into pots containing equal parts peat and sharp sand, and keeping them at 18°C (64°F). When the cuttings are rooted, pot them up into small pots and overwinter in a cold frame. In spring, set them out in a nursery bed for three or four years before transplanting to their final positions.

Below: Chamaecyparis lawsoniana 'Lutea'
A beautiful golden conifer, raised in North America more than one hundred years ago. It requires a sunny position for the golden-yellow foliage to keep its colour throughout the year.

Right: Catalpa bignonioides 'Aurea' *The beautiful, soft-textured, woolly, heart-shaped leaves of this deciduous tree retain their golden-yellow colour throughout summer. They are a perfect match for the purple and yellow flowers.*

Chamaecyparis lawsoniana 'Lutea'

This golden-yellow-foliaged form of the evergreen conifer, Lawson's Cypress, is a well-tried favourite for small gardens. It has an upward, relatively narrow stance, with a drooping, spire-like top and flattened, somewhat feathery sprays of slightly drooping foliage.
Height: 9m (30ft)
Spread: 1.5-1.8m (5-6ft)
Cultivation: Well-drained garden soil and an open but sheltered position suit it best. In shady positions it tends to become green. No pruning is required, except during early years, when you should cut out second-leader shoots during spring.
Propagation: Seeds can be sown in spring, but the seedlings will not necessarily reflect the nature of the parent. Named forms are best raised in spring from heel cuttings 10cm (4in) long, inserted into pots containing equal parts of peat and sharp sand and kept at 16°C (61°F). When the cuttings are

---

Catalpa bignonioides 'Aurea' is excellent for a small garden. It can be grown in a lawn, or mixed with other plants in a border. However, do not place high plants in front of it, or they spoil its shape.

Chamaecyparis lawsoniana 'Lutea' can be grown as a specimen in a grouping with other conifers, or in a mixed border where its size and colour will break up visually long vistas.

Propagation: Seeds can be sown when ripe in late summer, but they take up to two years to germinate. Often the plant has low-growing roots and these can be layered in late summer and early autumn. They take about two years to produce roots. Another method is to take 7.5-10cm (3-4in) long half-ripe heel cuttings in mid to late summer. Insert them in equal parts peat and sharp sand and place in a propagation frame at 16°C (61°F). When they are rooted, place them in a cold frame.

Below: **Cornus mas** *The clusters of small golden-yellow flowers are a delight in late winter and early spring. The fruits of this European native have been used for sweetmeats and tarts. The Turks used the flowers to control diarrhoea, as a preventative for cholera, and for flavouring sherbet. The hard wood has been used to make forks and ladder-spokes.*

rooted, pot them up into small pots and plant them out into a nursery bed during the following year for three or four seasons before setting them in their final site.

Cornus mas

Cornelian Cherry (UK)
Cornelian Cherry Sorbet (USA)

This is a distinctive late winter and early spring flowering deciduous shrub. It is somewhat twiggy and bushy, with 1.2-2.5cm (½-1in) long clusters of golden-yellow flowers. These are borne along naked branches and are sometimes followed by bright red, edible cherry-like fruits. The dark green leaves turn reddish-purple in autumn. The form 'Aurea' has leaves suffused yellow.
Height: 2.4-3.5m (8-12ft)
Spread: 1.8-3m (6-10ft)
Cultivation: Any good garden soil, including clay, suits it. Position it in full sun, if possible, although it will tolerate light shade. No regular pruning is needed, other than an initial shaping when young.

Cornus mas is a delight in winter, but unfortunately its branches often spread to soil-level, making it impossible to set plants beneath it. However, it is possible to train on a long main stem.

TREES AND SHRUBS

Cupressus macrocarpa 'Goldcrest'

This beautiful, hardy, densely-foliaged, medium-sized evergreen conifer has rich yellow, feathery, scale-like foliage. It has a narrow, columnar outline which broadens slightly with age. It is excellent for coastal areas and can also be planted to form a hedge. In ten years, it should have grown 4m (13ft) high and 1m (3½ft) wide.
Height: 9-18m (30-60ft)
Spread: 1.5-1.8m (5-6ft)
Cultivation: Any well-drained garden soil and a sunny, open

Left: **Cupressus macrocarpa 'Goldcrest'** *This is a superbly-coloured form of the Monterey Cypress. It forms a striking focal point in a lawn or border, and also looks good in a colour-contrasting collection of conifers, especially blue ones.*

Cupressus macrocarpa 'Goldcrest' blends well in groupings with blue-foliaged conifers such as *Picea pungens* 'Koster' and silver-barked trees like birches. In a large garden, try a grouping of cupressus and silver birches, under-planted with daffodils.

position suit this lovely conifer. No regular pruning is needed, other than removing double leader shoots in spring.

Propagation: Seeds can be sown in spring, but the seedlings will not resemble the parent. Instead, take 7.5-10cm (3-4in) long heel cuttings during autumn, inserting them into pots of equal parts peat and sharp sand and placing them in a cold frame. When the cuttings are rooted, pot them up into small pots and plunge these in a nursery bed. Set the plants out into their final positions in the garden in autumn when they are well grown and sturdy.

Below: **Cupressus macrocarpa**
The golden form of this magnificent conifer forms an eye-catching hedge that can be used as a backdrop for dark-leaved plants, or as an attractive feature on its own. It looks best when positioned in good sunlight.

Above: **Cytisus scoparius 'Golden Sunlight'**
The rich yellow, pea-shaped flowers are dominant in early summer. The plant often appears bare when flowering is over, and is therefore best positioned in a mixed border with other plants.

Cytisus scoparius

Common Broom (UK)
Scotch Broom (USA)

This is an upright, free-flowering deciduous shrub with pea-shaped, rich-yellow flowers, 2.5cm (1 in) long, borne singly or in pairs during early summer. Although deciduous, its green stems give it an evergreen appearance. There are several superb forms, including 'Andreanus' (yellow and chocolate flowers), 'Burkwoodii' (shades of maroon, purple and red), 'Golden Sunlight' (rich yellow flowers) and 'Sulphureus' (sulphur-yellow flowers).

Height: 1.5-2.5m (5-8ft)
Spread: 1.5-2.1m (5-7ft)
Cultivation: Well-drained, deep, neutral or slightly acid soils are best, and plenty of sun. After flowering, cut off about two-thirds of the previous season's shoots. It is often easier to do this with a pair of garden shears.
Propagation: It can be increased from seeds sown in spring and placed in a cold frame, but it is easier to take 7.5-10cm (3-4in) long heel cuttings during late summer. Insert them into pots containing equal parts of peat and sharp sand and place them in a cold frame. Pot them into pots of peat-based compost when they have rooted, and plant out into the garden in autumn.

Cytisus scoparius is the parent of many forms, including the Moonlight Broom (*Cytisus scoparius 'Sulphureus'*). This is an attractive compact form, with creamy sulphur-yellow flowers, tinged red when in bud, during early summer.

TREES AND SHRUBS

Right: Forsythia x intermedia 'Spectabilis' *This is one of the most popular of spring-flowering shrubs, its rich yellow flowers appearing with the newly-emerging leaves. Forsythias are named in commemoration of William Forsyth, who was Superintendent of the Royal Gardens at Kensington, London about 200 years ago.*

Forsythia x intermedia

Few spring-flowering plants can match the colour impact of this vigorous, deciduous hardy hybrid shrub. It has golden-yellow, bell-shaped flowers, 2.5-3cm (1-1¼in) wide, in groups of up to six on the previous year's shoots. The leaves are lance-shaped, toothed and dark green. Several superb forms are available, including 'Spectabilis' with large rich yellow flowers, and 'Lynwood' with very large golden-yellow flowers. The form 'Spectabilis' can also be used to form hedges.

Height: 2.4-3m (8-10ft)
Spread: 2.1-2.4m (7-8ft)
Cultivation: Most garden soils are suitable, in sun or partial shade. They are a good choice for town gardens. If you want to grow a hedge of 'Spectabilis', set the plants 45-60cm (1½-2ft) apart in late autumn, cutting the shoots back to soil-level to encourage bushiness from ground-level. Because flowers are borne mainly on shoots which developed during the previous season, cut out a few of the oldest shoots from the base each spring after flowering. At the same time, remove dead wood and twiggy growths from the centre of the shrub. Hedges need a light clipping in spring.
Propagation: Home gardeners can readily increase forsythia in autumn, by taking hardwood cuttings, 25-30cm (10-12in) long, of the current year's growth. Insert them in a nursery bed in the garden; rooting takes about a year. Then plant in their final sites.

Forsythias are, to many people, the epitome of spring and the beginning of the gardener's year. The cheerful yellow flowers add to those of naturalized daffodils to paint a strongly-coloured spring picture.

Height: 60cm-1.2m (2-4ft)
Spread: 1.5-2.1m (5-7ft)
Cultivation: Give genistas a well-drained, slightly acid or neutral soil and a position in full sun. They do not like rich soil as this encourages soft growth, quickly damaged by frost. Because plants are difficult to transplant, use only container-grown ones. No regular pruning is required, other than thinning out congested and dead shoots after flowering. However, a light clipping at this time helps the development of further shoots, as well as maintaining an attractive and manageable mound-like shape.
Propagation: It can be increased from seeds, but the easiest method is to take 7.5-10cm (3-4in) long heel cuttings during late summer, insert them into pots of equal parts peat and sharp sand and place them in a cold frame. Pot the cuttings into peat-based compost when they are rooted, and transplant them into the garden in late autumn.

Below: Genista hispanica
This early summer-flowering shrub, native of south-west Europe, grows best on poor, well-drained soils. Rich soils encourage lush growth that is vulnerable to frost damage.

Left: Forsythia *As an added dimension, a forsythia can be grown on a stem and planted to blend with a white fence and to act as a focal point in the corner of a garden.*

Genista hispanica

Spanish Gorse (UK)
Spanish Broom (USA)

A dense, spiny and hairy deciduous shrub, best suited to warm areas. The deep green, exceptionally narrow leaves are borne on upright stems, and the golden-yellow, pea-shaped, 2.5m (1in) wide flowers appear from early to mid-summer. When it is in full flower, the colour is so intense that the whole shrub appears blessed with a golden glow.

Genista hispanica produces a dense, spreading display of startlingly yellow flowers. Its spreading habit makes it ideal for covering large, warm, dry areas, and its mounded shape is attractive.

TREES AND SHRUBS

Above: **Hamamelis mollis**
The spider-like fragrant, golden-yellow flowers of this small Chinese tree or large shrub have made it a firm favourite in many gardens. The branches have a zigzag spreading habit.

Hamamelis mollis

Chinese Witch Hazel (UK and USA)

Of all winter to early-spring flowering plants, this hardy deciduous small tree or large shrub is perhaps the most memorable. The sweetly-scented golden-yellow flowers, 2.5-3cm (1-1¼ in) wide, are formed of spider-like petals clustered along the base twigs. The broad, roundish, rather pear-shaped mid-green leaves are a delight in autumn, when they turn a beautiful yellow before falling. The form 'Pallida' bears large, sulphur-yellow and sweetly-scented flowers from late winter.

Height: 1.8-2.4m (6-8ft)
Spread: 1.8-2.4m (6-8ft)
Cultivation: Fertile, moisture-retentive, light to medium-textured neutral or slightly acid soil is best. Set the plant in full sun or light shade, and shelter it from cold winds. Little pruning is required, except for the removal in spring of dead or straggly branches.
Propagation: Although it can be increased from seeds, as well as 10cm (4in) long heel cuttings in late summer, the easiest way for home gardeners is to layer low-growing shoots in early autumn. Rooting takes about two years.

Hamamelis mollis has spreading branches, allowing plenty of light to reach plants close to it during winter and spring. The winter-flowering *Rhododendron mucronulatum* with funnel-shaped, rose-purple flowers makes an attractive contrast.

Hypericum 'Hidcote'

(*Hypericum patulum* 'Hidcote')

This is a hardy, semi-evergreen compact shrub, with wide, lance-shaped deep green leaves. During summer it displays 4-5cm (1½-2in) wide, saucer-shaped, golden-yellow flowers near the ends of the shoots. It is a reliable shrub, and justifiably one of the most popular. Many other hypericums can be grown in our gardens, including the well-known Rose of Sharon (*Hypericum calycinum*), also known as Aaron's Beard. With its golden-yellow flowers, up to 7.5cm (3in) wide, and its tough, durable nature, it is ideal for covering sunny, well-drained banks. Steep slopes in gardens become awash with colour from its flowers from early summer to early autumn. It forms a dense mass of ground-covering, bright-green leaves by sending out spreading roots.

Height: 90cm-1.8m (3-6ft)

Spread: 1.5-2.1m (5-7ft)

Cultivation: Hypericum prefers a fertile, well-drained but moisture-retentive soil and a sunny or slightly shaded position. It will tolerate slightly alkaline soils. Little pruning is required, although occasionally it may be damaged by frosts. If this happens, cut back the shoots to their bases in spring, and at the same time remove weak or diseased shoots.

Propagation: Softwood cuttings can be taken in summer, but it is often easier to take 10-13cm (4-5in) long cuttings in late summer, insert them into pots containing equal parts of peat and sharp sand and place them in a cold frame. The following year, the cuttings can be set out in a nursery bed and transplanted to their permanent sites when well-grown and sturdy.

Left: **Hypericum 'Hidcote'**
This is an exceptionally reliable shrub for the garden, with large saucer-shaped, golden-yellow flowers through most of the summer. The flowers appear slightly above the foliage.

Hypericum 'Hidcote' is useful for filling large areas in shrub borders with bright colour. It can also be positioned at the junction of paths, where it can be used as a focal point, however, it eventually needs plenty of space, if it is not to encroach on the path.

Left: Juniperus chinensis 'Aurea' *This golden form of the Chinese Juniper was raised at Young's Nursery in Surrey, England, thereby gaining one of its common names. It bears both juvenile and adult foliage simultaneously producing a two-tone effect.*

Right: Juniperus chinensis *A golden form of this spectacular evergreen forms an exciting focal point in a sea of heathers and with a background of dark-leaved conifers. The large yellow conifer at the left of the juniperus is Chamaecyparis lawsoniana 'Winston Churchill'.*

Juniperus chinensis 'Aurea'

Young's Golden Juniper · Golden Chinese Juniper (UK)

A distinctive slow-growing, tall, slender evergreen conifer with golden foliage, this shrub is ideal for small town gardens, reaching only 1.5m (5ft) high and 80cm (32in) wide in ten years. It has two types of foliage: needle-like young leaves, and scale-like adult ones.
Height: 6m (20ft)
Spread: 1m (3½ft)
Cultivation: Ordinary well-drained soil and a position in full sun are best. No regular pruning is needed.
Propagation: Seeds can be sown in late summer and autumn, but the plants do not come true from named forms. Therefore, in late summer take 5-10cm (2-4in) long heel cuttings, inserting them into pots containing equal parts of peat and sharp sand and place them in a cold frame. When rooted, pot up the cuttings singly into small pots and plunge these into a nursery bed. This helps to keep the compost moist and cool. Plant them out in the garden in late autumn while the soil is still warm, to encourage rooting.

Kerria japonica

Jew's Mallow (UK)
Japanese Rose (USA)

This is a beautiful spring and early summer flowering deciduous shrub with arching shoots. The long apple-green stems bear bright green, toothed, lance-shaped leaves. The 4cm (1½in) wide single flowers are borne on the ends of the previous season's stems. It is the form 'Pleniflora' that is chiefly grown, with double, 5cm (2in) wide, bright orange-yellow flowers. A variegated form is also available, with creamy-white edges to the leaves.
Height: 1.2-1.8m (4-6ft)
Spread: 1.5-1.8m (5-6ft)
Cultivation: Ordinary garden soil is suitable. As soon as flowering has finished, cut back the flowered shoots of 'Pleniflora' to encourage the development of strong shoots.
Propagation: It can be increased from 10cm (4in) long hardwood cuttings in autumn, inserting them into pots containing equal parts of peat and sharp sand. During the following spring, set the rooted cuttings in a nursery bed. An easier way is to dig up rooted stems during autumn or spring.

Below: Kerria japonica 'Pleniflora' *The deeply-toothed, bright green leaves are a perfect foil for the double orange-yellow flowers. Kerrias were introduced into the British Isles in 1804 by William Kerr the British plant-hunter.*

Kerria japonica 'Pleniflora' looks superb planted against a south or west-facing wall. In such a position, it is essential to encourage spring growths from soil level. Small blue-flowered bulbs, such as crocuses, do well at its base.

Juniperus chinensis 'Aurea' is superb in a heather
garden, contrasting with heathers and other conifers,
especially those with a spreading and prostrate
growth habit. It can also be positioned against blue
foliaged conifers.

TREES AND SHRUBS

Left: **Laburnum anagyroides**
When trained over a pergola, its pendulous flowers form a stunning canopy in late spring. But it is a tree that is poisonous, and should not be planted near a fish pool or in gardens with inquisitive children.

Potentilla x 'Elizabeth'

Cinquefoil (UK and USA)

Few shrubs display their flowers for such a long period as this hardy deciduous shrub. The 2.5cm (1in) wide, canary-yellow flowers appear from early summer to

Laburnum anagyroides

(Laburnum vulgare)
Common Laburnum (UK)
Golden Chain (USA)

This small deciduous tree bears golden-yellow, pea-shaped flowers in drooping sprays 15-25cm (6-10in) long, in late spring and early summer. The slightly hairy, dull green leaves are formed of three leaflets. As the tree ages, it tends to spread. For extra yellow colour, choose the form 'Aureum' with soft yellow leaves which slowly become green during the growing season. Occasionally, this laburnum is trained over a pergola to produce a tunnel of glorious colour when in full flower.
Height: 3-5.4m (10-18ft)
Spread: 2.4-3.5m (8-12ft)
Cultivation: Laburnums like a well-drained garden soil in full sun or slight shade. Ensure that the tree is well supported during its early years. The seedpods are poisonous to humans and to fish, so take care to prevent children from investigating them, and do not plant a laburnum tree near a fish pool. No pruning is needed, other than an initial shaping of the tree in summer.
Propagation: Seeds can be sown in autumn and placed in a cold frame. However, named forms do not come true from seed and are therefore grafted on to special rootstocks in the nursery.

Below: **Potentilla x 'Elizabeth'** *This shrubby Cinquefoil is one of the gems of the garden, with bright canary-yellow flowers from early summer to autumn. It is an extremely reliable shrub that needs little attention.*

Laburnums form a happy and colourful combination with lilacs, especially those with blue flowers. Even when planted several yards apart, the two trees create a beautiful picture.

autumn and are borne singly or in twos and threes. They stand slightly above the mid-green, deeply-cut leaves. There are several other superb forms, including 'Farreri' (bright yellow) and 'Katherine Dykes' (primrose-yellow).

Height: 90cm-1.2m (3-4ft)
Spread: 1.2-1.5m (4-5ft)
Cultivation: Any good well-drained garden soil suits it, and a position in full sun. No regular pruning is needed, other than cutting out dead and old stems during spring.
Propagation: Take 5-7.5cm (2-3in) long cuttings in spring, set them in pots containing equal parts of peat and sharp sand and place them in a cold frame. Alternatively, lift and divide large clumps in spring.

Below: **Laburnum anagyroides** *These bright-flowered trees are occasionally used as street trees. However, remember that all parts of the tree are poisonous, especially the seeds.*

Shrubby potentillas can be grown as informal hedges. Set the plants 75-90cm (2½-3ft) apart, but allow for their spread when positioning them alongside a path or boundary.

TREES AND SHRUBS

Robinia pseudoacacia 'Frisia'

Black Locust · False Acacia (UK)
Black Locust · Common Locust ·
Yellow Locust (USA)

This is a beautiful, small to medium-sized form of the Common Acacia. It has deciduous golden-yellow leaves. From spring to autumn it reveals pinnate leaves formed of up to eleven pairs of leaflets, first golden-yellow, then pale greenish-yellow in mid to late summer.

Height: 6-7m (20-26ft)

Spread: 3-3.5m (10-12ft)

Cultivation: Robinia thrives in any well-drained soil and a sunny position. Avoid cold and exposed areas. No regular pruning is required, but if any shaping is needed, it is best carried out during mid-summer when there is less chance of the tree bleeding.

Propagation: It is best to buy plants from a reputable nurseryman, as the propagation of the tree involves grafting the species on to stocks of *Robinia pseudoacacia* in spring.

Robinia pseudoacacia 'Frisia' is useful for providing colour contrasts. The 1.8-2.4m (6-8ft) high *Cotinus coggygria* 'Royal Purple', with dark plum-coloured foliage, makes an excellent companion.

Far left: Robinia pseudoacacia 'Frisia' *The golden-yellow leaves formed of many leaflets create a beautiful and graceful tree, even for small gardens. It provides continuing interest from spring to autumn.*

Left: Senecio 'Sunshine' *This New Zealand plant, with its daisy-like yellow flowers in early summer, is a delight in any garden. It is also attractive during winter when the silvery-grey leaves are covered with frost.*

Right: Taxus baccata 'Fastigiata Aurea' *A beautiful yew with golden foliage, especially attractive when planted in full sun. Initially, it suits rock gardens, but eventually becomes too large for a restricted site.*

Senecio 'Sunshine'

A widely-grown evergreen shrub, known for many years as *Senecio greyi* or *S. laxifolius*. It is a spreading, mound-forming – sometimes straggly – shrub, with silver-grey leaves that turn green with age. During early summer, it produces yellow, daisy-like flowers 2.5cm (1 in) across. During winter, the leaves look handsome when they are covered by frost or a light dusting of snow. Unfortunately, heavy snow falls can flatten and destroy the shrub's attractive mounded form.

Height: 1-1.2m (3-4½ft)
Spread: 1.2-1.5m (4-5ft)
Cultivation: Ordinary well-drained garden soil in full sun is ideal. It does well in coastal areas. Occasionally, it is damaged by severe frosts and heavy snow falls; if this happens, cut out the dead shoots in spring. Straggly plants should also be cut back in spring.
Propagation: During late summer, take 7.5-10cm (3-4in) long half-ripe cuttings. Insert them into pots of equal parts peat and sharp sand and place them in a cold frame. When they are rooted, transplant them to the garden.

Taxus baccata 'Fastigiata Aurea'

Golden Irish Yew (UK)
This is a neat, upright, golden evergreen conifer, a form of the Irish Yew. It has a solid appearance, with tight foliage. It is slow-growing, reaching 2m (6½ft) high and about 60cm (2ft) wide after ten years.
Height: 4.5m (15ft)
Spread: 75-90cm (2½-3ft)
Cultivation: Well-drained soil, acid or alkaline, suits it. A position in full sun is essential to encourage good foliage colour. No regular pruning is needed.
Propagation: It has to be increased by 7.5-10cm (3-4in) long heel cuttings in late summer and early autumn. Insert them into pots of equal parts peat and sharp sand and place them in a cold frame. Pot them on into pots of peat compost and plant them out in the garden when well-grown.

Senecio 'Sunshine' is best positioned near the front of a border or next to a path. Its mounded form becomes completely covered with flowers. It also looks good at a junction of two paths.

Taxus baccata, the Common Yew, is the parent of several golden-leaved forms, including 'Aurea' (slow-growing, compact, with young golden-yellow foliage) and 'Dovastonii Aurea' (leaves edged yellow).

TREES AND SHRUBS

Left: Taxus baccata '**Semperaurea**' *A beautiful golden form of the English Yew. It develops slowly into a medium-sized shrub, with the yellow colour at its most intense during spring.*

Taxus baccata 'Semperaurea'

This is a slow-growing, densely-packed, golden-foliaged version of the Yew. The new foliage is golden on first opening in spring, and slowly becomes rusty-yellow for the rest of the year. It grows to about 1m (3½ft) high in ten years.
Height: 3m (10ft)
Spread: 1.5-2.1m (5-7ft)
Cultivation: Most garden soils, in full sun or shade will do. Yews are very adaptable plants, able to thrive in peat-rich, acid soils and chalky soils alike. No regular pruning is needed, but it can be clipped to a preferred shape.
Propagation: Take 7.5-10cm (3-4in) long heel cuttings in late summer and early autumn. Insert them into pots containing equal parts of peat and sharp sand, and place them in a cold frame. Pot them on and plant out when they are well-grown and sturdy.

Ulex europaeus

Gorse · Whin · Furze · (UK and USA)

A hardy, sharply-spined, densely-branched evergreen shrub with scale-like leaves that soon fall. From spring to early summer it displays 1.8-2.5cm (³/₄-1in) long, pea-shaped, golden-yellow flowers. The flowers often appear intermittently until late winter. It is the double-flowered form 'Plenus', with compact hummocks of flowers, that is most often seen in gardens.
Height: 1.5-2.1m (5-7ft)
Spread: 1.5-2.1m (5-7ft)
Cultivation: Gorse needs a light, well-drained poor soil and a position in full sun. Little pruning is needed, but leggy shrubs can be cut back in spring to encourage

Taxus baccata 'Fastigiata Aurea' can be used to form an attractive hedge. Set the plants 38cm (15in) apart, sprinkling bonemeal in the planting holes to encourage rapid root development. Firm planting is essential to ensure quick establishment.

new growths from the base.

Propagation: Sow seeds in spring, placing them in a cold frame. Alternatively, take 7.5cm (3in) long cuttings in late summer and insert them into pots containing equal parts of peat and sharp sand. Place these in a cold frame and pot up the plants into pots of peat compost when rooted, transplanting them into the garden in late autumn.

Below: *Ulex europaeus*
This densely-spined, evergreen shrub is hardy in even the most severe weather. It forms an attractive windbreak or boundary. Bright golden-yellow, pea-shaped flowers appear during spring and early summer.

Further plants to consider

Berberis thunbergii 'Aurea'
Height: 90cm-1.5m (3-5ft)   Spread: 75cm-1.2m (2½-4ft)
A distinctive deciduous berberis, with yellow leaves turning pale green by late autumn.

Coronilla glauca
Height: 1.5-1.8m (5-6ft)   Spread: 1.2-1.5m (4-5ft)
A rounded, dense, bushy evergreen shrub, with glaucous leaves and rich yellow scented flowers from early to mid-summer.

Gleditsia triacanthos 'Sunburst'
Height: 5.4-7.5m (18-25ft)   Spread: 3-4.5m (10-15ft)
A deciduous tree with bright golden-yellow young foliage, each leaf formed of up to thirty-two narrow lance-shaped leaflets.

Halimium ocymoides
Height: 60-90cm (2-3ft)   Spread: 90cm-1.2m (3-4ft)
A small, hardy, compact, evergreen shrub, ideal for a large rock garden. During mid-summer, it boasts 2.5cm (1in) wide bright yellow flowers with chocolate blotches at the base of the petals.

Mahonia aquifolium
Oregon Grape
Height: 90cm-1.5m (3-5ft)   Spread: 1.5-1.8m (5-6ft)
A well-known and widely-grown mahonia, with dark green, leathery leaves. During early spring, it bears terminal clusters of fragrant rich yellow flowers, followed by bunches of blue-black berries.

Mahonia x 'Charity'
Height: 1.8-2.4m (6-8ft)   Spread: 1.5-2.1m (5-7ft)
A hardy evergreen with fragrant, rich yellow flowers borne at the tips of the shoots during winter and into early spring.

Rhododendron luteum
Height: 1.8-2.4m (6-8ft)   Spread: 1.5-2.1m (5-7ft)
A well-known deciduous shrub with fragrant, rich yellow flowers during early summer. It is an ideal plant for the wild garden, and does well in slight shade.

Rosa xanthina 'Canary Bird'
Height: 1.5-1.8m (5-6ft)   Spread: 1.2-1.8m (4-6ft)
A deciduous shrub rose, with beautiful clusters of semi-double bright yellow flowers during early to mid-summer.

Sambucus racemosa 'Plumosa Aurea'
Golden Cut-leaved Elder (UK)
Height: 2.1-2.4m (7-8ft)   Spread: 1.8-2.1m (6-7ft)
An eye-catching deciduous shrub with finely-cut golden leaves. During spring, it displays white flowers. It is a plant which looks good when set in front of a dark-leaved hedge, such as yew.

Ulex europaeus is native to western Europe including the British Isles, and north-west Africa. At one time, it was an important feature in the British landscape, where it formed 'furze-brakes' which were given local place names.

Bupleurum fruticosum

An unusual, attractive, dome-shaped, evergreen or semi-evergreen shrub, ideal for creating a background of sea-green leaves. During mid- to late summer, 3-4in (7.5-10cm) wide heads of small, yellowish flowers are borne.
Height: 4-6ft (1.2-1.8m)
Spread: 5-8ft (1.5-2.4m)
Hardiness: Zones 5-9
Cultivation: Plant in good, well-drained soil, including those that are slightly alkaline. It is ideal for

with green or glaucous-green foliage borne in broad, fan-like, slightly drooping sprays. Among the hundreds of cultivars are 'Columnaris', a narrow tree with blue-gray foliage; 'Ellwoodii', a slow-growing plant with blue-gray needles; 'Green Allar', a conical plant that has bright green foliage; 'Lanei', with beautiful golden-yellow needles; and 'Pembury Blue', which has pendulous blue-gray foliage.
Height: 25-35ft (7.5-10.5m)
Spread: 8-12ft (2.4-3.6m)
Hardiness: Zones 5-8

Above: Bupleurum fruticosum
The sea-green leaves of this evergreen shrub create a superb background for other plants. The yellow flowers provide a bright splash of color.

growing in coastal areas, where salt spray may be a problem.
Propagation: In mid- and late summer take 3in (7.5cm) long cuttings and insert them in equal parts moist peat and sharp sand. Place in a cold frame.

Chamaecyparis lawsoniana

Lawson False Cypress

This well-known evergreen conifer forms a large conical tree

Cultivation: As well as being grown as a specimen plant, this versatile conifer can also be used to form a hedge or windbreak. Plant in any well-drained soil, preferably in full sun or light shade. Plant golden-leaved varieties in full sun. No regular pruning is needed for plants grown as specimen, but if young plants develop two leading shoots, one of these must be cut out – preferably in spring.
Propagation: The ordinary all-green type can be raised from seeds sown in late winter and early spring, but named forms are raised from cuttings. Take 4in (10cm) long heel-cuttings in late spring and insert in equal parts moist peat and sharp sand.

Above: Chamaecyparis lawsoniana *The green or glaucous-green fans of evergreen foliage create a contrasting background for many plants. This versatile conifer can also be used to form a hedge or windbreak.*

Cornus alba 'Spaethii'

Tartarian Dogwood · Golden-variegated Dogwood

This deciduous willowy-stemmed and suckering shrub is superb for creating a wealth of variegated light green leaves with irregular golden-splashed edges. It has the bonus of bright red stems in winter. 'Elegantissima', another variety of this versatile shrub, may be easier

Bupleurum fruticosum eventually creates a dramatic display, but when young, pleasingly harmonizes with *Hebe* 'Blue Gem', framed against a background of *Tamarix* and *Spartium junceum*.

Chamaecyparis lawsoniana, native to southwest Oregon and northwest California, is a hardy, evergreen conifer, the parent of many colorful varieties, both large and dwarf.

irregular creamy-white edges.
Height: 2.1-2.4m (7-8ft)
Spread: 2.1-2.7m (7-9ft)
Cultivation: Plant in fertile, moisture-retentive soil in full sun or light shade. It is superb for planting around the edge of an informal garden pond or in a moisture-retentive wild garden, perhaps alongside a stream. Every spring, cut back all the stems to within a few inches of ground-level. This will encourage the development of new stems.
Propagation: In mid-summer take 7.5-10cm (3-4in) long heel-cuttings, inserting them in equal parts moist

Below: Cornus alternifolia 'Argentea' *This superbly variegated deciduous shrub is one of the best silver-foliaged border plants. Do not crowd other plants in front of it. The tiered outline of the branches is part of its appeal.*

Above: Cornus alba 'Spaethii' *The variegated leaves of the Golden-variegated Dogwood create welcome splashes of colour throughout summer. It often creates a sheet of colour from near soil-level to the uppermost shoots.*

peat and sharp sand. Place in a propagation frame with a temperature of 16°C (61°F). When rooted, pot up and later transplant to a nursery bed until large enough to be planted in a garden.

Cornus alternifolia 'Argentea'

Pagoda Dogwood · Green Osier (USA)

A superbly variegated deciduous large shrub or small tree (also known as 'Variegata') with horizontally spreading branches bearing small leaves with creamy-white edges. The prettily variegated leaves provide attractive splashes of colour throughout the summer months. It needs a position where the branches are not inhibited by nearby plants.
Height: 3-4.5m (10-15ft)
Spread: 3-3.6m (10-12ft)
Cultivation: Plant in moisture-retentive, but not waterlogged, soil in full sun or light shade. No regular pruning is required, other than occasionally cutting out a misplaced branch in spring.
Propagation: In mid-summer take 7.5-10cm (3-4in) long heel-cuttings, inserting them in equal parts moist peat and sharp sand. Place in a propagation frame with a temperature of 16°C (61°F). When rooted, pot up and later transplant to a nursery bed until large enough to be planted in a garden.

Cornus alba 'Spaethii' is mainly grown for its variegated leaves during summer, but the shiny, bright red stems in winter are equally welcome. Position in front of dark-foliage hedges.

Cornus alternifolia 'Argentea' looks superb when planted against a background of dark foliaged trees or shrubs. It is especially attractive when situated against a Yew (*Taxus baccata*) hedge.

Cotoneaster lacteus

An attractive evergreen shrub with leathery, deep green leaves that reveal hairy, grey undersides. It forms a dominant shrub – superb as a background for other plants. It has the bonus of developing creamy-white flowers in heads up to 7.5cm (3in) wide during mid-summer. These are followed in autumn and until mid-winter by clusters of red berries.

Height: 3.4-5m (10-15ft)
Spread: 2.4-3.6m (8-12ft)
Cultivation: Plant in any good garden soil in a sunny position. No regular pruning is needed, but cut out misplaced shoots in spring.
Propagation: It can be raised from seeds or by taking cuttings in mid-summer, but for home gardeners layering low-growing

Above: Cotoneaster lacteus can be grown to create an attractive hedge. Set the plants 60-75cm (2-2¹/₂ft) apart in a single row. After planting, cut off the top third of the plant to encourage bushy growth.

shoots in late summer is the easiest method. These take about a year to develop roots, when the young plant can be severed from the parent.

Cotoneaster lacteus This hardy, evergreen shrub creates a wealth of deep green leaves. Additionally, during mid-summer it bears creamy-white flowers, followed in autumn by clusters of red berries.

X Cupressocyparis leylandii

Leyland Cypress (UK and USA)

A vigorous, fast-growing evergreen conifer that rapidly creates a pleasing screen of grey-green foliage. The foliage droops slightly in sprays. It is frequently recommended for use as a hedge, but because of its rapid growth and high ultimate height it is only suitable for very large gardens.
Height: 7.5-9m (25-30ft) after 15 to 20 years.
Spread: 1.2-1.8m (4-6ft) after 15 to 20 years.
Cultivation: It grows well in most soils and positions, even those containing chalk and in coastal areas where salt spray may be a problem. When grown as a hedge, set the individual plants 75-90cm (2½-3ft) apart. In exposed areas, support young plants with strong canes. There is no need to prune this conifer.
Propagation: In late summer and early autumn take 10cm (4in) long cuttings. Insert them in equal parts moist peat and sharp sand, and place in a cold frame.

Below: X Cupressocyparis leylandii *The grey-green foliage, slightly-drooping towards its tip, creates a dense screen. It is the fastest-growing conifer, so take care not to plant it in a small garden.*

Elaeagnus pungens 'Maculata'

Thorny Elaeagnus (USA)

A beautiful slow-growing and widely-grown evergreen shrub with oval, leathery, glossy-green leaves irregularly marked along their centres with golden splashes. The leaves are borne on stiff, spiny stems. Other variegated forms include 'Dicksonii' (sometimes known as 'Aurea'), with irregular golden edges to the leaves, and 'Variegata' with narrow, creamy-white edges to the leaves.
Height: 2.1-3m (7-10ft)
Spread: 2.4-3.6m (8-12ft)
Cultivation: Ordinary well-drained soil suits it, in either full sun or light shade. Avoid poorly drained situations. No regular pruning is needed, other than occasionally cutting out misplaced shoots in spring. If all-green stems appear, cut these out immediately.
Propagation: In late summer take 10cm (4in) long cuttings. Insert them in equal parts moist peat and sharp sand, and place in a cold frame. By the following late spring either pot up the rooted cuttings or temporarily plant in a nursery bed until large enough to be transferred to a permanent position.

Above: Elaeagnus pungens 'Maculata' *looks especially bright in spring with bright yellow daffodils crowded around its base. It also forms a pleasing duo with the winter-flowering* Viburnum tinus.

X Cupressocyparis leylandii forms a dominant screen. Don't position other plants too close to it, as inevitably it scavenges the soil of food and moisture, as well as creating shade.

Elaeagnus pungens 'Maculata' The leathery, glossy-green leaves are handsome in winter when highlighted by low-angled rays of sun. It is dramatic when planted in a large tub and positioned on a patio, especially when filling a large corner.

Fagus sylvatica

Beech (UK)
European Beech (USA)

This well-known deciduous tree can be planted to form an attractive hedge. Set young plants 45-60cm (1½-2ft) apart, either in a single row or two lines spaced 45-60cm (1½-2ft) apart. The foliage is very attractive; bright green when young, slowly changing to mid-green and becoming darker as the season progresses. In autumn, the leaves assume yellow and russet tints before falling, although often they hang on the plant until spring.

Height: 1.5-6m (5-20ft), as a hedge.

Spread: 0.9-1.2m (3-4ft) as a hedge.

Cultivation: Plant in most soils except those that are heavy, wet and cold. Cut back newly-planted hedges by a quarter to encourage the development of shoots. If this initial pruning is neglected, the hedge becomes bare of shoots and leaves at its base. Once established, trim the hedge to shape during mid-summer.

Left: Fagus sylvatica *is the parent of several superbly coloured forms, as well as distinctive shapes. The Dawyck Beech* (Fagus sylvatica 'Fastigiata') *has a tall columnar stance, broadening with age.*

Above: Griselinia littoralis *has such softly-coloured foliage that it creates an ideal backcloth for pastel-coloured flowered and foliaged plants. When grown as a specimen in a border it has an informal outline.*

Fagus sylvatica When grown as a hedge, this deciduous tree creates a screen of bright green leaves in spring. In autumn they turn lovely yellows and russets.

Griselinia littoralis This slightly tender, slow-growing, evergreen shrub from New Zealand is ideal in coastal areas where salt spray may be a problem. Select a sheltered position for maximum protection against strong and cold winds.

Left: Ilex x altaclarensis
'Lawsoniana' *is best grown as a*
specimen shrub, perhaps near a
path so that it can be readily seen
during winter. There are many
other superb variegated hollies.

Ilex x altaclarensis 'Lawsoniana'

A superbly variegated hybrid holly with large, shiny, usually spineless, green leaves heavily splashed at their centres. It bears orange-red berries during winter.
Height: 3-5.4m (10-18ft)
Spread: 2.4-3.6m (8-12ft)
Cultivation: Plant in good soil in full sun or shade. Avoid soils that dry out during hot summers. Shoots often revert to being all-green, and these should be completely cut out as soon as they are noticed. Although no regular pruning is required, use secateurs to cut out spindly or misplaced

shoots in late summer
Propagation: During mid-spring take 7.5cm (3in) long heel-cuttings. Insert them in equal parts moist peat and sharp sand, and place in a cold frame.

Ilex aquifolium

Holly (UK) · English Holly
European Holly (USA)

This well-known, hardy, leathery-foliaged, evergreen shrub or tree has glossy, dark green leaves with wavy edges and sharp spines. Although most apparent at Christmas, when widely used in decorations, it is superb as a background for other plants. Some plants are male, others female. Female plants bear the well-known red berries in autumn and winter if a male specimen is planted near to it.
In addition to the all-green type, there is a wide range of colourfully variegated types that brighten gardens throughout the year. These are all less vigorous than the all-green type.
Height: 3.6-7.5cm (12-25ft) all-green type.
Spread: 2.4-3.6m (8-12ft) all-green type.
Cultivation: Plant in any good soil, in full sun or shade. However, avoid soils that dry out during hot summers. Protect young plants from cold winds. No regular pruning is needed, other than using secateurs during mid to late summer to remove spindly, misplaced shoots.
Propagation: The ordinary all-green type, as well as variegated forms, can be increased from 7.5cm (3in) long heel-cuttings taken during mid-summer. Insert in equal parts moist peat and sharp sand, and place in a cold frame. Named variegated forms can also be increased by budding in mid-summer. However, plants raised from cuttings are better, as they are not prone to develop sucker-like shoots.

Griselinia littoralis

A slow-growing evergreen shrub with leathery, shiny, yellowish-green leaves. The greenish flowers, which appear in spring, are insignificant and the plant is normally grown for its attractive leaves, which create a pleasing background for other plants. As well as being grown as a specimen plant, it can form an attractive and unusual hedge if its size is controlled.
Height: 2.4-4.5m (8-15ft)
Spread: 1.8-3m (6-10ft)
Cultivation: Plant in ordinary soil, in full sun or medium shade. It is not hardy in very cold areas, although once established it has a hardier constitution. It is tolerant of coastal areas, where salt spray may be a problem. If grown as a hedge, space the plants 45cm (1½ft) apart. Nipping out the growing tips of young plants encourages bushiness.
Propagation: During late summer take 7.5-10cm (3-4in) long cuttings and insert them in equal parts moist peat and sharp sand. Place in a cold frame. When rooted, pot up into small pots and place in a cold frame for a further year. Later, plant into a sheltered nursery bed for another year.

Ilex x altaclarensis 'Lawsoniana' This hardy evergreen shrub with dominantly yellow-splashed green leaves, is further enhanced in winter when seen against a background of snow. But it is equally attractive in summer, especially in strong sunlight.

Hollies are steeped in superstition. The normal prickly and all-green type is supposed to be lucky for men, whereas smooth-leaved and variegated forms are luckier for women, especially when combined with ivy.

TREES AND SHRUBS

Ligustrum ovalifolium

California Privet

This well-known semi-evergreen hedging plant has glossy, oval, midgreen leaves.

Ligustrum vulgare, European or common privet, is very similar to California privet but is hardy to Zone 4.

Height: 4-6ft (1.2-1.8m) as a hedge.

Spread: 2-3ft (60-90cm) as a hedge.

Hardiness: Zones 5-9

Cultivation: Plant in any good soil, in sun or shade. When planting a hedge, set the plants 1-1½ft (30-45cm) apart in a single row or staggered into two lines. In spring after being planted, cut back all hedging plants by one-third to a half. Regular clipping, in spring and autumn, is essential for established hedges.

Propagation: In autumn, take 10in (25cm) long hardwood cuttings and insert them to half their length in the soil. Do not position too close to other plants.

Below: Ligustrum ovalifolium
The glossy, oval, green leaves create a pleasing background for other plants, but do not plant them too close as privet depletes the soil of water and plant foods.

Ligustrum ovalifolium has several yellow-leaved forms; *Ligustrum ovalifolium* 'Aureo-marginatum' has green leaves with wide and irregular yellow edges, while 'Variegatum' has cream or pale yellow borders.

Liriodendron tulipifera 'Aureomarginatum'

Variegated Tulip Tree (UK and USA)

A distinctively variegated form of a well-known deciduous tree. The light to mid-green leaves have blunt, almost square tops and are edged and blotched in yellowish-green or yellow. During autumn the leaves assume rich autumn colours, but these are not as noticeable as the rich autumn colours seen in the all-green form.

Height: 5.4-7.5m (18-25ft)
Spread: 3-4.5m (10-15ft)
Cultivation: Well-drained soil in light shade or full sun. No pruning is needed, other than initially shaping the tree when young.
Propagation: The easiest way for home gardeners to increase this plant is to layer low-growing branches in spring.

Left: Liriodendron tulipifera 'Aureomarginatum' *(This variegated form of the Tulip Tree has light to mid-green leaves, blotched and edged in yellowish-green or yellow.*

Lonicera nitida

Japanese Honeysuckle (UK)

This well-known evergreen shrub is often grown as a hedge - the small, glossy-green leaves which crowd along the shoots create a superb background. If left unpruned, it grows up to 1.8m (6ft) high and eventually reveals a leggy, bare base. However, when grown as a hedge and clipped regularly it is much more pleasing.

Height: 0.9-1.5m (3-5ft) as a hedge.
Spread: 30-60cm (1-2ft) as a hedge.
Cultivation: Plant in well-drained soil, in full sun or shade. When grown as a hedge, set the plants 25-30cm (10-12in) apart, in a single row. After planting, cut back the top third of the shoots to encourage bushiness. During subsequent years, use shears to trim the plants in early and late summer.
Propagation: Take 10cm (4in) long cuttings in mid to late summer. Insert them in equal parts moist peat and sharp sand, and place in a cold frame. When rooted, transfer to a nursery bed until large enough to be planted into a garden.

Left: Lonicera nitida *The small, glossy-green leaves create a handsome foil for variegated subjects, as well as white and yellow plants. When not clipped, this evergreen has a pleasing, informal shape.*

Liriodendron tulipifera creates a dominant feature, either when planted as a focal point in a lawn or towards the end of a flower border, harmonizing with the white-flowered *Hydrangea arborescens* 'Grandiflora'.

Lonicera nitida is frequently grown as a hedge but tall, leggy specimens become bent over by heavy falls of snow. Clipping the top to form a slope helps to prevent light snow falls damaging the hedge.

TREES AND SHRUBS

Taxus baccata

Common Yew · Yew (UK)
English Yew (US)

For centuries this evergreen conifer has been used to create hedges, but even earlier it was widely planted in churchyards. Its foliage is very attractive; dark green with yellowish-green undersides.
Height: 1.5-1.7m (5-7ft) as a hedge.
Spread: 0.9-1.2m (3-4ft) as a hedge.
Cultivation: Plant in any soil, even those containing chalk, and in full sun or shade. However, avoid exceptionally wet and cold soils. When grown as a hedge, set the plants 45cm (1½ft) apart in a single row. At the same time, nip out the growing shoots to encourage bushiness at their bases. Established hedges need clipping with shears in late summer.
Propagation: It is often increased

Right: Viburnum davidii As well as creating an attractive backcloth with its green leaves, this evergreen shrub has white flowers in terminal heads during early summer, and turquoise-blue berries later in the year.

from seeds sown in late summer and placed in a cold frame. When the seedlings are about 5cm (2in) high, plant them into a nursery bed for three to four years. Alternatively, take 7.5-10cm long heel-cuttings in autumn. Insert them in equal parts moist peat and sharp sand. When rooted, plant into a nursery bed for about three years.

Below: Taxus baccata is the parent of many forms of Yew, including the Irish Yew (Taxus baccata 'Fastigiata') which has an erect habit with dark, blackish-green leaves. It is frequently seen in churchyards.

Viburnum davidii

An attractive evergreen shrub with prominently veined dark green leaves. It has the bonus of developing white flowers in heads up to 7.5cm (3in) wide in early summer. If male and female plants are present the flowers are followed by turquoise-blue berries.
Height: 60-90cm (2-3ft)
Spread: 1.2-1.8m (4-6ft)
Cultivation: Plant in good, moisture-retentive soil. Avoid light soils as they dry out rapidly in summer. No regular pruning is needed, other than cutting out misplaced or damaged shoots in spring.
Propagation: During late summer take 7.5-10cm (3-4in) long cuttings. Insert them in equal parts moist peat and sharp sand, and place in a cold frame. When rooted, pot up and place in a cold frame, later setting them into a nursery bed for two or three years.

Taxus baccata the Yew, was a sacred tree to the Druids, who built temples near to them. Later they were planted in Christian churchyards, a fashion that still continues today.

Weigela florida 'Variegata'

This beautifully variegated deciduous shrub with a compact habit, has light green, slightly wrinkled leaves with broad, creamy-white edges. It has the bonus of bearing clusters of tubular, foxglove-like, 2.5cm (1in) wide, pale pink flowers during early and mid-summer. The form 'Foliis Purpureis' also has attractive leaves, but all the same colour. These are purple, with the bonus of pink flowers in early and mid-summer.

Height: 1.2-1.5m (4-5ft)
Spread: 1.2-1.5m (4-5ft)
Cultivation: Plant in well-drained but moisture-retentive soil, in full sun or partial shade. It is ideal for filling borders up to 1.5m (5ft) wide between walls and paths. Every year, as soon as the flowers fade, cut out to ground-level a few of the old stems.
Propagation: During mid-summer take 10cm (4in) long half-ripe heel-cuttings from non-flowering shoots. Insert them in equal parts moist peat and sharp sand, and place in 16°C (61°F). When rooted, pot up and over-winter in a cold frame. Plant out into a nursery bed in spring.

Below: Weigela florida 'Variegata' *Although this variegated form does not have the flower-power of the ordinary species, it more than compensates for this with colourful leaves.*

Further plants to consider

Cornus controversa 'Variegata'
Height: 4.5-6m (15-20ft)   Spread: 3.6-4.5m (12-15ft)
A distinctive deciduous tree with mid-green leaves variegated silvery-white and borne on distinctively tiered branches. It is best when other plants are not crowded in front of it.

Euonymus fortunei 'Sunspot'
Height: 30-45cm (1-1½ft)   Spread: 38-50cm (15-20in)
A slow-growing dwarf evergreen shrub with glossy, dark green leaves boldly splashed at their centres with bright golden-yellow. It is a superb shrub creating colour throughout the year.

Griselinia littoralis 'Variegata'
Height: 2.4-4.5m (8-15ft)   Spread: 1.8-3m (6-10ft)
This beautifully variegated evergreen shrub is not fully hardy, and best grown in sheltered and warm regions. It is ideal for planting in coastal areas, as it tolerates salt spray. The leathery, apple-green leaves are variegated white.

Olearia ilicifolia
Maori Holly (UK) · Daisy Bush (UK and USA) · Tree Aster (USA)
Height: 2.4-3m (8-10ft)   Spread: 2.4-3m (8-10ft)
An evergreen shrub, densely covered wlth narrow, leathery, grey-green leaves, sharply and coarsely-toothed along their edges. Their undersides have an attractive greyish-white felt. During mid-summer, fragrant white daisy-like flowers are borne in clusters up to 10cm (4in) wide.

Pittosporum tenuifolium
Height: 1.8-4.5m (6-15ft)   Spread: 1.5-2.1m (5-7ft)
This interestingly-foliaged evergreen from New Zealand is not fully hardy in cold areas, and best reserved for planting in mild climates. In cold weather it is likely to lose its pale green, wavy-edged leaves which are borne on blackish stems. It is often grown as a hedge in mild coastal areas – plant 38-45cm (15-18in) apart.

Rhamnus alaternus 'Argenteovariegata'
Height: 1.8-3m (6-10ft)   Spread: 1.5-2.1m (5-7ft)
This evergreen bushy shrub has a narrow stance, with marbled-grey leaves irregularly variegated with creamy-white edges. It is ideal for planting in a small garden, creating colour throughout the year. It is less hardy than the all-green type.

Stranvaesia davidiana
Height: 3.6-6m (12-20ft)   Spread: 4.5-6m (15-20ft)
A large and bold hardy evergreen shrub with dark green lance-shaped leaves. During mid-summer, white flowers are borne in heads up to 7. 5cm (3in) wide. Round crimson berries appear in late summer and early autumn.

Viburnum davidii, wlth its evergreen, glossy-green leaves is an attractive dome-shaped shrub that creates a pleasing background for many low, prettily-flowered plants.

Weigela florida 'Variegata', with superbly variegated leaves, harmonizes well with tall, blue-flowered, bearded irises and *Lunaria annua*, a white-flowered form of Honesty.

Amelanchier lamarckii

Snowy Mespilus · June Berry (UK)
Serviceberry · Sarviceberry ·
Shadbush · Shad · Sugar Plum
(USA)

Few spring flowering plants
surpass the beauty of this bushy,
spreading, deciduous shrub or
small tree. Starry, white flowers are
profusely borne amid young,
coppery-red and silky, oval leaves.
In autumn they turn orange and
red. The flowers are followed by
purplish-black, sweet and
succulent fruits up to 12mm (¹/₂in)
wide. Other amelanchiers bear
fruits, and these have been used
by North American Cree Indians in
both a fresh and dried state. They
formed a pleasant addition to
pemmican, a North American

Indian cake, as well as for making
puddings of a similar quality to
plum pudding. Indeed, a name
used by early North American
settlers for amelanchier was
Grape-pear, reflecting the then
botanical classification of this shrub
in the pear family.
Height: 3-4.5m (10-15ft)
Spread: 3-3.6m (10-12ft)
Cultivation: Any good well-drained
but moisture-retentive soil suits it,
in either light shade or full sun. No
regular pruning is needed, except
during its formative years to create
an attractive shape.
Propagation: The easiest way to
increase this shrub is by layering
low-growing branches in early
autumn. However, it may take up to
a year before rooting occurs and
the young plant can be planted in a
nursery border.

Below: Amelanchier lamarckii
*The starry white flowers are certain
to capture attention in spring, while
in autumn leaves assume rich
coppery tints.*

Amelanchiers native to North America were prized
by Cree Indians for their straight grained wood, used
for making arrows and pipe stems. Indeed, they were
known to Canadian voyageurs as *Bois de flétch.*

Above: Cornus kousa chinensis
During mid-summer, four white bracts cluster around purplish green flowers. It is best planted alongside a path, so that the flowers, fruits and coloured leaves can be readily appreciated.

Cornus kousa chinensis

An attractive and unusually flowered deciduous shrub with spreading growth bearing mid- to dark-green leaves which assume rich bronze and crimson tints in autumn. During mid-summer it bears purplish-green flowers surrounded by four white bracts, each up to 4cm (1½in) long. In late summer it bears strawberry-like fruits.
Height: 2.1-3m (7-10ft)
Spread: 2.1-2.7m (7-9ft)
Cultivation: Plant in good soil, preferably in bright light. However, avoid chalky, infertile soils. No regular pruning is needed, other than cutting out misplaced branches in spring.
Propagation: In late summer, take 7.5-10cm (3-4in) long cuttings. Insert them in equal parts moist peat and sharp sand, and place in 16°C (61°F). When rooted, pot up and place in a cold frame. In spring, plant into a nursery bed for two years before planting into a garden.

Eucryphia glutinosa

Spectacular, slow growing, deciduous or partially evergreen tree-like shrub with rich green leaves that turn orange-red in autumn. The 6.5cm (2½in) wide white flowers have masses of stamens that dominate them, and are further enhanced by yellow anthers. The flowers arise from leaf joints from mid- to late summer.
Height: 3-4.5m (10-15ft)
Spread: 1.8-2.4m (6-8ft)
Cultivation: Slightly acid or neutral, light and peaty soil and a lightly shaded and sheltered position ensure success with this slightly delicate shrub. It is not suitable for cold regions, as the young shoots become damaged.
-

Above: Eucryphia glutinosa *With white flowers, packed at their centres with stamens bearing yellow anthers, this shrub always attracts attention. Flowers are borne singly or in pairs.*

No regular pruning is required, but young plants should have the tips of their shoots removed in spring to encourage branching and bushiness.
Propagation: During late summer, take 7.5-10cm (3-4in) long heel cuttings from non-flowering shoots. Insert them in equal parts peat and sharp sand. Place in 16°C (61°F). An easier method is to layer low-growing shoots in late summer, but the development of roots takes much longer.

Cornus kousa chinensis attracts attention so easily that it seldom needs other plants to be positioned around – white bracts in mid-summer, strawberry-like fruits in late summer, coloured leaves in autumn.

Eucryphia glutinosa is ideal for planting in a lightly shaded woodland setting. When in flower it creates a dominant focal point. Ensure that a path is near by, so that the flowers can be admired close-up.

Eucryphia x nymansensis

This spectacular hybrid between *E. glutinosa* and *E. cordifolia* is an erect and fast-growing evergreen tree. During late summer and into early autumn it develops 6.5cm (2½in) wide, cup-shaped, white or cream flowers. Each of these has a large central crown of stamens, headed by pink anthers.

Height: 4.5-6m (15-20ft)
Spread: 1.8-2.4m (6-8ft)

Cultivation: Well-drained, light and fertile soil in slight shade, and a sheltered position, are needed. It tolerates lime in the soil, but grows best in neutral or slightly acid conditions. No regular pruning is required, but shoot tips damaged by frost must be cut out in late spring. Young plants can be encouraged to develop sideshoots by nipping out their growing tips in spring.

Propagation: During late summer, take 7.5-10cm (3-4in) long heel-cuttings from non-flowering shoots.

Above: Eucryphia x nymansensis
A slightly tender shrub with eye-catching cream flowers during late summer and into early autumn. These are borne in clusters of two or three, and make a stunningly attractive picture.

Insert them in equal parts peat and sharp sand, and place in 16°C (61°F). An easier method is to layer low-growing shoots in late summer, but the development of roots takes much longer.

Eucryphia x nymansensis looks superb when planted with blue lace-cap hydrangeas, such as 'Blue Wave'. It also harmonizes with the white-flowered, bulbous, Summer Hyacinth *(Galtonia candicans)*.

Left: Hydrangea arborescens
'Grandiflora' *The large flower heads of this deciduous shrub brighten borders from mid to late summer. The flowers are especially attractive when framed against a blue sky.*

in full sun or light shade is needed. It benefits from a mulch of compost or well-decayed manure in spring. In mid-spring, cut back the previous season's shoots by about a half. At the same time, cut out thin and wispy shoots growing from the base.

Propagation: In late summer take 10-15cm (5-6in) long cuttings from non-flowering shoots. Insert them in equal parts moist peat and sharp sand, and place in a cold frame. When rooted, pot up and later plant into a nursery bed until large enough to be transferred into a garden.

Hydrangea arborescens

Hills of Snow · Sevenbark (USA)

This hardy deciduous shrub has a rather lax habit, with bright green, slender-pointed leaves and dull-white flowers borne in flat heads from mid to late summer. The best form is 'Grandiflora', with pure-white flowers in more rounded clusters.

Height: 1.2-1.5m (4-5ft)
Spread: 1.5-1.8m (5-6ft)
Cultivation: Moisture-retentive fertile soil and a sheltered position

Below: Hydrangea paniculata
'Grandiflora' *The large flower heads are spectacular when highlighted by blue sky. It is one of the best white-flowered shrubs for late summer colour.*

Hydrangea paniculata 'Grandiflora'

A stunningly attractive hardy, deciduous shrub, which during late summer and into autumn develops large, pyramidal, terminal heads of creamy-white flowers. These large heads, up to 45cm (18in) long, usually weigh down the stems.

Height: 1.8-2.4 (6-8ft)
Spread: 2.1-2.4m (7-8ft)
Cultivation: Moisture-retentive fertile, loamy soil is required. Prune plants in spring, cutting back the previous season's shoots by about a half. If very large flower heads are desired, thin out the shoots to seven to ten on each plant. However, severe pruning and thinning decreases the shrub's life. For general garden display, just prune back the stems in spring.

Propagation: In late summer take 13-15cm (5-6in) long cuttings from non-flowering shoots. Insert them in equal parts moist peat and sharp sand, and place in a cold frame. When rooted, pot up and later plant into a nursery bed until large enough to be planted into a garden.

Hydrangea arborescens 'Grandiflora' makes a dominant display when in flower and is especially useful for creating a sheet of white, mid-summer flowers alongside a lawn. Blue sky enhances the blooms.

Hydrangea paniculata 'Grandiflora' has such large flower heads that they tend to weigh down stems and cause them to spread. Therefore, do not position it too close to paths or other large shrubs.

Left: Magnolia stellata *During spring this small tree creates a mass of star-like, many-petalled, fragrant, white flowers borne on naked shoots. In winter the buds are grey and hairy, and add to the tree's beauty.*

Magnolia stellata

Star Magnolia (UK and USA)

A superb deciduous, slow-growing tree for small gardens, where it creates a wealth of white, star-like flowers up to 10cm (4in) across during mid-spring. Earlier, this tree was thought to be a separate species, but is now considered to be a form of *Magnolia kobus* and therefore is occasionally sold as *Magnolia kobus stellata*.
Height: 2.4-3m (8-10ft)
Spread: 2.4-3.6m (8-12ft)
Cultivation: Well-drained, moderately rich, loamy soil is best, but it grows well in most soils. However, it benefits from a sheltered position away from cold north and east winds.
Propagation: During mid-summer take 10cm (4in) long heel-cuttings. Insert them in equal parts moist peat and sharp sand, and place in a warm propagator. When rooted, pot up the cuttings and overwinter in a cold frame.

Left: Prunus laurocerasus 'Otto Luyken' *This small form of the large and dominant Common Laurel is ideal for small gardens. It can be pruned in early summer. The white candles of flowers appear from mid-summer.*

Prunus laurocerasus 'Otto Luyken'

This hardy, evergreen low-growing form of the Common Laurel develops semi-erect, 7.5cm (3in) long, white candles from mid-summer onwards. The deep green, leathery leaves, 10cm (4in) long and 2.5cm (1in) wide, are tapered and pointed at both ends.
Height: 1-1.2m (3½-4ft)
Spread: 1.5-2.1m (5-7ft)
Cultivation: Ordinary well-drained

Magnolia stellata is a superb magnolia for a small garden. To brighten the soil around and under its extreme edges, plant a medley of small, spring-flowering bulbs such as crocuses.

Prunus laurocerasus 'Otto Luyken' creates superb ground cover and edging to the junction of an informal lawn and an area under tall conifers, where the soil is dry. Water plants regularly to establish them quickly.

Left: Pyrus salicifolius 'Pendula'
This deciduous ornamental pear tree creates a stunningly attractive focal point on a lawn. Take care not to crowd it with other shrubs and trees – they ruin its shape.

becoming green. During mid-summer it bears masses of yellow, daisy-like flowers. It is equally attractive in summer when peppered with flowers as in winter when covered with a light sprinkling of snow.

Height: 1.5-2.1m (5-7ft)
Spread: 1.8-2.4m (6-8ft)
Cultivation: Well-drained soil and a position in slight shade to full sun suits it. It grows well in coastal areas.
Propagation: During late summer take 7.5-10cm (3-4in) long half-ripe cuttings. Insert them in equal parts moist peat and sharp sand and place in a cold frame. When rooted, plant into a nursery bed until large enough to be set in a garden.

Below: Senecio greyi *A superb, popular, evergreen shrub, equally attractive in winter when covered with frost and snow as in summer when it becomes smothered with yellow, daisy-like flowers in crowded clusters. It is ideal for planting at path edges.*

soil suits it - even if slightly alkaline. It grows well under pines and is ideal for creating attractive ground-cover. Normally, pruning is not necessary, but large plants can be carefully cut back in early summer, using sharp secateurs.
Propagation: Take 10cm (4in) long cuttings in late summer and early autumn. Insert them in equal parts moist peat and sharp sand. Place in a cold frame. When rooted, plant into a nursery bed until large enough to be set in a garden.

Pyrus salicifolius 'Pendula'

Willow-leaved Pear (UK and USA)

An elegant, deciduous tree with a spreading crown and pendulous branches bearing narrow, lance-shaped, willow-like, silvery-grey leaves. Eventually, the branches hang down nearly to ground-level and create a dome completely covered with leaves. During spring it produces clustered heads of pure-white flowers.
Height: 4.5-6m (15-20ft)
Spread: 2.4-4.5m (8-15ft)
Cultivation: It is a tree that is tolerant of most conditions, flourishing in poor as well as rich soils. It also grows in areas deprived of moisture, as well as those which are relatively moist. No regular pruning is needed, but

staking the plant when young is vital.
Propagation: This is best left to professional nurserymen.

Senecio greyi

This beautiful evergreen shrub is often sold as, and confused with, *Senecio laxifolius*, which is rarer and reveals a smaller stance. It also has slender, more pointed leaves. There is further confusion with *Senecio* 'Sunshine', which is widely sold as *Senecio greyi*. This is a beautiful shrub, forming a broad, dome-shape with silvery-grey leaves when young, later

---

Pyrus salicifolius 'Pendula' looks best when planted in a slightly elevated position. When young and before branches reach the ground it benefits from an underplanting of low-growing, blue-flowered spring bulbs.

Senecio greyi is ideal for planting near to the edge of a lawn or path, its dome-shape neatly but informally creating a sloping edge. It blends well with old paving slabs, but avoid new, brightly-coloured types.

Left: Spiraea x arguta *Beautiful spring-flowering shrub, ideal for planting near gates, where it cloaks posts and creates a wealth of eye-catching flowers amid a backcloth of fresh-green lance-shaped leaves.*

Spiraea x arguta

Bridal Wreath (UK and USA)
Foam of May (UK)

Well-known and widely-grown hardy deciduous shrub, creating a wealth of pure-white flowers from mid to late-spring. They appear in tight, 5cm (2in) wide clusters along the slender, arching stems.
Height: 1.8-2.1m (6-7ft)
Spread: 1.5-2.1m (5-7ft)
Cultivation: Fertile, deep soil and full sun or light shade suits it best. Little pruning is needed, other than occasionally lightly trimming and thinning congested plants after flowering.
Propagation: Take 20-25cm (8-10in) long hardwood cuttings in autumn. Insert them in a sheltered border, where they take about a year to produce roots. Sharp sand at the base of each cutting encourages the formation of roots.

Spiraea x arguta creates a superb backcloth for other plants, even when not bearing flowers. The small, lance-shaped, fresh-green leaves are ideal for highlighting Sweet Williams (*Dianthus barbatus*).

Spiraea thunbergii is ideal for planting close to paths and lawn edges, where it produces a wall of white flowers. Yellow-flowered plants blend well with this spiraea, such as *Potentilla fruticosa* in early summer.

Spiraea thunbergii

This hardy, deciduous and twiggy shrub from China and Japan is a delight in any shrub or mixed border, creating a wealth of white flowers in dense clusters on slender branches in spring and early summer. The flowers are borne on naked branches, before the leaves appear.

Height: 1.5-1.8m (5-6ft)
Spread: 1.8-2.1m (6-7ft)
Cultivation: Deep, fertile soil and either full sun or light shade suits it. Those shrubs that become a tangled mass can be thinned after the flowers fade, but this is only occasionally necessary.
Propagation: Cuttings 7.5-13cm (3-5in) long of the current season's growth can be taken in mid-summer and inserted in equal parts moist peat and sharp sand. Place in a cold frame. However, it is easier for home gardeners to take 20-25cm (8-10in) long hardwood cuttings in autumn and to insert them in a sheltered nursery bed. They take about a year to form roots.

Styrax japonica

Snowbell Tree (UK)
Japanese Snowbell (USA)

Small, graceful, deciduous shrub or small tree with slender, often drooping branches bearing dark, glossy-green, oval leaves and pure-white bell-shaped flowers with yellow stamens during early summer. It looks best when the flowers can be viewed from below.

Height: 3-5.4m (10-18ft)
Spread: 2.4-3.6m (8-12ft)
Cultivation: Lime-free, moisture-retentive loam in full sun or light shade suits it best. Late frosts can prove disastrous for the flowers. No regular pruning is needed, other than initially shaping the plant and keeping its centre open.
Propagation: It can be raised from seeds or half ripe cuttings in summer, but if you already have this shrub in your garden it is easier to layer a low-growing shoot in late summer or autumn.

Viburnum opulus 'Sterile'

Snowball (UK and USA)

A well-known form of the widely-grown deciduous shrub Guelder Rose. This superb variety has maple-like, dark green leaves and large, rounded heads of snow-white flowers during early and mid-summer. Often, the flower heads are so large that they weigh down the stems.

Height: 1.8-3m (6-10ft)
Spread: 1.8-3m (6-10ft)
Cultivation: Plant in deeply-prepared, moisture-retentive soil. No pruning is needed, other than cutting out misplaced and straggly shoots after the flowers fade.
Propagation: Take 7.5-10cm (3-4in) long heel-cuttings in late summer. Insert in equal parts moist peat and sharp sand, and place in a cold frame. When rooted, plant into a nursery bed for two or three years. Alternatively, layer long low-growing shoots in autumn.

Styrax benzoin, a related species and native of Sumatra, Borneo, Java and Malaya, yields a resin called Benzoin that at one time was used in Roman Catholic churches in the composition of incense.

Viburnum opulus 'Sterile' is a dominant shrub when in flower, especially in strong sunlight. Hostas planted around its base help to create interest throughout summer. Plain-leaved types are best.

TREES AND SHRUBS

Viburnum plicatum 'Mariesii'

During early summer this popular deciduous shrub creates a wealth of white flowers up to 4.5cm (1¾in) wide on tiered branches. The flowers sit on small, erect stalks, resulting, from a distance, in the branches appearing to be covered with snow.

It is a shrub that needs space, so that the branches are unrestricted in their spread and not obscured by other plants. The form 'Lanarth' is similar, but bears slightly larger flowers on longer stalks, with branches less horizontally tiered.

Height: 1.8-3m (6-10ft)
Spread: 1.8-3m (6-10ft)
Cultivation: Moisture-retentive loamy soil in full sun or light shade suits it. Avoid planting it under overhanging trees. No regular pruning is needed, other than thinning out straggly shoots. Cut out dead wood after flowering.
Propagation: The easiest way is to layer low-growing shoots in late summer and early autumn. They take about a year to develop roots. When rooted, sever from the parent and plant in a nursery bed.

Left: Viburnum plicatum 'Mariesii' *This deciduous shrub seldom fails to brighten gardens in early summer. Its flowers are borne on tiered branches. The dull green, tooth-edged leaves develop beautiful wine-red tints in autumn.*

Viburnum tinus
Laurustinus (UK and USA)

Widely-grown and reliable, this bushy, dense, evergreen shrub has a round form. Masses of pink-budded white flowers are borne in 5-10cm (2-4in) wide heads from early winter to late spring. The form 'French White' is strong growing, with large heads of white flowers.

Height: 1.8-3m (6-10ft)
Spread: 1.5-2.1m (5-7ft)
Cultivation: Plant in moisture-retentive soil in a position sheltered from cold winds. It is superb for coastal areas, surviving slight salt spray. Also, it tolerates light shade. During late spring, cut out dead shoots, or those that are misplaced.
Propagation: Sow seeds during late summer or early autumn in well-drained seed compost, and place in a cold frame. Alternatively, take 7.5-10cm (3-4in) long heel-cuttings during mid-summer. Insert them in equal parts moist peat and sharp sand. Place in 16°C (61°F). When rooted, pot up the cuttings and place in a cold frame.

Left: Viburnum tinus *An easily-grown evergreen shrub that brightens winter months with white flowers. These are followed by blue fruits that turn black. It is ideal for planting in coastal areas, where salt spray can be a problem.*

Viburnum plicatum 'Mariesii' should not be obstructed by tall plants. However, when planted in a sea of relatively low-growing plants such as *Polygonum bistorta* 'Superbum', its beauty is further highlighted.

Viburnum tinus is a welcome evergreen shrub during winter and therefore best planted where the flowers can be readily appreciated - by the sides of paths and along the boundaries of gardens at the fronts of houses.

Yucca flaccida 'Ivory'

Distinctive evergreen shrub from southern North American States. It has bluish-green leaves up to about 53cm (21in) long and 4cm (1½in) wide. It is a stemless yucca, with leaves arising from soil-level and the whole plant spreads by sucker-like growths. The ends of the leaves bend down slightly, with curly, thread-like growths at their edges. From mid to late summer it produces erect, 5-6.5cm (2-2½in) long, creamy-white flowers in heads up to 1.2m (4ft) high.

Height: 0.9-1.2m (3-4ft)
Spread: 0.9-1m (3-3½ft)
Cultivation: Well-drained light soil and a position in full sun suits it. It grows well in coastal areas. No pruning is needed.
Propagation: During spring, remove and replant rooted suckers. Large ones can be planted directly into a border, while small ones benefit from a few years in a nursery bed.

Below: Yucca flaccida 'Ivory'
Few plants are as distinctive as yuccas, with their tall flower spires. This variety bears creamy-white flowers from mid to late summer, above sharply-pointed, bluish-green, sword-like leaves.

Further plants to consider

Abutilon vitifolium 'Tennant's White'
Height: 1.8-2.4m (6-8ft)　Spread: 1.5-1.8m (5-6ft)
Slightly tender deciduous shrub, best grown in the shelter of a south or west-facing wall. From early to late summer it bears pure-white flowers about 5cm (2in) wide.

Buddleia davidii 'White Cloud'
Butterfly Bush (UK and USA)
Summer Lilac · Orange-eye Buddleia (USA)
Height: 2.1-2.7m (7-9ft)　Spread: 2.1-2.4m (7-8ft)
Well-known deciduous shrub with long, arching branches that during mid and late summer bear large, dense, pyramidal heads of white flowers.

Choisya ternata
Mexican Orange Blossom (UK and USA)
Height: 1.8m (5-6ft)　Spread: 1.8-2.4m (6-8ft)
Slightly tender evergreen shrub wlth aromatic, glossy-green leaves and sweetly-scented white flowers up to 36mm (1½in) wide during late spring and early summer. In cold areas grow in the protection of a south or west-facing wall.

Deutzia x magnifica
Height: 1.8-2.4m (6-8ft)　Spread: 1.8-2.4m (6-8ft)
Widely-grown deciduous shrub with upright stems bearing double pompom-like white flowers during early and mid-summer. Other white-flowered forms include 'Nakaine', a semi-prostrate form growing no more than 45cm (1½ft) high and spreading to 90cm (3ft), with single, white flowers.

Exochorda macrantha 'The Bride'
Pearl Bush (UK and USA)
Height: 1-1.5m (3½-5-ft)　Spread: 0.9-1.2m (3-4ft)
Hardy, compact, deciduous shrub with arching branches bearing brilliant white flowers during late spring.

Philadelphus 'Beauclerk'
Mock Orange (UK and USA)
Height: 1.8-2.4m (6-8ft)　Spread: 1.5-1.8m (5-6ft)
Superb deciduous hardy shrub with single, fragrant, white flowers with slightly pinkish tinges at their centres during mid-summer. Other superb varieties include 'Manteau d'Hermine' (creamy-white, fragrant and double), 'Avalanche' (single, white and fragrant) and 'Virginal' (double, white and fragrant).

Halesia monticola
Snowdrop Tree (UK and USA)
Height: 4.5-6m (15-20ft)　Spread: 3.6-7.5m (12-25ft)
A hardy deciduous tree with pendulous, bell-shaped white flowers borne in clusters during late spring. *Halesia carolina* is similar, with silvery-white bell-shaped flowers.

Yucca flaccida 'Ivory' creates an exotic scene in a garden, as well as having a strong 'architectural' appearance. Do not use them excessively, and position at the corners of borders, where they can be seen from several directions.

GARDEN PLANS

Planning the positions and arrangements of plants is an essential part of designing a garden. The fourteen garden plans detailed on the following pages will help you create attractive colour harmonies and contrasts – as well as rich fragrances – throughout your garden. There are ideas to brighten patios, courtyards and porches, as well as flower and shrub borders.

Flowers, as well as leaves and berries, create a virtually inexhaustible colour palette for gardeners. In addition, plants with variegated leaves help bring further interest to borders, often throughout the year and there

are many robust and hardy variegated evergreen shrubs and climbers to choose from.

The garden plans feature plants taken from a particular part of the colour spectrum. The colour schemes we have selected are gold and yellow, red and pink, blue and purple and green and white. There are also plans that detail the planning of scented borders.

Each plan indicates the size, colour and shape of each plant. An outline drawing identifying each plant through its common and botanical names accompanies each illustration.

Key:
1 Rose 'The New Dawn'
2 Clematis 'Ernest Markham'
3 *Buxus sempervirens* 'Suffruticosa'
4 *Helianthemum nummularium* 'Wisley Pink'
5 *Begonia semperflorens* (red)
6 *Lobelia erinus* (blue)

Right: *Bright and attractive porches are essential to all homes. This pink and red theme is especially eye-catching when seen against a white background. Small, urn-like containers complete the design.*

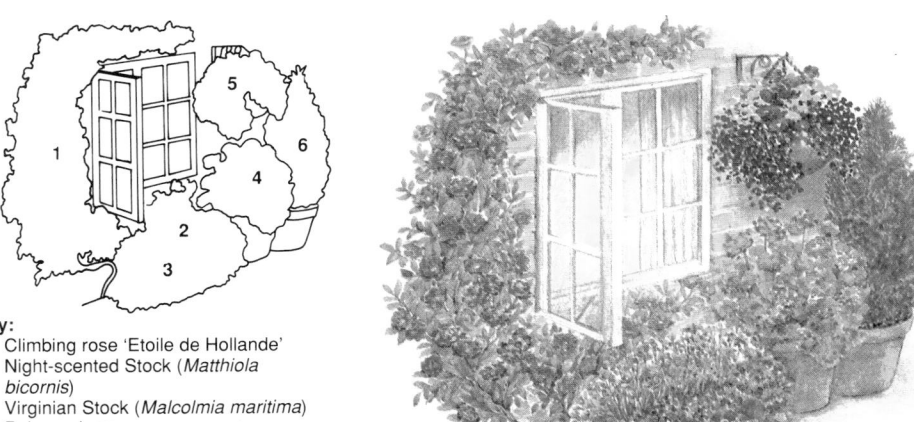

Key:
1 Climbing rose 'Etoile de Hollande'
2 Night-scented Stock (*Matthiola bicornis*)
3 Virginian Stock (*Malcolmia maritima*)
4 Pelargoniums
5 Trailing lobelia, petunias, geraniums and marigolds
6 *Chamaecyparis pisifera* 'Boulevard'

Above: *Scented flowers planted near windows enrich rooms during the day and at night.*

Key:
1 Petunias and trailing lobelia
2 *Cupressus macrocarpa* 'Goldcrest'
3 *Chamaecyparis lawsoniana* 'Pembury Blue'
4 *Betula pendula* (Silver Birch)
5 *Chamaecyparis lawsoniana* 'Green Pillar'
6 *Chamaecyparis lawsoniana* 'Lutea'
7 *Chamaecyparis lawsoniana* 'Allumii'
8 *Juniperus squamata* 'Meyeri'
9 *Chamaecyparis lawsoniana* 'Lanei'
10 *Thuja occidentalis* 'Sunkist'
11 *Erica vagans* 'Mrs D. F. Maxwell'
12 *Tsuga canadensis* 'Pendula'
13 *Thymus praecox* 'Annie Hall'

Below: *Reds and pinks create a warm, bright and glowing garden.* These colours contrast well with yellow and gold plants.

GARDEN PLANS

Above: *Blue plants are eye-catching but can, if used too freely , dominate a garden. Here they contrast well with yellow plants.*

Key:
1 *Picea pungens* 'Thomsen'
2 *Pinus sylvestris* 'Aurea'
3 *Picea pungens* 'Globosa'
4 *Hydrangea macrophylla*
5 *Salix x chrysocoma*
6 *Cotinus coggygria* 'Notcutt's Variety'
7 *Robinia pseudoacacia* 'Frisia'
8 *Chamaecyparis lawsoniana* 'Columnaris'
9 *Cedrus deodara* 'Golden Horizon'
10 *Juniperus chinensis* 'Pyramidalis'

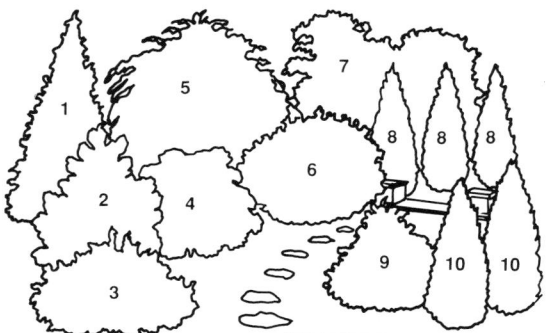

Below: *Patios steeped in scent and colour throughout summer create a superb outside living area*

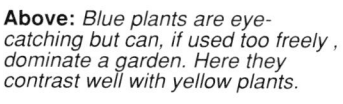

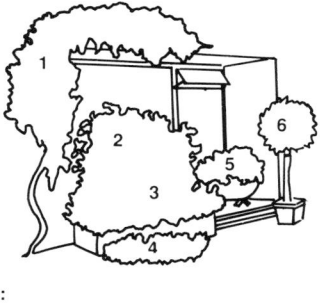

Key:
1 *Wisteria floribunda* 'Macrobotrys'
2 *Nicotiana alata* 'Lime Green'
3 *Malcolmia maritima* (Virginian Stock)
4 *Alyssum maritimum* 'Wonderland' (*Lobularia maritima*)
5 Container of scented, half-hardy annuals
6 Bay Tree (*Laurus nobilis*)

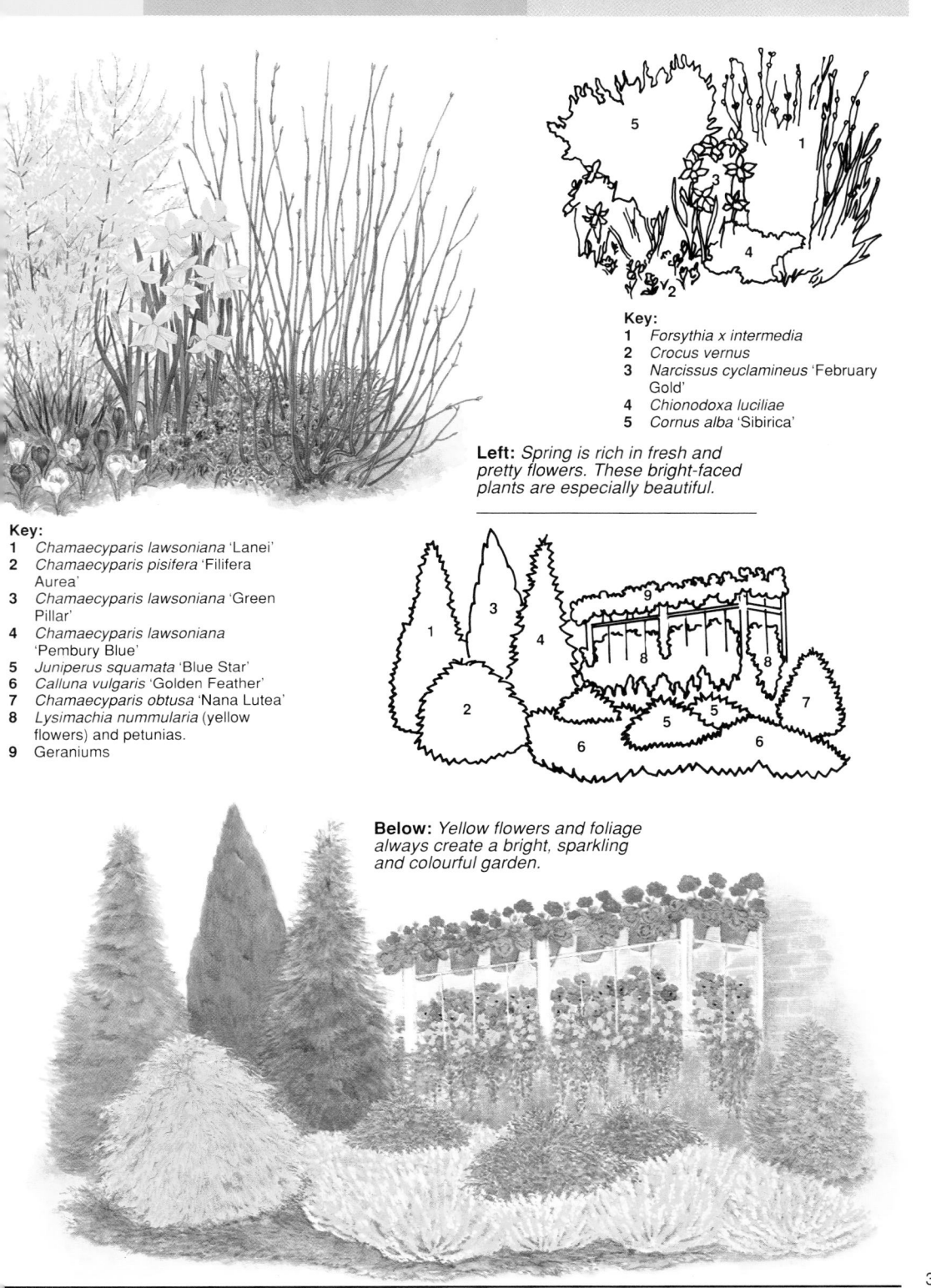

Key:
1. *Forsythia x intermedia*
2. *Crocus vernus*
3. *Narcissus cyclamineus* 'February Gold'
4. *Chionodoxa luciliae*
5. *Cornus alba* 'Sibirica'

Left: *Spring is rich in fresh and pretty flowers. These bright-faced plants are especially beautiful.*

Key:
1. *Chamaecyparis lawsoniana* 'Lanei'
2. *Chamaecyparis pisifera* 'Filifera Aurea'
3. *Chamaecyparis lawsoniana* 'Green Pillar'
4. *Chamaecyparis lawsoniana* 'Pembury Blue'
5. *Juniperus squamata* 'Blue Star'
6. *Calluna vulgaris* 'Golden Feather'
7. *Chamaecyparis obtusa* 'Nana Lutea'
8. *Lysimachia nummularia* (yellow flowers) and petunias.
9. Geraniums

Below: *Yellow flowers and foliage always create a bright, sparkling and colourful garden.*

GARDEN PLANS

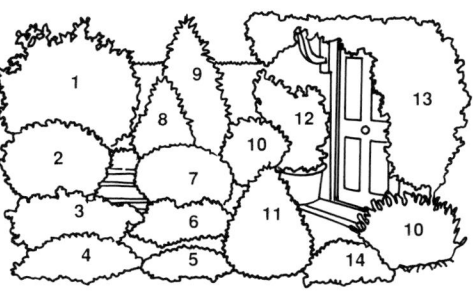

Above: *Small courtyard gardens can become pleasing oases of scent and colour throughout summer. Position plants especially rich in scent near windows and doors, as this is where they are most appreciated. In addition brightly coloured dwarf and slow-growing conifers create eye-catching features throughout the year.*

Key:
1. *Philadelphus* 'Beauclerk'
2. *Lavandula stoechas*
3. *Limnanthes douglasii*
4. *Thymus x citriodorus* 'Aureus'
5. *Thymus x citriodorus* 'Silver Queen'
6. *Helianthemum nummularium* 'Beech Park Scarlet'
7. *Ruta graveolens* 'Jackman's Blue'
8. *Chamaecyparis pisifera* 'Boulevard'
9. *Chamaecyparis lawsoniana* 'Lutea'
10. *Lavandula* 'Hidcote'
11. *Chamaecyparis lawsoniana* 'Minima Aurea'
12. *Tropaeolum majus* (Nasturtium)
13. *Lonicera tragophylla*
14. *Helianthemum nummularium* 'The Bride'

Right: *White borders create a cool and refreshing ambience, and look especially attractive when planted with a background of green foliage plants. Take care not to position plants too close to large hedges, as around their bases the soil may have become dry.*

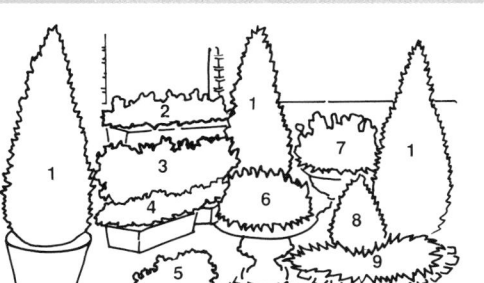

Key:
1 *Chamaecyparis lawsoniana* 'Ellwood's Gold'
2 Tulips and hyacinths
3 Daffodils
4 Polyanthus
5 *Saxifraga* 'Cloth of Gold'
6 *Muscari armeniacum*
7 Tulips, crocuses and hyacinths
8 *Chamaecyparis lawsoniana* 'Minima Aurea'
9 *Juniperus horizontalis* 'Blue Moon'

Above: *Window-boxes, tubs and troughs create 'instant' colour on a patio. Containers can be planted with bulbs and bedding plants, initially placed in an out-of-the way area and later, when creating a bright display, moved into position on a patio or terrace, or in a courtyard. Large, wooden tubs make ideal homes for dwarf and slow-growing conifers.*

Key:
1 *Anaphalis triplinervis*
2 Rose 'Madame Alfred Carriere'
3 Rose 'Iceberg'
4 *Gypsophila paniculata*
5 Hosta – variegated form
6 *Iberis sempervirens*

GARDEN PLANS

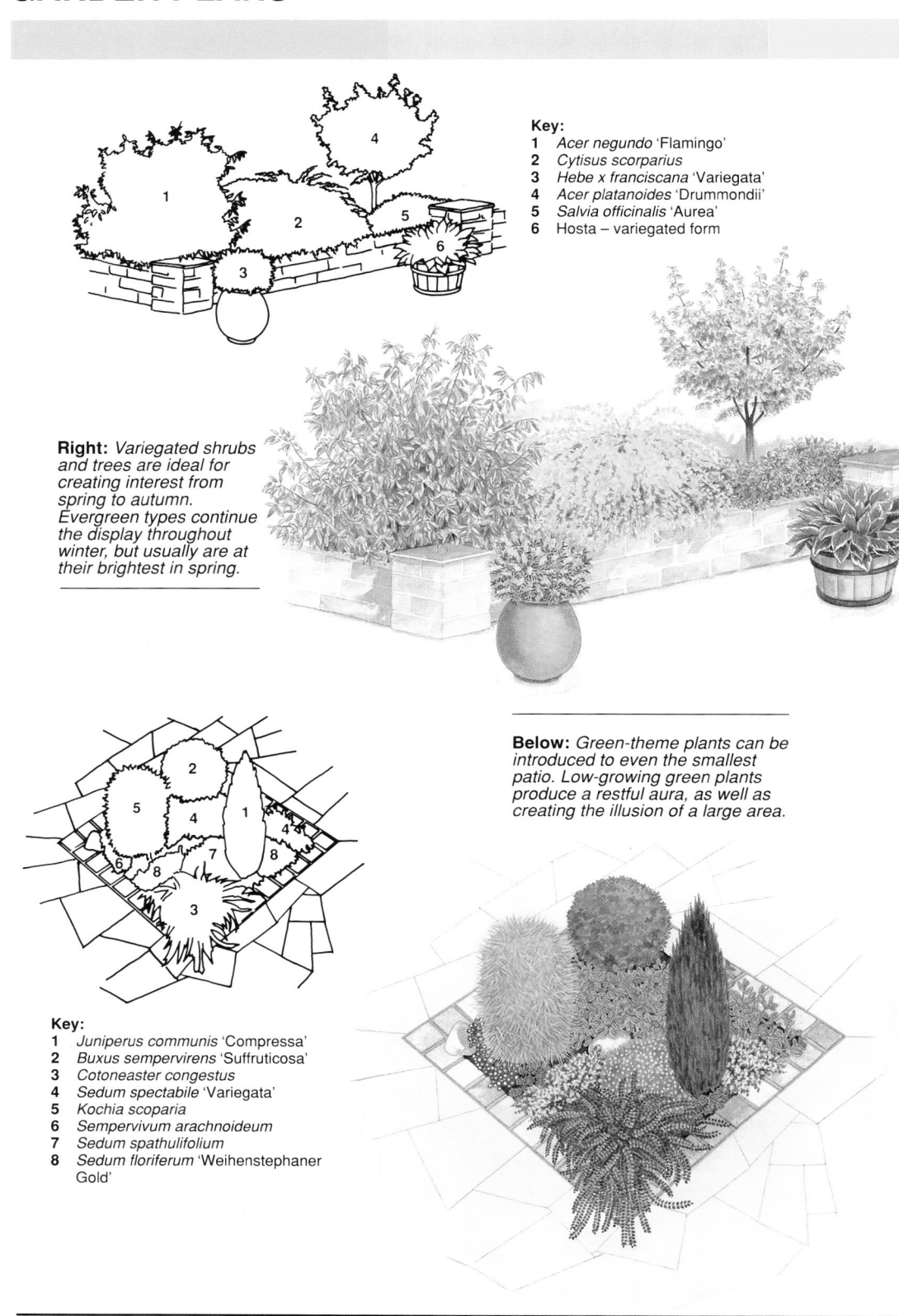

Key:
1. *Acer negundo* 'Flamingo'
2. *Cytisus scorparius*
3. *Hebe x franciscana* 'Variegata'
4. *Acer platanoides* 'Drummondii'
5. *Salvia officinalis* 'Aurea'
6. Hosta – variegated form

Right: *Variegated shrubs and trees are ideal for creating interest from spring to autumn. Evergreen types continue the display throughout winter, but usually are at their brightest in spring.*

Below: *Green-theme plants can be introduced to even the smallest patio. Low-growing green plants produce a restful aura, as well as creating the illusion of a large area.*

Key:
1. *Juniperus communis* 'Compressa'
2. *Buxus sempervirens* 'Suffruticosa'
3. *Cotoneaster congestus*
4. *Sedum spectabile* 'Variegata'
5. *Kochia scoparia*
6. *Sempervivum arachnoideum*
7. *Sedum spathulifolium*
8. *Sedum floriferum* 'Weihenstephaner Gold'

Above: *Courtyards can be brightened with flowering climbers as well as those with variegated leaves. Tubs packed with small shrubs bring further interest and colour.*

Below: *Walls and paving benefit from hanging-baskets, climbers, stone toughs and tubs. Also, many annuals and small shrubs can be planted into gaps left between the paving.*

GLOSSARY

Acid Refers to soils and compost with a pH below 7.0. Most plants grow best in slightly acid soil, about 6.5. However, a few such as azaleas and rhododendrons prefer acid conditions. (*see* pH)

Activator A chemical, usually in granular or powder form, that speeds up the decay of vegetable material in a compost heap.

Alkaline Refers to soils or composts with a pH above 7.0. (*see* pH)

Alpine Correctly, a plant that grows on mountains and above the level at which trees normally grow. Usually however, it means any small plant that can be grown in a rock garden or alpine meadow. Many delicate alpines can also be grown in an alpine house, a form of greenhouse that is unheated, which provides a plentiful circulation of air around the plants and prevents their foliage being continually moist, especially in winter.

Annual A plant that grows from seed, and flowers and dies within the same year. There are two types of annual; hardy and half-hardy. The hardy ones can be sown outdoors in spring, in the position where they are to flower. The half-hardy ones are sown in seedboxes or pots in the warmth of a greenhouse in late winter or early spring and subsequently planted into a garden as soon as all risk of frost has passed. However, many plants that are not strictly annuals, are treated as such. For instance, *Lobelia erinus* is a half-hardy perennial usually raised as a half-hardy annual, and *Mirabilis jalapa* (Marvel of Peru) is a perennial grown as a half-hardy annual.

Aquatic Correctly, a plant that grows entirely in water. However, it is generally taken to mean any plant that grows wholly or partly submerged in water, or in wet soil at the edges of a pond.

Anther The pollen-bearing part of a flower. A small stem, known as a filament, supports an anther. Collectively, they are known as stamen. This is the male part of a flower.

Aphids Also known as aphides, aphis, blackfly and greenfly. These are the most common of all garden pests. They also invade houseplants. Aphids breed rapidly, sucking sap and transmitting viruses from one plant to another.

Asexual Non-sexual; usually used to refer to the propagation of plants through cuttings and other vegetative methods, rather than by seeds.

Basal The lower leaves on a plant. Sometimes these differ in size and shape from those borne higher up on the plant.

Bedding plant A plant that is raised to create a display at a specific time of year. Spring-flowering bedding plants are planted in autumn for flowering the following spring, and include such plants as Wallflowers and Double Daisies. Summer-flowering bedding plants are raised in late winter or early spring and planted into a garden to create colour throughout summer.

Biennial A plant that makes its initial growth one year, flowers during the following one and then dies. However, many plants are treated as biennials, although strictly they are not. For instance, the Double Daisy (*Bellis perennis*) is a hardy perennial usually grown as a biennial. The Sweet William (*Dianthus barbatus*) is another perennial invariably raised as a hardy biennial.

Bi-generic hybrid A plant produced by crossing two plants from different genera (plural of genus). This is indicated by placing an X before the plant's botanical name. For instance, the fast-growing X *Cupressocyparis leylandii* has *Cupressus macrocarpa* and *Chamaecyparis nootkatensis* as its parents.

Blind A plant whose growing point has not developed properly and may be distorted.

Bloom This has two meanings; either a flower or a powdery coating, usually on the leaves and stems.

Bog plant A plant that grows in perpetually moist conditions. These are usually found around a pond or alongside a ditch.

Bottom heat The warming, from below, of compost in which cuttings are inserted when encouraging them to form roots. The warmth is usually provided by electric wires buried under a layer of well-drained and aerated rooting compost. Cuttings inserted in this root rapidly, while seeds sown in boxes and placed on top are often encouraged to germinate quickly.

Bract Botanically, a modified leaf. Some plants have brightly-coloured bracts that are more attractive than the proper flower. For example, the eye-catching flowers on the shrub *Cornus kouca chinensis* are bracts.

Budding A method of propagation, whereby a dormant bud is inserted into a T-cut in the stem of a root-stock. Roses and fruit trees, as well as some shrubs, are often increased in this way.

Bulb A storage organ with a bud-like structure. It is formed of fleshy scales attached to a flattened basal plate. Onions, daffodils and tulips are examples of bulbs. Erroneously, the term is often used to include other underground storage organs, such as corms, tubers and rhizomes, which have different structures.

Bulbil An immature and miniature bulb at the base of a mother bulb. However, some plants, such as the Mother Fern (*Asplenium bulbiferum*), develop plantlets on their leaves that are also known as bulbils.

Calcicole A plant that likes lime in the soil or compost.

Calcifuge A lime-hating plant.

Chlorophyll The green colouring material found in all plants, except a few parasites and fungi. It absorbs energy from the sun and plays a vital role in photosynthesis; the process by which plants grow.

Chlorosis A disorder, mainly seen in leaves, when parts reveal whitish areas. It is caused by viruses, mutation or by mineral deficiency in the compost or soil.

Clone A plant raised vegetatively from another, and therefore identical to its parent.

Compost This has two meanings. One of these is the growing medium normally formed of loam, peat and sharp sand in which plants are rooted and grown. The other meaning is the mixture of vegetable waste which is normally formed into a heap, allowed to rot down and decay, and then either dug into the soil or applied as a mulch for covering the soil around plants.

Compound leaf A leaf formed of two or more leaflets. Compound leaves are characterized by not having buds in their leaf-axils (leaf-joints). All true leaves have buds in their leaf-axils.

Conifer A cone-bearing plant usually with a tree or shrub-like stance, although some are miniature and slow-growing. Includes such plants as pines, firs and spruces. Most conifers are evergreen, but a few such as larches and *Ginkgo biloba* (Maidenhair Tree) are deciduous.

Cultivar A variety raised in cultivation (*see* Variety).

Container-grown plants A plant grown in a container for subsequent transplanting to its permanent position in a garden. Plants sold in containers include trees, shrubs and rock garden plants. They can be planted into a garden whenever the soil is not waterlogged, frozen or very dry. Because a plant experiences little root disturbance when being transplanted, it soon establishes itself in the soil.

Corm An underground storage organ formed from a laterally swollen stem base. A good example of a corm is a gladiolus. Young corms, cormlets, form around its base, and can be removed and grown in a nursery bed for several seasons before reaching a size when they can be planted into the garden.

Dead heading The removal of faded and dead flowers to encourage the development of further flowers. It also helps to keep plants tidy and to prevent diseases attacking dead and decaying flowers.

Deciduous A plant that loses its leaves at the beginning of its dormant season. This usually applies to trees, shrubs and some conifers. (*see* Conifers).

Division A vegetative method of increasing plants by splitting and dividing roots. It is usually done with herbaceous plants with fibrous roots.

Double flowers These have more than the normal number of petals in their formation.

Evergreen A plant that continuously sheds and grows new leaves through the year, and therefore at any time appears to be 'evergreen'.

Fertilization The sexual union of the male cell (pollen) and the female cell (ovule). Fertilization happens after pollen has alighted on the stigma (pollination), grown down the inside of the style and entered an ovule.

F1 The first filial generation; the result of a cross between two pure-bred parents. Fl hybrids are large and strong plants, but their seeds will not produce replicas of the parents.

Frond The leaf of a palm or fern.

Genus A group of plants with a similar botanical characteristic. Some genera contain many species, others just one and are known as monotypic.

Germination The process that occurs within a seed when given adequate moisture, air and warmth. The coat of the seed ruptures and the seed-leaf (or leaves) grows up towards the light. At the same time a root develops.

Glaucous Greyish-green or bluish-green in colour. Usually used to describe the stems, leaves and fruits of ornamental trees and shrubs.

Ground cover A low, ground-hugging plant that forms a mat of foliage over the surface of the soil. It is useful for discouraging weeds, as well as creating a backcloth for other plants.

Half-hardy A plant that can withstand fairly low temperatures, but needs protection from frost. For example, half-hardy annuals raised in the warmth of a greenhouse early in the year and then planted out into the garden as soon as all risk of frost has passed.

Hardening off The gradual accustoming of protected plants to outside conditions. Garden frames are usually used for this purpose.

Hardwood cuttings A vegetative method of increasing plants such as trees and shrubs, as well as some soft fruits; blackcurrants, red currants and gooseberries. A piece of ripe wood is cleanly cut from the parent plant, usually in late summer and autumn, and inserted into a nursery bed in the garden. It is an easy way for home gardeners to increase plants.

Hardy A plant that does not need to be protected from the weather and will survive outside during the cold part of the year.

Heel A hardy, corky layer of bark and stem which is torn off when a sideshoot is pulled away from the main stem while creating a heel-cutting. The heel needs to have its edges cleanly trimmed with a sharp knife before the cutting is inserted into rooting compost.

Heeling-in The temporary planting of trees, shrubs and conifers while awaiting transfer to their permanent position in the garden. Heeling-in is usually necessary when plants have arrived from a nursery at a time when the soil is too wet or too dry to enable them to be planted immediately.

Herbaceous perennial A plant that dies down to soil-level in autumn. The plant remains dormant throughout winter and breaks into growth in spring, when the weather improves.

Herbicide A chemical formulation that kills plants and is generally known as a weedkiller. Some herbicides kill all plants they touch, while others are called 'selective' and kill only certain types.

Humus Microscopic, dark brown, decayed vegetable material. It is usually the product of a compost heap.

Hybrid The progeny from parents of different species or genera.

Inflorescence The part of the plant which bears the flowers.

Insecticide A chemical used to kill insects.

Layering A method of vegetatively increasing plants. It is an easy way for a home gardener to propagate plants. Low-growing shoots are lowered to ground-level and slightly buried in the soil. By twisting, bending or slitting the stem at the point where it is buried, the flow of sap is decreased and roots encouraged to form. Rooting may take up to eighteen months, when the new plant can be severed from its parent and planted into the garden.

Lime An alkaline substance used to counteract the acidity of soil. It also has the property of improving the structure of clay soils by encouraging small particles to group together.

Loam A mixture of fertile soil, formed of sharp sand, clay, silt and organic material.

Mulch A surface dressing of organic material. It conserves moisture in the ground, smothers weeds and increases the nutrient content of the soil.

Naturalize Usually used to refer to the planting of bulbs in an informal display and allowing them to remain there undisturbed. This term can also be applied to other plants which can be left in informal groups, perhaps in a woodland setting or in a 'naturalized' garden.

Neutral Refers to soil that is neither acid nor alkaline. On the pH scale this would be 7.0. (*see* pH).

Nursery bed An area of the garden, in a sheltered and warm position, where newly-rooted and unestablished plants can be grown for several years before they are planted into the garden.

Organic The cultivation of plants without chemical fertilizers or pesticides being used.

Peat Partly decayed vegetable material, usually acid. It is frequently used as a constituent of compost, as well as to form a mulch around acid-loving plants.

Perennial Usually used to refer to herbaceous plants, but also to any plant that lives for several years, including trees, shrubs and climbers.

Pesticide A chemical used to kill insects and other pests.

Photosynthesis The food-building process by which chlorophyll in the leaves is activated by sunlight. It reacts with moisture absorbed by roots and carbon dioxide gained from the atmosphere to create growth.

pH A logarithmic scale used to define the acidity and alkalinity of a soil-water solution. Chemically, neutral is 7.0, with figures above indicating increasing alkalinity, and below increasing acidity. Most plants grow well in 6.5-7.0, invariably taken by gardeners to be neutral, rather than the scientific neutral at 7.0.

Pollination When pollen from the anthers falls on the stigma (female part of a flower). Not all pollen grains germinate and develop tubes which grow down the style and fertilize the ovules.

Propagation The raising of new plants.

Pruning The removal, with a sharp pruning knife or secateurs, of parts of woody plants. With fruit trees and bushes this is done to encourage better and more regular fruiting. With shrubs and woody climbers it is carried out to encourage better flowering, as well as to create an attractively shaped plant.

Rhizome An underground or partly buried horizontal stem.

Scree A freely-draining area of grit and small stones for alpine plants. These are plants that need very good drainage.

Shrub A woody perennial with stems growing from soil-level. Unlike a tree, it does not have a trunk. However, some plants can be grown as a tree or as a shrub, depending on their initial training or propagation.

Single flowers These have the normal number of petals, arranged in a single row.

Softwood cutting A non-woody cutting with a soft texture.

Species A group of plants with the same characteristics.

Spit The depth of a spade's blade, usually 25-30cm (10-12in).

Stamen The male part of a flower, formed of anthers and filaments.

Stigma Part of the female part of a flower, on which pollen alights and causes pollination.

Stomata A minute hole, usually on the undersides of leaves, enabling the exchange of gasses. During respiration a plant takes in air from the atmosphere, retaining oxygen and giving off carbon dioxide. During photosynthesis the plant absorbs air, using carbon dioxide and giving off oxygen. The plural of stomata is stoma.

Strain Seed-raised plants from a common ancestor.

Stratify A method of helping seeds with hard seed coats to germinate. The seeds are placed between layers of sand and kept cold, usually during the extent of winter.

Sucker A basal shoot arising from the rootstock of a grafted or budded plant. They should be cut out close to the roots. If necessary, remove soil from around the bases of the suckers so that they can be cut right back to the roots.

Systemic Used to refer to chemicals that are absorbed into a plant's tissue. The time they remain active within a plant depends on the chemical, type of plant and the temperature.

Tender A plant that is damaged by low temperatures.

Thinning The removal of congested seedlings to enable those that remain to grow strongly and to have more space. It can also refer to the removal of surplus shoots, again to allow more light and air to reach those that remain.

Tilth Surface soil which has been broken down, usually in preparation for sowing seeds.

Top-dress Spreading and lightly hoeing-in fertilizers to the surface of the soil around plants.

Top-soil The upper layer of soil, often taken to be the top 25-30cm (10-12in).

Transpiration The loss of water from a plant through stoma. The roots absorb water, which rises through the stems and passes into the atmosphere through the stoma. This is an essential process and has several purposes including helping to keep the plant cool and keeping the plant turgid.

Tuber An underground storage organ, such as a dahlia.

Variegated Multi-coloured. Usually referring to the leaves.

Variety A naturally occurring variation of a species. However, the term variety is commonly used to include both true varieties, as well as cultivars. Cultivars are plants which are variations of a species and have been raised in cultivation.

Vegetative A method of propagation, including layering, grafting, budding and cuttings.

Windbreak A shrub, tree or conifer used to create a barrier that reduces the speed of wind and provides shelter for small plants.

INDEX

INDEX

LATIN NAMES

315

CREDITS

PRINTED IN BELGIUM BY

proost
INTERNATIONAL BOOK PRODUCTION